Editors/ Advisory Board

To the Reader

In publishing ANNUAL EDITIONS we recognize the enormous role played by the magazines, newspapers, and journals of the *public press* in providing current, first-rate educational information in a broad spectrum of interest areas. Within the articles, the best scientists, practitioners, researchers, and commentators draw issues into new perspective as accepted theories and viewpoints are called into account by new events, recent discoveries change old facts, and fresh debate breaks out over important controversies.

Many of the articles resulting from this enormous editorial effort are appropriate for students, researchers, and professionals seeking accurate, current material to help bridge the gap between principles and theories and the real world. These articles, however, become more useful for study when those of lasting value are carefully *collected, organized, indexed,* and *reproduced* in a *low-cost format*, which provides easy and permanent access when the material is needed. That is the role played by *Annual Editions*. Under the direction of each volume's *Editor*, who is an expert in the subject area, and with the guidance of an *Advisory Board*, we seek each year to provide in each *ANNUAL EDITION* a current, well-balanced, carefully selected collection of the best of the public press for your study and enjoyment. We think you'll find this volume useful, and we hope you'll take a moment to let us know what you think.

This book is the seventh edition of an anthology on state and local government. From its first edition that appeared in 1984, the book as been designed for use in courses on state and local government and in state and local government segments of courses on American government. The educational goal is to provide a collection of up-to-date articles that are informative and interesting to students studying the area.

The 50 state governments and approximately 83,000 local governments in the United States have a great deal in common. They also exhibit remarkable diversity. The contents of the book as a whole inevitably reflect this theme of commonality *and* diversity. Some of the selections treat individual states or localities in considerable detail. Other articles focus on particular aspects of more than one state or local government. Still other articles explicitly compare and contrast regions, states, or localities. Taken together, the selections provide an overview of similarities and differences among state and local governments in the United States.

Keeping the idea of similarities and dissimilarities in mind can help students who are beginning their study of state and local governments. In many state and local government courses, a home state or region is given special attention. In such courses, the theme of commonality and diversity can serve to highlight what is and is not typical about the home state or region.

When Newt Gingrich became Speaker of the House of Representatives and Republicans assumed majority control of both houses of Congress in January 1995, the possibility of substantial change in intergovernmental relations seemed to increase. As this book goes to press, there are signs that the Republican 104th Congress will pass a variety of laws that will make the states more important and more autonomous actors in the American federal system. The so-called "unfunded mandates" act, signed into law by President Clinton in late March, seems to be one such measure. Proposals to drastically reshape various social welfare programs, if enacted, would give states and, if the states so authorize, their localities dramatically bigger roles in the area of social welfare policy.

The book is divided into seven units. Unit 1 is devoted to several eighteenth- and nineteenth-century commentaries on American federalism and state and local governments. Unit 2 treats relations among national, state, and local governments. Unit 3 covers elections, political parties, interest groups, referenda, and related matters, and it pays considerable attention to unusual features of state and local "linkages." Unit 4 turns to government institutions. Cities and suburbs provide the subject matter for unit 5, while unit 6 is devoted to finances and economic development. Unit 7 concludes the book with an examination of privatization and of selected policy issues facing state and local governments.

The book generally groups articles treating particular aspects of the governing process, be it state *or* local government, in the same units or sections. For example, unit 4 covers governmental institutions at both state and local levels, with subsections treating state *and* local legislatures, executives, courts, and corruption respectively. Unit 5, which treats metropolitan areas, is an exception to this rule in that it focuses primarily on issues involving local governments.

Deciding what articles to use in this revised edition was not an easy task. I tried to assess articles according to significance and relevance of subject matter, readability for students, and utility in stimulating students' interest in state and local government. Potential selections were evaluated not only as they stood alone, but also as complements to other likely selections. I want to thank the Advisory Board members who provided detailed critiques of the sixth edition of *Annual Editions: State and Local Government* as well as suggestions for improvements to the seventh edition.

The next edition of this book will bring another opportunity to make changes. I earnestly solicit reactions to this book as well as suggestions of articles for use in the next edition. Readers are cordially invited to become advisors and collaborators in future editions by completing and mailing the postpaid article rating form at the end of this book.

Bruce Stinebrickner

Bruce Stinebrickner
Editor

Unit 1

Early Commentaries

Three selections provide historic perspectives on federalism and on state and local governments in the United States.

Unit 2

Intergovernmental Relations

Seven selections discuss relations among national, state, and local governments in the three-tier system of government in the United States.

The concepts in bold italics are developed in the article. For further expansion please refer to the Topic Guide and the Index.

Unit 3

Linkages between Citizens and Governments

Thirteen articles explore various mechanisms that are supposed to help make state and local governments responsive to citizens: elections, political parties, referenda, initiatives, and so forth.

Unit 4

Government Institutions

Twelve selections treat the functioning of legislatures, executives, courts, and other institutions in state and local governments.

Unit 5

Cities and Suburbs

Seven selections comment on issues, problems, and opportunities facing governments of metropolitan areas.

Unit 6

Finances and Economic Development

Fourteen articles examine revenue-raising methods that state and local governments use, as well as challenges and problems of development that state and local governments face.

The concepts in bold italics are developed in the article. For further expansion please refer to the Topic Guide and the Index.

Unit 7

Service Delivery and Policy Issues

Eleven selections treat the means that state and local governments use in delivering services to the public and policy issues in such areas as education, zoning, abortion, and so forth.

The concepts in bold italics are developed in the article. For further expansion please refer to the Topic Guide and the Index.

Topic Guide

This topic guide indicates how the selections in this book relate to topics likely to be treated in state and local government textbooks and courses. It is useful for locating articles that relate to each other for reading and research. The guide is arranged alphabetically according to topic. Articles may, of course, treat topics that do not appear in the topic guide. In turn, entries in the topic guide do not necessarily constitute a comprehensive listing of all the contents of each selection.

TOPIC	TREATED IN:	TOPIC	TREATED IN:
Abortion	61. Abortion: The Never Ending Controversy	**Election and Electoral Systems**	11. Mirage of Campaign Reform 12. Seismic Shift in the South 13. It Isn't the Gender 14. Dickering Over the Districts 15. If Term Limits Are the Answer 16. Should Judges Be Elected? 17. My Life as a School Board Candidate
Adoption	63. Failure of the Adoption Machine		
Boycotts	20. Boycott Madness		
Cities	32. View from the Bench 36. Business Flees to the Urban Fringe 37. Impossible Commute 38. Bend or Die 39. Tale of Two Suburbias 40. Indianapolis and the Republican Future 41. Block Watch 42. Sweet Smell of Secession 55. Wild about Convention Centers 56. Government at Bat 62. Desire Named Streetcar	**Ethics and Ethics Laws**	34. In Search of the Toughest State Ethics Law 35. Buddy System
		Federalism	1. *The Federalist*, No. 17 2. *The Federalist*, No. 45 3. Nature of the American State 4. *New* Federalism 5. Federal Government Mandates 6. Tightening the Screws 7. Gorilla That Swallows State Laws 9. Local Options 10. Should States or Regions Set Clean Air Rules?
Courts	6. Tightening the Screws 16. Should Judges Be Elected? 31. States' Lead in Rights Protection 32. View from the Bench 33. Justice by Numbers	**Governors**	29. Wisconsin's 'Quirky' Veto Power
		Interest Groups	11. Mirage of Campaign Reform 18. All Politics Is Local 65. Of LULUs, NIMBYs, and NIMTOOs
Criminal Justice System	32. View from the Bench 60. Do We Need More Prisons?	**Item Veto**	29. Wisconsin's 'Quirky' Veto Power
Economic Development	19. Store Wars 36. Business Flees to the Urban Fringe 52. Third Wave of Economic Development 53. Romancing the Smokestack 54. Strange Career of Enterprise Zones 56. Government at Bat	**Land Use**	6. Tightening the Screws on 'Takings' 66. Taking Old McDonald to Court 67. Communities, Fearful of Importing Crime
		Lotteries	45. It's Not a Miracle, It's a Mirage
		Mandates	5. Federal Government Mandates 8. Declaration of War

Early Commentaries

The American political system includes three levels of government—national, state, and local. Although not unique among nations today, this arrangement was unusual in the late eighteenth century when the United States became independent. Early commentaries on the American political system paid considerable attention to each of the levels of government as well as to relations among the three levels. These writings suggest the important role that state and local governments have always played in the United States.

Debate about the desirability of the proposed new Constitution of 1787—the Constitution that remains in force to this day—often focused on the relationship between the national government and the states. Some people thought that the states were going to be too strong in the proposed new union, and others argued that the national government would be. Three prominent supporters of the new Constitution—Alexander Hamilton, James Madison, and John Jay—wrote a series of articles in 1787–1788 explaining and defending it. Many of these articles, which came to be known as The Federalist Papers, treated the federal relationship between the national government and the states. So did many of the writings of other early observers. This shows the importance that was attached to the new federal relationship right from the start.

Local government was also the subject of considerable attention in early commentaries on the American political system. Alexis de Tocqueville, a French nobleman visiting the United States early in the nineteenth century, recorded his observations in a book entitled Democracy in America (1835). Tocqueville remarked on the extraordinary vitality of American local government institutions, comparing what he saw in the United States with European institutions at the time. Today American local government still plays a prominent role in the overall governing process, probably more so than in any other nation in the world.

Later in the nineteenth century, a second foreign observer, James Bryce, published another historic commentary on the United States, The American Commonwealth (1888). Bryce, an Englishman, discussed American federalism and American state and local governments. He described the similarities and differences among local government structures in different regions of the country, the nature of the states, and the lamentable performance of city governments. Like Tocqueville, Bryce was able to identify and analyze distinctive elements of the American system of government and make a lasting contribution to the study of the American political system.

Selections in this first section of the book come from The Federalist Papers and Bryce's American Commonwealth. These historic observations on American federalism and state and local governments provide a baseline against which to assess the picture of contemporary state and local government that emerges in the rest of the book.

Looking Ahead: Challenge Questions

How does the picture of local governments provided by Bryce compare with American local governments today?

Do you think that the observations of Hamilton, Madison, and Bryce are out of date by now? Why or why not?

Students of politics frequently refer to the "historic" writings of Plato, Aristotle, Machiavelli, Hobbes, Locke, Rousseau, and others. Selections in this section are examples of early or historic writings on American politics. Why do you think that those who study politics so often look to the classics, even centuries after they were first written?

Do you find the arguments and logic of Federalist No. 17 and No. 45 persuasive? Can you detect any flaws or mistakes?

Which author do you find most interesting and helpful—Hamilton, Madison, or Bryce? Why?

THE FEDERALIST
NO. 17
(HAMILTON)

To the People of the State of New York:

AN OBJECTION, of a nature different from that which has been stated and answered, in my last address, may perhaps be likewise urged against the principle of legislation for the individual citizens of America. It may be said that it would tend to render the government of the Union too powerful, and to enable it to absorb those residuary authorities, which it might be judged proper to leave with the States for local purposes. Allowing the utmost latitude to the love of power which any reasonable man can require, I confess I am at a loss to discover what temptation the persons intrusted with the administration of the general government could ever feel to divest the States of the authorities of that description. The regulation of the mere domestic police of a State appears to me to hold out slender allurements to ambition. Commerce, finance, negotiation, and war seem to comprehend all the objects which have charms for minds governed by that passion; and all the powers necessary to those objects ought, in the first instance, to be lodged in the national depository. The administration of private justice between the citizens of the same State, the supervision of agriculture and of other concerns of a similar nature, all those things, in short, which are proper to be provided for by local legislation, can never be desirable cares of a general jurisdiction. It is therefore improbable that there should exist a disposition in the federal councils to usurp the powers with which they are connected; because the attempt to exercise those powers would be as troublesome as it would be nugatory; and the possession of them, for that reason, would contribute nothing to the dignity, to the importance, or to the splendor of the national government.

But let it be admitted, for argument's sake, that mere wantonness and lust of domination would be sufficient to beget that disposition; still it may be safely affirmed, that the sense of the constituent body of the national representatives, or, in other words, the people of the several States, would control the indulgence of so extravagant an appetite. It will always be far more easy for the State governments to encroach upon the national authorities, than for the national government to encroach upon the State authorities. The proof of this proposition turns upon the greater degree of influence which the State governments, if they administer their affairs with uprightness and prudence, will generally possess over the people; a circumstance which at the same time teaches us that there is an inherent and intrinsic weakness in all federal constitutions; and that too much pains cannot be taken in their organization, to give them all the force which is compatible with the principles of liberty.

The superiority of influence in favor of the particular governments would result partly from the diffusive construction of the national government, but chiefly from the nature of the objects to which the attention of the State administrations would be directed.

It is a known fact in human nature, that its affections are commonly weak in proportion to the distance or diffusiveness of the object. Upon the same principle that a man is more attached to his family than to his neighborhood, to his neighborhood than to the community at large, the people of each State would be apt to feel a stronger bias towards their local governments than towards the government of the Union; unless the force of that principle should be destroyed by a much better administration of the latter.

This strong propensity of the human heart would find powerful auxiliaries in the objects of State regulation.

The variety of more minute interests, which will necessarily fall under the superintendence of the local administrations, and which will form so many rivulets of influence, running through every part of the society, cannot be particularized, without involving a detail too tedious and uninteresting to compensate for the instruction it might afford.

There is one transcendent advantage belonging to the province of the State governments, which alone suffices to place the matter in a clear and satisfactory light,—I mean

From *The Federalist Papers*, Alexander Hamilton, 1787.

the ordinary administration of criminal and civil justice. This, of all others, is the most powerful, most universal, and most attractive source of popular obedience and attachment. It is that which, being the immediate and visible guardian of life and property, having its benefits and its terrors in constant activity before the public eye, regulating all those personal interests and familiar concerns to which the sensibility of individuals is more immediately awake, contributes, more than any other circumstance, to impressing upon the minds of the people, affection, esteem, and reverence towards the government. This great cement of society, which will diffuse itself almost wholly through the channels of the particular governments, independent of all other causes of influence, would insure them so decided an empire over their respective citizens as to render them at all times a complete counterpoise, and, not unfrequently, dangerous rivals to the power of the Union.

The operations of the national government, on the other hand, falling less immediately under the observation of the mass of the citizens, the benefits derived from it will chiefly be perceived and attended to by speculative men. Relating to more general interests, they will be less apt to come home to the feelings of the people; and, in proportion, less likely to inspire an habitual sense of obligation, and an active sentiment of attachment.

The reasoning on this head has been abundantly exemplified by the experience of all federal constitutions with which we are acquainted, and of all others which have borne the least analogy to them.

Though the ancient feudal systems were not, strictly speaking, confederacies, yet they partook of the nature of that species of association. There was a common head, chieftain, or sovereign, whose authority extended over the whole nation; and a number of subordinate vassals, or feudatories, who had large portions of land allotted to them, and numerous trains of *inferior* vassals or retainers, who occupied and cultivated that land upon the tenure of fealty or obedience to the persons of whom they held it. Each principal vassal was a kind of sovereign within his particular demesnes. The consequences of this situation were a continual opposition to authority of the sovereign, and frequent wars between the great barons or chief feudatories themselves. The power of the head of the nation was commonly too weak, either to preserve the public peace, or to protect the people against the oppressions of their immediate lords. This period of European affairs is emphatically styled by historians, the times of feudal anarchy.

When the sovereign happened to be a man of vigorous and warlike temper and of superior abilities, he would acquire a personal weight and influence, which answered, for the time, the purposes of a more regular authority. But in general, the power of the barons triumphed over that of the prince; and in many instances his dominion was entirely thrown off, and the great fiefs were erected into independent principalities or States. In those instances in which the monarch finally prevailed over his vassals, his success was chiefly owing to the tyranny of those vassals over their dependents. The barons, or nobles, equally the enemies of the sovereign and the oppressors of the common people, were dreaded and detested by both; till mutual danger and mutual interest effected a union between them fatal to the power of the aristocracy. Had the nobles, by a conduct of clemency and justice, preserved the fidelity and devotion of their retainers and followers, the contests between them and the prince must almost always have ended in their favor, and in the abridgment or subversion of the royal authority.

This is not an assertion founded merely in speculation or conjecture. Among other illustrations of its truth which might be cited, Scotland will furnish a cogent example. The spirit of clanship which was, at an early day, introduced into that kingdom, uniting the nobles and their dependents by ties equivalent to those of kindred, rendered the aristocracy a constant overmatch for the power of the monarch, till the incorporation with England subdued its fierce and ungovernable spirit, and reduced it within those rules of subordination which a more rational and more energetic system of civil polity had previously established in the latter kingdom.

The separate governments in a confederacy may aptly be compared with the feudal baronies; with this advantage in their favor, that from the reasons already explained, they will generally possess the confidence and good-will of the people, and with so important a support, will be able effectually to oppose all encroachments of the national government. It will be well if they are not able to counteract its legitimate and necessary authority. The points of similitude consist in the rivalship of power, applicable to both, and in the CONCENTRATION of large portions of the strength of the community into particular DEPOSITS, in one case at the disposal of individuals, in the other case at the disposal of political bodies.

A concise review of the events that have attended confederate governments will further illustrate this important doctrine; an inattention to which has been the great source of our political mistakes, and has given our jealousy a direction to the wrong side. This review shall form the subject of some ensuing papers.   PUBLIUS

THE FEDERALIST NO. 45
(MADISON)

To the People of the State of New York:

HAVING shown that no one of the powers transferred to the federal government is unnecessary or improper, the next question to be considered is, whether the whole mass of them will be dangerous to the portion of authority left in the several States.

The adversaries to the plan of the convention, instead of considering in the first place what degree of power was absolutely necessary for the purposes of the federal government, have exhausted themselves in a secondary inquiry into the possible consequences of the proposed degree of power to the governments of the particular States. But if the Union, as has been shown, be essential to the security of the people of America against foreign danger; if it be essential to their security against contentions and wars among the different States; if it be essential to guard them against those violent and oppressive factions which embitter the blessings of liberty, and against those military establishments which must gradually poison its very fountain; if, in a word, the Union be essential to the happiness of the people of America, is it not preposterous, to urge as an objection to a government, without which the objects of the Union cannot be attained, that such a government may derogate from the importance of the governments of the individual States? Was, then, the American Revolution effected, was the American Confederacy formed, was the precious blood of thousands spilt, and the hard-earned substance of millions lavished, not that the people of America should enjoy peace, liberty, and safety, but that the government of the individual States, that particular municipal establishments, might enjoy a certain extent of power, and be arrayed with certain dignities and attributes of sovereignty? We have heard of the impious doctrine in the Old World, that the people were made for kings, not kings for the people. Is the same doctrine to be revived in the New, in another shape —that the solid happiness of the people is to be sacrificed to the views of political institutions of a different form? It is too early for politicians to presume on our forgetting

that the public good, the real welfare of the great body of the people, is the supreme object to be pursued; and that no form of government whatever has any other value than as it may be fitted for the attainment of this object. Were the plan of the convention adverse to the public happiness, my voice would be, Reject the plan. Were the Union itself inconsistent with the public happiness, it would be, Abolish the Union. In like manner, as far as the sovereignty of the States cannot be reconciled to the happiness of the people, the voice of every good citizen must be, Let the former be sacrificed to the latter. How far the sacrifice is necessary, has been shown. How far the unsacrificed residue will be endangered, is the question before us.

Several important considerations have been touched in the course of these papers, which discountenance the supposition that the operation of the federal government will by degrees prove fatal to the State governments. The more I revolve the subject, the more fully I am persuaded that the balance is much more likely to be disturbed by the preponderancy of the last than of the first scale.

We have seen, in all the examples of ancient and modern confederacies, the strongest tendency continually betraying itself in the members, to despoil the general government of its authorities, with a very ineffectual capacity in the latter to defend itself against the encroachments. Although, in most of these examples, the system has been so dissimilar from that under consideration as greatly to weaken any inference concerning the latter from the fate of the former, yet, as the States will retain, under the proposed Constitution, a very extensive portion of active sovereignty, the inference ought not to be wholly disregarded. In the Achæan league it is probable that the federal head had a degree and species of power, which gave it a considerable likeness to the government framed by the convention. The Lycian Confederacy, as far as its principles and form are transmitted, must have borne a still greater analogy to it. Yet history does not inform us

From *The Federalist Papers*, James Madison, 1788.

that either of them ever degenerated, or tended to degenerate, into one consolidated government. On the contrary, we know that the ruin of one of them proceeded from the incapacity of the federal authority to prevent the dissensions, and finally the disunion, of the subordinate authorities. These cases are the more worthy of our attention, as the external causes by which the component parts were pressed together were much more numerous and powerful than in our case; and consequently less powerful ligaments within would be sufficient to bind the members to the head, and to each other.

In the feudal system, we have seen a similar propensity exemplified. Notwithstanding the want of proper sympathy in every instance between the local sovereigns and the people, and the sympathy in some instances between the general sovereign and the latter, it usually happened that the local sovereigns prevailed in the rivalship for encroachments. Had no external dangers enforced internal harmony and subordination, and particularly, had the local sovereigns possessed the affections of the people, the great kingdoms in Europe would at this time consist of as many independent princes as there were formerly feudatory barons.

The State governments will have the advantage of the Federal government, whether we compare them in respect to the immediate dependence of the one on the other; to the weight of personal influence which each side will possess; to the powers respectively vested in them; to the predilection and probable support of the people; to the disposition and faculty of resisting and frustrating the measures of each other.

The State governments may be regarded as constituent and essential parts of the federal government; whilst the latter is nowise essential to the operation or organization of the former. Without the intervention of the State legislatures, the President of the United States cannot be elected at all. They must in all cases have a great share in his appointment, and will, perhaps, in most cases, of themselves determine it. The Senate will be elected absolutely and exclusively by the State legislatures. Even the House of Representatives, though drawn immediately from the people, will be chosen very much under the influence of that class of men, whose influence over the people obtains for themselves an election into the State legislatures. Thus, each of the principal branches of the federal government will owe its existence more or less to the favor of the State governments, and must consequently feel a dependence, which is much more likely to beget a disposition too obsequious than too overbearing towards them. On the other side, the component parts of the State governments will in no instance be indebted for their appointment to the direct agency of the federal government, and very little, if at all, to the local influence of its members.

The number of individuals employed under the Constitution of the United States will be much smaller than the number employed under the particular States. There will consequently be less of personal influence on the side of the former than of the latter. The members of the legislative, executive, and judiciary departments of thirteen and more States, the justices of peace, officers of militia, ministerial officers of justice, with all the county,

corporation, and town officers, for three millions and more of people, intermixed, and having particular acquaintance with every class and circle of people, must exceed, beyond all proportion, both in number and influence, those of every description who will be employed in the administration of the federal system. Compare the members of the three great departments of the thirteen States, excluding from the judiciary department the justices of peace, with the members of the corresponding departments of the single government of the Union; compare the militia officers of three millions of people with the military and marine officers of any establishment which is within the compass of probability, or, I may add, of possibility, and in this view alone, we may pronounce the advantage of the States to be decisive. If the federal government is to have collectors of revenue, the State governments will have theirs also. And as those of the former will be principally on the sea-coast, and not very numerous, whilst those of the latter will be spread over the face of the country, and will be very numerous, the advantage in this view also lies on the same side. It is true, that the Confederacy is to possess, and may exercise, the power of collecting internal as well as external taxes throughout the States; but it is probable that this power will not be resorted to, except for supplemental purposes of revenue; that an option will then be given to the States to supply their quotas by previous collections of their own; and that the eventual collection, under the immediate authority of the Union, will generally be made by the officers, and according to the rules, appointed by the several States. Indeed it is extremely probable, that in other instances, particularly in the organization of the judicial power, the officers of the States will be clothed with the correspondent authority of the Union. Should it happen, however, that separate collectors of internal revenue should be appointed under the federal government, the influence of the whole number would not bear a comparison with that of the multitude of State officers in the opposite scale. Within every district to which a federal collector would be allotted, there would not be less than thirty or forty, or even more, officers of different descriptions, and many of them persons of character and weight, whose influence would lie on the side of the State.

The powers delegated by the proposed Constitution to the federal government are few and defined. Those which are to remain in the State governments are numerous and indefinite. The former will be exercised principally on external objects, as war, peace, negotiation, and foreign commerce; with which last the power of taxation will, for the most part, be connected. The powers reserved to the several States will extend to all the objects which, in the ordinary course of affairs; concern the lives, liberties, and properties of the people, and the internal order, improvement, and prosperity of the State.

The operations of the federal government will be most extensive and important in times of war and danger; those of the State governments in times of peace and security. As the former periods will probably bear a small proportion to the latter, the State governments will here enjoy another advantage over the federal government. The more adequate, indeed, the federal powers may be rendered to the national defence, the less frequent will be those scenes of danger which might favor their ascendancy over the governments of the particular States.

If the new Constitution be examined with accuracy and candor, it will be found that the change which it proposes consists much less in the addition of NEW POWERS to the Union, than in the invigoration of its ORIGINAL POWERS. The regulation of commerce, it is true, is a new power; but that seems to be an addition which few oppose, and from which no apprehensions are entertained. The powers relating to war and peace, armies and fleets, treaties and finance, with the other more considerable powers, are all vested in the existing Congress by the articles of Confederation. The proposed change does not enlarge these powers; it only substitutes a more effectual mode of administering them. The change relating to taxation may be regarded as the most important; and yet the present Congress have as complete authority to RE-

QUIRE of the States indefinite supplies of money for the common defence and general welfare, as the future Congress will have to require them of individual citizens; and the latter will be no more bound than the States themselves have been, to pay the quotas respectively taxed on them. Had the States complied punctually with the articles of Confederation, or could their compliance have been enforced by as peaceable means as may be used with success towards single persons, our past experience is very far from countenancing an opinion, that the State governments would have lost their constitutional powers, and have gradually undergone an entire consolidation. To maintain that such an event would have ensued, would be to say at once, that the existence of the State governments is incompatible with any system whatever that accomplishes the essential purposes of the Union.

PUBLIUS

Nature of the American State

James Bryce

. . . As the dissimilarity of population and of external conditions seems to make for a diversity of constitutional and political arrangements between the States, so also does the large measure of legal independence which each of them enjoys under the Federal Constitution. No State can, as a commonwealth, politically deal with or act upon any other State. No diplomatic relations can exist nor treaties be made between States, no coercion can be exercised by one upon another. And although the government of the Union can act on a State, it rarely does act, and then only in certain strictly limited directions, which do not touch the inner political life of the commonwealth.

Let us pass on to consider the circumstances which work for uniformity among the States, and work more powerfully as time goes on.

He who looks at a map of the Union will be struck by the fact that so many of the boundary lines of the States are straight lines. Those lines tell the same tale as the geometrical plans of cities like St. Petersburg or Washington, where every street runs at the same angle to every other. The States are not natural growths. Their boundaries are for the most part not natural boundaries fixed by mountain ranges, nor even historical boundaries due to a series of events, but purely artificial boundaries, determined by an authority which carved the national territory into strips of convenient size, as a building company lays out its suburban lots. Of the States subsequent to the original thirteen, California is the only one with a genuine natural boundary, finding it in the chain of the Sierra Nevada on the east and the Pacific ocean on the west. No one of these later States can be regarded as a naturally developed political organism. They are trees planted by the forester, not self-sown with the help of the seed-scattering wind. This absence of physical lines of demarcation has tended and must tend to prevent the growth of local distinctions. Nature herself seems to have designed the Mississippi basin, as she has designed the unbroken levels of Russia, to be the dwelling-place of one people.

Each State makes its own Constitution; that is, the people agree on their form of government for themselves, with no interference from the other States or from the Union. This form is subject to one condition only: it must be republican.[1] But in each State the people who make the constitution have lately come from other States, where they have lived under and worked constitutions which are to their eyes the natural and almost necessary model for their new State to follow; and in the absence of an inventive spirit among the citizens, it was the obvious course for the newer States to copy the organizations of the older States, especially as these agreed with certain familiar features of the Federal Constitution. Hence the outlines, and even the phrases of the elder constitutions reappear in those of the more recently formed States. The precedents set by Virginia, for instance, had much influence on Tennessee, Alabama, Mississippi, and Florida, when they were engaged in making or amending their constitutions during the early part of this century.

Nowhere is population in such constant movement as in America. In some of the newer States only one-fourth or one-fifth of the inhabitants are natives of the United States. Many of the townsfolk, not a few even of the farmers, have been till lately citizens of some other State, and will, perhaps, soon move on farther west. These Western States are like a chain of lakes through which there flows a stream which mingles the waters of the higher with those of the lower. In such a constant flux of population local peculiarities are not readily developed, or if they have grown up when the district was still isolated, they disappear as the country becomes filled. Each State takes from its neighbours and gives to its neighbours, so that the process of assimilation is always going on over the whole wide area.

Still more important is the influence of railway communication, of newspapers, of the telegraph. A Greek city like Samos or Mitylene, holding her own island, preserved a distinctive character in spite of commercial intercourse and the sway of Athens. A Swiss canton like Uri or Appenzell, entrenched behind its mountain ramparts, remains, even now under the strengthened central government of the Swiss nation, unlike its neighbours of the lower country. But an American State traversed by great trunk lines of railway, and depending on the markets of the Atlantic cities and of Europe for the sale of its grain, cattle, bacon, and minerals, is attached by a hundred always tightening ties to other States, and touched by their weal or woe as nearly as by what befalls within its own limits. The leading newspapers are read over a vast area. The inhabitants of each State know every morning the events of yesterday over the whole Union.

Finally the political parties are the same in all the States. The tenets (if any) of each party are the same everywhere, their methods the same, their leaders the same, although of course a prominent man enjoys especial influence in his own State. Hence, State politics are largely swayed by forces and motives external to the particular State, and common to the whole country, or to great sections of it; and the growth of local parties, the emergence of local issues and development of local political schemes, are correspondingly restrained.

These considerations explain why the States, notwithstanding the original diversities between some of them, and the wide scope for political divergence which they all enjoy under the Federal Constitution, are so much less dissimilar and less peculiar than might have been expected. European statesmen have of late years been accustomed to think of federalism and local autonomy as convenient methods either for recognizing and giving free scope to the sentiment of nationality which may exist in any part of an empire, or for meeting the need for local institutions and distinct legislation which may arise from differences between such a part and the rest of the empire. It is one or other or both of these reasons that have moved statesmen in such cases as those of Finland in her relations to Russia, Hungary in her relations to German Austria, Iceland in her relations to Denmark, Bulgaria in her relations to the Turkish Sultan, Ireland in her relations to the United Kingdom. But the final causes, so to speak, of the recognition of the States of the American Union as autonomous commonwealths, have been different. Their self-government is not the consequence of differences which can be made harmless to the whole body politic only by being allowed free course. It has been due primarily to the historical fact that they existed as commonwealths before the Union came into being; secondarily, to the belief that localized government is the best guarantee for civic freedom, and to a sense of the difficulty of administering a vast territory and population from one centre and by one government.

I return to indicate the points in which the legal independence and right of self-government of the several States appears. Each of the forty-two has its own—

Constitution (whereof more anon).

Executive, consisting of a governor, and various other officials.

Legislature of two Houses.

System of local government in counties, cities, townships, and school districts.

System of State and local taxation.

Debts, which it may (and sometimes does) repudiate at its own pleasure.

Body of private law, including the whole law of real and personal property, of contracts, of torts, and of family relations.

Courts, from which no appeal lies (except in cases touching Federal legislation or the Federal constitution) to any Federal court.

System of procedure, civil and criminal.

Citizenship, which may admit persons (*e.g.* recent immigrants) to be citizens at times, or on conditions, wholly different from those prescribed by other States.

Three points deserve to be noted as illustrating what these attributes include.

I. A man gains active citizenship of the United States (*i.e.* a share in the government of the Union) only by becoming a citizen of some particular State. Being such citizen, he is forthwith entitled to the national franchise. That is to say, voting power in the State carries voting power in Federal elections, and however lax a State may be in its grant of such power, *e.g.* to foreigners just landed or to persons convicted of crime, these State voters will have the right of voting in congressional and presidential elections.[2] The only restriction on the States in this matter is that of the fourteenth and fifteenth Constitutional amendments, ... They were intended to secure equal treatment to the negroes, and incidentally they declare the protection given to all citizens of the United States.[3] Whether they really enlarge it, that is to say, whether it did not exist by implication before, is a legal question, which I need not discuss.

II. The power of a State over all communities within its limits is absolute. It may grant or refuse local government as it pleases. The population of the city of Providence is more than one-third of that of the State of Rhode Island, the population of New York city more than one-fifth that of the State of New York. But the State might in either case extinguish the municipality, and govern the city by a single State commissioner appointed for the purpose, or leave it without any government whatever. The city would have no right of complaint to the Federal President or Congress against such a measure. Massachusetts has lately remodelled the city government of Boston just as the British Parliament might remodel that of Birmingham. Let an Englishman imagine a county council for Warwickshire suppressing the muncipality of Birmingham, or a Frenchman imagine the department of the Rhone extinguishing the municipality of Lyons, with no possibility of intervention by the central authority, and he will measure the difference between the American States and the local governments of Western Europe.

III. A State commands the allegiance of its citizens, and may punish them for treason against it. The power has rarely been exercised, but its undoubted legal existence had much to do with inducing the citizens of the Southern States to follow their governments into secession in 1861. They conceived themselves to owe allegiance to the State as well as to the Union, and when it became impossible to preserve both, because the State had declared its secession from the Union, they might hold the earlier and nearer authority to be paramount. Allegiance to the State must now, since the war, be taken to be subordinate to the Union. But allegiance to the State still exists; treason against the State is still possible. One cannot think of treason against Warwickshire or the department of the Rhone.

These are illustrations of the doctrine which Europeans often fail to grasp, that the American States were originally in a certain sense, and still for certain purposes remain, sovereign States. Each of the original thirteen became sovereign when it revolted from the mother country in 1776. By entering the Confederation of 1781-88 it parted with one or two of the attributes of sovereignty, by accepting the Federal Constitution in 1788 it subjected itself for certain specified purposes to a central government, but claimed to retain its sovereignty for all other purposes. That is to say, the authority of a State is an inherent, not a delegated, authority. It has all the powers which any independent government can have, except such as it can be affirmatively shown to have stripped itself of, while the Federal Government has only such powers as it can be affirmatively shown to have received. To use the legal expression, the presumption is always for a State, and the burden of proof lies upon any one who denies its authority in a particular matter.[4]

What State sovereignty means and includes is a question which incessantly engaged the most active legal and political minds of the nation, from 1789 down to 1870. Some thought it paramount to the rights of the Union. Some considered it as held in suspense by the Constitution, but capable of reviving as soon as a State should desire to separate from the Union. Some maintained that each State had in accepting the Constitution finally renounced its sovereignty, which thereafter existed only in the sense of such an undefined domestic legislative and administrative authority as had not been conferred upon Congress. The conflict of these views, which became acute in 1830 when South Carolina claimed the right of nullification, produced Secession and the war of 1861-65. Since the defeat of the Secessionists, the last of these views may be deemed to have been established, and the term "State sovereignty" is now but seldom heard. Even "States rights" have a different meaning from that which they had thirty years ago.[5] . . .

The Constitution, which had rendered many services to the American people, did them an inevitable disservice when it fixed their minds on the legal aspects of the question. Law was meant to be the servant of politics, and must not be suffered to become the master. A case had arisen which its formulae were unfit to deal with, a case which had to be settled on large moral and historical grounds. It was not merely the superior physical force of the North that prevailed; it was the moral forces which rule the world, forces which had long worked against slavery, and were ordained to save North America from the curse of hostile nations established side by side.

The word "sovereignty," which has in many ways clouded the domain of public law and jurisprudence, confused men's minds by making them assume that there must in every country exist, and be discoverable by legal inquiry, either one body invested legally with supreme power over all minor bodies, or several bodies which, though they had consented to form part of a larger body, were each in the last resort independent of it, and responsible to none but themselves.[6] They forgot that a Constitution may not have determined where legal supremacy shall dwell. Where the Constitution of the United States placed it was at any rate doubtful, so doubtful that it would have been better to drop technicalities, and recognize the broad fact that the legal claims of the States had become incompatible with the historical as well as legal claims of the nation. In the uncertainty as to where legal right resided, it would have been prudent to consider where physical force resided. The South however thought herself able to resist any physical force which the rest of the nation might bring against her. Thus encouraged, she took her stand on the doctrine of States Rights: and then followed a pouring out of blood and treasure such as was never spent on determining a point of law before, not even when Edward III and his successors waged war for a hundred years to establish the claim of females to inherit the crown of France.

What, then, do the rights of a State now include? Every right or power of a Government except:—

> The right of secession (not abrogated in terms, but admitted since the war to be no longer claimable. It is expressly negatived in the recent Constitutions of several Southern States).
>
> Powers which the Constitution withholds from the States (including that of intercourse with foreign governments).
>
> Powers which the Constitution expressly confers on the Federal Government.

As respects some powers of the last class, however, the States may act concurrently with, or in default of action by, the Federal Government. It is only from contravention of its action that they must abstain. And where contravention is alleged to exist, whether legislative or executive, it is by a court of law, and, in case the decision is in the first instance favourable to the pretensions of the State, ultimately by a Federal court, that the question falls to be decided.[7]

A reference to the preceding list of what each State may create in the way of distinct institutions will show that these rights practically cover nearly all the ordinary relations of citizens to one another and to their Government.[8] An American may, through a long life, never be reminded of the Federal Government, except when he votes at presidential and congressional elections, lodges a complaint against the post-office, and opens his trunks for a custom-house officer on the pier at New York when he returns from a tour in Europe. His direct taxes are paid to officials acting under State laws. The State, or a local authority constituted by State statutes, registers his birth, appoints his guardian, pays for his schooling, gives him a share in the estate of his father deceased, licenses him when he enters a trade (if it be one needing a licence), marries him, divorces him, entertains civil actions against him, declares him a bankrupt, hangs him for murder. The police that guard his house, the local boards which look after the poor, control highways, impose water rates, manage schools— all these derive their legal powers from his State alone. Looking at this immense compass of State functions, Jefferson would seem to have been not far wrong when he said that the Federal government was nothing more than the American department of foreign affairs. But although the National government touches the direct interests of the citizen less than does the State government, it touches his sentiment more. Hence the strength of his attachment to the former and his interest in it must not be measured by the frequency of his dealings with it. In the partition of governmental functions between nation and State, the State gets the most but the nation the highest, so the balance between the two is preserved.

Thus every American citizen lives in a duality of which Europeans, always excepting the Swiss, and to some extent the Germans, have no experience. He lives under two governments and two sets of laws; he is animated by two patriotisms and owes two allegiances. That these should both be strong and rarely be in conflict is most fortunate. It is the result of skilful adjustment and long habit, of the fact that those whose votes control the two sets of governments are the same persons, but above all of that harmony of each set of institutions with the other set, a harmony due to the identity of the principles whereon both are founded, which makes each appear necessary to the stability of the other, the States to the nation as its basis, the National Government to the States as their protector.

Notes

1. The case of Kansas immediately before the War of Secession, and the cases of the rebel States, which were not readmitted after the war till they had accepted the constitutional amendments forbidding slavery and protecting the freedmen, are quite exceptional cases.

2. Congress has power to pass a uniform rule of naturalization (Const. Art. i. § 8).

Under the present naturalization laws a foreigner must have resided in the United States for five years, and for one year in the State or Territory where he seeks admission to United States citizenship, and must declare two years before he is admitted that he renounces allegiance to any foreign prince or state. Naturalization makes him a citizen not only of the United States, but of the State or Territory where he is admitted, but does not necessarily confer the electoral franchise, for that depends on State laws.

In more than a third of the States the electoral franchise is now enjoyed by persons not naturalized as United States citizens.

3. "The line of distinction between the privileges and immunities of citizens of the United States, and those of citizens of the several States, must be traced along the boundary of their respective spheres of action, and the two classes must be as different in their nature as are the functions of their respective governments. A citizen of the United States as such has a right to participate in foreign and inter-state commerce, to have the benefit of the postal laws, to make use in common with others of the navigable waters of the United States, and to pass from State to State, and into foreign countries, because over all these subjects the jurisdiction of the United States extends, and they are covered by its laws. The privileges suggest the immunities. Wherever it is the duty of the United States to give protection to a citizen against any harm, inconvenience, or deprivation, the citizen is entitled to an immunity which pertains to Federal citizenship. One very plain immunity is exemption from any tax, burden, or imposition under State laws as a condition to the enjoyment of any right or privilege under the laws of the United States. . . . Whatever one may claim as of right under the Constitution and laws of the United States by virtue of his citizenship, is a privilege of a citizen of the United States. Whatever the Constitution and laws of the United States entitle him to exemption from, he may claim an exemption in respect to. And such a right or privilege is abridged whenever the State law interferes with any legitimate operation of Federal authority which concerns his interest, whether it be an authority actively exerted, or resting only in the express or implied command or assurance of the Federal Constitution or law. But the United States can neither grant nor secure to its citizens rights or privileges which are not expressly or by reasonable implication placed under its jurisdiction, and all not so placed are left to the exclusive protection of the States."—Cooley, *Principles,* pp. 245-247.

4. It may of course be said that as the colonies associated themselves into a league, at the very time at which they revolted from the British Crown, and as their foreign relations were always managed

by the authority and organs of this league, no one of them ever was for international purposes a free and independent sovereign State. This is true, and Abraham Lincoln was in this sense justified in saying that the Union was older than the States. But what are we to say of North Carolina and Rhode Island, after the acceptance of the Constitution of 1787-89 by the other eleven States? They were out of the old Confederation, for it had expired. They were not in the new Union, for they refused during many months to enter it. What else can they have been during these months except sovereign commonwealths?

5. States rights was a watchword in the South for many years. In 1851 there was a student at Harvard College from South Carolina who bore the name of States Rights Gist, baptized, so to speak, into Calhounism. He rose to be a brigadier-general in the Confederate army, and fell in the Civil War.

6. A further confusion arises from the fact that men are apt in talking of sovereignty to mix up legal supremacy with practical predominance. They ought to go together, and law seeks to make them go together. But it may happen that the person or body in whom law vests supreme authority is unable to enforce that authority: so the legal sovereign and the actual sovereign—that is to say, the force which will prevail in physical conflict—are different. There is always a strongest force; but the force recognized by law may not be really the strongest; and of several forces it may be impossible to tell, till they have come into actual physical conflict, which is the strongest.

7. See Chapter XXII. ante.

8. A recent American writer well observes that nearly all the great questions which have agitated England during the last sixty years would, had they arisen in America, have fallen within the sphere of State legislation.—Jameson, "Introduction to the Constitutional and Political History of the States," in *Johns Hopkins University Studies.*

Intergovernmental Relations

Three levels of government—national, state, and local—coexist in the American political system. They not only survive alongside one another, but they also cooperate and conflict with each other in carrying out functions.

Legal bases for relationships among governments in the American political system include the United States Constitution, 50 state constitutions, court decisions by both state and federal courts, and state and national legislation. But legal guidelines do not prevent complications from arising in a system of government with three tiers. Problems requiring attention often overlap more than one state or local jurisdiction. Governments closest to the scene seem best able to handle certain kinds of problems, but at the same time higher, more "distant" levels of government often have access to better sources of revenue with which to finance such government activities. Citizens give different degrees of loyalty and support to different levels of government, and competing ambitions of politicians at different levels of government obstruct needed cooperation.

The formal relationship between the national government and the states is quite different from that between the states and their local governments. The national-state relationship is formally "federal" in character, which means that in theory the states and the national government each have autonomous spheres of responsibility. In contrast, the state-local relationship is not a federal one. Local governments are mere "creatures" of the states and are not on equal footing with their creators and masters. In practical terms, however, the national government has gained the upper hand in its dealings with the states, and often localities are more nearly on equal footing with state governments than their inferior legal position suggests.

The three tiers of American government have often been likened to a layer cake: three layers in one overarching system of government. Still using the cake analogy, political scientist Morton Grodzins argued that a marble cake better represents the interactions of local, state, and national governments. According to Grodzins, these interactions are far less tidy than the model of a layer cake suggests.

It is easy to think, for example, that public schooling is a local government function. This impression is supported by the prominent role of special-purpose local governments called "school districts" in governing public education. But, as Grodzins pointed out, such a view overlooks the powerful role that state governments play by providing financial aid, certifying teachers, prescribing curriculum requirements, regulating school safety and pupil health, and generally overseeing what school districts do. The national government is also involved in public schooling. In the last 40 years, the United States Supreme Court and lower federal courts have made numerous decisions aimed at ending racial segregation in public schools. In addition, for several decades national government grants have helped finance various activities such as school breakfasts and lunches and special education programs. (As this book goes to press in 1995, proposals to alter many of these national grant programs were being considered by the U.S. Congress.) Even this brief review of local, state, and national involvement in one area, schooling, can show why Grodzins believed that a marble cake better reflects the reality of the American three-level system of government than a layer cake does.

Intergovernmental transfers of money are an important form of interaction among local, state, and national governments. "Strings" are almost always attached to money that one level of government transfers to another level. For example, when the national government provides grants to states and localities, requirements concerning the use of the money accompany the funds, although the extensiveness and specificity of requirements vary greatly in different grant programs. Similarly, state governments aid local governments, and state money also brings strings of one kind or another.

Presidents and other government leaders often set forth proposals about how to structure relations and divide responsibilities among national, state, and local governments. President Ronald Reagan's "new federalism" was aimed at shifting greater responsibility back to the states and localities, thereby reversing a long-term trend toward greater national government involvement in providing an increasing number of services. Moreover, the amount of revenue that the national government transferred to states and localities was significantly reduced during the Reagan years. The change in direction begun under Reagan continued under President George Bush, and state and local governments had to operate in the context of what has been called "fend-for-yourself federalism." Whatever changes in intergovernmental relations that the Clinton administration tried to make faded into obscurity with the coming of a Republican-controlled House of Representatives and Senate in January 1995. Newt Gingrich, the first Republican Speaker of the House of Representatives in 40 years, made shrinking the size of the national government and giving increased responsibilities to the states an important part of the campaign promises that contributed to the Republicans' impressive victory in the November 1994 congressional elections. In the 104th Congress, the Republican House of Representatives passed a number of bills fulfilling Gingrich's cam-

paign promises. One such bill, later passed by the Senate and in March 1995 signed into law by President Clinton, was designed to make it very difficult for Congress to mandate state and local governments to do something without providing the necessary funding. Another bill passed by the House and, as this book goes to press, about to be considered by the Senate, would give the states responsibility for assisting households in which poor children reside, providing school lunches for poor children, and other such social welfare services. Along with these responsibilities would come lump sums (or "block grants") of money from the national government, but it would be up to the states (and possibly their localities) to devise and implement ways to assist poor people in their jurisdictions. It is just possible that the United States is beginning a new era of intergovernmental relations that will result in substantial changes in the activities of state and local governments.

Selections in this unit treat various aspects of relationships among national, state, and local governments.

Looking Ahead: Challenge Questions

Do you think that the current state of intergovernmental relations in the United States is satisfactory or unsatisfactory?

Which level of government do you think is contributing the most to the welfare of Americans? Why?

Under what circumstances do you think the national government should try to impose national standards on state and local governments? Under what circumstances do you think state governments should impose state standards on local governments?

Should states and localities have responsibility for performing more tasks and for raising money to pay for them? Why or why not?

The *New* Federalism

Is New Federalism an idea whose time has finally come? Maybe, but figuring out what it really means or would do is about as easy as nailing Jell-O to the wall.

ROCHELLE L. STANFIELD

New Federalism is back. Again. But this time—the third try—may be the charm. New schemes to take power away from the federal government and give it to states and localities are mostly retreads from the Nixon and Reagan Administrations. It's everything else that makes this time different.

"For the last 30 years, most of the talk about New Federalism has been intellectual—the kind of thing that one-tenth of 1 per cent of the people were interested in," Lamar Alexander, former college president, Tennessee governor, Education Secretary and would-be Republican presidential candidate in 1996, said in a recent interview. "What happened on Nov. 8 was just a huge scream from the gut about the arrogance of Washington, D.C. It's moved from the head to the stomach, and therefore is something that can't be ignored."

To depict New Federalism as a primal scream may not be far off the mark. The notion of a federal system with power shared between federal and state governments is among the most basic in Ameri-

can politics. That's what *The Federalist Papers*—recently returned to vogue by House Speaker Newt Gingrich, R-Ga.—are all about. But what New Federalism really means or would do remains elusive. Is the purpose to make all government smaller? Or better? To make the federal government smaller by shifting responsibilities to states and localities? Or to make all government work better by clearly defining responsibilities and assigning tasks to the level that does them best?

"If you simply transfer power from bureaucracies in Washington to bureaucracies in Madison [Wis.] or Sacramento [Calif.], that is a mistake and won't satisfy people," William Kristol, the chairman of the Project for the Republican Future and one of Gingrich's top idea men, said in an interview. "People want problems addressed in new ways. They want government cut back at all levels."

Not all Republicans, though, aim simply to make all government smaller. Whatever the end, how do you get there? Everybody uses the same terms—devolution, block grants, swaps, no "unfunded

Rep. William F. Goodling, R-Pa.
"I'm not just for block-granting money back and saying, 'Here, do your thing.'"

John Eisele

mandates"—but the meaning shifts with the speaker, the context and the audience.

Most participants in the discussion agree that there are overarching national goals the federal government is obligated to seek. But whose goals—the liberals' commitment to housing integration or the conservatives' commitment to reducing illegitimacy?

These differences over practicalities are likely to slow down and complicate the process of passing New Federalism legislation, but the pervasive, gut-level feeling that something needs to be done could provide the momentum—this time—to push it through in some form.

"The point is that for the American democracy to continue in its most effective form, there needs to be a reexamination of the basic questions that were asked by Hamilton, Jefferson and Madison about who does what," Gov. Mike Leavitt, R-Utah, said in an interview. He and Gov. E. Benjamin Nelson, D-Neb., are promoting a bipartisan conference of the states to consider fundamental issues of federalism and to recommend constitutional amendments that would shift power to the states. *(See box.)*

But probably the most important factor in New Federalism's favor is the ascension of Republicans in Congress.

Most of the federal programs and approaches in question were the product of Democratic Congresses that stepped in with money and orders to meet domestic needs and demands that had been left unmet by states and localities. Regardless of subsequent state and local reforms, program obsolescence and changing times, Democratic Congresses were loathe to give up these brainchildren.

Republican control of both chambers of Congress sweeps many of those obstacles away. In his opening remarks as Senate Majority Leader on Jan. 4, Robert Dole, R-Kan., spoke of federalism and the 10th Amendment, which reserves to the states all powers not delegated to the federal government. "But there are some in Washington—perhaps fewer this year than last—who believe neither our states nor our people can be trusted with power," Dole said. "Federalism has given way to paternalism—with disastrous results. If I have one goal for the 104th Congress, it is this: that we will dust off the 10th Amendment and restore it to its rightful place in our Constitution."

In his opening speech, Gingrich alluded to federalism only indirectly—noting that "there was much to what Ronald Reagan was trying to get done; there is much to what is being done today by [various Republican governors]"—but returning power to the states is one of his frequent themes.

This time around, New Federalism isn't only a Republican thing; it's also a central feature of the New Democrat theology. Sorting out intergovernmental responsibilities is a key item on an alternative contract with America developed by the Democratic Leadership Council.

President Clinton has jumped on the bandwagon. In December, he proposed to reorganize the Housing and Urban Development (HUD) Department along New Federalist lines. The Office of Management and Budget (OMB), the White House's Domestic Policy Council and Vice President Albert Gore Jr.'s National Performance Review are looking for similar steps to take in other departments.

OMB director Alice M. Rivlin, who wrote a book on the subject in 1992, when she was a scholar at the Brookings Institution, is one of the most enthusiastic New Federalists in the Administration. "I was persuaded early in my career, when I worked at what was then the Department of Health, Education and Welfare, that the federal government was trying to do too many different things," she said in a recent interview. "Even then, it would have made sense to rethink the relationship between the federal government and the states. I think that's even more true now."

Things are also different on the other side of the federalism equation. The November elections put 30 governorships in Republican hands—including 9 of the nation's 10 largest states (all but Florida); Republicans control both chambers of 19 state legislatures and one chamber in 13 states. The substantial influence of governors in presidential politics and the raw power of state legislatures in ratifying constitutional amendments (like one to require a balanced federal budget) dramatically increase their clout with the new Congress. On a policy level, the states have demonstrated over the past decade that they can manage programs as well as or better than the federal government. As many governors like to point out, the states have instituted both education reform and welfare reform—while balancing their budgets every year.

OMB director Alice M. Rivlin
"It's not easy to measure outcomes of public programs..."

Richard A. Bloom

Meanwhile, city and county governments have also changed. Regardless of party, mayors and county officials are more businesslike. Because they can no longer rely on Congress to bail them out financially, they've begun to look to themselves, their states and to the private sector. Thus—and perhaps most important—they've decided to join forces with the states rather than fight them as they did during the previous two rounds of debate over a New Federalism.

"I was part of that whole business of dealing with New Federalism [in 1982]," Gov. George V. Voinovich of Ohio, a Republican who was the mayor of Cleveland at the time, recalled at a recent news conference in Washington. "At that time, we didn't do too well, because the organizations [representing state and local governments] negotiated individually with the Reagan Administration." After the states, counties and cities cut deals at odds with each other, New Federalism proposals fell apart.

"So we have decided," Voinovich said, "that to the very best of our ability, we're going to work together as a team." He announced the formation of a coalition of five state and local government organizations (the National Governors' Association [NGA], the National Conference of

GETTING THE STATES TOGETHER

Of the many variations on the theme of New Federalism, one is truly a back-to-basics move. Two governors, Republican Mike Leavitt of Utah and Democrat E. Benjamin Nelson of Nebraska, are promoting a "Conference of the States" to consider fundamental reforms to shift power from the federal government to the states.

"Much of the discussion about devolution is focused on rearranging boxes—which program is handled by which area," Leavitt said in an interview. "The Conference of the States is focused on the broader picture of how do we recreate that delicate balance between states and the national government." *(See NJ, 1/28/95, p. 40.)*

The proposals that Leavitt and Nelson contemplate are so basic and long-range that they're not as controversial as the New Federalism proposals for converting welfare into block grants, for example. But ultimately, they would have a far greater effect on the balance of power between the federal government and the states.

One item, for example, would make it easier for the states to initiate a constitutional amendment. Currently, the only route open to the states is to call for a constitutional convention, a politically impractical path because, some fear, such a convention could get out of hand. Another item would be to allow two-thirds of the states to kill federal legislation.

As Leavitt sees it, getting specific about such programs as welfare or such special-interest issues as abortion would destroy the effectiveness of the conference, as would partisanship. "Those three things—I call them the three deadly sins—would kill the capacity of the conference to succeed," he said.

Both the National Governors' Association and the National Conference of State Legislatures have endorsed the idea. Officials of the organizations said that most legislatures have plans to adopt a formal resolution to call the conference, which would take place by fall.

No formal role is contemplated for local governments, which are the creatures of the states and have no official status under the Constitution. And that could disrupt the newfound partnership that state and local government organizations have formed. Leavitt and others say that they want local governments to participate by bringing proposals to the conference, but not by voting in it. That may not be enough for the locals.

"We intend to have a word [in the conference]," said Mayor Victor Ashe of Knoxville, Tenn., the president of the U.S. Conference of Mayors. "We're not going to let a meeting be held and cities and counties not be represented."

State Legislatures, the National Association of Counties, the U.S. Conference of Mayors and the National League of Cities).

"I think the next couple of years are going to be the greatest opportunity to restructure federal-state relations since the New Deal," Raymond C. Scheppach, the NGA's executive director, said in an interview. "If it's done right, I think you can have a win-win-win situation for the federal government, the states and the beneficiaries [of government services]. If it's done badly, I think everybody loses."

THE DEVIL IN THE DETAILS

On the basic themes of New Federalism, everyone sings the same tune: smaller, more efficient government; less federal micromanaging; greater flexibility for states and localities. It's when you try to pin down what those concepts mean in practice—and exactly how to achieve them—that divisions appear everywhere.

Republican governors are unified in their support for a balanced budget amendment and opposition to unfunded mandates (programs that Washington has imposed on state and local governments without providing the money to pay for them), for example, but split over whether language that would prohibit unfunded mandates should be incorporated in the proposal for a balanced budget amendment.

With their Contract With America, House Republicans appear to be a united front, marching under the flag of the Gingrich Revolution. But there are cracks in that facade.

When asked in an interview about some of the far-reaching block grants and the social agenda that some conservative lawmakers contemplate, for example, Rep. William F. Goodling, R-Pa., a moderate who chairs the Economic and Educational Opportunities Committee (formerly Education and Labor), replied, "As an authorizing committee, we will have a major responsibility in making sure that those who haven't dealt with these programs day in and day out don't make any mistakes that would come back to embarrass us."

State and local officials—Democrats and Republicans alike—insist that they will gladly exchange less federal aid for more flexibility in running the programs. But how much less and how much more? "If we get fewer dollars and we also get fewer regulations, we will be able to spend the dollars we get directly on services," Democratic state Rep. Jane L. Campbell, the assistant minority leader of the Ohio House, said in a joint interview with other legislators. "Actually, we want less federally."

But another Democratic state representative, Daniel T. Blue of North Carolina, said in the same interview: "We realize, too, that simply saying the states are going to assume greater responsibility is an empty promise if there are not resources that come with that."

And what exactly does *flexibility* mean? Everyone agrees that if Congress hands taxpayers' money to states or localities, some form of federal audit is necessary to avoid fraud and abuse. Beyond that, it gets very fuzzy.

"In areas where there is a need to have an across-the-board federal policy—safe drinking water is a good example—[the federal government could] set the standard and then let the state legislatures determine how to meet that standard," Campbell said. "If [Congress] just simply said, 'We want to make sure that children in this country don't starve and that people have a safe place to live and parents have an opportunity to be educated and trained and have child care, here's how much money there is to do it, now do it,' I think you would get extraordinarily better service. The accountability mechanism in the states is established: It's the state legislatures. We're elected by our constituents to make appropriate policy for the state."

Goodling, however, has a very different view of the extent of accountability. While he acknowledged that federal laws have "denied any local creativity" and that "we've tied the hands of local people," he said: "We should not have the right to send federal taxpayers' money anywhere unless they know what it is we expect to accomplish. I'm not just for block-granting money back and saying, 'Here, do your thing.' There has to be a purpose and goals . . . and oversight to see that's what's happening."

The Clinton Administration and the New Democrats see the federal government playing an additional role whenever it gives out money: promoting management reform. "We're really trying to reward effort," said Kathleen Sylvester, the vice president for domestic policy of the New Democrats' Progressive Policy Institute. "We've got to figure out what is the federal government's role to leverage change when there's an appropriate federal interest in something."

To some state and local officials, that smacks of the same old paternalism. "You can't just say, 'OK, this is yours, but by the way, you got to do it between A and Z,'" said New York state Sen. James J. Lack, a Republican. "Send us the unfettered authority. We'll do it. That's our job."

There's general agreement that whatever federal standards are imposed should require certain outcomes rather than set the specific practices or procedures to arrive at those outcomes. But setting outcome standards is easier said than done. "There is some glibness," Rivlin said. "It's not easy to measure outcomes of public programs, and one has to be careful not to produce counterproductive measures."

The theorists of federalism believe that the dilemma of flexibility versus accountability can be solved in the design of New Federalism legislation, and as was the case with New Federalism I and II, three general approaches are under discussion: block grants, swaps and turnbacks. But politics rarely accommodates such neat theories.

Republicans on the House Ways and Means Committee, for example, are working on a series of six block grants to consolidate as many as 300 welfare, child care, food and nutrition and other programs. But Nancy Landon Kassebaum, R-Kan., who chairs the Senate Labor and Human Resources Committee, has her eye on a swap: The federal government would take over total financing of medicaid (the states now contribute about $57 billion a year) while the states would accept total responsibility for aid to families with dependent children (AFDC), food stamps and a few small programs to make the swap at least equal and, preferably, to save the federal government money.

"It isn't just a question of sending money to the states and letting them, with a block grant, have the flexibility to run it," Kassebaum said on NBC News's *Meet the Press* on Jan. 15. "I would sever Washington's involvement."

No turnbacks have been formally introduced, but several people, including Alexander, have suggested eliminating federal elementary and secondary education programs along with a specific federal revenue source—taxes on alcoholic beverages or cigarettes, for example,

Democratic state Rep. Jane L. Campbell, the assistant minority leader of the Ohio House
"The accountability mechanism in the states is established: It's the state legislatures."

which states could in turn enact to pay for the additional education expenses.

"Block grants are a temptation [to Congress] to micromanage," Jeffrey Eisenach, the president of the Progress & Freedom Foundation and an adviser to Gingrich, said. "Complete devolution approaches [like swaps or turnbacks] really and truly get the federal government out of it. Once the money's in Washington, the power's in Washington, and you can't get around it."

But Eisenach acknowledged a drawback in terms of equity. Some states have a greater capacity to raise revenues than other states. "Part of the purpose of federal welfare programs, I suspect, is to hide the cross-state subsidies," he said.

For others, like Stuart M. Butler, the Heritage Foundation's vice president and director of domestic policy, the primary goal must be to reduce federal involvement. The Kassebaum swap would be "a disaster," Butler said, because the federal government would be left holding the entire bill for medicaid. "Once you've got a swap, you've got it," he said. Block grants, on the other hand, allow Congress to relinquish a program gradually. "You start by saying, 'You'll get a block grant with all the flexibility, but I'm going to cut funding by 15-20 per cent'—whatever you can get away with," Butler said. "Then the pressure is on Congress to look for ways of cutting that back further over time."

New York state Sen. James J. Lack, a Republican
"Send us the unfettered authority. We'll do it."

Photos by John Eisele

Richard A. Bloom

**Jeffrey Eisenach of the Progress & Freedom Foundation
"Block grants are a temptation to micromanage."**

"Everyone in state and local government knows what happens to block grants," said the Progressive Policy Institute's Sylvester. "They get whittled away and then there's less money to [provide services]."

Which is exactly why the NGA's Scheppach doubts that most governors would go along with a block grant for AFDC, food stamps or medicaid unless the grant is budgeted as an entitlement, in which the size of the grant is tied to the number of recipients. "If you're talking about a block grant that's fighting through the Appropriations Committees every year for its funding," he said, "I think that's a potential real problem."

But some governors say they want freedom so much that they're willing to risk future losses.

"I can't speak for all the governors, but I can for my governor," said Gerald H. Miller, the director of Michigan's Department of Social Services, who is handling welfare negotiations for Republican Gov. John M. Engler. "Clearly, to get the kind of flexibility we think that we need, we would be willing to give that [entitlement] up."

After meeting with House Republicans, a group of Republican governors said that they would agree to eliminating entitlements for individuals as long as Congress guaranteed that the state grants would not be reduced for five years. Republicans on the Ways and Means Committee were unwilling to make such a guarantee.

But Gov. Howard Dean of Vermont, a Democrat who's serving as the NGA's chairman this year, objected to the elimination of the entitlement. "No way, that's bad for everybody," he said in an interview.

Local officials recognize that however these proposals are structured, they ultimately will be left holding the bag. "It's the cities and counties of America where the local people will come to get help," Michael Hightower, a vice chairman of the Fulton County (Atlanta) Commission, said. "We're not saying 'Gimme, gimme gimme,' but we're also not saying, 'Give us less money.' We need the resources, because it's our hospitals and homeless shelters where the people come."

For this reason, Donald J. Borut, the executive director of the National League of Cities, sees some of these block grant proposals as "the mother of all unfunded mandates."

WHOSE AGENDA?

The flexibility of New Federalism doesn't mean abrogating national goals and principles, its exponents agree. The difficulty comes in defining just what are the nation's goals and principles.

Some are pretty generally accepted. The state and local organizations agreed, for example, to exempt civil rights from the unfunded mandates legislation. "Clearly, in the area of civil rights, I don't think anyone would even question that," said Mayor Victor Ashe of Knoxville, Tenn., the president of the U.S. Conference of Mayors. "That's basic." But some might question the definition of civil rights—whether it extends to affirmative action, for example, or to gays.

The Clinton Administration's redesign of HUD addresses the issue up front. At a news conference to explain the Administration's proposal, HUD Secretary Henry G. Cisneros spoke of "a long-standing tension between the rights of the states and the role of centralized government to deal with national goals and national ideals that the federal government has, for the last generation at least, been the protector of." Among these he listed fair housing, promoting housing mobility for the poor and attention to such special populations as the homeless, the elderly and the disabled.

Cisneros acknowledged that "in the white-hot heat of local politics, it is not possible for local government to act on these questions without some strong push from the federal government." Others argue that the results of the Nov. 8 elections call into question whether most Americans really want the federal government pushing on social welfare issues.

Nonetheless, the Administration carefully avoided using the term "block grants" to describe the three pots of money it envisions to replace 60 or so of HUD's programs. Instead, it called them "performance-based funds" to signify its "contractual agreement" with states and localities.

The conservatives also have a social agenda that conflicts with their notions of flexibility and devolution. The Contract With America, for example, is very specific on tough anti-crime legislation—traditionally the province of state government—and who should receive welfare. Left out of the contract but high on the agenda of some conservative lawmakers is a detailed list of what schools should and should not teach. This conflict shows up frequently in Republican rhetoric.

"Republicans . . . believe that our country's increasingly desperate fight against crime is an area where more freedom is needed at the state level," Dole told his colleagues on Jan. 4. And then, in the next breath, he said: "Our crime bill will impose mandatory minimum sentences on those who use guns in the commission of a crime, and make sure the jails are there to lock them up."

Similarly, on welfare reform, while contemplating the best way for the federal government to get out of the public assistance business, some Republican lawmakers insist that no money go to the illegitimate children of teenagers or to illegal immigrants.

Some conservative Republicans see a danger in this approach. "We've got to resist all these efforts that some Republicans are involved in that say we ought to fix welfare in Washington or we ought to show we're tough on crime by setting the state sentences," Alexander said. "That is absolute nonsense. The vote on Nov. 8 was about the arrogance of Washington, and the greatest danger that we have is that we'll replace their arrogant empire with one of our own."

Federal Government Mandates

WHY THE STATES ARE COMPLAINING

Martha Derthick

Martha Derthick, formerly director of the Brookings Governmental Studies program, is the Julia Allen Cooper Professor of Government and Foreign Affairs at the University of Virginia. She thanks John Dinan for research assistance.

Hard pressed by recession, state governments have been complaining that Congress keeps passing laws ordering them to undertake expensive new programs—but without providing the money to do so.* Complaints about federal mandates are not new. In 1980 New York City Mayor Edward I. Koch wrote bitterly of the "mandate millstone" in an article in *The Public Interest*, giving currency to the term.

The main concern of state officials is political: who will pay the costs of government? But their complaints raise constitutional issues as well. In various ways the Constitution protects the states' existence as governments, having their own elected officials and the power to raise taxes and to enact, enforce, and interpret laws. How far can federal mandates be pushed without infringing on the states' governmental character?

The federal government influences state governments in four main ways—through court decrees, legislative regulations, preemptions, and conditional grants-in-aid. As a quick review will show, all four have grown significantly more coercive in the past half century.

Judicial Decrees

Until the mid-1950s federal courts interpreting the Constitution had habitually told the states what they might *not* do. They had struck down literally hundreds of state laws. But they had refrained from telling states what they *must* do. This changed with school desegregation. In 1955, with *Brown v. Board of Education II*, the Supreme Court gave federal district courts responsibility for entering the orders and decrees to desegregate public schools. The Court's ruling initiated a judicial effort to achieve racial integration with affirmative commands, telling school districts how to construct their attendance zones, where to build schools, where to bus their pupils, and how to assign their teachers.

Once courts and litigants discovered what could be done (or attempted) in the schools, other state institutions, especially prisons and institutions for the mentally ill and retarded, became targets. Nearly all state prison systems now operate under judicial decrees that address overcrowding and other conditions of prison life, and federal judges routinely mandate construction programs and modes of prison administration.

Needless to say, federal judicial mandates come without money, because courts have no way of raising money.

Legislative Regulations

Congress is also a source of affirmative commands to the states. When it imposes taxes and regulations—such as social security payroll taxes, wages-and-hours regulation, and emissions limits—on private parties, it must decide whether to cover state governments as well, for they and their local subdivisions are employers and, in some respects, producers.

For much of the nation's history, Congress did not tax and regulate state governments because it conceived of them as separate, sovereign, and equal. In a leading statement of this constitutional doctrine, the Supreme Court ruled in 1871 (*Collector v. Day*) that a federal income tax could not be levied against a county judge in Massachusetts. An earlier decision of the Court (*Dobbins v. The Commissioners of Erie,* 1842) had settled that the states could not tax the salary of an officer of the United States. Under 19th-century conceptions of federalism, it followed that the federal government could not tax the salaries of officers of the states.

When the Social Security Act of 1935 was passed, states as employers were routinely exempted from paying the payroll tax. Similarly, when the Fair Labor Standards Act of 1938 set maximum hours and minimum wages for industrial employers, no one would have imagined extending such regulation to state and local governments.

Yet as these New Deal measures were being enacted, the doctrine of sovereign immunity that had protected the states was collapsing. The Supreme Court overruled *Collector v. Day* in 1939. Eventually, under the nationalizing impact of the New Deal, Congress began regulating state governments just as if they were private parties. For example, Congress extended wages-and-hours regulation to some state and local employees in 1966, to the rest in 1974. The Supreme Court at first upheld the move, but then, in response to the law of 1974, changed its mind. In 1976 the Court forbade Congress from exercising its commerce power so as to "force directly upon the States its choices as to how essential decisions regarding the conduct of integral governmental functions are to be made" (*National League of Cities v. Usery*). But the standard proved impractical and was abandoned in 1985 (*Garcia v. San Antonio Metropolitan Transit Authority*). Speaking for the Court, Justice Blackmun wrote that the "political process ensures that laws that unduly burden the States will not be promulgated." The Court seemed to wash its hands of the subject, leaving the states to the mercy of what Justice O'Connor in dissent called Congress's "underdeveloped capacity for self-restraint."

Preemptions

Preemptions are commands to the states to *stop* doing something and let the federal government do it. They are sanctioned by the supremacy clause of the Constitution, which requires that state laws yield to federal ones in case of conflict. Historically, preemptions have been not so much a calculated technique of intergovernmental relations as something that "just happened" as a byproduct of congressional action. It was left to the courts to rule, in response to litigation, whether preemption had taken place.

Recently preemptions have become both more frequent and more explicit. Congress passed more than 90 new preemptive laws in the 1970s and again in the 1980s, more than double the number for any previous decade. Partly because of pressure from the courts to be explicit, Congress now often does declare an intention to preempt. And the states naturally experience such declarations as coercion, even if they are being prevented from doing things rather than commanded to do them.

There is also a modern variant on the use of preemption, called by students of federalism "partial preemption." In the 1970s, as it enacted a new wave of regulation, Congress hit on a way of making use of the states for administration. It would preempt a field—say, occupational health and safety or surface mining or air pollution control—but permit the states to continue to function providing that they adopted standards at least as exacting as those it stipulated. The Supreme Court upheld this technique (*Hodel v. Virginia Surface Mining and Reclamation Association,* 1981).

Technically, the states can refuse the federal government's invitation to serve as administrators of its regulations. But in practice they have responded. "Each State shall . . . adopt . . . a plan which provides for implementation, maintenance, and enforcement" of federal air quality standards, the Clean Air Act says—and each state does. Better to be subordinate governments than empty ones.

Grant-in-Aid Conditions

Federal grant-in-aid conditions addressed to the states have been around at least since the Morrill Act of 1862, which gave the states land—30,000 acres for each member of Congress—to endow colleges in the agricultural and mechanic arts.

In theory, states have always been able to refuse federal grants. In practice, they have generally found them irresistible. And as time passed, states' dependence increased: aid was habit-forming. In 1965 federal highway grants passed $4 billion a year. In 1970 federal

grants for public assistance, including Medicaid, passed $7 billion a year. Altogether federal grants in 1970 amounted to nearly 30 percent of states' own-source revenues. It is absurd to hold, as constitutional doctrine formally does, that such grants can be rejected, and the burden of the accompanying conditions thereby avoided.

Over time, the conditions of grant programs expanded in scope and detail. Successful political movements left their mark on grant programs through conditions that apply to all or most grant programs. The rights revolution of the 1960s and 1970s, for example, left a legacy of anti-discrimination requirements, and the environmental movement a requirement that environmental impact statements be prepared for federally aided projects.

Similarly, conditions have multiplied program by program. Section 402 of Title IV of the Social Security Act of 1935 took 2 brief paragraphs to describe what should be contained in state plans for aid to dependent children. By 1976 section 402 had grown to 9 pages; by 1988, to 27.

Also, Congress in the 1970s began threatening to withhold grants, particularly those for Medicaid and highways, to achieve objectives connected only loosely or not at all to the underlying purpose of the grant. When Congress set a national speed limit of 55 miles per hour in 1974 and a minimum drinking age of 21 in 1984, it did so by threatening to withhold highway grants from states that failed to comply.

Finally, the language of grant-in-aid statutes has become more coercive. Federal law makes some Medicaid services "mandatory" and Congress keeps adding to the list.

From time to time presidents, especially Republicans, have tried to reduce and simplify grant conditions. The revisions that Nixon, Ford, and Reagan achieved, in the form of revenue sharing and block grants, have been modest and, in the case of general revenue sharing, short-lived. Conditioned grants for specific purposes have persisted and always predominated.

Historically, grant-in-aid conditions could be enforced only by administrative action, primarily the threat to withhold the grant. Because withholding was self-defeating, it was not often used. Federal administrators got what compliance they could through negotiation. However, with the rights revolution and the rise of judicial activism, many grant-in-aid conditions became judicially enforceable, particularly in programs of AFDC and education of handicapped children. A whole new set of commands emanated from an awe-inspiring source, the courts.

As grant conditions became more coercive, grants did not keep pace. Grants as a share of states' own-source revenues reached a peak at 32 percent in 1976 and then began to fall.

Do Mandates Matter?

The rise of the affirmative command, occurring subtly and on several different fronts, constitutes a sea-change in federal-state relations. The states have been converted from separate governments into subordinate

Congress is not much inclined to contemplate the deeper issues of federalism and to ask, self-critically, whether or where it should exercise restraint in its use of mandates.

ones, arguably mere "agents" in some programs. In constitutional significance, the change is comparable to the transformation by which the federal government ceased over the course of many years to be a government of limited, specified powers and became free to engage in any domestic activity not prohibited by the Bill of Rights.

That mandates developed only in the past 40 years does not necessarily mean that they are contrary to the Framers' intentions. That depends on which Framers one consults. Today's federalism is what the losing side of 1787 feared, but arguably what the winning side hoped for. Madison, after all, went into the Constitutional Convention saying that the states should be retained because they would be "subordinately useful." That is precisely what they have become. And there is at least a hint in *The Federalist* that affirmative commands would be acceptable. Number 27, written by by the ardently nationalistic Hamilton, anticipated that the federal government would employ the states to administer its laws. It is hard to see how that could have happened in the absence of mandates.

Yet most fundamentally, *The Federalist* saw federalism as a way to safeguard the public against abuses of governmental power and to sustain republicanism, the great central principle of the American regime. As Hamilton argued in number 28, "Power being almost always the rival of power, the general government will at all times stand ready to check the usurpations of the state governments, and these will have the same disposition towards the general government. The people, by throwing themselves into either scale, will infallibly make it preponderate. If their rights are invaded by either, they can make use of the other as the instrument of redress."

Indeed, the institutions of federalism can be used by the people to play different levels of government—and through them different policy choices—off against each other. One sees this happening most vividly in the prolonged contest over abortion policy, in which the federal courts "corrected" the restrictive excesses of state laws in the early 1970s and state legislatures responded by "correcting" the libertarian excesses of *Roe v. Wade*, and so on—in a heated intergovernmental exchange that threatens to be endless because the rival political movements are incapable of compromise.

Today mandates come in so many different forms and with so many different purposes that it is difficult to speak of them as a class. Limited, for the sake of discussion, to those that compel expenditure, they clearly raise important questions about republicanism. Judicial mandates come from a body that is not elected at all; congressional mandates, from a body that is not responsible to the various state electorates. When the federal judiciary commands the states to spend more on prisons and Congress commands them to spend more on Medicaid, they are making decisions that state electorates have no way to review. State officials lose their ability to weigh competing claims on state budgets. Of course, no such weighing is done at the federal level, where mandates are produced in isolation

from one another. Neither the courts nor Congress, framing commands to the states, asks the question, "how much, compared to what?" that is crucial to rational, responsible policymaking. At some point, federal commands to the states may come to implicate the guarantee clause of the Constitution: "The United States shall guarantee to every state in this Union a Republican Form of Government."

Can Mandates Be Curbed?

How strongly state officials oppose mandates may be questioned. Accepting subordination as a fact of life, they have produced scattered complaints but not concerted or doctrinaire opposition. Although the loss of budgetary discretion is a serious problem for governors, it is hard for all 50 of them to get together on anything, much less take a public stand *for* overcrowded prisons or *against* medical care for pregnant women.

Largely devoid of interest in constitutional issues except for its own battles with the president, today's Congress is not much inclined to contemplate the deeper issues of federalism and to ask, self-critically, whether or where it should exercise restraint in its use of mandates. If it can expand the benefits of government while imposing much of the cost on other governments in the system, why not do it?

By contrast, the Supreme Court, habituated to thinking in constitutional terms, and made conservative by a series of Republican appointments, is engaged in a wide-ranging retreat from the use of mandates. In school desegregation, prison administration, and enforcement of grant-in-aid conditions, not to mention voting rights, abortion, and *habeas corpus*, the Court has signaled that it will show more deference to the states. But it is one thing for the Court to practice self-restraint and quite another for it to attempt to restrain Congress. The Court does not lightly challenge a co-equal branch of government, nor has it had much success in the past in devising practical and enduring standards to protect the state governments.

There remains, nonetheless, a strong case for federalism, as Alice Rivlin, for one, has urged in the 1991 Webb Lecture before the National Academy of Public Administration and in *Reviving the American Dream*. As Madison foresaw, the task of governing so vast a country is too formidable for one government alone. It is significant that someone as thoughtful and experienced as Rivlin, whose whole career has been based in Washington and devoted to shaping national policy, should conclude that national uniformity is a liability in some areas of government. She names education and skills training, child care, housing, infrastructure, and economic development as activities that are "likely to succeed only if they are well adapted to local conditions, have strong local support and community participation and are managed by accountable officials who can be voted out if things go badly."

Rivlin's vision of revitalized state government calls, appropriately, for interstate equalization of revenues, to be achieved—and here her proposal becomes radical—by the states' adopting "one or more common

By contrast, the Supreme Court, habituated to thinking in constitutional terms, is engaged in a wide-ranging retreat from the use of mandates.

taxes (same base, same rate) and sharing the proceeds." She suggests a single state corporate income tax or a uniform value-added tax, shared on a per capita basis and substituted for state retail sales taxes. To achieve this, the states would need the "blessing and perhaps the assistance of the federal government."

Indeed. There is no plausible mechanism, formal or informal, by which the 50 states could voluntarily agree on a common tax. It would have to be imposed by Congress in a fresh stroke of centralization—a mandate, if you will—entailing preemption of a particular tax source and dedication of the proceeds to the states, with no conditions attached. The absence of conditions proved not to be politically durable when general revenue sharing was tried in the 1970s. State political leaders might be forgiven if they doubt whether Congress would be willing to take the heat for imposing a new tax while turning the proceeds over to them.

Perhaps no other of our governing institutions has been subject to so much change and yet so resistant to planned, deliberate reform as federalism. Its history is one of centralization, steady and seemingly irreversible. Yet the case for lodging a large measure of domestic responsibility and discretion with the states and their local subdivisions remains strong. So is the case for the states having governments—republican governments chosen by state electorates and accountable to them, and capable of raising their own revenues and deciding how those revenues should be spent. It is one of the ironies of federalism that deliberate acts of decentralization, such as Rivlin proposes, depend on centralization as a precondition.

---

*In response to such complaints, the Republican-controlled 104th Congress passed a so-called "unfunded mandates" bill that was signed into law by Democratic President Clinton in March 1995. The legislation makes it very difficult for Congress to pass laws that impose requirements *and* accompanying costs on states. *Editor*

Tightening the Screws On 'Takings'

**The Supreme Court has been siding with property owners.
The lesson: Governments need to craft land use actions with care.**

JONATHAN WALTERS

Should governments have broad power to regulate land use in the name of public welfare and safety? Or are we a country that holds the rights of the private property owner preeminent? In the minds of advocates on both sides, it is nothing less than a struggle for the soul of America.

That struggle has led in recent years to a number of high-profile U.S. Supreme Court cases in which landowners have claimed that government has overstepped the bounds of that power. "Taking" is the term landowners apply when they believe a government is setting conditions—such as development bans or easement requirements—that unfairly deny them full use of their property.

The most recent takings decision to come down from the Supreme Court, issued at the end of June, was yet another in a string of court decisions slapping governments on the wrist for failing to justify a taking or compensate a landowner adequately.

While the ruling is not likely to send localities into headlong retreat on land use laws or wholesale review of permit conditions, it does serve notice that the high court is paying attention and that states and localities had better craft their land use laws and permitting conditions with care.

By a 5-4 vote, the court ruled in *Dolan v. City of Tigard* that officials of the Oregon city had not adequately proved that commandeering a slice of commercial property was an appropriate condition of a construction permit. The case was remanded back to the city, where officials either have to come to terms with the landowner or demonstrate conclusively that the taking was justified.

Another takings case pending before the U.S. Supreme Court involving a town in Southern California was remanded shortly after the *Dolan* decision. The court told Culver City to carefully review the permitting requirements at issue in light of *Dolan*.

The facts in *Dolan* will ring very familiar with local officials nationwide: Florence Dolan, a Tigard landowner who wanted to double the size of her plumbing business, was told that the construction permit would be contingent upon her setting aside 10 percent of her 1.7-acre lot for flood mitigation and also for a bike path at the rear of the parcel.

Tigard officials justified the floodplain requirement on the grounds that the increased size of the store would reduce the lot's rain absorption capacity and therefore increase runoff and the chance of flooding in the creek behind the store. The city also argued that doubling the store's size would mean a significant increase in traffic at the site, and that a bike path would help mitigate the traffic impact.

Dolan argued that the city was blackmailing her into providing it with free land for recreational use and that the city had not made the case that the environmental and transportation impacts of the new development merited what she characterized as seizure of a tenth of her property without compensation.

THE RIGHT OF GOVERNMENTS to demand that private landowners bear the burden of mitigation in cases where development will have a clear negative impact on some area of the public welfare or safety has long been established and upheld by the courts. And developments that have environmental and traffic impacts have long been prime candidates for special mitigation requirements.

That mitigation can come in many forms. It can involve easements, as in the Dolan case, or it can involve mitigation fees. It can also involve requiring supplemental construction (such as road improvements and the like), or even an outright development ban or moratorium.

But the cases decided by the Supreme Court over the past decade have served notice to local officials that such conditions have to meet fairly stringent tests of both "nexus" and "proportionality." That is, any remedy called for by a government has to be directly related to the negative impact government believes will result from a particular land use, and the remedy called for has to be in some proportion to that impact.

The nexus test is fairly straightforward. If, for example, a proposed development will clearly increase traffic flow in an area, the court has ruled that it is perfectly reasonable for a government to require a developer to tone down the project or ante up for road improvements. It would not be so reasonable for a government to require extensive landscaping or some form of public access to the property, both of which would be unrelated to a concern about traffic.

The proportionality test is a bit trickier to grade. If a developer wants to build a small coffee shop on a corner, it is probably not reasonable under the proportionality test to ask the developer to set aside acres of land for floodplain preservation. If the developer is putting in a Wal-Mart, on the other hand, then it might be. But weighing the remedy versus harm for the proportionality test requires some sophisticated calculation and some solid forecasting.

Governments have flunked both the nexus and the proportionality tests in the U.S. Supreme Court lately.

Recent takings rulings in no way threaten government's ultimate right to regulate land use.

In *Dolan*, the court ruled that the city had simply not made the case that the taking of a tenth of the land was proportional to the forecasted environmental and traffic effects of construction, or that the proposed remedies would actually address the perceived impacts.

Some experts in land use regulation believe that the bike path requirement, in particular, made the whole proposition vulnerable. "That was the real weak link," says Gerald Kayden, a senior fellow at the Lincoln Institute of Land Policy in Cambridge, Massachusetts, a non-partisan, not-for-profit group that studies and consults on land use issues. "It's one thing to say you can't build on land because of the potential for flooding. It's quite another to say that not only can you not use the land but it has to be turned to public access."

SINCE THE *DOLAN* RULING, spin doctors on both sides of the case have been busy. Private landowner interests are casting it as a huge victory. "It was a great decision," says Robin L. Rivett, director of environmental law with the Pacific Legal Foundation, a Sacramento-based advocacy group that works the property-owner-rights side of the takings street. "It provides some real help to property owners down the road; it forces government to really relate a development's impact with the permit requirements."

The land-use-control factions are scrambling to make the best of the decision themselves, to somewhat comical effect in some cases. For example, the Rails-to-Trails Conservancy, a not-for-profit organization that supports turning abandoned railroad rights of way into bike paths, and which filed an amicus brief on behalf of Tigard, ginned up a press release in the wake of the ruling with the heading: "U.S. Supreme Court Recognizes Bicycle/Pedestrian Paths as Useful Means of Transportation." The court did mention in passing that a bike path in some cases might be considered a legitimate traffic congestion mitigation tool. But in this particular case, the court said, that was a dubious proposition.

The response of Paul Edmondson, an attorney with the National Trust for Historic Preservation, which also filed an amicus brief in the case, is more measured. He contends that the city of Tigard could have justified its action (and still could, as it had successfully done in two state courts) if it had simply articulated its case better.

More important, Edmondson points out—and Kayden agrees—that the ruling in no way threatens government's ultimate right to regulate land use. But Kayden says the cumulative effects of recent U.S. Supreme Court rulings in takings cases cannot be dismissed so easily, even if they are decided on a fairly narrow reading of the facts of the cases at hand.

Three cases in particular have shaped the recent takings landscape. In *First English Evangelical Lutheran Church v. County of Los Angeles*, the high court ruled in 1987 that governments could be held liable for damages in a takings case (the county eventually won the actual takings case, however). That same year, in *Nollan v. California Coastal Commission*, the court ruled that the commission had failed the nexus test in requiring a landowner to provide public access across his property to an adjacent beach. And in 1992's *Lucas v. South Carolina Coastal Council*, the court ruled that preventing a landowner from building a house on a lot in an area previously zoned for residential construction represented a taking.

While the first case served notice to states and localities that their actions might prove expensive, the other two were decided strictly on their merits and set no particular precedent one way or the other. But taken together, along with *Dolan*, they do send a message, Kayden argues. "If you look at *Dolan* in isolation," he says, "it actually mirrors many state court opinions dealing with conditions for permission for development; it's in the mainstream of state court jurisprudence. So in isolation, one might say that it's no big deal. But it's hard to see it in isolation. Since 1987, there has been a steady drumbeat of decisions from the Supreme Court leaning somewhat in the direction of property rights. I see this opinion as another example of the court placing its thumb on the scales of justice on the side of property owners."

WHETHER THE U.S. SUPREME Court's thumb continues to rest on the property-owner side of justice's scales obviously depends a great deal on the makeup of the court.

Justices Harry Blackmun, Ruth Bader Ginsburg and John Paul Stevens probably can be counted on to support state and local government in most takings cases (David Souter was the other dissenter in the *Dolan* case, but is not considered a sure friend). But Blackmun is retiring, likely to be replaced by federal Judge Stephen Breyer, so at best the pending change in the court this fall will be a wash.

Rather than count on a friendly Supreme Court, Kayden says localities had better try another tack: "You could characterize this ruling as the Local Planners Full Employment Act. Localities need to hire more planners, and use those planners better. They need to be less complacent about asking for goodies without backup evidence for those goodies. Localities need to do their homework."

The Gorilla that Swallows State Laws

ELLEN PERLMAN

It never did make sense that all of the taxpayers in Norwich, Vermont—more than 3,000 people—would choose to become tax delinquents in the space of a short time. But there the town clerk was, day after day, fielding calls from banks and mortgage companies all over the country, wanting to know whether the deadbeats of Norwich had straightened out, paid their back property taxes and cleaned up their credit records.

As it turned out, there were few if any genuine deadbeats in Norwich that summer of 1991. It was all the result of a foul-up at a credit reporting company. A woman hired by the firm to copy public records had mistakenly sent it every name on the tax receipt book rather than the delinquent list the company had asked for.

When the state legislature heard about the slur in Norwich—and the fact that it had happened before in several other Vermont towns—it struck back hard with a new state law. Since 1992, all citizens of Vermont have been entitled to one free report on their credit status every year. And they have to be asked for their consent before a credit company can pass their records along to anyone else.

As far as Vermont legislators were concerned, that should have been the end of the issue. But it wasn't. For much of the next two years, the state found itself in a three-way struggle with Congress and the credit industry, fighting off efforts to

Federal preemption sounds like a technical term. But when Congress starts talking about it, states are well advised to defend themselves.

wipe its law out with a new federal statute. Banks, retailers mortgage companies and other consumer lending agencies all joined in a massive lobbying campaign to have regulations such as Vermont's rendered unenforceable by a superseding act of Congress.

As of this summer, the congressional debate was still going on. Vermont appeared to have staved off defeat with a grandfather clause allowing its law to stay on the books. But by that time, officials all over the state had been reminded of the importance of a concept they are encountering more and more: preemption.

Not too long ago, the subject of federal preemption was strictly the province of the intergovernmental community and a scholarly matter of constitutional federalism. In recent years, it has become something very different. It is a bargaining chip for industries and consumer groups to use in leaning on members of Congress and in playing off one level of government against the other. In this year's congressional session, preemption language has cropped up in bills dealing with product liability, telecommunications, health care, banking, transportation, pesticides and many other subjects.

The U.S. Constitution makes it clear that an act of Congress takes precedence over state law, but for most of the nation's history, the federal government moved into regulatory issues not to supersede the states but because the states hadn't acted at all. The collisions between Washington and state government that punctuated the New Deal years nearly all came because Congress chose to move into areas of state neglect. In fact, during the two centuries that federal government has existed in America, fewer than 500 state laws have been preempted. But nearly half of those preemptions have been enacted during the past two decades.

One reason for that is the faster pace of regulation in general and its spread into areas where neither the states nor Congress intruded very much before 1970. Environmental issues are foremost among them. The further government moves into a policy area, the more likely it is that a state will do something Washington may want to overrule with a statute of its own.

You might assume the Reagan and Bush years, in which the White House devoted much rhetoric to the importance of state and local initiatives and the folly of federal intrusion, to have been a time when preemption slowed down. But if there was a slowdown, it was tiny. All told, there were 100 federal preemptive strikes against the states in the 1980s, according to the federal Advisory Commission on Intergovernmental Relations. That was only eight fewer than in the decade between 1970 and 1979. The truth was that the Republican administrations of the 1980s were more concerned about getting rid of regulation at all levels than they were about protecting states' rights.

And what few on any side anticipated was how aggressively states would jump into the regulatory void left by the federal government. At the start of the 1980s, consumer activists and liberal Democrats in favor of strong regulation feared there would be a breakdown in consumer protection as federal regulators went lax. But the states proved them wrong—and set the stage for a tug-of-war between Washington and the states that has only grown more intense.

In 1986, to cite one example, California passed the Safe Drinking Water and Toxic Enforcement Act. It requires all businesses that employ more than 10 people to warn consumers of cancer or birth defect risks in products they sell or produce. Soon after the law went on the books, warning signs began popping up in stores and restaurants about the potential danger in everything from alcohol to paperback books. Ever since, a coalition of dozens of industries has attacked the California law on the grounds that existing federal guidelines should be interpreted as preempting it.

So far the law has held, as have the laws enacted by many states in the 1980s challenging business on oil spill liability, nuclear power safety, workplace injuries and dozens of other issues. On oil spills alone, 19 states enforced laws during the decade exposing corporations to unlimited liability. Despite a prolonged and expensive lobbying campaign, Congress did not respond favorably to demands by the oil companies to set a liability cap preempting state oil spill laws. Instead, a federal law was passed in 1990 allowing states to impose as tough a standard as

they want. For the most part, when Congress has passed such environmental laws as the Resource Conservation and Recovery Act, Superfund and the Clean Water Act, it has set minimum standards but allowed states to enact stricter ones.

In other areas, though, the preemption strategy has paid clear dividends. Last year, the cellular telephone industry succeeded in persuading Congress to put a few lines in its omnibus budget reconciliation bill that knocked states entirely out of the business of setting cellular rates or regulating who can offer any mobile communication services. Nine states had existing cellular rate laws wiped off the books; the other 41 were summarily preempted from enacting them in the future.

The provision was slipped into the bill without hearings, blind-siding state officials, who complained that the outcome would be higher rates for consumers and less control over shady business operators who bring down the quality of service. The cellular phone industry declared victory. "We're

pleased with congressional action," says Jo-Anne Basile, lobbyist for the Cellular Telecommunications Industry Association. "This technology doesn't recognize things like state borders."

But last year's surgical strike didn't quiet things down on the telecommunications front; it only generated new debate and new demands. This year, other communications companies are pushing Congress to carve out exemptions for them from future state regulation. In one bill that passed the House in June, 33 states would be taken out of the business of deciding if there is enough competition in a local market to allow telephone companies the flexibility to set their own prices. That job of setting policy would go to Washington. "A number of companies would love to have all those oversight regulatory roles shifted to the FCC and taken away from the states," says Debra Berlyn of the National Association of State Utility Consumer Advocates. "Not that the FCC would do a better job, but that the FCC could not do the job."

In fact, no industry comes to Congress with the argument that preempt-

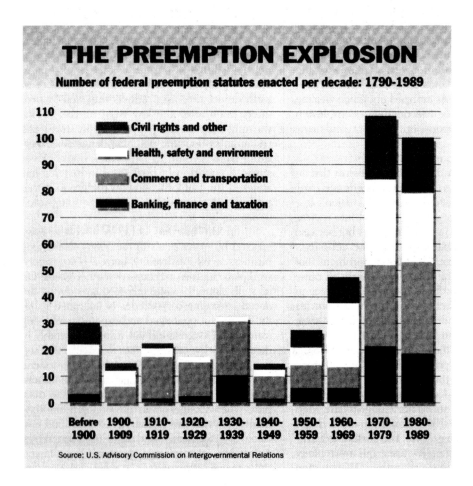

THE PREEMPTION EXPLOSION

Number of federal preemption statutes enacted per decade: 1790-1989

Civil rights and other

Health, safety and environment

Commerce and transportation

Banking, finance and taxation

Before 1900 | 1900-1909 | 1910-1919 | 1920-1929 | 1930-1939 | 1940-1949 | 1950-1959 | 1960-1969 | 1970-1979 | 1980-1989

Source: U.S. Advisory Commission on Intergovernmental Relations

ing state power is a good in itself. What they argue for is uniformity. The cumulative effect of the past decade of state regulation, insists Tyler Wilson of the U.S. Chamber of Commerce, has been a patchwork quilt of inconsistent law that is much more burdensome to business than anything the old federal ogre used to come up with. "All of a sudden," says Wilson, "instead of dealing with one 800-pound gorilla, we were contending with 50 attorneys general. Business found it more difficult."

The chamber and other business lobbying organizations make a case for uniformity that cuts across specific policy areas. A splintered system of state laws, they say, bogs down operations, brings on costly litigation and takes its toll on consumer costs, technology development and competitiveness. "When you have 50 sets of rules, it is extremely difficult to manage and operate a business in a manner to be in compliance with all 50 rules," says Dirk Van Dongen, president of the National Association of Wholesaler-Distributors. Sometimes, in his view, the only way to fight the regulatory maze is get it preempted in Washington by a uniform federal standard.

That standard, of course, can be either stronger or weaker than what the states have chosen to do. That business would like to make it weaker—and not merely uniform—is a point that its lobbyists rarely stress in their complaints to Congress. Consumer advocates, on the other hand, stress it all the time. Preemption, says Pam Gilbert of the lobby group Congress Watch, "doesn't give business uniformity. It just gives them an advantage they don't have today."

T he banking industry has leaned heavily on the uniformity argument in its campaign this year to preempt some of the strict credit laws that Vermont and other states have enacted. "If we have to abide by 50 state laws in fine-tuning credit reporting, it's a lawyer's dream," says Norman G. Magnuson, spokesman for Associated Credit Bureaus Inc. "We're not talking about the federal government usurping the power of the states. Set standards states can live with." In making that case, the credit bureaus have been helped by the American Bankers Association, which favors complete preemption of state credit reporting laws by federal statute.

Until recently, the bankers wouldn't have been much interested in the issue. The original Fair Credit Reporting Act of 1970 had little to do with banks—it regulated only a narrow section of the credit industry, the 800 or so credit bureaus that keep track of consumers' credit transactions and issue the reports that businesses use when deciding whether to extend additional credit.

But by 1992, when a move to update the credit act began gathering momentum in Congress, it was clear that the scope would be broadened considerably to include the companies that furnish the information to credit bureaus— banks, mortgage lenders, credit card companies, retail stores and anyone else whose customers turn in detailed credit applications. The theory was that those businesses should be held accountable if they make errors and furnish adverse information to the credit bureaus. State attorneys general and the Federal Trade Commission could take action against businesses that showed a pattern of submitting inaccurate information.

Expanded federal regulation of credit practices clearly posed a risk to the phalanx of businesses that had never been covered by it before. On the other hand, it offered these businesses a chance to take aim at—and possibly wipe out— state laws that seemed more onerous than the likely federal product. The momentum for credit legislation came from angry consumers and their advocates, but industry seized on the federal deliberations as a way to secure a less burdensome future at the state level. So, although the legislation as initially drafted contained no preemption provisions at all, the banking and credit industries lobbied hard to have them added, and at one point succeeded in having a broad range of preemption language tucked in. When U.S. Representative Esteban E. Torres, a California Democrat and key sponsor of the credit law revision, could not get the preemptions removed, he withdrew the bill altogether, calling the broad preemptions a poison pill, and nothing further took place in the 102nd Congress. "Industry was much too greedy," said an aide to Torres. This year, however, the issue is back. A new credit reform bill is working through Congress, and it appears that preemption of state law will remain in it on a few carefully targeted issues.

For one, the Federal Trade Commission would allow 30 days for a credit bureau to reinvestigate a credit report that a consumer says is in error. Within that time, the bureau must either verify or remove information a consumer has contested. Some states have shorter timetables. Also, the FTC would set the standard for disclosure forms consumers get when they've been turned down for a loan. These forms notify consumers of their rights.

Meanwhile, a broad range of business organizations has been arguing the uniformity issue in the maneuvering over product liability legislation, which may be the marathon preemption issue of all time. For the past dozen years, business and its allies have struggled to get a federal law that would govern their liability in damage suits relating to product safety and performance. "Our product liability law looks like a map of old Yugoslavia. It's a mess," says Victor Schwartz, counsel to the Product Liability Coordinating Committee, the main lobbying group on the business side. He and his allies have been saying this since the first Reagan term. And they have been opposed by trial lawyers and consumer advocates who complain that the real desire of business is not for uniformity but for escape from the high damage awards manufacturers have faced under strong state laws.

In the first years of the marathon, the industry coalition asked for overarching displacement of state liability laws but couldn't muster broad enough support to get it enacted. More recently, as in the case of credit reporting, the debate has focused on a less sweeping federal law that would preempt the states on some matters but keep their legislative rights intact on others. However, Senate legislation containing preemptions on statutes of limitation and punitive damage awards was shot down in June, and Senate sponsors have promised that it will be back in the next Congress.

On liability, as on most preemption issues, business and the consumer groups represent opposite ends of the pole. But the state government lobby is divided. The National Governors' Association sides with businesses, arguing that excessive litigation under the current patchwork system creates a less healthy economic development climate. The National Conference of State Legislatures, a significant number of whose members are trial lawyers, rejects product liability preemption on its face, saying legislatures and courts ought to have control of the issue.

On telecommunications, it is industry that sees things from more than one perspective. The cellular phone companies lean toward overall preemption of the states, as their lobbying over the past year has underscored. The United States Telephone Association, which represents local phone companies, favors federal price regulation for telephone service but state control over which local companies can provide long-distance service. "There's no general consensus on preemption universally," says Larry Clinton, lobbyist for the telephone association. "It depends on what's being preempted and how it's being preempted."

That could stand as a slogan for the entire debate. There is no grand plan for which level of government businesses prefer to have regulating them. It depends on the issue, the political climate and the myriad other forces at work each year.

Nor is there a grand plan for which branch of government business prefers. Vermont is learning at the moment that the federal preemption game extends beyond the walls of the Capitol. What Congress is unwilling to do for industries, the executive branch can sometimes be leaned upon to do in its place.

This spring, Vermont passed a law requiring milk and milk products to be labeled if the milk came from cows treated with artificial bovine growth hormone. Sponsors argued that consumers had a right to the information, since some studies had linked the hormone to stomach cancer and other ailments.

After the state law passed, a dairy industry coalition including the International Dairy Foods Association and the National Ice Cream Association filed suit alleging that the measure is unconstitutional because it is preempted by existing federal food and drug guidelines that do not require labeling. Vermont argues that nothing in the federal guidelines should be construed as telling states they can't go further. "It doesn't

say anything about our power," insists Julie Brill, the state's assistant attorney general. The case is pending.

In general, the states have done pretty well in recent years in fighting off federal preemption efforts involving the executive branch. In the 1980s, auto manufacturers went to the FTC with an argument that existing federal regulations preempted state "lemon laws" imposing strict quality standards on the sale of new cars. The FTC rejected the argument and told the states they could pass just about any new-car law they wanted. Vermont is hoping that the federal courts, in a somewhat different situation, take the same attitude.

In addition, states have been bolstered by some significant victories in the U.S. Supreme Court. For most of the 20th century, courts have tended to side with the federal government in virtually all disputes with the states, holding that state power in such cases consists of little more than the ability to try and persuade Congress to exercise restraint. As recently as 1988, in *South Carolina v. Baker*, the Supreme Court made clear its view that the Constitution provides no protection for the states against federal preemption. The court ruled that Congress could tax municipal bonds because it was not violating the doctrine of intergovernmental tax immunity by doing so.

More recently, though, the trend has been the other way. In 1991, the Supreme Court sided with the states in a case that pitted Missouri's law requiring judges to retire at age 70 against a federal age-discrimination law. Missouri's law was upheld. Justice Sandra Day O'Connor wrote in her opinion that if Congress intends to alter the constitutional balance between the states and the federal government, as the Constitution allows, Congress must make that "unmistakably clear in the language of the statute." Preemption could not be implied. "It is incumbent upon the federal courts," O'Connor wrote, "to be certain of Congress' intent before finding that federal law overrides this balance."

The fact is that, for all of the noise and intensity of the lobbying campaign, most efforts at federal preemption still don't work. There has never been a huge con-

gressional constituency in favor of eviscerating state laws. Liberal Democrats who favor regulation tend not to care whether it comes from Washington or the state capitols, and a fair number of conservative Republicans feel uncomfortable abandoning the concept of states' rights. More preemption campaigns wind up like the one on oil spill regulation—unsuccessful—than like the one on cellular telephones.

Still, preemption doesn't have to succeed most of the time to create a gradual erosion of state power in the federal system. One victory out of every four or five tries, and the balance of power in the federal system will change significantly over a long period. "After years and decades of doing this, how much room is left for states to maneuver?" asks Chris Zimmerman of the National Conference of State Legislatures. "Little by little you erode state sovereignty."

And as far as states are concerned, there is an even more ominous specter on the horizon: global preemption. As NAFTA, GATT and other trade agreements take full effect in the next few years, there is the real possibility that international organizations will have the power to declare that state regulations dealing with price or product quality represent trade discrimination against foreign countries. The states have already lost on one such issue. Two years ago, a GATT panel determined that state tax breaks for local beer and wine industries violated international trade law by discriminating against Canadian beer and wine imports.

More such cases, ranging further into the area of state regulatory power, seem certain in the next couple of years unless treaty language is changed. Tennessee Tax Commissioner Joe Huddleston, current president of the Federation of Tax Administrators, warns that a new World Trade Organization may eventually substitute for the U.S. Supreme Court on tax policy; 29 state attorneys general expressed similar fears in a recent letter to President Clinton. "It may have dangerous consequences for states," Huddleston says. And if that day comes, there will be another consequence as well: The federal government will get an idea of what it feels like to be preempted.

A DECLARATION OF
WAR

Local governments, tired of picking up the tab for state programs, are fighting back.

Linda Wagar

Officials in the oceanside community of Bar Harbor, Maine, feel a little queasy every time the Legislature meets. Their statehouse representatives have an endless supply of ideas on how to spend local dollars.

They have ordered landfills closed and demanded storage sheds for road salt. New equipment for firefighters and special education classes for public schools. Certification for a code enforcement officer and the hiring of a civil defense director.

Many of the ideas are good. But they have left Bar harbor struggling to pay for programs it never requested and had no choice but to accept.

"It's like someone taking your credit card at Christmas time and buying you a lot of stuff you always wanted but could never afford," said an expert on local government. "In the end you're still the one stuck with the bill."

By the end of fiscal 1993, Bar Harbor will have spent $671,000 or 9.5 percent of a $7 million budget, paying for unfunded state mandates. The impact these mandates have on property taxes, however, most likely will be blamed on Bar Harbor officials—not the legislators who approved them, said City Manager Dana Reed.

Local officials said the state has bent over backwards to hide its role behind local tax increases. The state flaunts the positive by requiring all local property tax bills to include the statement: "If it were not for state revenue sharing your local taxes would be 3 percent higher." But Bar Harbor devised a way to make the public more aware of the state's role. The city added another line to the tax bill. This one reads: "If it were not for state mandates your taxes would be 9.5 percent lower."

Frustrations over unfunded state mandates stretch far beyond the confines of this tiny New England town. They can be heard in almost any city in any state. The anger has reached a boiling point as the drying up of federal aid has prompted more and more states to turn to local governments to fund a growing number of programs.

Local officials describe the unfunded mandates as a double whammy since state laws often limit or exclude them from raising taxes to pay for these programs. The mandates befuddle local officials who wonder how states could argue fervently against unfunded federal mandates and then commit the same crime against local governments.

Desperate for relief, local governments in 10 states have successfully pushed for constitutional amendments prohibiting their states from forcing unfunded programs on them. In November, Maine voters became the latest to approve an anti-mandate amendment. Local government experts predict that other states will follow.

Amendment supporters said the constitutional change forces states to take responsibility for their actions by compelling them to pay for programs they require. But others warned against tinkering with state constitutions to resolve problems that they said could be better handled through lobbying and legislation.

They worried that financially-ailing states will lose their ability to require counties to meet minimum standards for education, infrastructure, the environment and health and human services. The result, they said, will be that the viability of government services will be dependent on the desires of local officials.

While local officials acknowledged the anti-mandate amendment has some flaws, they said state officials have pushed them into a corner, leaving amending the constitution as their only option.

Besides Maine, the nine other states with constitutional amendments are California, Florida, Hawaii, Louisiana, Michigan, Missouri, Montana, New Mexico and Tennessee.

The amendments vary in language and effectiveness, according to an independent study financed by the National League of Cities. Some permit states, such as California, to adopt unfunded mandates as long as local governments are reimbursed or allowed to raise taxes to finance them. Others, such as Maine, require the state to pay for the mandate. In most states the amendments can be overridden with a super-majority vote, e.g., two-thirds or three-fourths majority, in the legislature.

The survey of local officials deemed Washington and New Mexico as having the most effective amendments based on how well state officials upheld the language. Michigan and Missouri were given low marks.

Just a few months after its passage, Maine is feeling the effects of the anti-mandate amendment. A state statute requiring counties to offer welfare assistance may be stricken from the books since no money to fund the program over the next two years was included in the governor's proposed budget.

Portland, the state's biggest city, has threatened to drop its welfare program if the city becomes a magnet for the poor from towns who abandon their programs. Doug Porter, a deputy commissioner for the Maine Department of Human Services, said he sympathizes with local governments' concerns but is worried about what will happen to Maine's poor. "You don't eliminate the need when you eliminate a program," said Porter.

Portland officials also have threatened to sue the state mental institution, which has been releasing patients into the community in accordance with a court order. City officials said the actions have resulted in an unfunded mandate since the former patients still require services. The state maintains that the former patients have been released to local programs financed by the state.

Amendment supporters said the problems in Maine are not the fault of the amendment. They are, they said, part of a normal transition as the state comes to terms with the fact that it can no longer shift costs onto local government.

Local officials in Florida saw themselves in a similar bind when they pushed for a constitutional amendment in 1990. University of South Florida Professor Susan Mac-Manus calculated that between 1980 and 1988, Florida passed more than 225 requirements for local services costing up to $1 billion a year. The state didn't contribute a penny of the cost.

Ray Sittig, executive director of the Florida League of Cities, said no unfunded mandate has survived the legislative process since his state's amendment went into effect. (In fact, the League is pushing for a second amendment that would allow local government to raise taxes. Sittig acknowledged that voters could be the real sticking point on the passage of that amendment.)

Wayne Voigt, staff director of the Florida Senate Natural Resources and Conservation Committee, said the amendment has produced some real changes in the Legislature. He no longer sees pie-in-the-sky environmental legislation introduced by lawmakers who have given no thought to the cost. "It has really reduced those kinds of proposals that weren't thought all the way through," Voigt said.

Sen. Jon Johnson reported a similar situation in Louisiana, which passed a constitutional amendment in 1991. "There are many more cases of restraint because of the amendment," Johnson said.

Officials in other states also said the primary benefit of the amendment was that it made state government more aware of the serious financial impact state legislation has on local government.

But did it really take a constitutional amendment to get that message across? Local officials, two national studies and even state officials said it did. Officials in several states said they fought for a constitutional amendment only after state statutes — drafted to accomplish the same end — had failed. Florida had such legislation in place for 10 years.

State laws are easily ignored, because legislatures simply tack new mandates to the language: "Notwithstanding any provision to the contrary."

It was such legislative maneuvering that rated Illinois a ranking of "poor" on its anti-mandate law, by the National League of Cities' study. The state passes an average of 17 unfunded mandates per session. "There is no money to pay for anything anymore," said Roger Heubner, a lobbyist for the Illinois Municipal League.

The Illinois League tried for the last two years to add an anti-mandate amendment to the state's constitution, but the bill never made it through the Legislature.

Last year, however, the League placed an advisory question on the ballot asking voters if they wanted the state to impose unfunded mandates on local government. A total of 80 percent of the voters said "no."

Less than a month later, the Illinois House passed legislation increasing firefighters' pensions, but the Senate killed that particular unfunded mandate.

Equally ineffective have been laws requiring legislative proposals to include a statement outlining how much they would cost state and local governments.

Janet Kelly, a Bowling Green State University professor, who conducted the National League of Cities' mandate study, found that of 28 states with fiscal note requirements, the majority produces notes of "questionable accuracy." Nearly 60 percent of the states said the requirement to draft a fiscal note occasionally was ignored. Even when fiscal notes are drafted, "the legislature does not treat them seriously in its mandating decisions," Kelly said.

Heubner said part of the reason local government continues to get clobbered with unfunded mandates lies in its weak lobbying position. Elected officials, he said, listen to those who give them the most campaign money. As a campaign contributor, local government is way down the list. "Political action committee dollars are what is guiding public policy," Heubner said.

Howard Duvall, executive director of the South Carolina Municipal Association, said it's difficult to compete with special interests when the membership of an organization consists primarily of part-time officials with full-time second jobs. South Carolina has been criticized by Kelly for having a particularly atrocious record of approving unfunded mandates.

"It's hard to organize our people and get them to the capitol to pack a committee room," said Duvall. "We are up against police and union officials that can fill a room at a moment's notice."

In addition, local government lobbying efforts are divided among dozens of issues, not just the one or two on which special interest groups concentrate their resources.

Despite local governments' happiness with anti-mandate amendments, Kelly warned they should be used as a last resort. "What cities and counties most want is to be recognized as legitimate governing bodies," said Kelly. "They want to work with state government to form better policy. Constitutional amendments try to force that issue. The problem is that you can't mandate cooperation."

This could be true particularly in states with the initiative process where the legislature has little or no input on the language of the constitutional amendment. In such a case, state-local relations could become further strained.

Recognizing this, the Florida League of Cities asked the Legislature for help in passing an anti-mandate amendment. When lawmakers refused, the League collected thousands of signatures, raising the threat of the initiative process, and convinced the Legislature to help mold an amendment the state could live with.

A policy analyst for the state, who asked not to be named, said that by involving the Legislature, local government had a "less vociferous opponent." But the analyst said even with legislative involvement, the amendment further exacerbated what was already a poor relationship between the state and its cities and counties. "Neither of them trusts the other," he said.

Hard feelings also resulted in Maine. Rep. Ruth Josephs was particularly troubled by the Maine amendment because it would void almost any law that requires local government to spend money. Josephs said she hadn't seen "a bill yet that doesn't have some fiscal impact on somebody."

"This will mean that all the work we're doing throughout the session could be voided because it can't be funded," she said.

Another problem with anti-mandate amendments is that they could result in a patchwork of government programs that vary from county to county, Kelly said. Programs could differ dramatically since state guidelines would not have to be followed unless funding was included.

"It's only been lately we've begun to think about the effect of this," Kelly said. "If we let these noncompliance options work is that a good thing? The answer may be 'no'."

Louisiana Rep. Quentin Dastugue had a similar concern when he voted against putting his state's anti-mandate amendment on the ballot. Dastugue, a Republican who represents part of New Orleans and its suburbs, worried in particular about the impact the amendment would have on environmental legislation.

Dastugue said the state could pass environmental cleanup laws that private industry would have to follow but local government could ignore. Even a state's ability to transport nuclear waste could be affected by the amendment, he said.

A national study showed that it was only when states faced the threat of an amendment that they began treating the problem seriously.

Dastugue said he opposes most unfunded mandates, but did not think passing an amendment was a wise choice. The amendment could usher in a whole host of problems the state will have difficulty resolving.

"This isn't some law we can go back and change," he said.

So far, however, the biggest problem with anti-mandate amendments isn't that they have hamstrung important legislation, but that lawmakers have figured out how to circumvent them.

The most common method for getting around the anti-mandate amendment has been to draft legislation that places responsibility on local government by default. For example, a bill in one state prohibited landfill operators from accepting recyclable materials. Although local government would become responsible for finding a new home for those recyclables, it was never mentioned in the legislation.

Some of these bills have forced cities and counties into lengthy court battles over who is responsible for carrying out such mandates. But Sittig of Florida said he has more faith in the courts than the Legislature.

There is good reason to believe that more states soon will be confronted with anti-mandate amendments. A national study (by MacManus of Florida) showed that it was only when states faced the threat of an amendment that they began treating the problem seriously.

In addition, the recession has worsened relations in states that traditionally had a good rapport with local government.

Massachusetts provides the best example. For years, Massachusetts was able to pass on millions of dollars to cities and counties. During the mid-1980s, local government saw state aid increase by $150 million a year.

But by 1989, Massachusetts found itself in the throes of the recession. By 1992, local aid had been cut by $610 million, said Geoffrey Beckwith, executive director of the Massachusetts Municipal Association.

Although the economy has improved in recent years, Beckwith said state funds to local government have not grown at the same rate as the budget.

To make matters worse, the state is considering an education reform package that will require more local dollars be spent on schools. The problem is that a voter-approved state proposition prohibits local government from raising taxes more than 2.5 percent.

"State-local relations have been in a tailspin," said Beckwith. "Unless there is a turnaround to ensure the citizens are well served, we may seek a constitutional amendment."

Kelly, of Bowling Green State University, said states like Massachusetts still have time to improve their relationship with local government so a constitutional amendment isn't needed.

Kelly said the state-local battle that has led to these amendments in other states is really more of a fight for legitimacy than for dollars. Local officials, she said, want a vital role in forming state policy that affects local government.

She stressed that greater cooperation on both sides will ensure that laws don't just sound good on paper, but work well in the towns and cities that must put them into practice.

LOCAL OPTIONS

Congress should return control of education
to states, school boards—and parents.

LAMAR ALEXANDER,

WILLIAM J. BENNETT,

AND DAN COATS

*Mr. Alexander, a former governor of Ten-
nessee and former secretary of education, is
a Nashville attorney and a senior fellow at
the Hudson Institute. Mr. Bennett, an* NR
*senior editor and a former secretary of edu-
cation, is a co-founder of Empower America.
Mr. Coats is a Republican senator from
Indiana.*

A S IT SETS out to repair the damage wrought by its prede-cessor, the new Republican majority in Congress needs to look hard at education. Among the least-no-ticed events of October's closing leg-islative rush was final passage of HR-6, the Elementary and Secondary Education Act (ESEA), a $65-billion measure that is bad for children, for education, and for American federal-ism. In 1,000-plus pages it sets back the cause of serious school reform, wastes billions of dollars, and erodes local control of American schools.

At a showy pre-election bill signing in Massachusetts, President Clinton and Senator Edward Kennedy said the law signals a national commitment to our children. Retiring Senate Majority Leader George Mitchell (D., Me.) cited education as one of the jewels in the crown of the 103rd Congress. Educa-tion Secretary Dick Riley said no one in Washington, perhaps in the whole country, was serious about education before Clinton's inauguration. And columnist Jack Anderson reported that Morgan Stanley's research department finds Clinton's "political stock . . . blue-chip when it comes to keeping its promises on education reform."

Like so much associated with this Administration, however, what sounds too good to be true turns out to be not entirely true and not very good at all. HR-6 was the legislative equivalent of a stealth bomber, heavily armed with dangerous weapons but scarcely visible save to its controllers and crew.

Part of a comprehensive education package, along with "Goals 2000" and measures such as a "school to work" program and expansion of Head Start, HR-6 did far more than reauthorize ESEA, the keystone of federal school aid since 1965. It reversed a decade of progress toward a coherent, bipartisan education-reform strategy as embodied in the Bush Administration's "America 2000" plan, which sought to roll back federal regulation and replace it with the initiative of teachers, communities, and parents, and which coupled vol-untary goals with good tests and ac-countability for results.

By signing off on HR-6 and Goals 2000, President Clinton transformed a nationwide reform movement into a federal program. The new regulations concern not only the standards and as-sessments that schools use but also how they discipline student offenders, the topics that teachers and parents must discuss with one another, the content of sex-education courses, and the (rare) circumstances in which denying a child the right to pray may be an infraction. Clinton has even cre-ated something akin to a national school board, the National Education Standards and Improvement Council.

Almost as worrying is the resurrec-tion of inputs, resources, and services as gauges of education quality. Three decades of research show no reliable link between what goes into schools and what children learn there. Yet Goals 2000 and HR-6 affirm the rou-tine assertion of the education estab-lishment: If we're not happy with school results, more money and regula-tions will improve them.

Political correctness pervades many sections of the bill. *Education Daily* matter-of-factly reports that "HR-6 is laced with language on gender equity, from authorizing grants to requiring schools to collect data." The bill also es-tablishes a post-modern definition of the "family," provides day care for the babies of unwed teenage mothers, and conflates school reform with health care, violence prevention, etc.

The law provides vast windfalls for colleges of education and authorizes funds for dozens of pork-barrel proj-ects. More troubling still is the bill's hypocrisy with respect to such promis-ing reform strategies as charter schools and parental choice. While al-lowing members of Congress to claim that they voted for them, HR-6 actu-ally immobilizes them with rules and conditions. What good, for example, is a school-choice program that lets the "sending school" veto the child's depar-ture? Furthermore, such shackles will help the enemies of school choice argue a few years down the road that these reforms don't work.

From *National Review,* December 19, 1994, pp. 42-44. © 1994 by National Review, Inc., 150 East 35th Street, New York, NY
10016. Reprinted by permission.

How It Passed

THE passage of this legislation reveals much about the opportunities and perils awaiting the new Congress. HR-6 spent more than a year on Capitol Hill after the White House sent it up. Hearings dragged on. The high-profile issues were how to adjust the Chapter One formula to direct more federal dollars toward poor communities and whether to keep or jettison Chapter Two, a block grant that was immensely popular with states and localities. Tucked away in the fine print—but seldom discussed or reported—were dozens of new programs and hundreds of changes in existing ones, as well as intricate linkages between ESEA and the Goals 2000 bill. The Administration's complex proposals were heavily embroidered by Bill Ford's House Education and Labor Committee, and Ted Kennedy's Senate Labor and Human Resources Committee.

Eventually, the House cranked out the most offensive piece of education legislation in memory, the Senate a somewhat milder version. The final edition was cobbled together behind closed doors during August and September in a "staff conference" dominated by Democratic congressional aides, some of them around since the days of LBJ. Lobbyists and Administration officials played key roles in the process, but nobody else was allowed into the room.

The vast bill emerged from conference about 48 hours before the House voted on final passage. Senators had a couple of additional days to try to get hold of copies and examine the bill. Few did. It is likely that not a single member of either body had actually read the full text of the final version.

The teachers unions and the Washington-based interest groups quietly did their part to round up votes, rousing their memberships with the promise of federal dollars. Business groups went along, perhaps because their education staffs consist mostly of establishment fellow-travelers. Governors, state legislators, and mayors, many of whom had fussed loudly about Goals 2000, were mute about HR-6, though it will cost them substantial control over their schools.

Conservative organizations sat this one out or focused on such narrow items as the school-prayer provisions. Editorialists naïvely supposed that any bill labeled "education" must be a good thing. As for congressional Republicans, most donned their "damage control" garb, curbing the worst Democrat-drafted excesses without challenging the measure's fundamental premises.

What can we do now? When it comes to education, decisions made in Washington are decisions *not* made by parents, teachers, and 15,000 local school boards. Mandates shaped in Washington are programs not fashioned by the states and communities, which foot most of the bill. Regulations crafted in Washington can be counted upon to respond to the demands of special interests rather than the needs of fifty million unique children attending some 110,000 distinctive schools across this diverse land.

Education is not an endeavor where one size fits all. Perhaps we can agree on a core of voluntary goals and standards that make sense for the nation, but it's folly to prescribe a single path to them, or to suggest that Uncle Sam knows best. Worse than folly, it saps initiative and responsibility, curbs creativity, and wrongly pretends that some of the touchiest and most localized issues in American society—the way our children are taught about religion and sex, the place of education in our communities—lend themselves to uniform national solutions. Decentralizing education policy is a way to strengthen communities, to rebuild the culture, to buttress families, and to diffuse—and perhaps defuse—volatile decisions.

Horse-Trading

IN 1986, when one of us was chairman of the nation's governors and another was education secretary, the governors proposed some "old-fashioned horse-trading," namely lifting the regulatory burden from American schools in return for better education results. In time this proposal turned into a consensus about how to reform the schools: local control coupled with gubernatorial leadership; voluntary national goals combined with responsibility for each state and locality to work toward them as it deemed best; wide-ranging choices for families among excellent schools that differ on many dimensions; the fundamental right to flee a bad, or unsafe school for a good one, (plus tests that make it possible to know which are which); and essential skills and serious content taught by talented individuals who are accountable for their results and rewarded for classroom excellence.

That's what America 2000 was all about. And that's still how the American people believe we should tackle our education problems. A recent survey by Public Agenda makes plain that a "safe, orderly environment and effective teaching of the 'basics'" head their list, joined by high standards and clear lines of accountability. But the public has serious misgivings about the trendy schemes beloved of today's education establishment—the very approaches on which money and legitimacy are lavished by HR-6 and the rest of the Clinton package. As Public Agenda reports, "the large majority of Americans are uncomfortable" with such things as "ending the 'tracking' of students, and replacing standardized, multiple-choice tests with new, more 'authentic' assessments." We also know from other surveys that the American people strongly favor school choice and are deeply mistrustful of the Federal Government's ability to improve our schools.

Today Washington is on a collision course with what the American people want and what they know to be right. The recent election results provide dramatic evidence. HR-6 is a large, ugly example of what has gone wrong and what the voters are rejecting. It should be repealed. The "national school board" should be canned, and local control should be restored. Education should be sent home to states, communities, and families.

Indeed, it's time for the Federal Government virtually to withdraw from elementary and secondary education and relinquish the authority it has seized in this domain. Dozens of federal programs ought to vanish. The resources they now consume should be made available—perhaps through a federal tax cut or an expanded version of Chapter Two—to states and localities to do with as they judge best. We're now drafting, and one of us plans in January to introduce, a short, simple bill to accomplish this. The new majority in Congress creates a more hospitable environment for such legislation than we've had since the Great Society pointed federal education policy in the wrong direction.

Insofar as any education functions stay in Washington, their guiding principles should be choice, deregulation, innovation, accountability, and serious assessment keyed to real standards in core subjects. The National Education Goals Panel, made up of governors and state legislators along with Executive Branch and congressional representatives, is where oversight responsibility should rest, not with civil servants, "experts," or the Federal Government. Today's Department of Education could be reduced to something far humbler and less costly.

That doesn't mean Presidents have nothing to say about education. In truth, they should say quite a bit. But they shouldn't try to run the nation's schools. They must not seek to control them. And they need to understand that acceptance of their education agenda depends on the power of their ideas, not on federal red tape. Bill Clinton should tell the country what he thinks a good school is. Those who agree with him can be trusted to create their own. Those who favor a different idea must be free to march to their own drummers.

Should states or regions set clean air rules?

Dean C. Marriott

Dean C. Marriott is commissioner of the Maine Department of Environmental Protection. He is a member of the Ozone Transport Commission and has served as its chair and vice chair. The commission covers: Connecticut, Delaware, the District of Columbia, Maine, Maryland, Massachusetts, New Hampshire, New Jersey, New York, Pennsylvania, Rhode Island, Vermont and Virginia.

The problem is air pollution. And in the Northeast and mid-Atlantic states it's a big problem. So big that Congress — our elected representatives in Washington — took it on.

Essentially, Congress said that for the good of all their constituents who live, travel, work and play in these 12 states and the District of Columbia, the air has to be cleaned up. Health is the issue.

Ground-level ozone is the major component of summertime smog. And it is a serious environmental and public health problem in this region of 65 million people. Even limited exposure to smog can have detrimental effects in the young and the old, the healthy and the infirm.

Ground-level ozone is not released directly from a source. It is produced by a chemical reaction in summer sunshine; it "travels," borne by wind patterns throughout our region; and, during the past 20 years, we have made no significant progress in reducing the unhealthy amount of ozone in the air.

That's bad enough, but consider that ground-level ozone isn't our only air pollution problem. Carbon monoxide and an alarming presence of toxics in the air justify serious concern.

Something innovative, aggressive and dramatically effective has to be done. When it comes to air quality in the Northeast and mid-Atlantic region, the traditional political process is simply not working. The solutions are not in place, and the needed improvements aren't being made. We have a regional problem and it is appropriate to seek a regional solution.

So who comes up with this regional solution? Each state legislature acting on its own with the hope that the puzzle pieces fit when all is said and done? Or would it be more efficient and effective to have a group of state officials and governors' appointees, a group specifical-

Joseph A. Petrarca and Richard J. Cessar

Rep. Joseph A. Petrarca, Westmoreland County, is Democratic chairman and Rep. Richard J. Cessar, Allegheny County, is Republican chairman of the Pennsylvania House Transportation Committee.

In 1980, Bill Clinton was defeated for re-election as governor of Arkansas in part because he raised automobile tag fees about $15. Imagine the uproar if he'd added up to $1,000 to a car's cost.

Further, the boost in the price of cars is only the beginning. California's plan for that state's severe ozone problem is being challenged in court. The plan could require motorists to use reformulated gasoline at an additional cost of up to 20 cents a gallon. And the plan could eventually lead to requiring the use of high-cost, low-performance, battery-operated vehicles.

That's exactly what could happen in the 12 mid-Atlantic and northeastern states and the District of Columbia that are members of the Ozone Transport Commission if that body — created by the 1990 Clean Air Act Amendments — imposes the California low-emission vehicle standards.

When the price hike hits new car stickers and possibly the gas pump, it will likely create a political and governmental Gordian Knot. But unlike in legend, there'll be no Alexander the Great with the power to cut through it. That's because the voters can't hold the Ozone Transport Commission responsible — its members are appointed by governors, not elected.

The voters may turn to elected officials for action. But since governors and legislatures won't have the power to undo or modify the Ozone Transport Commission's action, the result will be an angry public and a powerless government — not a happy combination.

Indeed, the combination is not only unhappy, but an unprecedented usurpation of state legislative powers. It would be the first major policy decision made by a group of executive branch appointees without the consent of the governed through their elected representatives. "Taxation without representation" comes to mind, or in this case, "legislation without representation."

Furthermore, the Ozone Transport Commission, by a majority vote, can override a member state whose leg-

Point

ly created to focus on the issue at hand, work out the details?

Clearly, the latter. Acting as individual states, independent of each other, is a patchwork approach to air quality protection. It focuses attention only on what goes on inside state lines. It permits the assumption that "somebody else" is going to address the issue and invest in the solutions: It lets the rest of us sit idly by.

That kind of buck passing gets us nowhere. A complex, cross-boundary problem is not going to be solved in piecemeal fashion. What it is going to do is further disrupt local economies. Working together to develop and implement a regional solution to air pollution gives no state a competitive edge. What it takes to make air quality improvements should not be an undue burden borne by a few, but the shared responsibility of all.

A regional approach is the right approach to cleaner air. State delegations to Congress recognized that. In the Clean Act Amendments of 1990, those delegations created the Ozone Transport Commission. Its members are appointees of the top elected officials of every mid-Atlantic and Northeast state and the District of Columbia. Its mission is to work out regional strategies for improving air quality.

The commission provides the level playing field. It is the place where the unique needs and circumstances of each entity are acknowledged and taken into account in the search for solutions. It enables states to hear and be heard in the debate over plans and programs.

The commission is working to come up with something all can live with. Working this way will give us a plan that is comprehensive, integrated and appropriate. It is an efficient approach, inclusive of participants' interests, that will get the job done.

"Who should set clean air rules" is not a states' rights issue. Clearly, in many debates and perhaps on most issues, states are in the best position to decide how to approach a problem. But we have a regional problem here, one that knows no political boundaries.

We must address the issue in a collective way.

Counterpoint

islature has voted against adoption of the California plan, or whose representative on the commission votes against it.

Further, the commission's decision would be an ongoing usurpation. Every time California officials modify their plan, the Eastern region's states would be automatically bound by the change.

A fourth objection to the commission's actions concerns the negative economic effects from a slump in new car sales in reaction to price hikes and vehicle performance problems.

Further, a study by DRI/McGraw-Hill estimates that if the California low-emission vehicle and reformulated gasoline programs are adopted, states across the country would suffer significant job losses. Pennsylvania would lose 55,000 jobs by the turn of the century. Neighboring Maryland would lose an estimated 20,000 jobs, New Jersey 35,000, New York 60,000, and, to the south, Virginia 35,000.

Finally, the costly California plan is probably unnecessary to solve the 12-state region's ozone problems. California remedies were devised to cope with far greater ozone problems than are found on the East Coast. California, for example, exceeds the federal ozone smog standard 10 times more frequently than New York does.

Studies in several states have found the California program is not cost effective and that state and federal ozone-control programs are drastically reducing pollution. In Pennsylvania, for example, environmental standards are curbing volatile organic compound emissions by 57 percent and nitrous oxide emissions by 23 percent. Adoption of the California plan will make only incremental reductions in pollution.

In summary, for the Ozone Transport Commission to impose California's low-emission vehicle program on the 12-state Northeast and mid-Atlantic region would increase the costs of owning and operating an automobile, destroy political accountability, transfer authority away from state governments, harm state and national economies and — after all that — is probably unnecessary.

As a regional commission prepares to set clean-air rules for the Northeast, its critics are crying foul. They maintain decisions of such import should be made by elected officials in each state. But commission supporters maintain that a regional solution is the only way to ensure clean air. At stake is not just clean air, but states' rights and the powers of elected vs. appointed officials.

Linkages between Citizens and Government

- **Political Parties and Elections, (Articles 11–17)**
- **Interest Groups, Protests, Boycotts, and News Media (Articles 18–21)**
- **Referenda, Initiatives, and Recalls (Articles 22 and 23)**

The American political system is usually classified as a representative democracy. Top officials are elected by the people and, as a result, government is supposed to be responsive and accountable to citizens. Both the theory and practice of representative democracy are of interest to students of American politics. Political scientists study various processes that seem essential to the functioning of representative democracy: parties, interest groups, election laws, campaign techniques, and so forth. Attention is not limited to the national government; state and local governments are also examined to assess responsiveness and accountability.

State and local governments operate under somewhat different institutional arrangements and circumstances than the national government. In many states and localities, voters can participate directly in the policy process through mechanisms known as *initiative* and *referendum*. In addition, some state and local voters can participate in removing elected officials from office by a procedure called *recall*. In many localities in the New

England states, an open meeting of all local citizens, called a town meeting, functions as the local government legislature. These mechanisms provide additional avenues for citizens trying to influence state and local governments.

Generally speaking, party organization is strongest at the local level and weakest at the national level. Party "machines" are a well-known feature of the local political landscape in the United States, and colorful and powerful "bosses" have left their mark on local political history. While the heyday of "bosses" and "machines" is past, noteworthy examples of contemporary political machines still exist.

National elections, especially for the presidency, are usually contested vigorously by the two major parties and, over the long haul, the two parties tend to be reasonably competitive. This is less true in states and localities, because voters in some states and many localities are decidedly oriented toward one party or the other. Thus, in some states and localities, closer and more significant competition can occur within the nominating process of the dominant party than between the two parties in general elections.

Party labels do not appear on the ballot in many localities, and this may or may not affect the way elections are conducted. In "nonpartisan" elections, candidates of different parties may, in fact, openly oppose one another just as they do when party labels appear on the ballot. Another possibility is that parties field opposing candidates in a less than open fashion. As yet another alternative, elective offices may actually be contested without parties or the political party affiliations of candidates playing any part. One cannot assume that formally nonpartisan elections are accompanied by genuine nonpartisanship; nor can one assume that they are not.

One last feature of state and local political processes deserves mention here. While members of the Senate and House of Representatives in Washington, D.C., hold well-paid, prestigious positions, their state and local counterparts often do not. Many state legislators are only part-time politicians and earn the bulk of their livelihoods from other sources. This is also true of most general-purpose local government officials. In addition, most local school board members are unpaid, even though many devote long hours to their duties. Because many elected state and local officeholders do not get their primary incomes from their positions in government, it may well affect the way they respond to constituents. After all, while they and their families typically live in the community that they are representing, their livelihoods do not depend on being reelected.

Selections in the first section of this unit focus on parties and elections. The second section covers the roles of interest groups, protests, boycotts, and news media in state and local politics. The third section treats referenda, initiatives, and recalls—three procedures that give voters in many states and localities a direct role in determining policies and overseeing the performances of elected officials during their terms in office.

Looking Ahead: Challenge Questions

If you were the head of an interest group, would you use different techniques in trying to influence a state government than in trying to influence a local government? What would the differences be?

Do you think there is much difference between running for office in a small town, running for a seat in a state legislature, and running for a Congressional post?

Do you think people are more or less knowledgeable when they vote in state and local elections than in national elections? Why?

Which level of government seems most responsive to citizens—national, state, or local? Why?

Do you think citizens should be allowed to participate in policy making through the initiative and referenda processes? Why or why not? What do you think about allowing citizens to recall officials during their term in office?

The Mirage of Campaign Reform

We've spent the past 20 years talking about how to keep money from corrupting the political process. The more we talk, the worse the problem seems to get.

ROB GURWITT

Let's start with a short test.

Imagine a state somewhere in the Midwest. The public's disgust with politics has boiled over. A small band of reformers, arguing that campaign money has been corrupting the legislature, seizes the moment and puts a measure on the ballot to stifle the influence of private interests in the campaign process.

They propose setting aside enough public money every two years to give every candidate with a serious campaign as much as it takes to conduct it. Private funding would be legal, but everything possible would be done to discourage it; if your opponent took private funds, you would get public funds to match.

The campaign gets raucous. Some opponents of the measure argue that public funds have no place in campaigns. Others bombard radio talk shows with complaints that taxpayers' money shouldn't go to support politicians. The reformers counter that only when there's enough public funding to run a full-scale campaign will candidates stop bellying up to the special-interest bar. Even better, they say, candidates won't have any incentive to turn to fat cats in a close race because all it would do is generate more public money spent against them.

Throughout the fall, polls show a cynical electorate going back and forth on the question. Half the streets in the state are festooned with bright blue signs reading, "We Deserve Better. Yes on Public Financing," and red signs countering, "Your Money? For Politicians??? Vote No!" A to-do erupts when newspapers reveal that the opposition is being funded by the state's major corporations, but it quiets down after a report that the other side has been tapping the liberal Democratic network in Hollywood. Finally, Election Day rolls around. Early returns show the measure going down narrowly, but it pulls ahead when the numbers start flowing in from the cities, and finally passes.

Here's the question. It's now 2002, a decade later. Which of the following has happened?:

(A) The reform law has served mainly to create a multimillion-dollar industry of consultants, pollsters and campaign professionals, all of them skilled at running "independent expenditure" campaigns for the corporations, unions, trade associations and ideological groups that just want to "participate" on behalf of their favored candidates. The Supreme Court says it is unconstitutional to prohibit these expenditures. Because of them, special interests are as powerful in the state as ever.

(B) Legislators, faced with tight budgets, seem chronically unable to find enough money to fund the provision guaranteeing extra public funding for candidates whose opponents use private contributions. So the public money turns out to be nothing more than a floor. When a campaign is really close and hard-fought, private funding is what makes the difference.

(C) Campaign costs, which were supposed to go down after the reform law passed, keep going up. Candidates with rich friends believe their chances of winning go up if they spend every dollar of private money they can raise, even if their opponents are given public money to match them. The reform law not only hasn't controlled costs—there is talk that it is going to bankrupt the state.

(D) Nobody really knows what the reforms would have accomplished, because the Supreme Court has thrown them out. The court said that the provision matching public money against excess private funding violates the free speech rights of the person who wants to spend the extra private money.

(E) The reformers were right: The system survives all its court challenges, it wrings private money out of campaigns and holds costs down, it allows candidates to spend their time campaigning rather than raising funds, and it gives legislators the freedom to cast their votes without worrying about their campaign budgets. All in all, it is a tonic for democracy.

And now that you've made your choice, here's the real question: Why did you just snicker when you got to E?

I t has been almost 20 years since the campaign reform movement built up its first real head of steam in the aftermath of Watergate. At the time, there was a widespread feeling of optimism, a belief that effective reform was just a matter of legislating the appropriate limits and disclosure laws. Congress passed them, states passed them, and now it is hard to find anyone who believes it's that simple anymore. A problem that seems as though it ought to be solvable—how to keep campaign money from influencing the decisions of government—is proving an enormously frustrating puzzle.

True, the country has made some progress since Watergate. There was a time when it was next to impossible to find out where candidates got their money. Now, every state requires disclosure of the amounts and sources of campaign contributions, although some—Ohio, for example—make gathering the information an unpardonable

SEARCHING FOR THE CHEAP SEATS

I f you're hoping to break into politics with a run for the state legislature, you might want to think about heading for someplace as sparsely populated as Montana or Idaho. House seats in both states are flat-out bargains—winning one consumed less than $5,000 on average four years ago, and hasn't gone up much since.

There are plenty of other states where campaign costs haven't risen beyond the reach of ordinary folk, but identifying them can be difficult. Because the states treat campaign disclosure forms differently, it's almost impossible to compare legislative campaign costs for all 50 of them. The accompanying chart shows average and median costs for state House seats in 11 states—those covered in a joint project led by political scientists Anthony Gierzynski of Northern Illinois University and Gary Moncrief of Boise State.

In all cases, the average cost is higher than the median, or the mid-point of all campaigns, because a few high-spending contests have pulled the figure up.

Different costs among states can be traced to anything from varying district sizes to the expense of media markets to the degree of campaign professionalization that has taken place. It would be unthinkable, for example, to run for the California Assembly without paid staff, consultants and pollsters;

THE COST OF RUNNING
State House Campaign Expenditures, 1988

State	Average	Median
California	$370,722	$302,128
Idaho	4,425	2,244
Minnesota	13,244	13,144
Missouri	9,618	6,921
Montana	2,692	2,265
New Jersey	48,033	33,670
North Carolina	12,085	10,025
Oregon	35,982	30,333
Pennsylvania	18,462	13,944
Washington	25,811	20,145
Wisconsin	14,868	11,812

Sources: Created by Anthony Gierzynski from data collected in a joint project with David Breaux, William Cassey, Keith Hamm, Malcolm Jewell, Gary Moncrief and Joel Thompson.

in Montana, where legislative careerism has yet to take hold, you'd probably be laughed out of the state for using them.

There are other forces at play as well. Minnesota and Washington are close to each other in number of people and professionalization, but it costs a fair bit less to run in Minnesota. The reason probably is Minnesota's public financing law, which generally keeps spending down.

The escalation of campaign expense varies within states as well. Moncrief has found, for instance, that the cost of winning a House seat in Washington State grew by about 25 percent between 1980 and 1990, controlling for inflation. But the cost of a Senate seat rose by an inflation-adjusted 300 percent. The reason: The House remained under firm Democratic control during the decade, while the Senate became the crucial battleground between the parties.   —R.G.

endurance test for the public.

In addition, some 20 states prohibit candidates from accepting direct corporate donations, and more than half the states have tried to curb the undue influence of any one contributor by limiting individual donations; a smaller number limit giving by political action committees. Twelve states provide direct public financing to individual candidates, although several of those systems have proved irrelevant in practice.

Still, it is hard to find people who think the system is significantly better; many insist it is worse. Private money is ubiquitous in all its forms—direct contributions, independent expenditures, "soft money," "bundled" donations—and the routes it travels to candidates only multiply with each new effort to restrict them. Campaigns continue to become more expensive. Legislators complain that the pressure of raising money is giving them less and less time for legislating or engaging voters. Donors complain that they are under increasing pressure to give to legislators who preside over their interests.

Perhaps most important, the voters themselves are increasingly cynical about the role of money in elections. They are convinced that monied interests can buy whatever they need in the legislative process, and they believe that the elections system perpetuates the status quo. "Most people perceive that politicians become careerists because the campaign finance system gives them the advantage as incumbents," says Gary Moncrief, a Boise State University political scientist.

In short, it's hard to escape the feeling that much of the campaign reform effort has been a waste of time. "The terms of the debate have not changed much since the early 1970s, when I first got into it," says Daniel Lowenstein, a law professor at UCLA and the first chairman of California's Fair Political Practices Commission. "And to the extent they have, they've changed for the worse: More prominence is being given to even more simple-minded ideas."

That may stem from simple frustration. If anything, the past two decades of campaign finance reform have given the country a lesson in the difficulties of legislating change. They have demonstrated that good intentions have little to do with actual results, that it's hard to keep reform efforts from falling prey to political maneuvering, that Republicans and Democrats diverge fundamentally in the way they view the issue, and that beyond a certain point no one seems able to agree even on what they want to accomplish.

Above all, they have made it clear that trying to force the system to conform to some preconceived set of ideals is doomed to fail. "We live in a democratic and pluralistic society, and you just cannot structure a regulatory system that will cover everything," says Herb Alexander, a campaign finance specialist and director of the Citizens' Research Foundation in Los Angeles.

The elections process is like a minor ecosystem; changing one small part of it can yield entirely unforeseen results elsewhere. Wisconsin, for instance, is one of three states that provide public financing for state House and Senate campaigns (the others are Minnesota and Hawaii). The idea was to level the playing field for incumbents and challengers, and to cut reliance on PAC contributions. But the system has gone off-kilter. Not only have legislative candidates been ignoring it routinely in close contests, opting to forego public money in exchange for freedom from spending limits, but the parties have been using it mainly to subsidize nuisance challenges to incumbents on the opposing side.

"If you want to keep an incumbent busy in some seat," says Democratic state Senator John Medinger, "you get a sacrificial lamb. He or she gets $8,000 or so of public money and keeps the incumbent home, and then the parties target the eight or nine seats where they're willing to blow the limits." Those eight or nine crucial elections, of course, are fought out with private funding.

"Public financing is a nice ethical thing to do," says Medinger, who is retiring this year, "and it's certainly good government. It just may not be good politics in every case." What has happened in Wisconsin is certainly not what the state's reformers had in mind.

One reason reforms can be counted on to produce unanticipated consequences is that campaign money is remarkably protean, not unlike the liquid-metal robot in *Terminator 2*. Just when you think you've dealt with it, it rises from the floor behind your back.

Take Arizona. The state has the strictest contribution limits in the country, $240 per candidate for individuals and most PACs this year. (The amount is indexed for inflation.) With contribution ceilings so low, you'd think that no legislator would feel a debt to any individual donor, and that interests trying to influence the legislature would look for some means other than campaign giving. You would, of course, be wrong.

For one thing, political committees don't sit still once they've given all they can to candidates. Instead, some mount independent expenditure campaigns— that is, campaigns on behalf of or against a particular candidate that are separate from the candidate's own campaign. In the 1990 elections, for example, the political action committee run by US West Corp. gave maximum contributions to the candidates it was supporting, and still had half of the money it had raised left over. But there were about a dozen key races that would decide the majority in each house, so the PAC mounted independent campaigns in several of them, trying to help the GOP win control. "I refused to sit back and not have the opportunity for US West to participate in the political process," says Barry Aarons, the PAC's director.

At the same time, Arizona's strict contribution limits have hardly wrung individual influence brokers out of the system. Since putting a viable campaign together in $240 increments is hard work, anyone who can convince others to contribute to candidate X is bound to become a pretty valuable friend of X's. In fact, some candidates are bypassing PACs altogether and searching out people—somehow, many of them turn out to be lobbyists—who can persuade donors who might have contributed to a PAC to contribute directly to the candidate instead. As one Arizona lobbyist points out, "Some candidates make a great to-do about the fact that they don't accept PAC contributions, but then they solicit individual PAC members for direct contributions."

The problem is by no means unique to Arizona: Donors and candidates all across the country have shown endless inventiveness in getting around contribution limits. A few years ago, the *Charlotte Observer* in North Carolina told the story of a party activist who reported being handed an envelope containing $15,000 in checks from optometrists to a statewide candidate. Each check was for less than $100, the level at which it would have had to be reported; the total amount, however, was well in excess of the $4,000 to which an optometrists' PAC would have been limited. The head of the state optometric association saw nothing wrong with that sort of "bundling." "The Optometric Society has not functioned politically as a group," he said. "If we were, we would be organized legally as a PAC."

In essence, says Alexander, "some of these laws just exchange the big giver for the big solicitor." Or as Paul Gillie, research director for Washington State's Public Disclosure Commission, puts it, "Money is like water: It will find its way no matter what obstacles it encounters."

This would be a sobering thought even under the most statesmanlike of circumstances, with incumbents committed to improving the system regardless of the impact on their own careers and parties willing to ignore partisan advantage in the interest of doing the right thing. But of course, we don't have those circumstances. We have incumbents who don't want to do anything to help challengers, and Democrats and Republicans whose main goal in legislative life is to achieve—or to keep—majority status.

That shouldn't be very surprising. "If you're in political office and like it and want to get reelected, why should you help your opponent?" asks Alan Rosenthal, director of the Eagleton Institute at Rutgers University. "There aren't many areas in which we believe that people should encourage their competition—we don't believe that Johnson & Johnson should go out and help Merck."

That applies to parties at least as much as it does to individuals. Democrats control most state legislative bodies in this country. They want the leaders of those bodies to continue to be able to shift money from their own campaign funds—stocked with PAC donations—to the campaigns of Democratic allies. Republicans have no trouble raising money from individual private donors. They do not like the idea of limiting the amount of money in private contributions that a candidate will be allowed to accept. "Campaign finance is a cutthroat business, and each party will try to devise a system that helps it best," says Ran Coble, who directs the North Carolina Center for Public Policy Research.

That dynamic is on display this year in Washington State, where two separate campaign reform initiatives have been proposed for the November ballot. One of them, backed by the GOP, qualified after a petition campaign in which people were paid to gather signatures—a new practice in Washington. The other, supported by a coalition that includes the League of Women Voters, Common Cause and a variety of prominent Democrats, collected barely enough signatures to qualify.

The Republicans' measure places limits on the size of contributions, prohibits transfers between candidates, and requires unions to get the written permission of members before using their payroll deductions to fund a PAC. It in no way tries to restrict spending, or

the overall amount a candidate can raise.

The rival measure, on the other hand, would involve spending limits. Candidates would not have to abide by them, but if they did, they would be given the reward of being allowed to take larger contributions. In addition, no candidate could get more than a third of his or her money from PACs and party caucuses.

No one knows whether variable contribution limits could pass constitutional muster—the Supreme Court essentially equates political spending with free speech—but Mark Brown of the Washington Federation of State Employees insists that spending limits are vital. "Campaign finance reform without expenditure limits will clearly favor Republicans," he says. That is because, he argues, the groups that support Democrats are currently being priced out of the market. "The labor movement in recent years has come to realize that we simply cannot remain competitive in the political arena with the cost of campaigns skyrocketing as they have," Brown says.

There are some problems with spending limits quite apart from the constitutional questions. There is evidence, for instance, that spending limits tend to hurt challengers. "Over the years," says Daniel Lowenstein, "we have found out that spending a substantial amount of money is more crucial to challengers than it is to incumbents. So spending limits are more of a problem than they may once have seemed." Moreover, as Herb Alexander once pointed out, "It is altogether impossible to prevent a savvy election lawyer from finding a hole in expenditure ceilings wide enough to drive a campaign message through."

The debate over spending limits, though, does serve to highlight a basic conflict between equally respectable political values: Trying to keep the barriers to entering politics as low as possible, versus giving challengers the freedom to spend whatever they need in order to win.

But there is another conflict that goes even further to explain the frustrations of campaign finance reform, and that is the discord between its fundamental aim—removing the influence of special interests from the legislative process—and the notion that everyone ought to be able to participate in elections by

giving money to his or her candidate of choice. "The problem in campaign finance," says Larry Sabato, a political scientist at the University of Virginia, "is that people will not accept the fact that we can't have it all. We want completely clean elections with no tainted money, and we want full and unfettered rights of free speech and association. You cannot have both. If you're not going to tinker with the First Amendment, you have to accept the fact that you can't dam the flow of political money."

Does that mean that effective campaign finance reform is a dead end? Given the conflicts between basic political values, the fluid dynamics of political money and the difficulties inherent in asking legislators and political parties to tackle the matter, it's understandable that many people think so. But despite all the disappointments and unpleasant consequences of the campaign reform movement over the past two decades, the fact remains that there is still useful work to be done.

At the very least, it is time to recognize that in this field, as in many others, there are limits to what government regulation can accomplish—that "good enough" is the best we can hope for. That is not to say that reform efforts are pointless. There are regulations, such as contribution limits and even public financing, that have helped temper some of the grossest excesses of the past, and proposals for free television time and cut-rate mailing costs may also help. But it's naive to expect new legislation to produce a perfect system, especially since campaigns have evolved to the point where every new limit seems to hurt as much as it helps. Boosting individual contributions at the expense of "special interest" donors, for example, has obvious public appeal, but it may also harm groups, such as teachers or anti-abortionists or women's rights advocates, whose ability to have an impact on a campaign rests in pooling many small donations. In the long run, legislation that works to keep the various sources of funding in balance, rather than trying to eliminate one or another, may prove the most stable reform.

It may also go the farthest toward

protecting the one element of reform that seems most in need of safeguarding: the system's openness. With strong disclosure laws, the system at least has a chance to correct itself. As Larry Sabato once wrote, disclosure "is the greatest single check on the excesses of campaign finance, for it encourages corrective action, whether by the politicians themselves, by the judiciary through prosecution in the courts, or by the voters at the polls."

"You've got to let the voters see what's going on, and then let them make their own decision," says Kent Cooper, a longtime official of the Federal Elections Commission. "If they want to re-elect a guy who's representing a cash constituency more than them, fine: If they make an informed choice, the system's not corrupt." Perhaps the most basic reform mechanism, in other words, is to make it as easy as possible for the public to find out who's getting money from whom, and to avoid reforms that force money underground.

That seems like an obvious idea, but you couldn't tell by looking at its reception in many legislatures. Most states require all candidates for statewide and legislative office to file campaign disclosure reports in a central state office,

> **Maybe we can't cut out special interest campaign money. But we can do a better job of tracking it.**

although a few—Ohio, North Carolina, Vermont and Nevada—do not. But only 20 states require listing the occupation and principal place of employment of contributors, and only five—Florida, Louisiana, Maryland, Ohio and Wyoming—require all contributions to be itemized, regardless of the amount. There are even some states—Ohio and Wisconsin, for instance—that allow so-called "conduits," which are set up by special interest groups to funnel contributions by their members to candidates; the group can take credit for the money, but all that gets reported is the individual's contribution.

Even more important, in those states that have watchdog disclosure agencies, they are treated like poor stepchil-

dren. They rarely have the staff or resources to analyze what is happening to the campaign finance system as a whole, to perform specific audits of candidates' returns or even to make the data available in a form that allows people to figure out, say, how much the dairy industry has contributed to a particular candidate. Even the most highly regarded campaign disclosure agencies—New Jersey's Election Law Enforcement Commission and California's Fair Political Practices Commission, for example—have had to withstand severe budget cuts over the past few years. "We were like a thin man entering a famine as we went into this recession," says Fred Herrmann, director of New Jersey's ELEC. Until states get serious about disclosure, nothing else they do will amount to much.

That is especially true because, short of outlawing all private money—which the Supreme Court would not allow—money will always be a factor in elections. Reform legislation can force it further underground, or it can pull it into the open, but, as Cooper says, "the schemes will be there and the people operating in the gray area will be there." Disclosure is no ideal answer; it may simply be the best one we have.

Seismic Shift in the South

GOP strength has been growing in the once solidly Democratic South—and suddenly the region begins to look solidly Republican instead.

Garry Boulard

Garry Boulard, a free-lance writer from New Orleans, La., writes for The Christian Science Monitor *and the* Los Angeles Times.

For W. G. "Bill" Bankhead, Florida's former Senate Republican leader, the massive GOP sweep of state legislatures across the South is less revolutionary than evolutionary, and distinctly reminiscent of author James Michener's description of how land was formed in his 1959 epic *Hawaii*.

"Land was finally born, yes," Michener wrote. " . . . stubbornly inch by painful inch, it grew. In fact, it was the uncertainty and agony of its growth that were significant."

"That's exactly how it happened for us Republicans here in Florida," said Bankhead, where the GOP on Election Day finally broke a painful 20-20 tie in the state Senate to emerge with a narrow two-vote margin for control at 21 to 19. They also picked up eight new seats in the state House for an overall total of 57 to the still-ruling Democrat's 63.

"The victory is big for us because it comes on top of years and years of slow progress," continued Bankhead. "And best of all I think that growth for us is going to continue for the next few election cycles."

But Bankhead may be modest; while it is undoubtedly true that the Sunshine State's GOP path to political viability has been a long and arduous one, it is equally true that its working control of the Senate and the narrow four-vote gap it still needs to win control of the House (where just four years ago the party was down by 11 seats) represents an historic divide, what the *Miami Herald* after the election called a "seismic power shift."

Indeed, the Republicans' advance in Florida, where they have never before in this century been in the majority in either chamber, is easily symbolic of the overall GOP firestorm that rolled through the Old Confederacy on Election Day, breaking records and precedents in its wake from North Carolina to Texas and Florida to Tennessee.

A COMPLETE REALIGNMENT

"In some ways the Republican advance in the South seems almost too grand and sweeping to take in entirely," said Charles Bullock, a professor of political science at the University of Georgia. "We may well be looking at an historic moment in time—the complete political re-alignment of the once Democratic South to the now solidly Republican South. It was that big a victory."

And the numbers support such assertions—Election Day 1994 in Dixie saw the GOP emerge overall with 669 state legislative seats, up from the 538 they held in 1992, and 1990's 474. In just four years the party has gained almost 200 new seats in state legislatures in the South.

But in some states the Republican victories were beyond seismic—they were cataclysmic, shaking to its foundation the serene world of Democratic-controlled legislatures that have governed virtually unchallenged for generations. In South Carolina, Republicans have control of the House by a 62 to 58 margin, the same chamber where in 1990 they held only some 42 seats. The good news for the GOP in the Palmetto State didn't end with the November election. In its immediate aftermath, two conservative lawmakers in the House who won re-election to their seats as Democrats announced they were switching their allegiance to the GOP, thus providing the final two votes needed for a shift in party control.

"We had talked with both of the members about coming over to our side before," said Chris Neeley, a top official with the South Carolina Republican party who helped coordinate the 1994 successful legislative races. "But we weren't sure when they might make their decision to join us. That they did it when they did was obviously a great help to us."

Both of the lawmakers—C.D. Chamblee and Harold Worley—said they were joining the GOP because it was more in line with their own political philosophy. But Neeley said he expects to see at least two additional members change from the Democratic to the Republican party in the near future, thus strengthening the GOP's control of the

House. "And it wouldn't surprise me if we see this same sort of thing happening in other Southern states too," Neeley predicted.

NERVOUS DEMOCRATS

In North Carolina, the Republican blowout was even more stunning: an unprecedented and unexpected 13-seat gain in the Senate where they will now breathe down the necks of nervous Democrats who hold only a two-seat margin at 26 to 24. But in the House elections, the Republicans won a massive new 26 seats—one of the biggest state legislative party shifts in modern history—to emerge with 68 seats to the Democrats' 52.

"I hope I'm wrong about this, but it is just now possible that the cycle has been completed," said Dewey Grantham, professor of history at Vanderbilt University. He is the author of *Life and Death of the Solid South*, a 1988 examination of how the Democratic party reigned supreme in the South for more than a century. "My hope has always been that we would eventually have a genuine two-party competition in this region. But with this election there are strong signs that we are just going to swap one solid South for another, that what was once all-Democratic is now, as this election shows, about to become all-Republican."

Certainly for the 1994 Republicans, all of the elements were in their favor for a strong showing. A mid-term election during the first term

VOTERS REBEL AGAINST STATUS QUO

The Republican sweep in the November elections that signalled voter disdain for the status quo was reinforced by a number of ballot measures across the country on term limits and campaign spending reform.

Many of the policy reforms that united Republicans in both congressional and state races—tax cuts, term limits and crime—were big ticket items again this year when voters faced more ballot measures—142—than at any time in recent history. Tax issues, as usual, topped the list, crime and term limits followed.

Placed on the ballot in 23 states by citizen petition or legislative action, the measures give voters a say in public policy issues.

WATCHED NATIONALLY

Few things marked voter rebellion as well as two unique ballot measures approved by narrow margins in Oregon and California that took the states onto uncharted political and ethical ground.

Oregon voters approved by a slim 52 percent majority "a death with dignity" law that allows doctors to prescribe lethal drugs to consenting adults. Efforts are already under way in California, New Hampshire and Iowa to introduce bills in the legislatures patterned after the Oregon measure.

One of the most watched initiatives in the nation—Proposition 187 in California—was approved 2-to-1 by state voters. The measure bars illegal immigrants from government services including education and nonemergency health care. Though presently stymied by court action, the amendment will probably drive debate on immigration issues in Washington, D.C., and state capitols across the nation. Organizers who put the amendment on the California ballot say they have been contacted by groups in Florida, Washington, New York, New Jersey and Texas that want similar measures passed in those states.

TAX AND SPENDING

Tax limitation measures were narrowly defeated in Oregon, Missouri and Montana. In Nevada, lawmakers will now have to muster a two-thirds majority in both houses to raise taxes or create new ones. Sponsored by Nevada Assemblyman Jim Gibbons, the measure was approved by 78 percent of voters. Legislative supermajority requirements for all tax increases were adopted in 1992 in Arizona, Colorado and Oklahoma and in Washington in 1993. Already, proposals requiring supermajorities or voter approval of all taxes are circulating for the 1996 ballot in at least five states.

Some tax issues went down by wide margins. South Dakota voters

opposed by 58 percent a constitutional amendment to limit prope taxes, and 73 percent of Oregon voters said no to a more extre plan to replace the entire state and local tax system with a 2 perce "equal tax" on all trade.

Voters weren't in the mood for paying taxes, either. Oklahoma didn't like a proposal for a penny tax on every dollar spent for mov and other entertainment; Colorado said no to a cigarette tax; Mas chusetts rejected a graduated income tax; Montana voters repealed $73 million tax increase; Arkansas's soft drink tax was nixed; and Iowa, voters repealed taxes on soft drinks and food.

TERM LIMITS

Idaho, Massachusetts, Nebraska and Nevada voters restricted ter of state and federal officials. Colorado voters toughened limits House candidates and restricted terms for various state and lo officeholders. Alaska and Maine passed federal limits. Only in Ut where legislators passed term limits on themselves this past sessio did voters refuse stricter limits.

CRIME

Voters took a tough stance on sentencing measures. Georgia vot approved the nation's toughest sentencing law by a 4-to-1 marg The "two-strikes measure" mandates life in prison without parole a second violent felony. In California, voters approved a law alrea on the books. The "Three Strikes, You're Out" law orders prison ter of 25 years to life for three-time offenders. Passage by the vot makes it impossible for lawmakers to alter the measure witho another ballot referendum.

Wyoming and Oklahoma voters passed constitutional amendme that allow their legislatures to get tough on crime. Wyoming's pro sion lets the Legislature create a criminal sentence of life imprisc ment without parole and limits the governor's power to commut death sentence. The Oklahoma measure gives the Legislature t power to set minimum prison terms for all convicted felons, who w have to serve the minimum term before being paroled.

Oregon voters also cracked down, enacting measures to stiffen man tory sentences for violent crimes and to put prisoners to work. And O voters said yes to an issue that toughens death penalty appeals.

While gun control measurers failed in several cities around t country, Alaskans voted to amend their constitution and expli give citizens the right to bear arms.

Voters in Alaska, Alabama, Maryland, Idaho, Ohio and Utah said yes

of a new president nearly always brings marked gains nationally and locally for the opposition. In 1990, during President Bush's first term, the Democrats gained more than 50 legislative seats across the country. But in the case of this election and this president, the gains were all the more profitable not only because President Clinton suffered throughout the year from low popularity ratings, but also because he has remained consistently unpopular in the South since his election. Even in 1992 as Clinton won 32 states and 43 percent of the national vote, he lost the South overall to Bush, and—not counting his native state of Arkansas and vice-presidential candidate Al Gore's

measures that will guarantee crime victims the right to take part in prosecuting the offenders. Vermont made it easier for judges to deny bail to people accused of violent crimes. And Colorado voters approved a referendum that prohibits bail for violent felons awaiting trial.

GAMBLING

As some state officials eye the revenue rewards of casino gambling, now legalized in 23 states, and state-run lotteries, legal in 36, new measures were introduced.

New Mexico approved a state lottery and video gambling while Missouri will allow riverboat casinos to carry slot machines. In a continuing battle, South Dakota voters again approved a video lottery that had been ruled illegal by the state Supreme Court.

But voters opposed a casino proposal in Florida. The Navajo Nation rejected casino gambling on its vast reservation, and Wyoming voters refused to legalize games of chance in the Cowboy State. Rhode Island said no to casinos proposed in five cities and towns, but approved a separate measure that made a law requiring a vote on gambling part of the state constitution. Minnesota voters turned thumbs down on off-track betting, and Colorado nixed proposals to expand gambling.

ONE OF A KIND

Though not as high profile as the suicide and illegal immigrant ballot measures approved in Oregon and California, there were several one-of-a-kind proposals taken to voters.

A measure to move the state Capitol from Juneau to Wasilla, population 4,300, was defeated by a 55 percent majority of Alaska voters.

In the only abortion vote this election, Wyoming voters rejected a measure that would have prohibited physicians from performing abortions and provided criminal penalties for doctors who performed such operations.

West Virginia voters eliminated a constitutional ban on racially integrated schools—40 years after the U.S. Supreme Court declared segregation unconstitutional.

Environmental groups applauded a decision by Arizona voters who rejected, 60 percent to 40 percent, a "takings" ballot measure that would have required state regulators to assess the cost to private interests of every regulation they issue.

Oklahoma gave two wineries permission to use out-of-state grapes. And Washington state denture makers won the right to sell false teeth directly to the public without going through licensed dentists.

native Tennessee—won only two states of the Old Confederacy (Georgia and Louisiana).

CONSERVATIVE VOTERS

But even without the juicy targets of Clinton and Washington to run against, state Republicans running for legislative office were nicely positioned to make strategic gains simply because their party comes closer to reflecting the religious, conservative, anti-government views of a vast segment of the region's voters.

"Our priorities have ended up being the same priorities of the people here," said Representative C. Robert Brawley of North Carolina, who helped engineer the GOP statehouse takeover there. "The people around here are most concerned about crime, taxes, holding down spending and welfare reform, and all of those were the main features of the platform all of the Republican legislative candidates ran together on as a team."

But other currents have also laid the groundwork for an eventual Republican state legislative sweep in the South, and the two most prominent have been ratios and race.

"You don't have the old ratio of several members to a district, which helped perpetuate Democratic seniority in the Southern legislatures," said Blease Graham, a professor of political science at the University of South Carolina. "Instead, now there are single-member districts and that has made it easier for Republican candidates to beat the Democratic candidates one-on-one."

Population shifts also support Republican gains—old-time big cities like Atlanta, New Orleans and Miami still almost exclusively send Democrats to represent them at the statehouse, but the faster growing and more affluent suburban districts surrounding those cities have been the principal GOP domain for more than a generation now, with all signs pointing toward continued success: "The only real battleground areas in the South today are the real rural areas," said Bullock. "These are the places where if there are any 'yellow dog Democrats,' this is their final hideout. But even here, we're seeing substantial Republican gains."

RACIAL POLARIZATION

The question of race, however, in a region where blacks make up nearly 25 percent of the population, compared with just over 12 percent nationally, sometimes seems to sear itself into nearly every political equation. Moves to pump up the number of black state lawmakers through reapportionment, by requiring districts with larger numbers of black voters, did indeed produce more black legislators. But the new districts also came at the expense of moderate or centrist white Democrats who frequently entered into biracial legislative coalitions with the African American lawmakers.

"Now we're just getting more and more racial polarization down here in our legislatures, and caught in between are the centrist white Democrats," said Robert Sheheen, who numbers himself among the latter as he gives up his position as speaker of the South Carolina House because of the Republican takeover. "Our group is getting smaller and smaller, and ultimately it is just going to mean the death of the Democratic party as we've known it in the South."

But despite all of their bountiful good fortune, the Republicans in the South have not yet attained mythic status—they can still go wrong and make mistakes. Some lawmakers believe the biggest land mine awaiting them is whether or not they produce not only on the

1995 LEGISLATIVE CONTROL

STATE	TOTAL LEGIS.	SENATE DEM	SENATE REP	SENATE OTHER	HOUSE DEM	HOUSE REP	HOUSE OTHER	CONTROL	GOVERNOR
Alabama	140	23	12	0	74	31	0	Dem	Rep
Alaska	60	8	12	0	17	22	1i	Rep	Dem
Arizona	90	11	19	0	22	38	0	Rep	Rep
Arkansas	135	28	7	0	88	12	0	Dem	Dem
California	120	21	17	2i	39	41	0	Split	Rep
Colorado	100	16	19	0	24	41	0	Rep	Dem
Connecticut	187	17	19	0	90	61	0	Split	Rep
Delaware	62	12	9	0	14	27	0	Split	Dem
Florida	160	19	21	0	63	57	0	Split	Dem
Georgia	236	35	20	1v	114	65	1u	Dem	Dem
Hawaii	76	23	2	0	44	7	0	Dem	Dem
Idaho	105	8	27	0	13	57	0	Rep	Rep
Illinois	177	26	33	0	54	64	0	Rep	Rep
Indiana	150	20	30	0	44	56	0	Rep	Dem
Iowa	150	27	23	0	36	64	0	Split	Rep
Kansas	165	13	27	0	45	80	0	Rep	Rep
Kentucky	138	21	17	0	64	36	0	Dem	Dem
Louisiana	144	33	6	0	86	17	1i,1v	Dem	Dem
Maine	186	16	18	1i	77	74	0	Split	Ind
Maryland	188	32	15	0	100	41	0	Dem	Dem
Massachusetts	200	30	10	0	125	34	1o	Dem	Rep
Michigan	148	16	22	0	53	56	1v	Rep	Rep
Minnesota	201	43	21	3v	71	63	0	Dem	Rep
Mississippi	174	36	14	2v	89	31	2i	Dem	Rep
Missouri	197	19	15	0	87	76	0	Dem	Dem
Montana	150	19	31	0	33	67	0	Rep	Rep
Nebraska	49	Nonpartisan			Unicameral			NA	Dem
Nevada	63	8	13	0	21	21	0	Split	Dem
New Hampshire	424	6	18	0	112	286	2L	Rep	Rep
New Jersey	120	16	24	0	28	52	0	Rep	Rep
New Mexico	112	27	15	0	46	24	0	Dem	Rep
New York	211	25	36	0	94	56	0	Split	Rep
North Carolina	170	26	24	0	52	68	0	Split	Dem
North Dakota	147	20	29	0	23	75	0	Rep	Rep
Ohio	132	13	20	0	43	56	0	Rep	Rep
Oklahoma	149	35	13	0	65	36	0	Dem	Rep
Oregon	90	11	19	0	26	34	0	Rep	Dem
Pennsylvania	253	21	29	0	101	102	0	Rep	Rep
Rhode Island	150	40	10	0	84	16	0	Dem	Rep
South Carolina	170	29	17	0	58	62	4i	Split	Rep
South Dakota	105	16	19	0	24	46	0	Rep	Rep
Tennessee	132	18	15	0	59	40	0	Dem	Rep
Texas	181	17	14	0	89	61	0	Dem	Rep
Utah	104	10	19	0	20	55	0	Rep	Rep
Vermont	180	12	18	0	86	61	2i,1o	Split	Dem
Virginia	140	22	18	0	52	47	1i	Dem	Rep
Washington	147	25	24	0	38	60	0	Split	Dem
West Virginia	134	26	8	0	69	30	1v	Dem	Dem
Wisconsin	132	16	17	0	48	51	0	Rep	Rep
Wyoming	90	10	20	0	13	47	0	Rep	Rep
TOTALS	7,424	1,021	905	3i,6v	2,817	2,604	11i,1u, 2o,2L,3v	18D, 19R, 12S	

L – Libertarian
i – Independent
o – Political party other than Democratic, Republican or Independent

u – Undecided race
v – Vacancy

Source: National Conference of State Legislatures, Dec. 1, 1994

state level, but in Washington as well. "The ball has been passed to us, and now we have to prove that we know how to govern," said David Wilkins, the Republican speaker pro tem of South Carolina who is set to take over Sheheen's office once the new legislature meets in January. "It is a risk for us, because I think the expectations out there are high."

Others worry about potential conflicts between the agendas of Republicans in Washington and those back home. "If the Republicans in Washington decide they want to hold down federal costs for projects by handing down to us a whole series of unfunded mandates, then that's going to be a problem for us," said North Carolina's Brawley. "That isn't at all part of our agenda down here."

MIDDLE VS. RIGHT?

Meanwhile the emergence of lawmakers embracing the tenets of the religious right could also cause problems for Republicans determined to legislate from the middle. Calling the 1994 elections a "sea change in American politics," Ralph Reed, executive director of the Christian Coalition in Washington, said hundreds of candidates aligned with conservative religious groups were elected on both the state and national levels this time around. The People for the American Way, a Washington group that spends a lot of its time monitoring the electoral successes of the religious groups, said that 60 percent of some 600 candidates backed by such groups for national and state office won in the 1994 election.

But Representative Harold Brubaker of North Carolina, who will be the next speaker of the House, said the potential for conflict between Southern Republican lawmakers and religious right lawmakers is overstated. "There won't be any division between us because a great number of us agree with many of their issues," he said. "I think they've got some good ideas, and I just want to wait and see what they come up with."

Even if the newly muscular state Republicans manage to achieve their overall goals and maintain or build upon recent electoral victories, nearly everyone agrees Southern legislatures will continue to be more rancorous places to make law than they have been in the past.

"Politics is getting more confrontational, more partisan," Georgia Democratic House Majority Leader Larry Walker told the *Atlantic*

Constitution the day after the election that saw six new GOP seats in the Georgia Senate and 14 new seats in the House. "It's just the times we live in."

MORE PARTISANSHIP

"Things have been just much more partisan in recent years," noted Joe Brown, long-time secretary of the Florida Senate. The new Senate president, Republican Jim Scott, has promised to work to minimize some of the partisan edge of recent years in Tallahassee. "It used to be where it was kind of natural to have more of a coalition kind of effort. But that just seems to be a lot harder to pull off these days between the Republicans and Democrats," Scott said.

But South Carolina's Wilkins thinks complaints about partisanship in Southern legislatures is more a manifestation of Democratic frustration over having to share power than anything else. "As we gained strength in the House, suddenly they said there was too much partisanship going on because they were just always used to getting their way," he said.

Wilkins even thinks closely contested legislative battles—a phenomenon unheard-of in years past under one-party, courtly Southern rule—could actually lead to more harmony between Democrats and Republicans. "If both parties have enough members and votes to block legislation against each other, then that means both parties will eventually have to be more reasonable, trying to find a middle ground in order for things to get passed," he said. "It could be a good thing."

But even if the partisan rancor increases and the newly Republican Southern state legislatures fail to live up to their billing, most experts believe the future bodes well for the GOP in Dixie anyway.

"Really, when you get down to it, just about everything is playing into their favor down here," said Vanderbilt's Grantham. "There are so many ideological, philosophical and traditional predispositions among people in this region that fit into current day Republicanism, I think this is just the beginning of their era. What I don't know is how long that era will last."

It Isn't the Gender

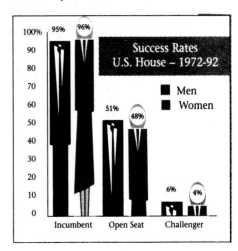

Percentage of Candidates and Officeholders Who Are Women

■ Candidates since 1972
■ Officeholders in 1994

State House 21% 22%
State Senate 17% 17%
U.S. House 7% 11%
U.S. Senate 7% 7%
Governors 6% 8%

In politics a man usually bests a woman, or so the conventional wisdom goes. Polls

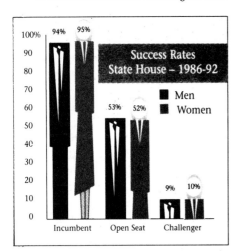

Success Rates State House – 1986-92

■ Men
■ Women

Incumbent: Men 94%, Women 95%
Open Seat: Men 53%, Women 52%
Challenger: Men 9%, Women 10%

show that people by overwhelming margins believe women have a tougher time getting elected to public office than men do, and even those who say they are more likely to vote for a woman predict the man will win.

But a new study by the National Women's Political Caucus (NWPC) says electoral success has nothing to do with gender and everything to do with incumbency. The NWPC studied the election rates of 50,563 candidates—all the majority party candidates, men and women, who ran in general elections for state house and senate from 1986 to 1992 and for U.S. House, Senate and governor from 1972 on.

In state house races incumbent women won 95 percent of their races, incumbent men won 94 percent. In the state senates, female incumbents won 91 percent of

their elections and male incumbents 92 percent. In the U.S. House the numbers were similar—96 percent of incumbent women won, 95 percent of men. Incumbency is clearly the important factor, not gender.

Just 53 women have run for the U.S. Senate and 33 for governor in general elections since 1972. The number is too small to make meaningful generalizations. But the study found no evidence that women were less likely than men to win these races.

Women are 51 percent of the population and 53 percent of the voters, but they make up only 21 percent of state legislators, 11 percent of U.S. House members, 7

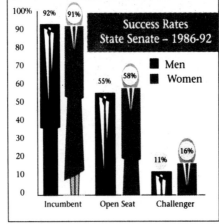

Success Rates State Senate – 1986-92

■ Men
■ Women

Incumbent: Men 92%, Women 91%
Open Seat: Men 55%, Women 58%
Challenger: Men 11%, Women 16%

percent of U.S. senators and 8 percent of governors. And those are roughly the percentages by which women have been candidates for those offices.

The study also calculated the outcomes for state legislative races when a woman

ran against a man for an open seat. It found:

• Women won 55 percent and men 45 percent of state senate open races between a man and a woman.

• Women won 52 percent and men 48 percent of open state house seats when a man faced a woman.

• Female challengers in state senate races beat male incumbents 17 percent of the time, while male challengers beat female incumbents only 11 percent of the time.

Most incumbents are men, at every level of office. This fact, coupled with the fact that incumbents are almost assured of reelection, explains why women have a tougher time winning office.

"Women do win less often than men," says Jody Newman, author of the study, "not because they are women, but because they are less often incumbents."

Success Rates U.S. House – 1972-92

■ Men
■ Women

Incumbent: Men 95%, Women 96%
Open Seat: Men 51%, Women 48%
Challenger: Men 6%, Women 4%

Dickering Over the Districts

You can take redistricting out of the legislature but the politics remain.

Tim Storey

Tim Storey is NCSL's expert on redistricting.

Most states now have new state legislative district maps in place for the upcoming fall elections, but at least 23 of them are being challenged in court.

Every 10 years the U.S. Census Bureau counts Americans, and then states begin the arduous and often agonizing task of redrawing political boundaries for state legislative and congressional seats. In most states, it's the lawmakers who do the map drawing, and routinely they do it in a politically charged, contentious atmosphere. Inevitably, passing a redistricting plan comes down to the closing days of the session and is adopted in a cloud of partisanship. Not long after, disgruntled members, editorialists and public interest groups call for reform. "There must be a better way," they declare.

But is there?

Donald Stokes, dean of Princeton's Woodrow Wilson School, points out that the United States is the only nation with representative districts that leaves remapping to the normal legislative process. As a two-time member of New Jersey's redistricting commission, he argues that the public interest—not political interests—is served best when law-

Redistricting Via Commission

State	Members	Selection Requirements
Ark.	3	Governor, secretary of state and the attorney general serve.
Colo.	11	Legislature selects 4, governor 3, judiciary 4. Maximum of 4 from legislature; 6 from the same party. Each congressional district must have at least 1 but no more than 4 representatives; at least 1 member must live west of the Continental Divide.
Hawaii	9	Senate president selects 2, speaker 2, minority Senate 2, minority House 2. These 8 select 9th member to chair. No member may run for legislature in the two elections following redistricting.
Mo.	House— 18 Senate— 10	There are two committees. Governor picks 1 person from 2 lists submitted by the main political parties in each Congressional district to form the House committee. Governor picks 5 from lists of 10 submitted by the two parties to form the Senate committee. No member may hold legislative office for next 4 years.
Mont.	5	Majority and minority leaders of both houses each select a member. Those 4 select a 5th chair. If the 4 cannot select a 5th within 20 days, then a majority of the Supreme Court selects the chair. Public officials may not serve. Members may not run for office for 2 years.
N.J.	10	The chairs of the two major parties select 5 members each. If they cannot develop a plan in the allotted time, the chief justice of the Supreme Court appoints an 11th member.
Ohio	5	Board is the governor, auditor, secretary of state and 2 members selected by the legislative leaders of each major party.
Pa.	5	Majority and minority leaders of both houses each select 1 member. These 4 select a 5th to chair. If they fail to do so within 45 days, a majority of the Supreme Court will select the 5th. Chair may not be a public official.
Wash.	4	Majority and minority leaders of both houses each select 1. These 4 select a non-voting chair. If they fail to do so by a specific date, the Supreme Court selects the 5th. No commission member may be a public official.

Todd Rosenkranz, NCSL

makers are removed from redistricting. And indeed, nine states rely on commissions to redraw district lines, contending that lawmakers' priorities are to maximize partisan control and entrench incumbents rather than develop fair plans that can stand up in court.

But others argue that politics will never be absent from a process inherently political. For after all, commission members are appointed by politicians and bring their own agendas to the table. Some in Pennsylvania have called for an overhaul of their commission system and suggested that redistricting be brought back into the legislative process because they believe that the commission system invests too much power in the hands of too few people. Pennsylvania has a five-person commission for legislative redistricting.

Nevertheless, the appeal of removing redistricting from the legislative environment can be particularly tantalizing at least once every 10 years.

Following a contentious redistricting battle in Virginia in 1991, Delegate Steven Agee announced that he would introduce a bill during Virginia's next regular session calling for the creation of a redistricting commission. In Louisiana, several prominent public figures such as former governor Buddy Roemer and Senator Dennis Bagneris, who chairs the committee that handled redistricting, have been joined by various newspaper editorial writers in calling for the creation of some sort of entity to draw Bayou State districts that will take the process out of the hands of the Legislature.

Currently, redistricting of legislative seats is the responsibility of the legislature in 39 states. (In Alaska the governor is charged with redistricting, and Maryland's governor submits legislative maps to the legislature.) Reformers contend that redistricting done within the normal legislative process creates a clear conflict of interest since the outcome will have so many political ramifications.

Nine states have lifted the task of redistricting out of the legislature and given an independent commission the initial responsibility for redrawing the lines. The states are Arkansas, Colorado, Hawaii, Missouri, Montana, New Jersey, Ohio, Pennsylvania and Washington. The makeup of these commissions varies. Arkansas has a three-member commission composed

of the governor, secretary of state and attorney general. In Washington, the redistricting commission comprises four members, one each appointed by the minority and majority leaders in each house of the Legislature. None of the commissioners may hold public office while serving on the commission. The four appointed members select a fifth non-voting chairman. Several states have specific restrictions barring commission members from running for the legislature in subsequent elections.

Of the states that completed redistricting in 1991, several used the commission system successfully. New Jersey held legislative elections in November under districts drawn by an 11-member commission earlier in the year. The New Jersey commission adopted plans that have not been challenged in court, and no challenge is expected. Each of the two state party chairmen appoints five members to the commission, and the 10 commissioners have 30 days to produce new district maps. If they are unable to do so, an 11th commissioner is appointed by the chief justice of the state Supreme Court to break the tie and ensure the adoption of a fair plan with the public's interest as its top priority.

In 1991, as in 1981, Princeton's Donald Stokes was tapped by the chief justice as New Jersey's 11th member. Stokes lauds the New Jersey system as a model because it infuses the process with the wisdom of politics yet eliminates the conflict of interest that he believes is inherent when the legislature redistricts itself. Stokes says that the conflict of interest is so clear that "legislatures have been catching hell for the mischief that results (since) the early 19th century period in which Elbridge Gerry gave us the term *gerrymander.*"

In 1981, Stokes was joined by the commission's five Democrats to pass a plan, and in 1991, the five Republicans voted with Stokes.

Iowa's method of redistricting is the most radical of the states. The Iowa approach seeks to eliminate political concerns as the main force behind the line drawing. During the '60s and '70s, the courts repeatedly threw out redistricting proposals from the Iowa legislature; and in 1972, the Iowa Supreme Court imposed its own plan. With the frustrations of the past clear in their minds,

Iowa lawmakers enacted the current redistricting statute in 1979.

Under Iowa law, the non-partisan Legislative Service Bureau submits a set of proposed redistricting maps to the legislature, which must approve or deny the plans without amending them. If the legislature rejects the first set of plans, the bureau supplies a second set also to be voted up or down without amendments. If the legislature rejects the second set, it gets a third set that it may amend. Only by stretching out the process to the third round can the legislature retake control of the line drawing.

Iowa's redistricting statute prohibits the Legislative Service Bureau from using any political data such as voter registration or past election results when drawing up the plans. Neither may the bureau take into consideration the residences of incumbent legislators. The bureau may use only population figures provided by the Census Bureau and apply criteria such as creating compact districts and preserving communities of interest.

Using this unusual system, Iowa became the first state in 1991 to adopt both state legislative and congressional districts, and no court challenges have been filed. Wyoming was actually the first state to complete redistricting using a process of apportioning seats out to counties, but their plans were thrown out by a federal court for violating the one person, one vote rule.

The Iowa experience was not without its anxious moments. One local television station declared the plans dead on arrival once the political results of the plans were revealed. The Iowa plans paired 20 of 50 incumbent senators and 40 of 100 incumbent representatives in the same districts; the Senate majority and minority leaders and the House speaker and majority leader were not spared. Nevertheless, the Iowa General Assembly accepted the first plans.

Iowa's ability to remove politics from redistricting is unusual. Even states with a commission or board admit that politics still play a key role. Mark McKillop, who was the supervisor of the Senate Democratic reapportionment project in Pennsylvania, responds to those wanting to strip the process of politics by saying, "They're kidding themselves if they think they can take politics out of it." He does endorse a commission system like the one used in Pennsylvania on the grounds of efficiency. "If this were done in the legislature, we would still be doing it," McKillop said.

Anne Lee, the reapportionment chair for the League of Women Voters in Hawaii, agreed that politics were still very evident in the commission process used in her state. She did point out that the commission lifted the contentious process from the Legislature, thus allowing them to focus on substantive issues rather than being consumed by redistricting. She also noted that each political party had an equal voice on the Hawaii commission instead of one party dominating the process, which might occur if it were done within the Legislature.

Many states successfully adopt each decade redistricting plans that stand up in court and are produced within the crucible of the normal legislative process. Virginia Delegate Ford Quillen pointed out that his state "produced a good product using the typical legislative committee system." He also said that it would be very difficult "to design a pure commission system where the commission members don't have their own agendas." One of the principal criticisms of commissions is that the members invariably have political motives, and it merely concentrates substantial power in the hands of a smaller group than the legislature.

Using a commission system does not guarantee that new district plans will not be challenged. The Hawaii commission had its plans thrown out in 1982 and replaced by temporary court-drawn plans. Missouri, Ohio and Pennsylvania are currently in court defending plans drawn by commissions.

It is certain that redistricting will continue to be a divisive and time-consuming chore for legislatures every 10 years. Redistricting plans, whether drawn by the legislature or an independent commission, will always have dramatic political results. Whether you are a winner or loser in the redistricting sweepstakes may determine which system you advocate.

If Term Limits Are the Answer, What's the Question?

They are designed to solve a problem that may no longer exist.

ALAN EHRENHALT

Decades from now, when term limits are given their legitimate place as a loony footnote to 20th century political history, some alert scholar may want to look back to the town of South Pasadena, Florida, as the place where they began to self-destruct, and to Fred G. Held Jr. as the man who helped it happen.

When it came to enacting term limits, South Pasadena, a suburb of St. Petersburg, was ahead of just about everybody in the country. A decade ago, when the town approved a new charter, it provided that from that point on, all members of its city commission would be limited to three consecutive three-year terms. This spring, the law finally kicked in. Fred Held, who went on the commission the same day the charter was enacted, duly stepped down and went back to private life.

That was on a Wednesday. The next day, Held got a phone call from the city clerk. She told him something he already knew, which was that the commission had a problem. With one member having resigned, and given the effects of some defeats in the past couple of elections, the four incumbent commissioners had a combined total of two years' experience in government. They didn't know a whole lot about running South Pasadena.

In fact, the four of them had been mulling over their problem, and one of them made a very logical point. The charter said you had to leave office after nine years. It didn't say how long you needed to be out before you could come back in.

In South Pasadena, it turned out that two days was enough. On Friday morning, having spent 48 hours as a private citizen in accordance with the term-limit law, Fred Held was unanimously elected by the commission as the city's mayor, filling a vacancy. His return increased the combined total of governmental experience on the commission by 550 percent. His colleagues were glad to see him. "As a commission," one of them admitted, "we are very green."

I don't want to be flippant about this. It may well be that in his two days of retirement, back home amongst the people, Held picked up some morsels of grassroots wisdom he would have missed if he had stayed on the job continuously. But if you think that's unlikely, maybe you will agree with me that term limits in South Pasadena are an example of a public policy absurdity.

It's especially absurd because South Pasadena uses the commission form of government. There is no professional manager to run the day-to-day community affairs; the commissioners, seasoned or not, have to do all the heavy lifting. One of them is in charge of parks, one takes safety, one handles finance and one is the building commissioner. The mayor is officially in charge of administration.

For this work, the four commissioners are paid a total of $275 a month, plus $125 for expenses. The mayor gets an extra $100. Now, given that South Pasadena has fewer than 6,000 people, and that a majority of its citizens are retirees, it's true that managing its affairs is not the most stressful job in American government. Still, taking care of a park system or a town budget, even a small one, is more than part-time work if there is no manager in overall charge. And the pay never seems to go up with the responsibilities. In the past decade, the voters turned down salary increases for the commissioners several times.

Any idiot should be able to see that, under circumstances like those, South Pasadena's problem isn't getting rid of venal careerists—it's finding anybody willing to take the jobs at all.

The two commissioners who joined the group a year ago had to be drafted by their colleagues. Nobody had volunteered to run.

What everyone seemed to realize was that in Fred Held, the town had a gem of a politician. A retired insurance executive from Philadelphia, Held moved to South Pasadena 15 years ago, found himself with some extra time and discovered that local government fascinated him.

Not only that, but Held turned out to have some badly needed skills as a conciliator. Small as it is, South Pasadena has been riven in recent years, like many South Florida towns, by conflict between pro-development and anti-development factions. Held, at the time the term-limit law forced him out, appeared to be the only player in local politics with enough credibility on both sides to keep the debate civil. "He excels at government," says Joe Catalfamo, the commissioner who seems to have come up with the idea of ignoring the law and bringing Held back after two days.

ENOUGH ABOUT FRED HELD AND SOUTH PAS-
adena. The question is why anybody would think a law like this is a good idea. In an institution such as Congress, where it has been routine for members to arrive early in life and stay until old age, the case for term limits may at least be rational (although it still isn't very persuasive). When it comes to communities—small suburbs, like South Pasadena, or even big cities or counties—term limits are just silly. The problem they are designed to solve doesn't even exist.

Unfortunately, that will not prevent the idea from spreading all over the map of American local government. New York City now has a term-limit law for its city council; San Francisco has one for its county supervisors.

A few weeks ago, state legislators from Cobb County, Georgia, one of the nation's monster suburban jurisdictions at nearly half a million people, proposed that Cobb become the first of Georgia's 159 counties to impose term limits on its county commissioners.

To a certain extent, this was partisan politics: The legislators are Democrats and most of the commissioners are Republicans. But it still reflects the continuing spread of the term limit virus into all sorts of inappropriate corners of government.

All it takes to show the inappropriateness of term limits in Cobb County is a few facts of its recent history. There was a time within modern memory when local officials really did stay on forever at the Cobb courthouse in Marietta. Ernest Barrett was chairman of the commission for 20 years before his death in 1984. But since then, Cobb voters have shown no desire to keep anybody in office very long. There have been three chairmen since Barrett's death; none has been reelected; no one on the current commission has even been there the eight years it would take to get mustered out under the proposed term-limit law. As the Cobb County commission's current chairman, Bill Byrne, says, "It's not a viable alternative here. The voters take care of it." Or, in the words of one of the county's veteran politicians, "The suburbs eat their young."

The truth is that term limits on local government just about anywhere are, at best, a solution to yesterday's problem. They are a cure for a careerism that is all but disappearing on its own.

In modern local politics, there really have been two kinds of self-perpetuating careerism worth worrying about. One was the "courthouse crowd" careerism, in which a small network of cronies, relatives and hangers-on could essentially lock up a county and its government for a generation or more. This was true over much of the South for the better part of this century, but as Cobb County and countless other jurisdictions have demonstrated during the past decade, it is now an anachronism. Elections are volatile, new players and interests move in and out, a job as a commissioner is not a lifetime sinecure. If term limits are meant to stamp out good-old-boy hegemony at the county courthouse, they are a decade or so too late.

There is, of course, a very different kind of careerism in local politics: the careerism of the lifetime political animal who begins organizing campaigns in high school, graduates from college determined to run for office and views election to office, a few years later, as a precious gift worth not only savoring but perpetuating. These are the professionals who arrived in local government all over the country in the 1980s, turned councils and commissions from part-time into full-time institutions, and honed the tools of incumbency to the point where they became virtually impossible for a challenger to dislodge.

THIS IS THE CAREERISM THAT THE TERM-LIMITS
activists seem most sincerely disturbed about, in Congress and in state legislatures and in local government as well. But there is a question that these crusaders ought to ponder, and that is whether this form of careerism, too, may become a thing of the past.

The political professionalism of the 1980s was very largely a phenomenon of a generation—of Baby Boomers and those slightly older who grew to maturity in the activist years of the 1960s, were imbued with the spirit of government as social problem-solver, and decided that a lifetime in politics would be not only fun but absolutely self-justifying in a moral sense. Thus we have the Bill Clintons and the Gary Harts and the Jerry Browns of the most recent cohort in national politics.

But will the same supply of professionals emerge from a generation that has grown up disillusioned with government, resigned to its limited possibilities, besieged by scandal, and drawn to tales of entrepreneurialism and the free market rather than to complex schemes of government regulation? Is this group of people really going to set its sights on local government and stay there so immovably that it will take term-limit laws to blast them out? I think the answer is far from clear.

And if the next generation turns out to be different, it is worth asking just who it is that term-limits are supposed to save us from. If the purpose is to save us from people like Fred Held, then they are not only useless but corrosive to the political system.

Should judges be elected?

Point ▶▶▶▶▶▶▶▶▶▶   ◀◀◀◀◀◀◀ **Counterpoint**

Richard Lee Price

Richard Lee Price is an acting justice of the New York State Supreme Court in the Bronx and is president of the American Judges Association.

Although accused of politicizing what should be the branch of government above politics, most states still maintain that the best way to select judges is at the voting booth. I agree.

Those opposed to judicial elections say elected judges are politicians, beholden to their backers and special interest groups. They fail to acknowledge that judicial appointees suffer from the same fate.

One does not become appointed to a judicial position without cultivating supporters among the politicians with the power of appointment.

Gubernatorial appointments, the most common method of merit selection, do not routinely go to unknowns who, though bright and industrious, have no ties to the governor's office. Similarly, the members of judicial screening committees, who sometimes pick the pool from which the governor or other appointing official may select, are themselves either politicians or chosen by politicians.

Once one admits that both elected and appointed judges are politicians, it becomes clear that the public is better off with an elected judge. Such judges are accountable to the public and may be removed from office if their constituency is dissatisfied with the performance.

Take the case of the 1987 defeat of California Chief Justice Rose Bird, who was appointed to her post by Gov. Jerry Brown. During her tenure, she voted to reverse all 61 death sentences she reviewed.

When she ran in a retention election, she was ousted from judicial office. The lesson to be learned is that although the governor agreed with her death penalty reversals, the public was dissatisfied with her apparent refusal to enforce a law that the people supported.

Opponents of judicial elections insist that the judiciary must be capable of making decisions that may not, in some cases, adhere to the majority's ideas. Elected candidates, they proclaim, may be forced to compromise justice for the sake of pleasing their constituency.

While this concern may have some validity, judges should be re-elected not on the basis of a few decisions but on the basis of the body of work performed during their term. Moreover, public debate about controversial

Evan A. Davis

Evan A. Davis is a partner in the law firm of Cleary, Gottlieb, Steen and Hamilton. From 1985 through 1990, he served as counsel to New York Gov. Mario M. Cuomo.

Judges should apply the law, not make it. They should apply it objectively — without regard to the status or popularity of the parties before them.

Litigants should not need an ideologically "correct" position to get justice, nor should they feel they lost because the other side had political connections.

The way we choose judges has a lot to do with how well we live up to these goals of objectivity, of fairness in fact and appearance and of wise judicial decisions.

New York chooses its judges in two ways — some by election, some by appointment. The election of judges is riddled with politics. Indeed, the process is controlled by the leaders of the two political parties in each county.

This approach is one of the last vestiges of patronage for the party leaders, who are accountable only to the party committee. Their job is to keep the party strong, ensure enough workers to get the party candidates elected, and raise money for the party.

Although there is technically an election, it is really these party leaders who choose the judges. First, they control the process for getting on the ballot. They are naturally inclined to choose people who have been active and helpful in the party.

Second, with other party leaders in the state, they control the party organization, an important resource for getting elected. For example, in New York state judicial candidates generally have to run in large, multi-county, multimember districts.

It is hard for many of them to raise money and remain within the bounds of the Code of Judicial Conduct. But political parties can raise money, and they have access to volunteers who will ring doorbells, hand out fliers and get out the vote. So in upstate New York, which the Republicans control, the Republican candidate wins. The Democrats have the same good fortune in New York City.

The rare contested election for a judgeship, is not a pretty sight. The soundness of the law a judge is required to apply becomes grist for the political millstone. Aid to parochial education can become a hot topic, as well as labor vs. management issues and criminal justice matters. One campaign commercial featured the sound of jail doors clanging shut.

Point

or unpopular decisions is healthy and should not be discouraged simply because the office to be filled is that of judge.

Judges perform a constitutional, as opposed to a majoritarian, function, and it is constitutional for the public to vote out a judge who does not enforce the laws passed by the majority.

Another benefit is that judicial elections can be scrutinized for discrimination, thereby encouraging minority candidates. This especially has become the case since the U.S. Supreme Court determined in 1991 that Section 2 of the Voting Rights Act, which prohibits the dilution of minority voting strength, applies to judicial elections. Gubernatorial and other judicial appointments do not have to comply with the provisions of the Voting Rights Act.

The right to contest a judicial election that appears to discriminate against minorities is a legitimate method of redressing discrimination in the judicial selection process.

Elections force candidates to go public with their qualifications, allowing voters to select a candidate with the qualifications and attributes they believe necessary.

Running for judicial office has drawbacks, most notably the expense. But judges invest more than money in their candidacy; they spend years in many beneficial, professional and community activities earning a reputation that entitles them to run for a judicial position.

Once elected, judges base decisions on their best understanding of the law. Because all judges are influenced by their own values and opinions and have varying degrees of ability, each performs differently.

However, when a term expires and re-election is sought, once again the public has the right to consider the candidate's qualifications.

The third branch of government, not unlike the other two, represents the people and upholds the laws. Excluding the public from the process of judicial selection is anti-democratic. The importance of a judgeship mandates application of a critical constitutional right — the right to vote.

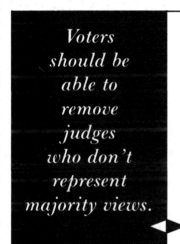

Voters should be able to remove judges who don't represent majority views.

Elections taint judicial objectivity and embroil judges in politics.

Counterpoint

In light of such a history, the appointment process begun in 1979 for judges on New York's highest court, the Court of Appeals, was a breath of fresh air. A nominating commission composed of diverse members forwards to an accountable elected official a list of names. The official then chooses an appointee from the list with the advice and consent of the state Senate.

The advantages of this process are numerous:

• **Scrutiny.** Interested applicants must pass scrutiny at three levels: the commission, the appointing authority and the confirming authority. The bar association and the public have an opportunity for input at each level.

• **Accountability.** The list of names forwarded to the appointing authority and the makeup of the nominating commission are matters of public record. The elected official responsible for choosing an appointee is accountable to the voters for his or her choices. And the Senate is accountable for its decision about whether to confirm the appointee.

• **Diversity.** The bench needs a mix of race and gender to maintain public confidence and to be true to our constitutional principles of pluralism and inclusiveness. If the nominating commission is diverse and under a mandate to consider the need for improved diversity — which should be the legal requirement — that goal is likely to be achieved.

On the other hand, with racially polarized voting all too prevalent, many parts of the state are unlikely to elect a minority judge.

• **Judicial independence.** Merit selection greatly improves judges' independence. Judges can apply the law without acting as if they are politicians writing it. They are chosen for their competence and not because of their opinions of certain laws.

They can pledge faithful and impartial performance of their duties as judges, without worrying whether the party leader will approve and accordingly support them in the future.

• **Opportunity.** A lawyer or lower court judge without political connections can aspire to become a judge or gain a higher judicial office.

This does not mean that those with political connections will not become judges. But it does mean more competition, and from this better choices emerge.

To set out these two approaches is enough. Now, you be the judge.

MY LIFE AS A SCHOOL BOARD CANDIDATE: LESSONS LEARNED IN LOCAL POLITICS

ALLEN D. HERTZKE

Assistant Director **Allen D. Hertzke** ran for the Norman, Oklahoma school board. Although public office was not to be one of them, he found many rewards along the way. Now fully restored to academic life, he is involved in the Religion in Politics Section of the American Political Science Association, assembling twelve panels for the 1994 APSA convention.

I'm not sure when I actually began to think of running for the local school board. I do recall the thought teasing its way into my consciousness last summer. During little league baseball games, the bleacher talk turned to the schools. People were sharing experiences, comparing notes, commiserating. As a concerned parent and professor, perhaps I had something to offer.

In early December 1993 I took the plunge, filing as a candidate for the February election. In the next two months as a "participant observer" I learned a lot about the challenges and rewards of local politics. In an abbreviated form, the following are some of those lessons.

Lesson #1: THE DECISION TO RUN IS NOT A TRIVIAL THING.

There is something both exciting and daunting about walking into the election board and filing one's candidacy. I found myself thinking: Would I make a fool of myself? Where would I find the time to run a decent race? How would I get my regular work done? What would this do to family life? Would my candidacy put some friends and colleagues in an uncomfortable position? And, most importantly, what if I actually won?

Say what you will about it being "just" a school board race, becoming a candidate sparks a rather powerful chain of events. Filing for office, I had mounted a roller coaster. I lost sleep, my teaching suffered, and I missed a chapter deadline by over a month. Tired, I started taking vitamins and Ginseng. In the early days of the campaign there was arduous work to do with frustratingly little tangible result. "What have I gotten myself into?" was the feeling.

But as the campaign got rolling, as volunteers began to meet every Saturday in our house before canvassing, I also experienced the exhilaration of being the spark for something bigger than myself. I found my public voice, gained backers I respected deeply, and forged friendships with the kind of people who make a community work. What kept me going, indeed, was the realization that these fine people were going door to door for me in the middle of winter. If they could do that, I had a responsibility to do my best.

Lesson #2: IT AIN'T EASY BEING A CANDIDATE

I have worked in campaigns, written books, and lectured to four hundred students at a time. But running for the school board was one of the most intense, emotionally demanding, intellectually challenging experiences I've had.

In part this is because school board politics is intense, buffeted by deep clashing philosophies and profound equity issues. A veteran state senator explained it to me this way: "You are running for the toughest job there is, because if you mess with people's kids or their dogs you hit them where they live."

People demand a lot from prospective school board members. During the two month campaign, for example, we candidates attended six forums, answered four detailed questionnaires, shared two radio programs, met with the editorial staff of the local newspaper, and fielded numerous pointed questions over the phone from voters.

For a hotshot professor the experience in local democracy was humbling. I thought I knew the issues, but I had to go "back to school" when I got a questionnaire from a citizen's group with such fare as: What is your view of the Renzulli method of appropriate pacing? What is your understanding of a board member's liability under the Open Meetings Act? Then there was the League of Women Voters' question: What is your five-year goal for the Norman Public Schools? (*75 word limit!*). Now that requires some parsing.

Another thing I learned is that there is a profound difference between giving a lecture in a classroom and standing up in public and offering your views and vision. After my first forum with the other candidates one of my graduate students remarked, "Al, I've seen you lecture to hundreds of students, but tonight was the first time I've ever seen you nervous."

Yes, and then there was the TIME I WAFFLED. I learned just how hard politics can be one night when I appeared before the Republican Women's Club. Overconfident, I thought I was ready with tough answers on academic standards, self-esteem programs, sex education, and school-based clinics. Instead, the big issue of the night turned out to be a state constitutional question. On the basis of material I got from the "good government" types, I had told my volunteers I was in favor of the measure. But that night a speaker got up and blasted the amendment, to much whooping and cheering, giving examples of how voters elsewhere had used routine millage elections (to be eliminated by the amendment) to hold their school districts accountable. When the candidates were asked their position on the issue, the first three expressed their opposition, the fourth waffled so successfully that I thought he did too, and then it was my turn. I can only describe my answer as an *out-of-body-experience* in which part of me was watching as the other part was saying that perhaps we should defeat the measure.

That night I couldn't sleep. I thought to myself, "You gutless wonder—now what are you going to do?" I ultimately had to recant that waffling at the next forum, and I came away with a deeper understanding of why politicians act the way they do.

As the candidate, of course, I had to take full responsibility for what happened in the campaign. I'll never forget how, after a fitful night on election eve, I got a jarring phone call at 6:30 a.m.: "This is the election board and your signs are too close to the polling places. You need to remove them." So this is what being a candidate is like, pulling up yard signs during a sleet storm in the dark.

Lesson #3: LOCAL POLITICS IS REAL POLITICS

Looking back, I am struck by my own naivete. With only minimal discussions with a few close friends and without assessing the political landscape, I took the leap. I should have started much earlier, met with PTA officers and other community notables, and begun to build an organization prior to announcing. Which brings us to the lesson that school board politics is real politics. Running a credible race for this hotly contested seat required name identification, organization, strategy, time, and money—just like any other campaign.

The cash economy, for example, has reached the school board level. Norman, Oklahoma is a city of about 80,000, and the district covered only a fifth of that. Turnout in previous elections was as small as 900 votes, so we weren't talking about a big area or population. But to run a minimally credible campaign took at least $2,000 and probably more. I spent $2,500 on brochures, a few newspaper ads, yard signs, voter lists, xeroxing, and a small bit of mailing. The winning candidate spent over $8,000, and the second-place finisher over $4,000.

The problem is that you have to spend some money to reach a threshold of credibility so you can raise more. And as all the literature says, the candidate must take the leadership in fund raising. Thus to my chagrin I had to divert precious time away from organizational work or door to door canvassing to write fund-raising letters. I hit up departmental colleagues, campaign volunteers, and old buddies from graduate school. It was hard, slogging work, and I was amazed that it paid off.

But money was only one part of the puzzle. In talking with the other candidates, I found that we all struggled with the tasks of developing and sharpening a message, designing a strategy to get it across, and building an organization to achieve that goal.

Though all the candidates did pretty well by previous electoral standards, what none of us fully appreciated was that this wasn't a normal election. Not only were five candidates activating the local electorate as never before, but the eventual winner couldn't have been scripted as a more formidable candidate. His candidacy illustrates lesson #4.

Lesson #4: IT PAYS TO PAY YOUR DUES

Outside of the university community, I lacked public visibility. I had not paid my dues in the sense of being active in the PTA, serving on advisory committees, or attending school board meetings and speaking out. And though I ran a respectable campaign, that lack of visibility ultimately hurt me, especially in the compressed time of a short campaign.

The most formidable candidate, Mike Bumgarner, had clearly paid the most dues by extensive and visible involvement in the community and in the public schools. As a minister with the largest church in town, Bumgarner's activities naturally

placed him in contact with people in a variety of settings. But he had also spent untold hours as a school volunteer and had served as president of his school's PTA (unusual for an arena dominated by women). It also didn't hurt that he was from a well known Norman family (actor James Garner is one of the Norman Bumgarners). Gregarious and well liked, Mike was also backed by major establishment figures, including Democratic party insiders, who saw him as the perfect check on a possible "stealth candidate" from the Religious Right. He was organized, too, and at times it seemed to the rest of us that we were running against a machine. In some neighborhoods my volunteers found that practically everyone they knew had already been contacted by the Bumgarner organization.

Because of Bumgarner's strengths, the race took on a definite strategic shape. The only possible chink in Mike's armor was that he was perceived by some as the establishment's candidate at a time of rising discontent with the administration in some circles. But it was not clear that the majority felt that way, and the best any of Mike's opponents could hope for was to get into a runoff with him, unite the opposition, and eke out a win. I remember thinking that if Mike got only 40 percent of the vote, he might plateau there, and the second-place finisher would have the time and resources to overtake him in the runoff. But there were no tracking polls (thankfully) so none of us, including Bumgarner himself, knew exactly how it would come out.

The fog cleared on election day: Bumgarner received 1,211 votes (or 47 percent), followed by Kelley Lackey at 435 (17 percent), and myself with 389 (15 percent). Two other candidates received 10 and 8 percent respectively.

As I discovered, "real politics" did not end for me with the February election. Because no candidate had received a majority, a runoff was scheduled for April. Both Bumgarner and Lackey approached me with the same question: would I endorse? This forced me to do a lot of soul searching and strategic analysis. Irrespective of how I would personally vote, I knew I had a responsibility to those volunteers who had sat around the kitchen table, leaving it to go door to door in the middle of January for my campaign. I concluded that I couldn't speak for those who backed me, some of whom had strong reasons to vote for one or the other of the survivors. So I tried to play a constructive role, sharing my concerns and those of my backers with both candidates and hosting meetings for them.

Ironically, as a losing candidate I had become a more visible member of the community. Strangers congratulated me on the campaign; I was approached to serve on the parents advisory committee for the district. By running for the school board, in a sense, I have paid my dues

Lesson #5: BEING A CANDIDATE ENLARGES ONE'S PERSPECTIVE

Everything I have just written suggests this final lesson. Almost daily during the campaign I was confronted with my own ignorance, and my learning curve shot up. I got to know the community and the people in it in a way I could never have imagined. I also gained an appreciation for how complex school board issues are. As a candidate I was in a unique position to hear from lots of different people, and I learned that there are endless currents and cross currents, not to mention strange bedfellows, in school board politics. From that experience I concluded that the culture wars thesis—that the struggle over public education pits Christian fundamentalists against secular school authorities—is just too simple, too Manichean. But that is another story.

The campaign was also a great experience for the family. My wife and I shared the expansive encounter with the community, and our boys got into the act. Patrick, my older son, had been something of a polling expert, predicting right from the start that I would place third. But on election night he wanted to see the results, so we hopped into the car and drove to his elementary school, the polling place for our own neighborhood. He knew the strategic situation well by then, that we were competing for the second spot, so he was excited when Precinct forty-three's results were posted: Bumgarner 140 votes, Hertzke 75, Lackey 48, and the others on down. Though other precincts did not come in so well, I will treasure that moment with my son, standing in the dark with sleet falling, reading my own name on the tally sheet, or the "ballot shower," as Walt Whitman described it, that constitutes the poetry of democracy.

Most of all, what I gained from the campaign was a platform to speak my mind, a chance to encounter what Hanna Arendt argued was the uniquely revelatory nature of public life, and an opportunity to taste what Aristotle viewed as the distinctive human experience—full citizenship.

All politics *is* local

That's certainly the case in Arlington—and in your town, too

Dave A. Denison

Dave A. Denison is a former editor of
The Texas Observer.

For almost two years, I have been a spectator in the life and politics of one ordinary Massachusetts town. This does not qualify me to make pronouncements about New England folkways—two generations would put me in better standing—but it has led to a few thoughts about the state of democratic government, which may be of some concern now that we've been through another season of noisy electoral warfare.

Having recently completed a stint as editor of a local weekly, The Arlington Advocate, I've enjoyed an up-close view of politics at the level where it can be seen to have something to do with reality. The news, from this front at least, is not all bad. I have found little of the anger and futility we hear so much about in the national media. What I've seen has made me less pessimistic than the average Washington journalist chronicling the deterioration of representative government.

One advantage of covering town politics is that it affords a chance to observe politics without all the deformities we've become accustomed to on the national scene. In local politics there is no need to amass piles of money to run for office, no swirl of fancy-shoe lobbyists influencing every move government tries to make. Ideology and partisanship are less

important. Best of all, television plays no role, other than to provide undiluted cable-access coverage.

Local politics, it seems to me, is the antidote for one of the most debilitating notions plaguing the republic: that politics is something that comes through the media, as if it were just another bad sitcom. Politics becomes real, and useful, when it is experienced firsthand. A renaissance of political action probably can only start at the local level.

Arlington is a middle-class suburb of 44,000—the sort of place, it is said, the majority of American voters now inhabit. The average household income is about $50,000 a year. Violent crime is infrequent (the only murder last year was when a man killed his former wife). The schools are above average in most rankings, though they are not as highly regarded as those in more affluent suburbs nearby.

I should say up front that nothing much that happened in Arlington in my time as editor would qualify as "newsworthy" to an audience outside the town. In fact, the only story on my tenure that made national news was about a cat named Garfield, who was alleged to be so mean-spirited that he attacked the neighbors. The Wall Street Journal featured Garfield in an article about the aggressive-pet problem, and from there the story was pursued by a number of supermarket tabloids.

I would like to report that among the non-pet population a peaceful civility carries the day, but that was not

always the case. The Arlington School Committee, like school boards everywhere, provided the newspaper with more than enough material on how pettiness and division can get in the way of effective government. It didn't smooth things along when one committee member publicly referred to his colleagues as "a bunch of goons."

Lines drawn in blood or history

School Committee politics can be mysterious—in a way that local politics often is. A seasoned reporter covering Congress or a state legislature learns to understand political behavior by following the money trail, or by knowing the ideological or partisan motives of a given representative. But money and philosophy have less influence over local officials—which makes it sometimes more challenging to understand the pitched battles that take place.

Lines are drawn because of personality conflicts, or bad blood going back further than anybody but the aggrieved party remembers. The Arlington School Committee, for example, has long been divided. But about what? Not usually over identifiable issues, such as the need for more education financing, or less. For quite a while, it seemed to me the division was more social than political. A member of one bloc once told me that a member of the other had not even graduated from high school. As it turned out, a great battle erupted last year over whether to force the longtime superintendent into early retirement, and the camps divided into those loyal to him and those who wanted him replaced.

The superintendent was, in fact, replaced, and the committee is now in general agreement that the new one is a good choice. But while the issue was being fought out, it was not an occasion that made one swell with sentimental pride about the virtues of self-government. Parents complained about the "squabbling" on the committee and worried it was harming the schools. But something else happened last year that, I think, said just as much about the usefulness of an elected board of citizens running the school system.

Off and on for months, the idea had been floated that one and perhaps two of the town's seven elementary schools might have to be closed. Neighborhood schools have been an important feature of Arlington life, but with budgets growing tighter and the schools in need of renovation, there was a case to be made that seven schools were too many to maintain.

I am convinced that at a certain point there was a majority on the School Committee prepared to vote to close a school. But an active group of parents demanded that the case be argued on its merits. The Advocate published several columns and numerous letters from parents that spelled out reasons to keep all seven schools open. Self-interest was a factor, of course, but there was more than that. A sophisticated argument emerged that addressed the long-range financial and educational interests of the town and that noted, relevantly, that enrollments were on the increase.

In harmony with public consensus

At the same time, no one on the School Committee came forward with a rationale for closing schools. Public hearings drew hundreds of people, and it became clear that at least the part of the community that was participating in the decision was solidly opposed to closures. When it came time to decide, the committee wisely brought itself in harmony with the public consensus.

It's a homely vignette, and it's not meant to suggest that the people always triumph. The point is that a decision that was of vital concern to some citizens was not greeted with the sense of futility that is so often inspired by decisions at the state and national levels. Nor was it argued in the kind of simplistic terms one finds so often when well-financed interests take to the air waves in big-stakes battles. People were not left with that sour taste of frustration that has become part of national politics.

Arlington has a 252-member representative Town Meeting that meets every spring for two nights a week. In an earlier generation, it was mostly elderly gentlemen who gathered in Arlington's stately Town Hall auditorium to approve the budgets. Now a mix of men and women, with more young family members, participates.

Still, watching Town Meeting operate, one can't help being struck by how anachronistic it is. Who in this day and age would conceive that 252 people could get together to decide how a town should spend its money? It is time-consuming, inefficient and often preoccupied with budgetary complexity that only a few can comprehend.

Each season one can detect worry that the machinery of Town Meeting grinds too slowly—and that a few cranks can bring it near breakdown. It's true that the process suffers in direct proportion to how many oddballs and windbags take the floor. Trying to bolster confidence in the institution, I once editorialized (and with no one taking issue) that the ratio of solid citizens to jackasses in Town Meeting appeared to be about 20 to 1, no worse than in the general population, and certainly a better proportion than you would find in Congress or the state Legislature.

The more important point is that a citizen has less cause to complain about government spending or other action when he or she has the opportunity to take part in key decisions on the Town Meeting floor. Because the representative body is not a captive of

moneyed interests, town government is not a target of contempt the way the big government is.

In addition to Town Meeting, Arlington has a somewhat more unusual organization that attempts to include the citizen in decision-making. Four years ago, a group of local officials founded a group called Vision 2020 that is designed to get residents thinking about what kind of town Arlington should become over the next three decades. Several task groups now meet regularly, with dozens of consistent participants and hundreds more who plug into the work in at least a small way. Local officials, the thinking goes, get so caught up in the week-to-week crises of town affairs that long-range planning is almost always on the back burner. Vision 2020 attempts to give citizens some of the responsibility for planning.

Of course, the heart and soul of local politics has to do with immediate concerns. Nothing gets a person out of the living room and into a meeting hall as quickly as a perceived threat in her own back yard. Last year in the east end of Arlington, a sizable contingent took up a quixotic battle to keep a McDonald's from locating in an abandoned used-car lot. The sit is near a congested intersection, and nearby residents worried about traffic tie-ups and general disruption. From the start, handicappers weren't giving the neighborhood group much of a chance.

Where mother's milk is . . . milk

But this was not just any neighborhood group. Well-organized and vociferous, the East Arlington Good Neighbor Committee took the debate beyond the usual not-in-my-back-yard terms and asserted the community's right to help shape the commercial landscape. This does not often happen in suburbs, and endless car-choked strip malls have been the result. In Arlington, the Redevelopment Board and the Board of Selectmen must, by necessity, take a cautious approach to new development: the town is already densely populated, and there is not much open space for commercial projects. Consequently, residents tend to have as much political weight in these matters as business interests.

McDonald's must have concluded as much. With an apparent majority on the Board of Selectmen willing to side with the neighborhood group, the company quietly withdrew its offer to develop the controversial site. Less auto-intensive uses—a drugstore and a video store—are now in the works.

To a cynic, self-interest is 90 percent of politics—and the other 10 percent is cloaking self-interest in rhetorical finery.

At its worst, local politics can seem that way. A School Committee member votes to cut money from elementary education in just the year his daughter enters seventh grade. A prominent citizen wins a tax abatement from his friends on the Board of Assessors. An angry resident wants the Board of Selectmen to rein in his neighbor's cat.

In the fight against McDonald's, some of the neighbors, no doubt, joined the cause out of fear their property values would be adversely affected. Self-interest of that sort is a great motivator, it's true. But what of it? Every once in a while self-interest gives us a glimpse of what politics is at its best, too. These are the times when groups of people are pulled into the experience of politics, when they engage in public conversation, plan political strategy and assert their right to negotiate with powerful interests.

I don't mean to suggest that this happens all the time in Arlington—that

the town is some sort of Shangri-la of citizen activism. The threats to this community are not alarming, and most people are content to live lives of quiet uninvolvement. Out of the 44,000 people in town, the number of people who take an active role is not likely to be more than a few hundred. When a tax question or controversial ballot proposition comes up during local elections, there may be a 60 or 70 percent voter turnout. But when it's a matter of voting for a batch of local politicians, the turnout drops to 20 or 30 percent.

There is, even in local politics, a sometimes alarming lack of basic citizen competence. Yet for those who are not cowed or complacent, there is an enticement that is often missing in the national arena: In local causes it isn't so hard to win. It makes a huge difference that money is not the mother's milk of local politics. It is relatively easy for people to get organized in their own neighborhood or town. And it is instructive to see how even the most entrenched local officials sit up and take notice when a dozen citizens show up—and speak—at a public meeting.

Today's great frustration among the populace has to do with the belief that effective citizen action is no longer possible at the state house or in Congress. We are plagued by the feeling that the one surviving realm where democracy can still work is also the one where the root causes of national decline cannot be addressed. The business of local government begins to seem mostly about coping with larger

forces set in motion in distant centers of power.

Captives of the fat cats

Americans used to have ways of participating in state and national politics. This was one of the great functions of the two parties: to allow people to organize at the precinct level and feel a connection, through the party, to national decision-making. The voices of the rank and file were heard when their party leaders spoke. But now everyone knows the two parties are captive to the political professionals and fat-cat donors. Active membership, especially of the Democratic Party, has fallen off, and more people than ever consider themselves independents.

The feeling among citizens that they have lost influence over their elected representatives fuels the drive for term limits and the proliferation of ballot propositions and referenda. It leads to a misplaced anger at "government" or at politics itself. And yet when you watch people attempt to sort out public problems at the local level, you see them forced to make essential connections. Government is not necessarily an evil; politics is not by definition an odious activity.

Taking part in local politics is the starting point to restoring meaning to the national discussion. It is also probably the only way for citizens to begin regaining confidence in democratic governance. Seeing that active politics can make government work in your own town points the way to how it could be made to work elsewhere.

STORE WARS

Jonathan Walters

Elections in the village of East Aurora, in upstate New York, used to be quiet, staid affairs. "Country club elections" is the way the village administrator liked to describe them.

But he doesn't describe them that way anymore. Last March, after an intense, high-visibility purge campaign, four members of the board of trustees were swept out of office. They were swept out based on a single issue that has split the town like no issue before.

What subject could be so immediately galvanizing as to convert a pro forma village election into something resembling a Texas gubernatorial brawl—and turn quiet suburbanites into vengeful partisans? The answer lies in one hyphenated word: Wal-Mart.

The $67.3 billion corporate colossus that Sam Walton built is doing more than just reshaping the national retail landscape. It is creating a political protest phenomenon in diverse corners of small-town America. And the phenomenon is taking a lot of small-town public officials by surprise. "Developers have had a free reign in East Aurora," says Anne Leary, who is heading up the town's stop-Wal-Mart effort. "Now a lot of us are becoming involved in government affairs and we are stepping on some toes."

In an increasing number of places, the arrival of a Wal-Mart is just not being treated as the blessing it would have been a couple of years ago. To a growing corps of guerrilla-style activists, the big-box discount store has come to represent all the adjectives they don't want applied to their communities: sprawling, ugly,

> **There are a few corners of America where the mega-retailers have not yet penetrated, and there are guerrillas in those places fighting to keep them out.**

impersonal and cheap. It represents dollars that are shipped out of state each night instead of remaining in the community and recirculating in local hands. It represents Main Street merchants who can't support the Boy Scouts, the soccer league and the Rotary Club because the mega-store has driven them out of business.

This is not strictly a Wal-Mart issue. There are local development fights going on around the country right now involving Kmart, Costco, Target, Home Depot and just about all the national chains that like to build big boxes in and adjacent to small towns in a direct challenge to the local commercial order. But there is no question that Wal-Mart attracts the lion's share of controversy. When it comes to pouncing on small towns, Wal-Mart is in a league of its own.

Wal-Mart has always insisted it is not anti-small town and that it never tries to force itself in anywhere. "Of all the notions I've heard about Wal-Mart," Sam Walton wrote just before his death in 1992, "none has ever baffled me more than this idea that we are somehow the enemy of small-town America. If some community, for whatever reason, doesn't want us in there, we aren't interested in going in and creating a fuss."

Where Wal-Mart wants to go these days, however, a fuss tends to follow. By the estimate of one anti-Wal-Mart activist, the mega-retailer is currently involved in more than 100 fights in the United States, Puerto Rico and Canada. Wal-Mart, it should be noted, insists that it is involved in a mere handful, and that those are being waged by "1 percent of the people making 100 per-

If Lee Foster gets his way, there will be no Wal-Mart in Lake Placid, and his garden store will have a better chance of survival.

cent of the noise." But it does not take very long to come up with an extensive list of noisy places. Battles over Wal-Mart are either heating up or are in full swing in towns and cities from Cottage Grove, Oregon, to Newton, Iowa, Okeechobee, Florida, Lancaster County, Pennsylvania (where four Wal-Marts and a Sam's Club have been proposed), and Chestertown, Maryland, among many others.

Meanwhile, a national network of activists has sprung up, ready to assist these and any other towns in fighting mega-store development, particularly on the outskirts of town. The nexus of the network is the National Trust for Historic Preservation, which is taking the issue of sprawl head-on as a preservation concern. A Trust-sponsored meeting in early December drew more than 100 attendees from around the country.

The real hotbed of resistance is in upstate New York and New England, one of the few regions left where discount stores do not already crowd the small-town landscape. At the moment, there are active anti-Wal-Mart campaigns in East Aurora, Ithaca, Hyde Park, New Paltz, Sharon Springs, Catskill and Lake Placid, New York; Keene, New Hampshire; St. Albans and Williston, Vermont; Sturbridge, Halifax, Quincy and Easthampton, Massachusetts; Branford, Connecticut; and North Kingston, Rhode Island, among others. In the past two years, plans for Wal-Marts have been rejected in Lebanon, New Hampshire; Bath, Maine; and Westford and Greenfield, Massachusetts.

If the movement has a birthplace, it is Greenfield, where Al Norman, a long-time resident and professional lobbyist, launched a grassroots public referendum campaign two years ago that overturned Wal-Mart's zoning approval by the local government.

Wal-Mart insists it was zoning laws, not citizen opposition, that kept it out of Greenfield. In fact, it was both. City offi-cials had already approved a zoning change for Wal-Mart when Norman mounted his drive to overturn the change and place a cap on the size of all future retail developments. When the referendum passed, Alfred "Bud" Havens, president of the Greenfield city council and a Wal-Mart ally, resigned.

The Greenfield episode has had consequences far beyond the town's borders. It has spawned dozens of similar battles, and a reasonable number of them have been successful.

And some jurisdictions are taking pre-emptive action. The city of Fort Collins, Colorado, recently declared a six-month moratorium on all construction of retail developments larger than 80,000 square feet—considerably smaller than the space the typical Wal-Mart occupies. Skaneateles, New York, which has watched Wal-Mart battles buzzing in every direction around it, is in the process of placing a permanent cap on the size of retail development it will allow in town.

The state of Vermont—the only state without a Wal-Mart—recently invited a contingent of Wal-Mart management up to discuss the company's plans for its push into the Green Mountains. The message to Wal-Mart, delivered by Governor Howard Dean himself, was clear: We'd love to have you, but only if you locate in existing downtowns. Vermont doesn't want the Arkansas retailer paving over cornfields when there are plenty of vacant lots in the centers of Vermont towns that need filling. In the

Bob Trostle is one of the Lake Placid residents trying to keep Wal-Mart out: Is the anti-mega-store movement a conceited form of elitism?

wake of the trip, Wal-Mart has expressed non-committal interest in looking at a handful of Vermont downtowns. At the same time, however, it continues to press its claim on meadowland in St. Albans and Williston.

Even if Wal-Mart does accept the governor's terms, it may be in for a fight. Some merchants in St. Johnsbury, one of the cities that Wal-Mart says it is con-

from the fact that the town is the site of Old Sturbridge Village, a nationally known living museum depicting rural New England life in colonial times.

In Muir's view, this has virtually nothing to do with the question. As Muir sees it, Wal-Mart will bring in more jobs and tax dollars. It has met all of the town's zoning requirements and has filed a thorough environmental impact statement.

traffic to the narrow streets of Lake Placid on a daily basis. In addition, he points out, the site sits in a viewshed framing the dominant geographical feature of the town: Whiteface Mountain. At a stop-Wal-Mart rally in Lake Placid last November, Trostle and the rest of the crowd tended to express one dominant view above all others: They live in a small town because small-town life is what they prefer to lead. They don't want what has happened to other over-developed communities to happen to them.

Even when the fight over a mega-store is over, town politics rarely returns to what it was before.

sidering, argue that their vision for the town does not include a huge retailing powerhouse at the south end of the city's main street. They do know one thing, though, says local clothier Peter Russell: "If they locate downtown, some of us might be for them, some of us might be against them. But if they try to locate out in Mr. Jones' cornfield, nobody will be for them."

The ultimate outcome of these skirmishes is hard to predict. Wal-Mart is a formidable opponent, and the corporation plays and seems to enjoy a good game of hardball. And in most places, anti-Wal-Mart campaigns have to fight another influential group besides Wal-Mart: their own local officials, most of whom seem focused primarily on sales tax revenues and who argue that "if we don't get it, some other town will."

Nobody represents that point of view better than Bill Muir, chairman of the planning board in Sturbridge, Massachusetts, a town of 8,000 residents in the west-central part of the state. For 15 years, Muir, an affable lifetime resident of the town, has helped oversee Sturbridge's steady growth. Planning hasn't exactly been a high priority there—the two main Sturbridge roads are disjointed agglomerations of malls, mini-malls, fast-food joints and gas stations—but development has meant jobs, and Muir and his colleagues on the planning board have welcomed it eagerly.

It turned out that Muir's eagerness to get a Wal-Mart was not shared by all Sturbridge residents, however. And so the town spent the last year engaged in a bitter argument that gained intensity

The developer has committed at least $1 million for sewage expansion.

Town Selectman Charlie Blanchard, on the other hand, starts from an entirely different premise. His vision for Sturbridge is as a tourist destination anchored by Old Sturbridge Village. He is not convinced that dumping 8,000 cars a day onto the town's already overburdened Routes 20 and 131— 9,000 cars a day on weekends—is going to do much to enhance that vision. "I'm afraid a lot of people are going to say, 'Why should I go to Sturbridge to visit the village or the antique shops? All I'll be doing is fighting traffic.'"

The odds are that Muir will win and that Wal-Mart will get its store. In mid-November the planning board voted 4-2 to approve the project. Opponents have not yet decided whether to appeal. But even when the fight is over, the politics of the community will not return to "normal" for a long time. Wal-Mart has that effect.

It is having a similar effect in Lake Placid, New York, where Kim Daby, who has the interesting job of being both tax assessor and head of the planning board, evinces a bit of annoyance with his local anti-Wal-Mart activists. For years, Lake Placid's Main Street has oozed out both sides of town with strip development. As far as Daby is concerned, Wal-Mart merely represents one more big box along the road. What's the big deal all of a sudden?

The big deal, says Bob Trostle, one of the local residents fighting the superstore, is that the Wal-Mart will bring 8,000 cars and tons of tractor-trailer

Those who support Wal-Mart and the other mega-stores in the current warfare have one word for that attitude: "elitist." They accuse the activists of being smug dilettantes who have arrived from somewhere else and seek to dictate lifestyles to long-time residents.

That the movement is the purview of the well-educated and well-heeled is pretty clear. Anti-sprawl activists try valiantly to claim that their cause attracts a broad swath of socio-economic support. But the fact of the matter is, working-class and rural New York and New England residents don't spend a great deal of time worrying about the "built environment" or the "cultural landscape," to use just two of the phrases that preservationists like to toss around. They tend to be more impressed by the notion that clothes, towels and dishes will be a few dimes cheaper once the mega-store arrives, and that there will be a sizable increase in the number of part-time jobs available, albeit for low wages and spotty benefits.

And so town-and-gown-style divisions have begun to show up in virtually all of the places where there is a fight over Wal-Mart or other big-box retailers. In Lake Placid, many long-time residents already resented the fact that Main Street had been subsumed by the tourism trade, which has brought big-checkbook crowds and high prices. A Wal-Mart, a lot of residents think, might be the perfect antidote to that.

Given these divisions, the anti-Wal-Mart forces are unlikely to win many battles on the strength of environmental or quality-of-life arguments alone. To succeed, they need to make common cause with the element in town that stands to lose the most in the long run from the arrival of a mega-store. This is the Main Street business community.

Establishing this alliance is not as easy as it might seem. Many of the merchants in a typical small town tend to agree with the characterization of anti-development forces as elitist outsiders. Others are afraid to oppose a mega-store publicly for fear that their own customers will think them selfish. Still others cling to the idea that, no matter what the economics of the retail industry, they can survive the coming of Wal-Mart. The job of the activists is in part to convince them that this latter idea is simply not true.

The evidence that small-town merchants do not survive the mega-stores very well is fairly clear to anyone who chooses to look for it. It is available on the deserted streets of the downtowns in many areas of the country where Wal-Mart or other big-box retailers have moved in. And it has been documented in a string of studies conducted over the past few years. While Wal-Mart and other mega-stores tend to increase a region's retail pull, they suck dollars away from other local businesses.

A study of 30 Iowa towns by Iowa State University economist Kenneth Stone found that while the average Wal-Mart was doing $17 million worth of business in the first year after its opening, total sales in the communities where they located went up only $7 million. That meant the other businesses in town were losing $10 million. On average, according to Stone, Main Street is nicked for 12 percent of its retail sales.

But many towns are hit much harder. In Maine, retailers in the vicinity of a new Wal-Mart report as much as 25 percent losses in the first year. In Anamosa, Iowa, in the first year, three clothing stores, a shoe store, a drug store, a hardware store and a five and dime all closed. In Wal-Mart's home state of Arkansas, economist Thomas Muller notes, the corporation now accounts for 30 percent of all retail sales.

One who does not find that figure surprising is Ken Munsell, head of the Small Town Institute in Ellensburg, Washington. "Sam Walton's perverse genius," Munsell says, "was to realize that you don't need to generate new markets when you build a store. Local retailers simply can't compete. They'll go out of business. And Wal-Mart will just take the whole market."

That is why quality-of-life activists like Bob Trostle in Lake Placid have found allies in people like Lee Foster. Elitist isn't exactly the word that would spring to mind upon meeting Foster. In faded, grass-stained jeans, work boots, a windbreaker and a baseball cap, the thumbs of his hands hooked in his front pockets, Foster is the picture of a hard-working, independent small-town tradesman.

Foster owns and operates a garden and landscaping center in Saranac Lake, five miles west of Lake Placid. While Lake Placid's tourist-based Main Street would likely survive in the wake of Wal-Mart, Saranac Lake's already hurting downtown would probably be finished, Foster figures. "I don't know of one retail business here that isn't just squeaking by," he says. And Foster worries that his business—and the four jobs he provides to local residents—are in jeopardy as well, because the new Wal-Mart would include a garden center. Foster doesn't mind competing, he says, but he doesn't know how to compete with a company that buys gardening supplies by the railroad car when he buys them by the case.

And so, in Lake Placid and other towns across New York and New England in a similar situation, a fragile Chardonnay-and-Budweiser alliance has sprung up between environmentalists who don't think much of development and merchants who just don't want to be driven out of business. In Sturbridge, one of the most active and vocal Wal-Mart opponents has been Mark Palmerino, who runs a family-owned discount department store a few miles south of town. "I go to suppliers and ask them, 'How much are you charging for pink plastic wastebaskets?' " says Palmerino. "Wal-Mart goes to suppliers and says, 'This is how much we're going to pay you for pink plastic waste baskets, and if you don't like it, we'll find another supplier.' "

Wal-Mart has been campaigning to put out these brush fires of opposition with all the weapons available to a $67 billion corporation. It sometimes counsels small-town merchants on how to diversify and find "niche" markets (a tactic that Mark Palmerino in Sturbridge describes as the fox coming into the henhouse to teach the chickens self-defense). It has ginned up a substantial

public relations effort, noting, for example, that 65 of the country's 100 most livable towns (as judged by the book *100 Best Small Towns in America*), have Wal-Marts nearby. As the planning board vote drew near last fall, Wal-Mart peppered the Sturbridge area with mailings and ran radio spots and 7-minute television commercials on the local stations extolling the virtues of the big store.

And Wal-Mart has carefully cultivated some of the organizations that represent small towns and their elected officials. The National Association of Towns and Townships, which speaks for the interests of jurisdictions with fewer than 10,000 people, has never studied the potential impact of big-box retail stores on the economies of its members, nor does it have any plans to do so. What the association does do each year, though, is administer an annual "community leader" award contest. The contest is sponsored by Wal-Mart.

There are, moreover, some elected officials who sincerely endorse Wal-Mart's argument that the arrival of the mega-store does not have to be a disaster for Main Street business.

Shawn Hogan, mayor of Hornell, New York, is one of those. When he heard that Wal-Mart was nosing around a village just outside of Hornell, he demanded that the company locate within Hornell's borders so his town would get the sales tax proceeds of the store's business. Otherwise, he said, he would deny the Wal-Mart site the sewer and water extension that would have to come out of Hornell. So the adjacent village agreed to cede 80 acres to Hogan in exchange for a cut of the tax receipts.

Then Hogan got together with his local merchants and pointed out to them that all traffic going to and from Wal-Mart would have to pass through the city's downtown. "The merchants really agreed that it was up to them to take advantage of the increased traffic," says Hogan. "They started a business improvement district, and they have hired their first full-time retail recruiter and promotion specialist." With the advent of Wal-Mart, and the increased traffic it portends to generate, empty main street stores are now leasing up. Other developers are expressing interest in other parcels nearby.

But the Hornells of the world are rare. Not because they accepted a Wal-Mart, but because they actually thought about what getting one would mean, and the local elected officials engaged a broad segment of the community in that discussion. Most of their counterparts around the country have not yet learned how to do that.

In the end, the skirmishes now taking place between Wal-Mart and its critics will essentially be footnotes to the larger story of mass retailing and small-town decline. For hundreds of towns all over the country, the damage has long since been done. Wal-Mart will not go away, and the Main Street shops will not come back.

What does seem important, however, is the political change the movement is creating in those communities that have been able to hang on to some vestige of their Main Street ethic and core. When Fort Collins declared its recent development moratorium, it was for the purpose, city planner Claudia Benedict says, of buying some time to consider the economic, traffic, environmental and design impacts of superstores. "You cannot simply sit back and wait for development to come," says Benedict. "You have to put yourself in a position where you can deal with developers because they'll come in and overrun your community if you're not prepared."

In East Aurora, jockeying for position is intensifying. The village board will not vote on the Wal-Mart project until after trustee elections this March; their outcome will likely decide the project's fate. Whatever happens, one thing is certain: It's not going to be any country club affair.

BOYCOTT MADNESS

Charles Mahtesian

About two years ago, officials at the Greater New Orleans Tourist and Convention Commission received a curious letter. The Association for Supervision and Curriculum Development was considering holding its annual convention in New Orleans, so it wanted a little background information on Louisiana. Not the usual questions about possible meeting sites or available hotel rooms, but something a little more pointed. Such as the state's policies on abortion. And the Martin Luther King Jr. holiday. And capital punishment. And discrimination against gays and lesbians.

It was a letter that a lot of convention bureaus dread getting. Nowadays, conventioneers and tourists are asking less about local steakhouses, cultural events and strip joints and more about the politics and policies of a state or city. What makes the inquiries scary is that they are an ingredient in an emerging boycott fad, in which activists economically target cities and stats whose laws or policies they deem unsuitable. By taking their grievances out of the legislative and electoral arenas and into the economic realm, these activists can exact a heavy toll.

Colorado, for example, is weathering a boycott initiated by national gay and lesbian groups after a statewide measure prohibiting special civil rights protections for homosexuals was approved by

A high-profile, politically motivated boycott can cost a state or a city millions in convention and tourism business. There are ways to fight back, but they mostly amount to damage control.

the voters last year. In July, the Colorado supreme court upheld a temporary injunction preventing the amendment from taking effect, but so far the highly publicized boycott has cost the state between $50 million and $121 million, depending on whose estimate you believe. Denver alone estimates its loss in the neighborhood of $38 million.

And at a time when you would expect cities to be circling the wagons, some of them are even joining in the ambush. The U.S. Conference of Mayors yanked its 1993 summer meeting out of Colorado Springs; and Atlanta, Austin, New York City and

Philadelphia are among the cities and counties that have announced official bans on travel to Colorado for business or conventions in the wake of Amendment 2. The mayors of Denver and Colorado Springs, joined by the mayors of a handful of other major cities, retaliated by refusing to attend the mayors' conference meeting in its new location, New York City.

With many cities, including some of those snubbing Colorado, themselves vulnerable to charges of political incorrectness, it's hard to see where it all will end. At the present rate, says Richard J. Newman, president of the International Association of Convention and Visitor Bureaus, it won't be long before conventions will have nowhere left to go. "If they listen to every viewpoint in the organization, they'll never get anywhere. Maybe they'll go to some vanilla place with nothing to do and where no one wants to go to."

The convention business generated nearly $60 billion last year, from more than 82 million delegates who attended nearly 270,000 meetings in 349 different cities, so it's not hard to see why destination cities that depend on the travel and tourism industries fear each controversial new law, policy or ballot initiative that comes down the pike.

Every convention delegate spends an average of $623 over a four-day stay, and meeting organizers kick in about $65 per delegate. If a trade show is held in conjunction with a meeting, exhibitors spent an additional $330 per attendee, on average. The Chicago metropolitan area, for example, hosted 30,000 conventions, trade shows and corporate meetings in 1991, where delegates spent $2.5 billion. And Chicago ranks third among U.S. convention cities.

What strikes city officials as particularly unfair about the boycotts is that, typically, they indiscriminately target an entire state. In Colorado, the highly organized boycott has put the screws to every city and town, even those that long have had gay-friendly laws.

Business cannot afford to sit this one out either. Idaho's significant potato-growing industry sweated out boycott threats in 1991 as Governor Cecil D. Andrus mulled signing a restrictive abortion law. On one side, feminist and pro-choice groups began preparations for a potato boycott. Abortion opponents promised to eat more french fries to compensate if he signed the measure. In the end, Andrus vetoed the bill.

But as the Colorado vote demonstrated, the officials whose jurisdictions stand to lose the most from a boycott are often powerless to keep the offending law or policy off the books. And while the whole phenomenon is too new to have generated time-tested 10-point plans for combating a boycott threat, some cities are at least preparing for one, just in case.

There is likely to be plenty of opportunity for them to hone their anti-boycott techniques. The impulse to boycott is one that is becoming more and more popular, especially among activist groups on the political left. Just keeping track of which groups are boycotting which places or products is an exercise in itself—there are even competing publications that track boycotts.

The most prominent and tenacious boycotts of recent years have tended to focus on such issues as abortion, race and the rights of homosexuals. A network of liberal-leaning organizations helped expand the boycott in Colorado beyond gay and lesbian organizations.

Until recently, Miami was boycotted by African-American groups angered by the official snubbing of African National Congress leader Nelson Mandela in 1990. The city commission sparked the boycott when it rescinded a welcoming proclamation to Mandela over his refusal to repudiate Cuban leader Fidel Castro. Three years and $50 million in lost revenues later, the city began second-guessing its decision. Adjoining Miami Beach declared a Martin Luther King Jr. holiday and awarded Mandela a medal; the consolidated Metro-Dade government passed a proclamation honoring Mandela. Organizers agreed to end the boycott this summer, but not before extracting concessions from the tourism-dependent local business community.

Sensitivities surrounding the Martin Luther King Jr. holiday in Arizona provoked the boycott that set the modern-day standard. Unlike the Colorado boycott, which has been coordinated by national gay and lesbian organizations, Arizona felt the wrath of a grassroots effort that lacked a central organizing force but made up for it in intensity. "It's an unusual case," says Zachary Lyons, publisher of the the *Boycott Quarterly*, which follows boycotts for grocery co-ops and industry. "None of us tracking boycotts were ever able to find an organizer."

The first wave of meeting and convention cancellations came in 1987, after then-Governor Evan Mecham rescinded the paid King holiday for state employees. But it was the statewide ballot rejection of the holiday in 1990 that sparked a $400 million backlash. The National Football League responded by moving the 1993 Super Bowl from Phoenix to Pasadena, at a loss of $200 million to Arizona. Add another $190 million or so to that figure from the 166 conventions that pulled out. Voters approved a King holiday in 1992, but the aftershocks will be felt for some time, since the average large convention books its meeting place six to seven years in advance.

Louisiana and Utah, two states with restrictive abortion laws, have drawn the ire of abortion-rights activists. After the 1991 passage of Louisiana's abortion law, at least 17 groups canceled conventions that were expected to pump $116 million into the New Orleans economy. As the second-biggest convention spot after Washington, D.C., New Orleans is particularly vulnerable. Still, things could have been worse: According to one estimate, a victory by former Ku Klux Klan leader David Duke in Louisiana's 1991 gubernatorial race would have cost the state well over $1 billion in lost business investments and convention and tourism business.

Beyond abortion, race and gay rights, issues that have caused convention consternation include grapes, wolves, women's rights and the Persian Gulf War. When, in 1988, the San Francisco board of supervisors decided to support a United Farm Workers boycott of table grapes, agribusiness organizations decided to take their dollars elsewhere. The city faced another pullout three years later, from the American Petroleum Institute, which was angered by a resolution during the Gulf War declaring the city a sanctuary for anyone seeking to avoid military service.

Last year, Alaska thought it had narrowly averted an environmentalist-led boycott of its $1 billion-plus tourism industry by canceling, at least temporarily, plans to shoot hundreds of wolves from helicopters. But when state officials announced this summer that wolf-control efforts would be reinstituted, environmental groups quickly cobbled together a boycott coalition. Another state with a vibrant tourism sector, Montana, is the target of at least one environmental group, for its bison-killing practices.

And while some boycotts eventually fade away in practice without ever being officially called off, they can continue to have an impact on an area's economy for many years. Since the 1970s, some feminist activists have avoided Chicago and St. Louis in retaliation for their state legislatures' refusal to ratify the Equal Rights Amendment.

When Colorado mayors get together to commiserate over their lost convention and tourism business in the wake of Amendment 2, the mere mention of Atlanta gets their blood boiling. They are quick to point out that the city, which joined the official boycott of Colorado over the issue of gay rights, is the capital of one of the 23 states in which sodomy is still a felony. (Colorado isn't one of them.) Newman, the Association of Convention and Visitor Bureaus president, wonders if the host city of the 1996 Olympics will apply similar political-correctness litmus tests to countries that want to send teams to the games. "Is Atlanta going to take the moral high ground and say, 'We don't like what your government is doing at home'?" he asks.

WHERE THE BOYCOTT ACTION IS ...AND WAS

ACTIVE BOYCOTTS		
ISSUE	**PLAYERS**	**PLACES AFFECTED OR VULNERABLE**
ABORTION	National Abortion Rights Action League; National Organization for Women	Louisiana, Utah, North Dakota; for 1993 NARAL ranked 13 states as having "threat of any and all obstacles to abortion"; 35 states were ranked as having threat of "some obstacles."
GAY RIGHTS	National gay and lesbian organizations; American Civil Liberties Union; NOW; assorted businesses and localities	Colorado presently; 23 states have sodomy laws; at least 10 states could have gay rights-related measures on ballot in 1994.
ANIMAL RIGHTS Wolves	Fund for Animals; In Defense of Animals; Wolf Haven; Friends of Animals; environmental organizations	Alaska
Bison	Yellowstone Earth First!; environmental organizations	Montana

CONCLUDED OR DORMANT BOYCOTTS		
ISSUE	**PLAYERS**	**PLACES AFFECTED OR VULNERABLE**
EQUAL RIGHTS AMENDMENT	Feminist groups	15 states that did not pass the ERA
GRAPES	Agribusiness organizations	San Francisco
RACE (King holiday: Nelson Mandela)	Civil rights groups	Arizona and Miami formerly; in Louisiana, the governor can declare a King holiday; New Hampshire is now the only state without some version of King holiday.

Denver Mayor Wellington Webb tried to exact some small measure of revenge by requesting that the new site of the Conference of Mayors meeting not be any of the cities engaged in the boycott. The selection of New York City led Webb to announce that he would not attend. Robert Isaac, mayor of Colorado Springs, wrote to the membership of the mayors' conference in January to ask that "if we continue in this direction, will we not be viewed as hypocrites, and inevitably lose the credibility of the organization?" Isaac also questioned whether Miami and Cleveland—two cities which have not enacted gay civil rights protection—should be disqualified as 1995 and 1996 conference sites.

Portland and San Francisco, where the 1994 and 1997 mayors' meetings are scheduled, do have gay-rights laws in place, and part of Denver Mayor Webb's resentment stems from the fact that his city was one of several in Colorado that have long had similar laws on the books. Like some other Colorado mayors, he opposed the amendment—which would override local statutes—

from the outset. The mayors even joined in the suit against the amendment that so far has blocked its implementation.

Boycott Colorado, the Denver-based orchestrator of the embargo, has little sympathy for the mayors, insisting that they didn't work hard enough to defeat Amendment 2. "We don't believe the true education of Colorado has happened yet. It will not happen overnight," says Terry Schleder, president of Boycott Colorado. "We see this as a long-term process."

However tenacious Boycott Colorado and its allies prove to be, the boycott is not going to change the minds of Coloradans who voted for Amendment 2, says Roger Smith, president of the Denver Convention and Visitors Bureau. And meanwhile, he contends, the wrong people will be punished. "You're hurting the very people who had the legislation on the books already," says Smith. "The people they wanted to get are not even going to be affected."

Smith's point is well taken. Just as in Arizona—where the areas most affected were cities that already had municipal

King holidays in effect—the bulk of the Colorado vote in favor of Amendment 2 came from outside the cities, from areas less dependent on tourism revenues. Acknowledging that, Boycott Colorado is shifting gears. On top of the state boycott, the revised strategy is singling out the counties that voted in favor of Amendment 2—the group refers to them as the "hate counties"—and urging boycotts of businesses located in those areas.

But even opponents of Amendment 2 concede that if another vote was held today, the amendment probably would pass again. Will Perkins, chairman of Colorado for Family Values, the organization that proposed the measure, says it is not hard to figure out why. "People don't take kindly to boycotts, and they don't take kindly to blackmail. This is economic terrorism."

Clearly, however, the Colorado boycott has worked on an economic level, although it doesn't seem to have been as disastrous as some accounts would have it. The state's skiing and overall tourism revenues were actually up for the season. And convention officials say Denver's loss is just a fraction of the city's convention and tourism business. But it is worth noting that they cannot figure the toll on future convention business, since it is trickier to determine how many groups simply take a city out of consideration because it is a boycott target or to avoid a hassle.

W hile gauging the long-term impact of a boycott may be an inexact discipline, some ideas about how to prepare for one and fight it once it takes hold are emerging. Many cities are drawing up contingency plans—not just for boycotts but also for the accompanying negative publicity that also threatens the general tourism business.

Salt Lake City officials, for example, have an emergency plan designed to counter public relations disasters, whether they result from acts of nature or politics. If a weather-related mishap were to wreak havoc on the city or Los Angeles-style riots were to occur or a boycott was to take shape, officials would embark on an effort to convince visitors that their city was still operational. That means bringing in travel writers, contacting meeting planners who have sites booked in the next 90 days, and even paying the costs to fly in those planners if they want to take a look around. It is the cost of doing business these days.

Oregon did not have a contingency plan when its own anti-gay-rights initiative, which was defeated, was on the ballot last year. But rather than biting their nails waiting for the election results, business and political leaders, including Governor Barbara Roberts, campaigned strenuously to defeat the measure. Religious, business and political organizations were all enrolled in the effort.

To keep the controversy from tainting the state's image among potential conventioneers and tourists, the bureau took an extra step. During the campaign, it kept a database of the 1,800 angry letters it received on the issue. After the election, every letter-writer received a reply that explained how easy it is to get an initiative on the Oregon ballot. Enclosed in the envelope was a copy of the state tourism brochure.

Having a realistic assessment of potential damage is critical, says Rick

Colorado officials had an idea that Amendment 2 was a time bomb, but they underestimated its impact.

Davis, president of the Salt Lake Convention and Visitors Bureau. Since proponents of one side will often inflate their numbers, it pays to have some independent research on how your base audience will react. The response, if necessary, can then be tailored to them.

To get a feel for the impact of their state's new abortion law, for example, Utah travel and business officials commissioned a national survey. A small percentage of the people surveyed said they definitely would avoid the state. An even smaller number said they would make an extra effort to come there. But 86 percent of the respondents said the issue did not matter to them. Prior to the poll, a preemptive marketing campaign was under consideration. That idea was shelved when the results came in.

Only one major convention ended up taking its business elsewhere, and it was replaced by another that originally considered Salt Lake City *because* of the abortion law. For 1992, the year after the abortion law passed, the city actually saw a 60 percent increase in convention business over the previous year, a continuation of its recent emergence as a convention destination site.

Colorado officials had a pretty good idea that Amendment 2 was a ticking time bomb, but they underestimated its potential impact. Not much thought was given to coping with a boycott, at least not until celebrities such as Barbra Streisand began banging the drum and attracting media notice. At that point, the Coloradans were forced into a damage-control mode. The first order of business was a call to Phoenix, the oracle that most cities consult when the going gets tough. Phoenix's advice? Maintain high visibility. Confront the situation. Don't get spooked by the avalanche of negative press, for eventually it will die down. "When Somalia was on the front pages, calls to my office tapered off," says Terry Sullivan, president of the Colorado Springs convention bureau. "When Bill Clinton focused on gays in the military, calls surged. When Social Security dominated the news, calls dropped again."

In Colorado Springs, the people at the convention bureau sent out more than 300 letters to those who had booked space, explaining what exactly the amendment was about. Then they held a meeting with panicky hotel managers and sales directors to reassure and update them. "It's been a pretty interesting exercise in crisis management," says Sullivan. Officials embarked on publicity tours aimed at defusing the boycott. (As Denver Mayor Webb made the rounds—which included an appearance on the *Arsenio Hall* show—he was hounded by activists, including a group called the Lesbian Avengers.)

Tourism and convention officials are still unsure about what effect their counter-measures have had, if any, other than to assuage skittish convention and meeting planners or put a more favorable spin on media coverage. Of those who pulled out, says Rich Grant, communications director for the Denver bureau, some can be replaced. But, he adds, "we can't measure what we can't book."

But with groups in at least 10 states working to put measures similar to Amendment 2 on the ballot, prudence would dictate having a prepared counter-offensive. Four Oregon counties voted this June to prohibit local governments from "promoting" homosexuality or protecting gays against discrimination; similar measures in other counties will go before voters unless pending legislation to protect homosexuals from discrimination passes the Oregon House. California, Idaho, Florida, Michigan and Oregon— again—may be voting on statewide gay rights-related measures in 1994. If any of them pass, look for more boycotts and more elected officials embarking on national damage-control tours.

Or maybe they can try to persuade organizations threatening to boycott to follow the lead of the National Coalition to Abolish the Death Penalty, which, to give its members a chance to demonstrate and protest, tries to hold its annual conventions in states that *have* capital punishment.

SWISS CHEESE *Journalism*

Doris A. Graber

Doris A. Graber is a professor of political science at the University of Illinois at Chicago.

Swiss cheese makers will probably protest the analogy between news coverage at the state and local level and their prized product. They will be right. Swiss cheese has more substance than holes while the reverse is true for the press. In both cases, the holes arise naturally from the production process. Here is how state and local issues get such short shrift in journalism.

Compared to state and local levels, politics at the national level is far more glamorous and exciting. It also affects every American, rather than only a small fraction. This means it is easy for journalists, and for average Americans, to ignore state and local politics and focus on the larger arena.

The structure of the news business also contributes mightily to the holes in news coverage. Daily newspaper, and radio and television stations are primarily organized to serve "markets," rather than the political entities into which the nation has been divided. A market is the area in which a given print or electronic news outlet reaches enough people

to satisfy advertisers in search of potential customers. Market boundaries rarely coincide with the boundaries of political units. Except for a handful of journals and newsletters, and an occasional television and radio program, they are never structured to focus on entire states.

Typically, the local media emphasize the news in their primary publishing area, which means news from

An analysis of how the press operates shows there is little hope of curing the inadequate coverage most state and local governments receive.

the state's most populous cities. Outlying areas are covered rarely, if at all, because they are beyond the news beats that are routinely served by local journalists. On average, the market area covered by electronic and print media at the state and local levels extends over dozens of counties that often include more than 1,000 governmental units. These

units handle important public affairs, such as public education, sanitation and police, and they serve as electoral districts for national, state and local officials. Many have independent authority to levy taxes and all of them spend the public's money. Though the policies and politics of these units need attention, they rarely receive it.

The proliferation of suburban newspapers has not helped. There is simply too much important news to cover at all levels so that journalists are forced to make news choices. They favor national news and human interest stories and nearby city hall over outlying governmental units.

News audiences might argue that the media seem to find plenty of time and space to cover trivia, sports, and other soft news and that many stories are covered repeatedly. The profit-orientation of the media business means news enterprises cater to popular tastes for soft news. The soft news emphasis is even more prevalent at the local than the national level. For example, content analysis of local and national television news in 1990 and 1991 shows that 9 percent of their offerings consisted of sports, entertainment and soft news stories. The comparable figure for local news was 38 percent. Stations in larger communities, compared to smaller communities, tend to carry less fluff and more politics. Audience analysis reveals that the public's appetite for hard political news can be satisfied most readily by news about major national and local happenings. By and large, the public considers state news intrinsically boring, even though most people rate it as "very important" or "important" in public opinion surveys.

The fact that the FCC insists that local television and radio stations gear their programming to local needs has helped only marginally. More than three-fourths of the stories on local electronic media originate locally. But the primary local emphasis is on crime, disasters, entertainment, weather and sports. The ability of local stations to use new satellite and microwave technologies to tap into national news heralds further declines of attention to local and state concerns. However, local broadcasts of the national news often stresses local angles.

Market failure

Much political news is skipped because it would appeal to only a small portion of the audience in the market area. When state and local candidates' districts overlap several markets, or cover just one slice of a larger market, they may be unable to get the news coverage they need. Paid advertising coverage may be too expensive because rates are based on the entire market, not merely on the section that the candidates need to reach. The increasing availability of cable television may be helpful on that score.

The public considers state news intrinsically boring.

National news and soft news have more universal appeal and are easier to cover. Most national news comes from one geographical location — the nation's capital where all major news organizations deploy staffs. By contrast, state capitals are often in remote areas. Since recesses between legislative sessions are often long — and state news has traditionally focused more on legislatures than governors — many state capitals are news deserts for extended periods. No wonder that reporters shun them and prefer major cities instead.

Important differences between politics at the national and state and local level are other reasons for spotty coverage. State and local politics are conducted on a much smaller scale. Politicians find it easier, therefore, to stay in touch with each other and with their main constituencies. This reduces their incentive to use the press to inform the public about political happenings. When officials want to contact the press, they can easily reach members of the relatively tiny corps of reporters — making formal press conferences less necessary. The fact that reporters and officials have closer personal relationships at the state and local than the national level has often been cited to explain why national journalists are more harshly critical of public officials.

The nitty-gritty of government that occupies the bulk of public officials' time at state and local levels does not provide a steady stream of exciting news. Much of the work is highly technical and difficult to explain to the public. This discourages reporters and officials alike from trying to disseminate it.

Reporters may be reluctant to publish some news because they lack the expertise required to judge the merits of the story. Because state and local news establishments tend to be smaller, their reporters are less likely to be assigned to a single beat, which would permit them to become experts in an area. Instead, they usually rove among many different beats, covering routine news, with little chance to probe beneath the surface.

Skimpy media expertise

At the state and local level, fewer officials have public relations staffs to help them frame their stories so that they attract media coverage. While all governors have public infor-

mation staffs now, and most state legislatures have followed suit, it will be a long time before most other state officials will be able to handle media relationships comfortably. Meanwhile, many officials are loathe to give information to the press for fear that they may botch the job and suffer political damage.

Inept public relations practices abound among state and local officials, according to media scholar Phyllis Kaniss, who recently wrote a book on *Making Local News* (University of Chicago Press, 1991). Among common types are "paranoid media-avoiders" who shun the press entirely, "naive professionals" who talk too freely to a scandal-hungry press, and "dancing marionettes" who take their cues from press reports and editorials. Such names may evoke caricatures, but the gist of her characterizations is sound.

Kaniss recommends that state and local officials should study the media so that they can supply information in ways the media find attractive. This does not require deferring to journalists' preferences or sensationalizing news. It does require judicious choices of information for release and careful attention to framing stories.

A 1991 poll by political scientists Thad Beyle and G. Patrick Lynch of governors, lieutenant governors, attorneys general, secretaries of state and various legislators revealed that a majority in all the states deemed print media, rather than radio or television, the most effective transmitters of state and local news. State officials felt that broadcast stories were generally too brief and, in the case of television, too geared to visual elements. Since much of state and local news lacks visual appeal, it tended to be relegated to the tail end of broadcasts and given only cursory attention, if mentioned at all.

The reluctance of state officials to turn to electronic news, coupled with the reluctance of the electronic media to feature it, explains why gaps in state news have been particularly yawning in electronic news. This may be changing because officials are becoming increasingly aware that television is the best medium to mobilize public opinion and are therefore trying harder to get television coverage for themselves and their agencies.

In an earlier article ("Networks' Blind Spot," *State Government News,* May 1989), I wrote that state news is a double loser. The level of neglect of the state is even worse in the national media, particularly television, than it is locally. A re-analysis of the

---

Inept public relations practices abound among state and local officials.

---

same data shows that the situation has not improved. Content analysis of news programs on national newscasts in 1990 and 1991 showed no signs that the expanding national political role played by the states has focused more national media attention on state issues. State news on national television constituted barely 1 percent of all nightly news stories. A small number of states were spotlighted and the rest were neglected. The Pacific region was covered most amply and the Midwest the least, when amount of coverage was compared to population size.

There was little relation between the political importance of states and their stories and the amount of coverage they received. Again, coverage patterns are explained best by journalistic criteria. The states that received most coverage provided the most attractive story materials at a place and time that was most convenient for the national media. Accordingly, state news coverage on national television was not only sparse, it lacked political substance. The chief focus was on disaster, crime and trivia stories. State economic, political and social conditions and policies were largely ignored. Print media coverage of state news, as judged by content analysis of the *New York Times,* was much more ample and more substantive in its political content. But, like television news, it was imbalanced, with a few states receiving most of the coverage. Again, the Pacific region fared best and the Midwest worst.

Little change likely

What are the chances of getting more adequate coverage of state news? More media savvy officials, as mentioned, could improve the score. They could make many state news stories more appealing by casting them in terms of their national significance. They could package stories so that they have good visual and human interest appeal. Narrow-casting, thorough cable television and other developing technologies, may allow state and local officials and candidates for office to target their markets more effectively. Proliferation of channels dedicated to the use of specific governmental units could be encouraged.

Even if such changes are made successfully, subnational journalism is bound to remain full of holes for the foreseeable future — just like Swiss cheese. It simply is the nature of American journalism to cover the political scene lightly and unevenly. It would require a totally different process of news production to change coverage patterns. That is not likely to happen, given the deep historical roots of our current media system.

Civic Strategies
for Community Empowerment

JOSEPH F. ZIMMERMAN

Joseph F. Zimmerman is a professor of political science at the State University of New York at Albany, and editor of the NATIONAL CIVIC REVIEW Metro Trends department.

The past two decades have seen a serious erosion of "dynamic" democracy in many parts of the United States as eligible citizens vote less frequently and withdraw from other key aspects of local political life. Instead, we increasingly find a disturbing brand of "reluctant" democracy in which formal rights to participate are widely ignored in practice.

Among the explanations given for this phenomenon is a spreading sense of political impotency which discourages involvement. In many communities today, one routinely hears that "you can't fight city hall." While this theme is not new, when juxtaposed with a growing number of "private" preoccupations (e.g., multiple jobs to support the family or the explosion of recreational opportunities) and residential mobility, it provides good reason to keep out of the public arena.

However many communities (including larger jurisdictions) have effectively used certain structural mechanisms to combat feelings of political powerlessness and thus stem the potentially dangerous slide toward "reluctant" democracy. In this article we examine the record of such devices in three critical areas: the election system; ethics and openness in public affairs; and the degree of local discretionary authority. These areas offer future avenues for greater citizen participation.

Election Systems That Invite Participation

To encourage involvement, the formula used for electing officials must be generally perceived as fair. The criteria for measuring systems include effectiveness of ballots cast, responsiveness of elected officials, maximization of access to decision makers, equity in representation, and legitimization of the legislative body.[1] These canons can be used to evaluate six electoral structures: at-large; combined ward and at-large; limited voting; cumulative voting; and proportional representation.[2]

If an electoral system produces accurate community representation, government may satisfy voter needs. Unfortunately, no means for selecting officials accurately represents the views of all citizens on all issues at all times. The law making process can foster the illusion that each measure is scrutinized carefully and fully prior to its approval, amendment, or rejection. However, elected representatives—whether ethical or unscrupulous—are to a greater or lesser extent "trustees" who take many of their cues from non-constituent sources, thus producing results that never fully reflect voter consensus (if, indeed, there is one).

Three Mitigating Devices

Three devices can mitigate the problem: initiative, the referendum, and recall. Ideally, these mechanisms should be available on a standby basis as circuit breakers to be triggered only by gross misrepresentation of the electorate.

The Binding Initiative. This approach allows the electorate to place proposed laws on the referendum ballot. It can be traced to a 1715 Massachusetts law and to an 1898 constitutional amendment with respect to other areas of the United States.[3] Today 23 state constitutions authorize its use. Seventeen provide for constitutional and 21 for statutory initiatives. Placing a measure on the ballot requires petitions signed by a certain number of registered voters (from 3 to 15% of votes cast for Governor in the last election). Measures approved by the voters are not subject to gubernatorial veto. State statutes and municipal charters often authorize local initiative.

. . . elected representatives—whether ethical or unscrupulous—are to a greater or lesser extent "trustees" who take many of their cues from non-constituent sources, thus producing results that never fully reflect voter consensus . . .

This direct method for circumventing the legislative process attracts criticism. Opponents argue, for example, that elected representatives produce better laws or that popular measures are often poorly drafted, confusing to voters, and not coordinated properly with other statutes.[4]

An alternative, the indirect initiative, available in eight States including Massachusetts, empowers voters (with requisite signatures) to refer measures to the legislature for its consideration (akin to submitting a bill). If that body fails to approve the proposition within the stated time limit, in five states it is automatically placed on the ballot. In three states, sponsors of the proposal must collect additional signatures to force a popular vote. Five states authorize their legislatures to place a competing proposition on the ballot.

Advisory Initiatives. Non-binding questions may be placed on the referendum ballot to place pressure on law-making bodies to enact certain measures. The theory supporting this type of initiative suggests that elected representatives will act in accordance with the clearly expressed desires of the voters. In the late 1970s, the environmental and nuclear freeze movements often used such means to influence public opinion and law makers.

The Referendum. Plebiscitarian techniques in the United States are traceable to the Massachusetts Bay Colony where the General Court (legislative body) in 1640 authorized the use of the referendum.[5] However, this democratizing tool did not become established in most parts of the country until the early 1800s when state legislatures and constitutional conventions began to submit proposed constitutions for voter appoval. The first New York State Constitution of 1777, for example, was adopted in convention without popular vote.

In the late 19th century, several state legislatures, including New York's, so abused their powers that the public demanded (and won) the right to approve constitutional changes and a class of "conditional" laws which do not become effective unless approved by the voters. These restrictions are contained today in many state constitutions, including New York's, and typically involve taxation and the borrowing of funds.

A more dramatic development occurred in South Dakota in 1898 when voters amended the state constitution to authorize the electorate to employ the petition or protest referendum and the initiative.[6] This device allows voters to veto most laws enacted by a legislature. Exempted are laws designed to preserve "the public peace, health or safety, [and] support of the State Government and its existing institutions."[7]

The petition referendum, when signed by two to 15 percent of those voting in the last general election, suspends a law until a mandatory referendum on it can be held.

In 24 states, the protest referendum is authorized by the state constitution. In eight cases, it may be employed only to repeal an entire law while in the others it can be used like a line-item veto.

Specified topics (e.g., appropriation of funds, the judiciary, statutes applying to a single local government, and religion) usually are not subject to the petition referendum. The Commonwealth of Massachusetts excludes the largest number of items.[8]

Twenty states require a majority vote for repeal; the balance require from 30 to 50 percent of the vote in the last general election. Six constitutions forbid the state legislature to amend or repeal the voters' decision.

Local government charters and state statutes often allow for petition referenda to overrule municipal laws. The procedures are typically identical with those at the state level.

The Recall

This tool for popular involvement is a natural extension of the others. The recall or "imperative mandate" concept appeared in the Articles of Confederation and Perpetual Union, the national platforms of the Socialist Labor Party in 1892 and 1896, and the platform of the Populist Party in several states during the same period.[9] It was first authorized in the 1903 Los Angeles charter.[10] Currently, 14 state constitutions allow recall of state and certain local officers.[11] Also, 17 states authorize the recall of local officials by general law, special law, or a locally drafted and adopted charter. Although the California Constitution directed the State Legislature to provide for the recall of local officers, this provision does not affect cities and counties with "home rule" charters.

In Massachusetts, 52 locally drafted city and town charters allow recall. The Billerica town charter, for example, stipulates "any person who holds an elected town office, but not including an elected town meeting member, with more than six months remaining of the term of office, may be recalled from office by the voters"[12] The Oxford town charter simply states that "any elective officer of the town may be recalled and removed from public office by the voters of the town as herein provided."[13]

Charters of professionally managed cities typically include similar provisions to counterbalance the authority of that non-elected official. Although managers are theoretically accountable to the council, it is widely felt that intra-governmental politics can insulate them from popular opinion, thus requiring such protection.

In a few states, the recall ballot is also used to elect a replacement. If there is no prohibition, the target incumbent may simultaneously seek reelection (which, ironically, can occur if the other candidates split the opposing vote).

Like the initiative and the protest referendum, the recall process is launched by petition (usually requiring signatures equal to 25% of votes cast in the last election for governor or the position in question) and concluded by a special election.[14]

Several states require that recall petitions for statewide elected officials contain a geographical spread of signatures. California, for example, stipulates 1% of the last vote cast for the office in each of five counties.[15]

Typically a short justification for recall and defense appear on the ballot. San Francisco publishes a voter information pamphlet containing a sample ballot, the proponents' statement of reasons for the proposed recall, the officer's reply to the reasons, and paid advertisements. The 1983 pamphlet relative to the special recall election of the Mayor contained 49 paid advertisements (37 favoring the Mayor and 12 supporting recall).

In nine states, the electorate simply votes on the question of recalling an officer. In most jurisdictions, a majority affirmative vote *ipso facto* vacates the office which is then filled according to law, and may involve a second special election to select a successor.

In a few states, the recall ballot (e.g., Arizona) is also used to elect a replacement. If there is no prohibition, the target incumbent may simultaneously seek reelection (which, ironically, can occur if the other candidates split the opposing vote).

Arguments for and against the recall resemble those aimed at the initiative and petition referendum.[16] Not surprisingly, many elected officials oppose all three corrective devices. Yet it appears that their availability often promote dynamic democracy by enhancing governmental legitimacy and reducing feelings of political impotence.

Open and Ethical Government

These conditions are essential for effective, participatory democracy because citizens possess substantially fewer political resources than elected and appointed officials. As Aristotle insisted:

> If the citizens are to judge officers according to merit, then they must know each other's characters; where they do not possess this knowledge, both the election to office and the decision of lawsuits will go wrong![17]

Information and resulting citizen inputs alone, however, generally do not provide a sufficient antidote to unethical official behavior. Other, complementary mechanisms are needed.

So long as ethical problems remain clear-cut, the venerable English common law approach which relies on precedent-based judicial decisions may suffice. Nonetheless, today's issues often assume more subtle form, creating gray areas that require different treatment.

Codes of Ethics

While no one mechanism can ensure that governmental actions will be ethical, strong ethics codes and boards for rendering advisory opinions represent a critical first step.[18] Such codes establish essential guidelines for governmental officers, facilitate self-regulation, and bolster public confidence. Publication of advisory board opinions, with appropriate deletions to preserve the privacy of those making the requests, will in time build a case inventory to guide other elected governmental personnel contemplating similar actions.

Sunshine Laws

Sunshine laws are designed to throw light on governmental actions, the decision-making process, and attempts by individuals and interest groups to influence it. They include mandatory financial disclosures by public officers, open meetings of public bodies, and citizen access to public records.

Financial Disclosure. Requirements that public officers publish information about their personal and family finances are related closely to conflict-of-interest laws and codes of ethics. Manditory disclosure preferably should be restricted to a listing of income sources rather than specific amounts, and also might be limited to specified sources of income exceeding a stipulated amount. The required statement should contain the name and address of each creditor to whom a minimum amount is owed, due date, interest rate, date and original amount of the debt, existing special conditions, and a statement indicating whether or not the debt is secured. Mortgage debt on a personally occupied home and retail installment debt might be exempted from the disclosure requirement.

3. LINKAGES BETWEEN CITIZENS AND GOVERNMENTS: Referenda

A thorny question is whether financial disclosure should apply to all part-time citizen officers in small municipalities who serve without compensation or receive only minor stipends. There is no denying that service on a non-paid board of commission represents a sacrifice of time and money, and may also subject the officers to abuse and criticism by the public. A mandatory disclosure requirement for all officers might discourage candidacies — something to be avoided when the aim is to encourage wider participation by qualified individuals. Thus, in the case of part-time positions, it seems wise to limit disclosure requirements to candidates for bodies with regulatory powers such as planning boards.

A thorny question is whether financial disclosure should apply to all part-time citizen officers in small municipalities who serve without compensation or receive only minor stipends . . . A mandatory disclosure requirement for all officers might discourage candidacies — something to be avoided when the aim is to encourage wider participation by qualified individuals.

Open Meetings. Informed citizen participation is hindered by *in camera* decision-making. Many local governments and state legislatures have enacted open meeting laws designed to throw light on the policy process while, at the same time, permitting closed-door executive sessions for certain sensitive issues as property acquisition, disciplinary action, salary negotiations, or matters that could prejudice a government's position in a law suit.

Care must be exercised in defining the term "meeting" when adopting such laws. The Council of State Governments recommends that the concept refer to "the convening of a governing body for which a quorum is required in order to make a decision or to deliberate toward a decision on any matter."[19] It is also important to require that adequate public notice be given to interested persons and organizations of the place and time of meetings, and to specify exceptions to the open meeting requirements. In addition, complete and accurate records of meetings should be kept so that citizens unable to attend can examine proceedings.

Freedom of Information. A third type of "sunshine" law attempts to ensure that citizens will have ready access to most official records of government. Such devices are desirable because excessive confidentiality can shield unethical or prejudicial actions from cure. Yet the matter of what information should be released and under what conditions raises delicate questions which should not be addressed haphazardly. In 1977, the New York State Legislature addressed this problem by creating the Committee on Public Access to Records, charged with developing guidelines for the release of official information by state and local government agencies, and providing advice in cases of disputes.[20] The Committee's performance of its duties has been excellent.

A conflict can exist between freedom of information and privacy laws. The Federal Privacy Act of 1974, for example, requires executive agencies to keep confidential personal information, yet the Federal Freedom of Information Act requires agencies to make executive branch records available for inspection or duplication except "to the extent required to prevent a clearly unwarranted invasion of personal privacy."[21]

Balancing these two elements is a challenge for which no universal solution exists, indicating that communities must experiment with alternatives within the current legal framework until they find one which serves local needs.

Local Discretionary Authority

As suggested earlier, citizen participation tends to increase as communities gain greater control over their own public policy process. Historically, the legal relationship between states and their political subdivisions was governed by the *Ultra Vires* (beyond powers) concept, also know as Dillon's Rule, which denied inherent powers of local self-government and emphasized the plenary authority of the state legislature.[22] Fortunately, most states have modified the *Ultra Vires* Rule and provided for increased local discretionary authority by the adoption

of provisions for an *Imperium in Imperio* (empire within an empire). New York State employs the three approaches simultaneously, thereby producing considerable confusion relative to the legal powers of various local jurisdictions.

Clearly, local governments that deliver most public services and operate on a relatively small scale offer greater participatory opportunities. When these institutions lack substantial autonomy, citizen interest obviously wanes.

Retention of broad powers over local governments makes the state legislature a target of interests unable to achieve their goals at the grass roots. In general, state legislatures have been responsive to such demands, enacting many laws that mandate courses of action for more accessible political subdivisions.

The only national survey of this phenomenon reveals that most states have imposed numerous mandates upon their local governments, with New York in the lead. There, the legislature imposed its will in 66 of the 76 functional areas studied.[23] In contrast to the national government which still provides most financial assistance to subnational units with conditions attached, New York State is generous in sharing its income tax revenues with its political subdivisions with few conditions attached. However, the separate enactment of state mandates by the New York State Legislature over the years has reduced significantly the discretionary authority of the local units.

To what extent do states reimburse local governments for mandated expenditures? Currently, 12 provide full or partial support. California's Initiative Proposition 4 of 1979 and Massachusett's Initiative Proposition 2-1/2 of 1980 make this a requirement.

Mandates fall into 11 categories: entitlement; structural; service level; tax base; personnel; due process; equal treatment; ethical; good neighbor; informational membership; and record-keeping. A strong case can be made that the states should not be forced to reimburse costs associated with the last six types, since these are relatively inexpensive functions which (in spite of state intervention) should remain under maximum local control.

Conclusion

This review reveals that a substantial range of formal, participatory instruments have been devised to make state and local governments more responsive and accountable to their electorates. Unfortunately, not all of these mechanisms are everywhere available. Moreover, legal and other impediments often prevent their best use to overcome widespread feelings of political impotence and achieve "dynamic" democracy.

Given their greater authority and scope, state legislatures remain the prime key to establishing broader participatory "rights." They are still in the best position to initiate statutes and constitutional amendments for corrective devices to expand potential citizen influence on the governance process. They can increase the discretionary authority of local governments and establish general mechanisms for furnishing ethical advice to public officials. While not sufficient by themselves, such democratizing actions would set the stage for enlarged, more satisfying citizen participation.

Notes
[1]For details, see Joseph F. Zimmerman, "Electoral Systems and Direct Citizen Law Making." A paper presented at the University of Wurzburg, Federal Republic of Germany, July 1, 1987.
[2]Joseph F. Zimmerman, *The Federated City: Community Control in Large Cities* (New York: St. Martin's Press, 1972), pp. 65-79.
[3]*The Acts and Resolves of the Province of the Massachusetts Bay* (Boston: Wright and Potter, 1874), vol. II, p. 30, and *Constitution of South Dakota,* art. III, I (1898).
[4]Joseph F. Zimmerman, *Participatory Democracy: Populism Revived* (New York: Praeger Publishers, 1986), pp. 91-95.
[5]Nathaniel B. Shurtleff, ed. *Records of the Governor and Company of the Massachusetts Bay in New England* (Boston: From the Press of William White, Printer to the Commonwealth, 1853), vol. I, p. 293.
[6]*Constitution of South Dakota,* art III, I (1898).
[7]*Ibid.*
[8]*Constitution of the Commonwealth of Massachusetts,* Articles of Amendment, art. XLVIII, The Referendum, 2.

[9]*Articles of Confederation and Perpetual Union,* art. V.

[10]Frederick L. Bird and Frances M. Rayan, *The Recall of Public Officers: A Study of the Operation of the Recall in California* (New York: The Macillan Company, 1930), p. 22.

[11]Alaska, Arizona, California, Colorado, Georgia, Idaho, Kansas, Louisiana, Michigan, Nevada, North Dakota, Oregon, Washington, and Wisconsin.

[12]*Town of Billerica* (Massachusetts) *Charter,* art. VI, pp. 6-4.

[13]*Town of Oxford* (Massachusetts) *Charter,* chap. VII, p. 6.

[14]For details on signature requirements, see *The Book of the States* (Lexington, Kentucky: The Council of State Governments, latest edition).

[15]*Constitution of California,* art. II, p. 14 (b) and *California Elections Code,* p. 27211 (b).

[16]For details, see Zimmerman, *Participatory Democracy: Populism Revived,* pp. 122-26.

[17]Benjamin Jowett, trans., *Artistotle's Politics* (New York: Carlton House, n.d.), p. 288.

[18]Joseph F. Zimmerman, "Preventing Unethical Behavior in Government," *Urban Law and Policy,* vol. VIII, 1987, pp. 335-56.

[19]*Guidelines for State Legislation on Government Ethics and Campaign Financing* (Lexington, Kentucky: The Council of State Governments, 1984), p. 4.

[20]*New York Laws of 1977,* chap. 933 and *New York Public Officers Law,* pp. 84-90.

[21]*Freedom of Information Act,* 88 Stat. 1986, 5 U.S.C. p. 552 (a) (2).

[22]For details on the legal relations existing between state and local governments today, see Joseph F. Zimmerman, *State-Local Relations: A Partnership Approach* (New York: Praeger Publishers, 1983), pp. 15-48.

[23]Joseph F. Zimmerman, *State Mandating of Local Expenditures* (Washington, D.C.: United States Advisory Commission on Intergovernmental Relations, 1978).

Is the initiative process a good idea?

Point ▶ ▶ ▶ ▶ ▶ ▶ ▶ ▶ ▶ ▶ ▶

Douglas P. Wheeler

Douglas P. Wheeler is the California secretary for resources.

When Hiram Johnson was elected governor of California in 1910, he promised to rescue state government from special interests, especially the Southern Pacific Railway Co., and to "restore absolute sovereignty to the people."

After his election, Johnson called for establishment of the initiative, referendum and recall. California voters agreed with him and approved the measures in a special election in 1911.

Initiatives, especially in recent years, have had a profound effect on the course of California's — and in some cases the nation's — history by providing a means for frustrated voters to speak out when entrenched political forces and the legislative process failed to respond to their needs.

In 1972, California voters passed an initiative to protect the coastline from excessive development when it seemed that coastal resources otherwise would be unprotected. Six years later, when state legislators failed to respond to their needs, voters passed Proposition 13, putting a lid on rapidly spiraling property taxes and setting off a national trend on tax limitations.

Recently, however, we have seen a spate of initiatives that represent not so much a response to failures of the Legislature or other officeholders to act in the public interest, but an attempt by special interests to bypass traditional legislative processes.

In a media age, the initiative process is prone to abuse, substituting sound bites and billboard advertisements for reasoned debate on the merits of the issue. The initiative's format calls for an aye or nay without benefit of constructive interaction among legislators, voters and interest groups.

Not only is there no opportunity for rational debate and sensible give-and-take in the pre-election stage of an initiative campaign, initiatives once enacted often are difficult or almost impossible to modify.

The result can mean that unreasonable, shortsighted or unwieldy concepts are established in law. The laws tie the hands of administrators, lock in spending requirements regardless of need and fail to provide for changing times.

◀ ◀ ◀ ◀ ◀ ◀ ◀ Counterpoint

Bill Owens

Sen. Bill Owens served three terms in the Colorado House prior to his election to the Senate in 1988.

Like most of my legislative colleagues, I used to be a critic of initiatives. I felt the initiative process threatened our system of representative government. I have changed my mind. A properly structured initiative process results in increased responsiveness by government to the will of the people, greater citizen participation and a better-informed electorate. Legislatures recognize this by passing legislation under the threat of initiative. This fear of being bypassed by the people was at least partially responsible for the passage of acid rain legislation in Massachusetts, abolition of the sales tax on food in Arizona and Wyoming's minimum stream flow legislation.

Initiatives also lead to a better-informed electorate as well as to greater voter participation. Surveys show that the voter has a better understanding of most initiative proposals than of the platforms of the candidates they elect. Turnout also improves when initiatives are on the ballot — not to mention the beneficial effect of involving in the political process the 500,000 citizens who circulate petitions and the 25 million citizens who sign them during each two-year election cycle.

Initiatives often spark lively public debate, much needed during a time when incumbency and attack ads stifle substantive policy discussion. They also allow the public to better understand the political candidate's position on issues since the candidates usually are forced to disclose their views on the ballot questions.

The initiative represents an important safeguard against undue concentration of political power. American history is no stranger to accounts of the abuse of power — and even honest government can be concentrated too much in the hands of a few at the expense of the people. California Speaker Willie Brown was taught this lesson last November when California voters limited legislative terms and rolled back legislative perks, despite the multimillion dollar campaign against the initiative. The initiative allows for new ideas to be placed on the political agenda. Through the initiative, the people can play a direct role in making policy, joining legislators, judges and the media in defining public debate.

Critics claim that the initiative leads to "ballot clutter" — yet legislators place four times as many proposals

Point

Counterpoint

The legislative process often is time-consuming and cumbersome, but it provides a forum in which all sides of an issue can be debated and fine-tuned to accommodate a range of interests. In addition, it is subject to the careful scrutiny of the governor. Finally, there is a continuing legislative oversight, both to assure compliance with original intent and to modify laws and policies as circumstances change.

There are few written works of any kind — novels, short stories, newspaper articles and even op-ed page pieces — that would not benefit from review, deliberation and debate.

Legislation benefits from this process, but initiatives don't. What you see is what you get. And what the public gets all too often is a bad law, a law that could not have survived the open debate, critical review and modification provided by the legislative process.

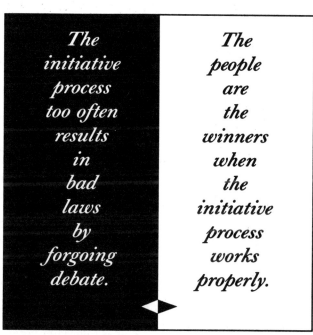

The initiative process too often results in bad laws by forgoing debate.

The people are the winners when the initiative process works properly.

In California, environmentalists recently have encountered growing voter resistance to the initiative process. Confronted last fall by a plethora of pro- and anti-environmental measures, including the nationally publicized "Big Green," voters rejected them all.

That defeat lead to speculation that Californians had abandoned their environmental sensitivity and left important capital programs, which routinely require voters' approval, without adequate funding. A more accurate assessment would reveal that the defeat of "Big Green" was evidence of growing awareness of the perils of "government by initiative."

I'll continue to defend the initiative process as a necessary last resort of the people when our elected representatives fail to act responsibly. But a far better strategy is to elect responsible public officials and to insist that they fulfill the trust we place in them.

on the ballot than do citizens. Since 1900, about 700 initiatives have passed in the United States — less than one-half of 1 percent of the hundreds of thousands of laws passed by our 50 state legislatures. Skeptics claim that initiatives "confuse" the electorate — yet the initiative questions on a ballot garner more votes — pro and con — than do most candidate races.

Critics charge that many initiatives are poorly drafted — yet of the 40 passed during two election cycles in the early 1980s only two have been held unconstitutional.

Opponents usually cite California when arguing against the initiative, and sometimes with good reason. I am not about to defend how the initiative is used in California. I would suggest that the safeguards built into the political process by California legislators designed to protect their incumbency has forced California's citizens to use the initiative to bypass their self-perpetuating Legislature. Common Cause reports that in 1986 California Senate incumbents outspent their challengers 75 to 1, while Assembly incumbents built up a 39 to 1 fundraising advantage. And guess what? No incumbent was defeated in 1986.

Combine this overwhelming spending advantage with safe, gerrymandered seats and large staffs — and it's no wonder the voters in California choose to influence public policy directly through the initiative rather than by running against entrenched incumbents.

The same is true in other states. The fact is that our political system is designed — with incumbents as the architects — to re-elect incumbents. And if you doubt that, just look around your legislature to see how many of your colleagues have been defeated recently. The initiative is a healthy response to the structural problems present in today's political process. While the initiative can be overused, or abused, it nevertheless provides a critical check on the powers of the three branches of government.

Government Institutions

- **Legislatures (Articles 24–28)**
- **Executives (Articles 29 and 30)**
- **Courts (Articles 31–33)**
- **Corruption, Contracts, and Related Matters (Articles 34 and 35)**

Government institutions are to state and local political systems what skeletons are to people. They shape the general outlines of policy processes in the same way that bones shape the outlines of human bodies. For state and local governments, as well as for the national government and most governments everywhere, institutions are critical factors in the governing process.

There are important variations among the states in executive, legislative, and judicial structures and in the degree to which citizens have access to the policy-making process. In "strong governor" states, chief executives hold substantially greater appointive, budgetary, and veto powers than in "weak governor" states. The roles of parties, committees, and leaders differ among state legislatures, as does the degree of "professionalization" among legislators themselves. The roles of state court systems vary according to the contents of state constitutions as well as state political and judicial traditions. In some states, the state's highest court plays a role that may be roughly comparable to that of the United States Supreme Court at the national level. The highest courts in most states, however, are generally less prominent. States also differ in whether judges are elected or appointed. With respect to policy making and government as a whole, some states allow for direct citizen involvement through the devices of initiative, referendum, and recall, while others do not. Many of these structural details of state governments are spelled out in each state's written constitution, although state constitutions generally do not play as prominent or symbolically important a role in state government as the United States Constitution does in national government.

Local governments do not incorporate the traditional three-branch structure of government to the extent that state and national governments do. Legislative and executive powers are often given to a single governing body, with the members choosing one of themselves to be the nominal chief executive. For example, school boards typically elect their own board "president" to preside over meetings, but they hire a professional educational administrator, called a superintendent, to manage day-to-day affairs. What is true of school districts also applies to many other local governments. In contrast, the structures of some "strong mayor" cities do resemble the executive-legislative arrangements in national and state governments. The traditional notion of an independent local judiciary as a "third branch" does not easily apply at the level of local government. Local courts, to the extent they exist, do not restrain the other branches of local government in the way that state and national courts are empowered to restrain their respective legislative and executive branches. As with state judges, some local judges are appointed and some are elected.

This unit on institutions is organized along traditional legislative, executive, and judicial lines. The first section treats state and local legislatures, which include town meetings, city and town councils, school boards, and, of course, state legislatures. The second section turns to governors and local government executives. The third section treats state and local courts, and the last section considers miscellaneous institutions and related matters that appear on the state and local landscape.

Looking Ahead: Challenge Questions

Compare and contrast the positions of president of a school board, elected chief executive of a small town, city manager, mayor of a large city, state governor, and president of the United States.

Compare and contrast the positions of school board member, member of a town meeting, town council member in a small town, city council member in a large city, state legislator, and member of the United States House of Representatives.

Get a copy of your state constitution and read it. How does it compare and contrast with the United States Constitution—in length, subjects covered, ease of reading, and familiarity?

Attend a meeting of your local school board. What was the meeting like? Did the meeting seem to consist of formally enacting decisions already made or of genuine give-and-take before board members actually made up their minds?

How many state governors and state legislators can you name? Do you feel you know enough about your own state governor and your representatives in your home state legislature to evaluate their performance?

Is it better to have well-paid and prestigious, elected positions as in the national government, or less well paid, part-time elected posts as are common in local governments and many state legislatures? Which makes for better government?

Do you think that it is a good idea to let citizens participate directly in the policy process by means of initiatives, referenda, or town meetings? Or is it better to leave legislating to elected representatives? Why?

In 1990, three states—Oklahoma, California, and Colorado—passed referenda establishing "term limits" for their state legislatures. In 1992 and 1994, many other states followed suit. What effects on the functioning of the state legislatures in these states do you expect term limits to have? Do you think it is a good idea to limit the number of terms or length of years that individuals can serve in one house of a state legislature? What about term limits for members of town councils, city councils, county councils, school boards, and other such elected bodies at the local level? Do you think that term limits will be put into operation in still more states? Why or why not?

The Legislature 2010: Which Direction?

Legislatures have made significant advances in the past 20 years. While some still have a ways to go, others are grappling with the question of whether they've gone too far.

Rich Jones

Rich Jones is NCSL's director of legislative programs.

Will legislatures in the 21st century be just like the U.S. Congress—full-time, professional bodies with long sessions, large personal staffs, career politicians and expensive media campaigns? Or will they be the more traditional, part-time legislatures with shorter sessions, smaller central staff organizations and members who hold down other jobs?

As is the case today, there are apt to be some of each. But lawmakers—and citizens—are more likely to decide consciously on a direction for their institution by taking stock of how the reforms of 20 years ago are affecting them today.

To a large extent, the modern state legislature is a product of reforms advocated by the legislative modernization movement in the mid-1960s. At that time, a series of studies conducted by universities, foundations and the Citizens Conference on State Legislatures characterized legislatures as ineffective, "sometime governments" that played little if any role in the development of state policy. They were not representative of the citizenry as a whole, met infrequently, experienced high rates of turn-

over among the members and depended for information almost exclusively on lobbyists and the executive branch. Partly because they were part-time bodies—in 1966, 30 states held biennial sessions—governors pretty much ran the show.

To correct these shortcomings, reformers advocated transforming state legislatures into more professional institutions. They recommended expanding the amount of time legislatures spent in session, providing legislatures with staff, improving legislative facilities, increasing lawmakers' pay, passing open meeting laws to make it easier for the public to participate in the process, improving legislative budget procedures to provide greater oversight of the executive branch and adopting statutes governing ethics and conflicts of interest.

The reformers succeeded; state legislatures are stronger. In 1988, there were over 33,000 staffers working in state legislatures, 40 percent of them full-time professionals. In 1990, all but seven states met in annual sessions. Legislative compensation has been increased in most states (although barely keeping pace with inflation) and legislators in 42 states are eligible for retirement benefits and in 46 states receive various insurance benefits such as health and hospitalization. The turnover in state legislatures has declined

from almost 40 percent in state houses during the 1950s to 28 percent in the early 1980s. In 1988, almost one out of every five legislators viewed the legislature as a career.

As a result of these changes, legislatures have been able to develop innovative state policies in areas as diverse as education reform, economic development, health care and the delivery of social services. The Kentucky General Assembly, for example, adopted a sweeping education reform and finance bill in 1990, and while Congress is at a stalemate, legislatures in Arizona, Iowa and Oregon have passed comprehensive groundwater protection statutes. During the coming decade, legislatures are likely to build upon their current policymaking capability to take on even more responsibilities. As they do, the already substantial demands on their time and attention will increase. How legislatures deal with these growing demands will determine the type of institutions they will become in the 21st century.

Legislators, political scientists and other observers point to current trends that suggest legislatures are on the path to becoming full-time, professional bodies like the U.S. Congress. Alan Rosenthal, director of the Institute of Politics at Rutgers University, observes

From *State Legislatures*, July 1990, pp. 22-24. © 1990 by the National Conference of State Legislatures. Reprinted by permission.

that "state legislatures are entering an era of congressionalization. If legislatures do not attend to the drift in where they are going institutionally, legislatures in a majority of the states will resemble mini–congresses." Rosenthal cites as evidence of this trend the growing number of full-time legislators, the rising costs of campaigns, the amount of time lawmakers must devote to fund raising and the decentralization of power within state legislatures, with individual members getting stronger and legislative leaders getting weaker.

Lawmakers such as Representative John Martin, speaker of the Maine House, and Kansas Senate Majority Leader Fred Kerr feel that pressures on modern legislatures are pushing them toward full-time status. "Kansas is in a free fall toward a full-time legislature," says Kerr. "You cannot have a commitment to a family and a complicated business and still serve in the legislature."

This trend toward full-time legislatures is not affecting all states uniformly. States can be grouped into three broad categories based on their level of professionalization such as time spent in session, legislative compensation, the amount of staff and turnover among the members. Using these criteria California, Illinois, Massachusetts, Michigan, New York, Ohio, Pennsylvania and Wisconsin are currently considered to be full-time, professional legislatures. There are 17 states that have purely part-time legislatures—New Hampshire, Nevada, Vermont and Wyoming, for example. Because such states have relatively small, rural, homogeneous populations with traditions of limited government, these legislatures are not likely to become full-time in the near future. In between are the 25 states whose legislatures have some full-time characteristics but not all.

"Over the next decade, the most interesting legislatures to observe will be those that fall in the vast middle between the professional and amateur extremes," writes Burdett A. Loomis, political science professor at the University of Kansas. "It is in these bodies where the tensions between the full-time legislature and the citizen legislature will play out most dramatically."

And these tensions are likely to run high. The notion of a full-time professional legislature is diametrically opposed to the traditional model in which citizens from all walks of life come

to the Capitol to conduct the people's business and then return to their other jobs.

Sentiment is strong among many legislators and some political scientists that the traditional, citizen-based legislature works best and should be preserved. They argue that these bodies are more representative of the general population, contain members who bring "real world" experience to the legislature and, because these members have to go back and live in that real world, provide a valuable, pragmatic perspective on issues. In addition, because their livelihood does not depend on their legislative salaries, members in traditional legislatures are more likely than their full-time colleagues to take greater risks by supporting responsible but unpopular positions that might cost them re-election.

At a recent conference on the future of state legislatures cosponsored by the National Conference of State Legislatures and the Eagleton Institute of Politics, the participants—current and former legislators, political scientists and media representatives—generally agreed that legislatures should try to avoid becoming highly professional bodies like the U.S. Congress. These observers thought the inability of congressional leaders to forge consensus on important issues such as the budget deficit, sky-high campaign costs, a heavy reliance on staff, and career members who become entrenched incumbents, make Congress a less than enviable model to follow. "There is a growing fear that the problems in Congress are moving into our own general assemblies," says Senator Steve Johnson of Indiana. "We need to find ways to avoid following the congressional model." One of the recommendations that came out of the conference was for legislators to consider closely any changes that would have the effect of increasing the professionalization of their legislatures.

But have the issues grown too complex and the time demands on legislators increased to the point that part-time service is unworkable in many states? Budgets in several states exceed those of some countries. As state bureaucracies have grown, so has the public's need for assistance in getting services. Difficult issues such as how to provide affordable health care to all the

people who need it, how to protect workers and the environment from hazardous pollutants while balancing the need to protect jobs, and how to finance and repair our aging infrastructure will require lawmakers who have the time, expertise and savvy to craft imaginative solutions. Will legislatures comprised of part-time members who meet for 30, 60 or 90 days a year be up to these tasks? If not, it is likely that the public will look to the governor, the courts or the initiative process to address their concerns.

"The central problem remains today what it was, in many ways, 20 years ago," writes Loomis, "how to balance the value of a citizen legislature against the need for enhanced expertise and experience in dealing with the increasingly large, difficult and complex problems facing the states."

Because of the strong emotional and philosophical commitment to the traditional part-time model, it is likely that legislatures will resist the trends pushing them toward full-time status. During the 1990s, legislatures are likely to experiment with various ways to improve the efficiency of their operations in an attempt to be effective without devoting any more time to legislative business.

Since 1985, studies aimed at improving legislative operations have been conducted in Alaska, Florida, Kansas, Minnesota, Nevada and Washington. A central focus of these studies was the question of time and how state legislatures can best use it. They emphasized the broad support for the traditional citizen legislature, recommended eliminating inefficient and ineffective procedures and advocated improving committee scheduling, holding more joint meetings between house and senate committees, strengthening interim committees and handling noncontroversial bills more efficiently as ways to make the legislature more effective.

In addition to streamlining and improving their procedures, legislatures in the 1990s are likely to use technology to increase their productivity. One of the objectives of the study of the Florida House of Representatives was to establish state-of-the-art technological solutions to problems of organization, administration and operations. The Michigan Senate has recently installed computers on the floor for every senator who wanted one. They can vote through the computer, review the bill being considered, as well as proposed amendments, send and receive messages through an electronic mail system and access the computer system in their offices to draft correspondence and communicate with their staff. California and New Jersey link computer systems in district offices with the main information system at the Capitol. A special task force in the Delaware House of Representatives is examining the use of fax machines, improved telecommunication systems and computers linking the legislators' homes to the Capitol as ways of increasing the effectiveness of their mostly part-time members.

But legislatures can only squeeze so much wasted time from the current process. The trends pushing legislatures toward becoming full-time institutions are strong and, as issues become more complex, are likely to get stronger.

"Legislatures have made considerable progress with respect to their competence in policymaking and the power they exert," says Rosenthal. "They want to continue to be professional as a legislature while avoiding complete careerism as legislators."

Although they want to resist this movement, it will be hard, because the problems confronting the states are not always open to quick solutions. Legislatures that meet in short regular sessions often must hold special sessions to complete their work. In Colorado and Oklahoma, for example, voters adopted constitutional amendments in 1988 shortening their legislative sessions. Both legislatures met in special session in 1989 to resolve issues left over from the regular session. Texas, which technically meets in regular session for 140 days every other year, has been in session over 270 days in 1989-90, holding three special sessions in 1989 and at least three in 1990.

When sessions convene in the year 2011 there are likely to be more full-time legislatures than in 1990, and fewer purely part-time bodies. The states in the middle of these two extremes, while not yet full-time, will likely be headed in that direction.

Our Beleaguered Institution

Reeling from voter anger and public distrust, can the legislative institution ever regain respect?

Karen Hansen

Karen Hansen is editor of *State Legislatures*.

In this era of political discontent, reality differs substantially from perception. State legislatures are stronger and more effective than at any time in history. Yet, according to public opinion polls, they are widely viewed as unresponsive and incapable. Changing that perception is one of the critical legislative challenges of the 1990s.

On the credit side of the legislative ledger are progressive and creative social policy and institutional accomplishments

> "The irony is that legislatures are doing a better job of handling bigger issues than ever, but getting less and less credit for it."

that rival the very best of federal legislation.

• Oregon convinced the federal government to give it a free hand to overhaul its health care system to cover 450,000 uninsured poor people; Florida enacted a managed competition approach, and at least seven other states have passed significant health care reform.

• Michigan is attempting to start from ground zero to reinvent and refinance K-12 education, Kentucky revamped its entire education system, and Oregon pioneered programs to better prepare kids for the workforce.

• In a special session that was the first of its kind in the nation, Colorado passed a tough new ban on kids possessing guns, and created a new penal system for hard-core juvenile offenders. Utah and Florida rewrote their laws covering kids and guns and dozens of other states are considering doing the same.

• Florida and Michigan leaders cast aside bitter partisan differences and worked out historic and surprisingly successful shared-leadership arrangements when the Florida Senate and the Michigan House became tied after the 1992 elections.

• Congress and the Environmental Protection Agency modeled the 1993 Clean Air Act Amendments on California's innovative air quality program that allows emissions trading in polluted areas and encourages the use of electric cars.

But despite these accomplishments, legislatures in the last few years have confronted a series of legal and ethical problems that cast a pall of corruption and distrust over the institution.

• The former Kentucky speaker and two other legislators were convicted in 1992 of extortion and racketeering in an FBI examination of gambling corruption.

• A New Mexico legislator was convicted of corruption in 1992.

• Seven Arizona legislators were indicted on charges of bribery, money laundering, conspiring to extort votes and other illegal acts in an FBI sting in 1991. Three went to prison, two did jail time and two got probation.

• In the worst Michigan scandal in 50 years, the director of the House Fiscal Agency was indicted this year in connection with allegedly siphoning off nearly $2 million of tax money for himself, his staff and his friends.

• In South Carolina, five lawmakers pleaded guilty or were convicted on bribery charges in connection with a phony gambling and dog racing bill, and 14 others were indicted.

Legislatures increasingly deal with complex problems that once were administered or financed by the federal government. With a huge demand for services and bitter taxpayer resistance to more state spending during this most recent recession, lawmakers have taken it on the chin from the public and the press.

"The irony," says Alan Rosenthal of Rutgers University's Eagleton Institute of Politics, "is that legislatures are doing a better job of handling bigger issues than ever, but getting less and less credit for it."

There is also "an incredible increase in lobbying and pressures at the state level," according to Rosenthal. Bribes from lobbyists have been at the root of ethics scandals in legislatures from California to South Carolina. And interest groups, by promising campaign help to individual legislators, can hobble the consensus building efforts of leaders. The public sees corruption and stagnation.

The Olden Days

It wasn't always like this. In the 1960s, under the powerful late Speaker Jesse

From *State Legislatures*, January 1994, pp. 12-15, 17. © 1994 by the National Conference of State Legislatures. Reprinted by permission.

Unruh, California set a new standard of professionalism. Legislatures up to that point were understaffed, paid a pittance and met only a few months every couple of years. They were, for the most part, the weakest branch of government. But Unruh ushered in a new, energized era. The California Legislature expanded its staff, increased its pay, lengthened its session, enlarged its research and budget analysis capacity, and became the model for many states. New York, Pennsylvania, Massachusetts, Michigan, Ohio, Illinois, Wisconsin and New Jersey followed suit as highly professional, well-paid, full-time legislatures. Many legislatures chose to remain part-time, citizen bodies, but they, too, professionalized their staff and strengthened their research and analysis abilities.

The 1970s, according to Rosenthal, after all of this was put in place, was a "very creative period" for state legislatures. In the 1990s, they're under siege.

Sixteen states have limited legislators' terms of office. Voters in 24 states increasingly bypass the legislature and settle public policy issues themselves through the initiative process. Public trust in government in the 1990s is at an all-time low, and citizens hold state legislatures, specifically, in lower esteem than they did 20 years ago.

"The more professional, the better-paid, the better-staffed and the closer to full-time a legislature is, the more it's suspect," says Jerome Lammers, former South Dakota House Majority Leader. "Look at California."

It's true. California voters are particularly hard on their Legislature. They passed one of the nation's strictest term limit initiatives, slashed the state budget by 40 percent and routinely decide dozens of issues through the ballot box. The governor even sponsored an initiative that would have given him unilateral authority to cut the state's budget in fiscal emergencies or whenever he reached an impasse with the Democratic-controlled Legislature. It failed.

Michigan voters enacted legislative term limits, and are now discussing an initiative that would make the Legislature unicameral and part-time. Observers believe if it gets on the ballot, it will pass.

But not all assaults on the legislature come from without. In Colorado, then-Senator Terry Considine, an insider, led the successful charge for term limits through an initiative after his bill failed in the General Assembly.

"Time was," says former Colorado Senate President Ted Strickland, "when part of our responsibility was to protect the institution of the legislature and maintain its integrity. That seems to have been forgotten."

Political scientist Malcolm Jewell thinks term limits are the most serious threat facing legislatures right now.

"Term limitations make legislators less effective, less experienced and more susceptible to lobbyists," Jewell says. "There's an erosion of legislative effectiveness in states where term limitations have passed.

"You need to repeal the term limitation initiatives."

The press, whose historic role toward those in government is adversary, often finds confrontation, scandal and acrimony more newsworthy than compromise, consensus and the tedium of lawmaking.

"A good story for a reporter is often a very bad story for the legislator involved or for the legislature as a whole," says former legislator and journalist Martin Linsky.

Assailed by the public, the press and in some instances its own members, the legislature is a beleaguered institution.

"It's all too easy, in stressful times, for everyone to forget how valuable—and how fragile—these representative institutions are," says nationally syndicated columnist David Broder.

So how do legislators go about making everyone remember?

Leadership, ethics and campaign finance reform are Malcolm Jewell's prescription for rebuilding respect for the legislature in today's hostile environment.

"Skilled, effective leadership is at the top of the list" to strengthen state legislatures, Jewell believes, followed closely by "higher standards of ethics—more sensitivity to ethical standards."

Jewell said the FBI sting in Kentucky "revealed some serious illegalities and a lack of sensitivity to the kinds of conditions that cause trouble. If relationships between legislators and lobbyists get careless enough, it's easy to slip into some kind of bribery or another.

"That hurts public support."

But Kentucky rose to the occasion. It created a bipartisan citizen ethics commission, prohibited legislators and leaders from forming PACs and required all legislative candidates to limit PAC contributions to 35 percent of the total funds raised or $5,000, whichever is greater, making the state's campaign financing law one of the strictest in the nation.

To Strengthen the Institution Leaders Can:

1. Educate each member about his or her responsibility to the legislative institution.

2. Conduct informal briefings and orientations for the media to help them understand the role and responsibility of the legislature and to help build support for the legislative process.

3. Enhance public input in legislative decisions. Strengthen support for legislative decisions by giving the public a greater voice in the process through hearings, town hall meetings or other devices.

4. Increase the efficiency of the legislative process and improve the quality of legislation that is passed. The rush at the end of the session does not enhance the legislature's public image nor does it result in high quality legislation.

5. Promote a sense of common values among the members and staff that embody the highest ideals of the legislative institution. Enforce compliance with these values even if it means supporting institutional needs at the expense of an individual member.

6. Create the circumstances in which all members, the media and the public have an interest in the legislative institution.

7. Ensure that leaders hold themselves and their legislature to standards which are at least as stringent as those applied to the rest of state government.

—from *Strengthening State Legislatures*

Indiana Senate President Pro Tem Robert Garton says legislatures today are stronger because of improved procedures and the generally high caliber of lawmakers now serving. But they are also more maligned because of the complexity of issues they handle.

"The issues have become more and more intractable," agrees Kentucky Senator Walter Baker.

Advice from *Strengthening State Legislatures*

To Raise Ethical Standards:

✳ Provide training to lawmakers, staff and lobbyists on the requirements of their state's ethics laws. This training should emphasize the highest ethical standards, not just meeting the minimum requirements of the ethics statute. It should also emphasize the importance of avoiding even the appearance of impropriety.

✳ Require that campaign contributions, gifts and money spent on lobbying be fully disclosed by legislators, staff and lobbyists.

✳ Educate members and staff about the acceptable standards of conduct in their state. Legislative leaders should take strong and decisive action to enforce these standards.

✳ Publish these standards of conduct and explain them to all members to avoid any confusion on the part of lawmakers or the public over what constitutes acceptable behavior.

To Improve Relations with the Media:

✳ Provide orientation programs for news personnel on both the legislative process and public policy issues pending before the legislature.

✳ Conduct bipartisan conferences with editorial boards and news managers regarding the legislature's activities and current issues. These meetings should focus media attention on the policy process and issues, not just on partisan differences and conflict.

✳ Set specific goals for the legislative session, articulate these goals to the media and discuss the legislature's performance with respect to these goals at the end of the session.

✳ Teach all legislators about the operations of the news media so they understand how best to work with it.

✳ Acknowledge when the media do a good job and pursue corrections of distortions in facts or other errors in stories.

To Improve Public Education and Understanding:

✳ Develop model curricula on state government and the legislative process to be used by schools.

✳ Meet with civics and government teachers to help them better understand the legislative process and issues before the legislature.

✳ Make it easier for the public to get information about legislative activities such as committee and session schedules, bill status, bill summaries and voting records.

✳ Take the legislature to the people by holding interim committee meetings in locations outside of the capital city.

✳ Use technology such as teleconferencing, interactive video and computer bulletin boards to facilitate communication with citizens in all regions of the state.

✳ Implement educational programs ranging from mock legislative sessions such as Boys' and Girls' State to internships for students.

✳ Distribute an annual report to the citizens that succinctly describes the actions taken by the legislature. This report could include a description of legislative action on major issues during the last session, budget data such as the amount and sources of tax revenue and the amount of state expenditures by function, measures of state government's performance during the past year, and a survey of citizen attitudes on current issues.

Senator Jim Lack of New York thinks so too. He believes legislatures are under fire because they are the "conduits and pass-throughs for other people's money—money we don't control, such as Medicaid and social services.

"States need more control over their financial destiny. They need to convince Congress that those 50 state legislatures are better able to monitor and handle the distribution of tax funds [than Congress is]."

Lack, like Professor Jewell, believes term limits will corrode the reputation of legislatures even more.

"A citizen lawmaker who reforms the legislature every session might be fine in movies—but it won't work in real life. There is the complexity of budgets, the relationships of the legislature with the federal and local governments.

"If they [term limit proponents] want to come out and say the Founding Fathers were wrong on representative democracy, then they need to come out with a parliamentary government like the European system.

"Of course that's heresy. But so are term limits when you come down to it."

In 1991, the National Conference of State Legislatures, concerned about the steep decline in public regard for the legislature, created the Legislative Institution Task Force to recommend solutions.

Its 1993 report, *Strengthening State Legislatures*, is a prescription for what ails the legislature most seriously—public perception, legislative organization and management, and leadership.

Educating the Public

Some states themselves have decided to educate the public about the legislature to dispel negative perceptions, and have done it quite successfully. In Georgia, for example, the Carl Vinson Institute of Government at the University of Georgia has developed a model curriculum and strategies for teaching courses about legislatures. Junior high and high school teachers in Minnesota receive a complete textbook written by legislators and staff for teaching about the legislative process. In Pennsylvania, the chief clerk of the House created a board game on the legislative process and distributes it free to public schools.

Most citizens learn about their legislature from the newspapers and television. The relationship between the legislature and the media is supposed to be adversarial, but that's no reason to look on the press as the enemy, the report suggests.

"Legislators and legislatures have it within their power to do something to restore their tarnished images," says Martin Linsky, "but they will have to begin by understanding the press, its drives and its constraints."

Linsky says tension between reporters and lawmakers is predictable, and legislators should accept it as a fact of life. But developing a professional relationship with the media is essential to creating a "more respected environment for legislators to do the people's business."

How to go about it? The NCSL report recommends briefing the media on both the legislative process and the important pending issues, conducting bipartisan meetings with editorial boards and news managers on activities and current issues, and discussing the legislature's goals and performance with the media at the end of each session.

Organization and Management

"Democracy is about means, not ends. It is about process, not product," says former Texas Congresswoman Barbara Jordan.

How legislatures conduct their business—passing the budget on time, debating issues fairly and openly, involving citizens—influences whether the public views them as legitimate bodies for resolving problems.

Most states are still reluctant to take on the mantle of a full-time legislature, and some, like Kentucky, revisit their decision.

The debate over a citizen versus full-time legislature "became a major league problem when we talked ethics," according to Speaker Joe Clark. "We decided we were a citizen legislature here, everybody's part-time."

But part-time needn't be unprofessional, the report states. Delaware and West Virginia recently examined their staffing needs to ensure they had a source of independent information to serve their citizen legislators. West Virginia added staff and reorganized func-

---

A New Report to Strengthen Legislatures

State legislatures in the 1990s get less respect than ever. The public believes they can't solve problems, they're unduly influenced by special interests, and that lawmakers as a whole are incompetent or dishonest.

Concerned by this negative public perception, the National Conference of State Legislatures in 1991 created the Legislative Institution Task Force to examine these problems and suggest solutions. Chaired by Maryland Delegate Nancy Kopp, the group consisted of 29 leaders, legislators and legislative staffers who met for two years. Their primary concern was building support for the legislative institution and the legislative process as the legitimate method for making public policy decisions.

This month, the task force published its recommendations in the report, *Strengthening State Legislatures*. It is available free to all legislators. Please call the NCSL Marketing Department at (303)830-2200 to receive your copy.

---

tions so lawmakers could get more help reviewing policy proposals and formulating alternatives.

The Florida House of Representatives conducted an extensive study of its operations that resulted, among other changes, in new deadlines for considering legislation, subjecting conference committees to open meeting rules, and reorganizing the committee system.

Leadership

Political scientists have long held that leaders shape the public image of the legislature and its success; they symbolize the institution in which they serve.

"Legislative leadership has a role that no one else in the legislature can perform," says Alan Rosenthal. "It is up to leadership to take a statewide perspective, deal with the other chamber and with the governor, represent the legislature to the press, serve and protect its members and help maintain the legislature as an institution."

A big responsibility. But by educating caucus members about their institutional responsibility, promoting a sense of common values among members and staff, developing agendas that lay out the policy priorities of their caucus, and attending to procedural and organizational responsibilities, leaders can preserve, promote and enhance the legislative institution.

"Legislatures really did transform themselves," says Rosenthal. "They are an institutional success story in terms of

> *Leaders shape the public image of the legislature and its success; they symbolize the institution in which they serve.*

where they were 20 years ago and where they are now."

If the public doesn't believe that, nobody else but legislators can convince them.

"The creation of representative legislatures, as a balance to the traditional strong individual leader, has been America's greatest contribution to free, democratic government," says U.S. Senator Paul Sarbanes, a former Maryland state lawmaker. "The freedom and liberties of our people depend on them.

"Other nations now struggle to create representative legislatures, which America has had for 200 years. Too often we foolishly take them for granted and assume that representative government is ours by birthright. But, in truth, we must continually work to strengthen our legislatures and, thus, to preserve our freedom and liberty."

A worthy goal.

The Political Virtue Of Partisan Deadlock

Is there any way to make this happen on purpose?

ALAN EHRENHALT

It sounds like a recipe for chaos: Democrats and Republicans mired in numerical deadlock in the California Assembly, with each party holding 40 votes and unwilling to budge an inch when it comes to electing the speaker or getting the place organized at all. Whatever happens when the Assembly meets again this month, it is unlikely to be a pretty sight.

Of course, California's most visible legislative body hasn't been a pretty sight for some time now. It has spent the past decade only a few steps ahead of outright dysfunction, with Speaker Willie Brown's Democrats in rebellion against two Republican governors, with Republican Assembly members practicing guerrilla warfare against Brown, and with some truly frightening legislative outcomes, such as the budget impasse a few years back that forced California to pay its employees with scrip for several weeks.

And that was in a relatively stable partisan situation—at least it was clear that Democrats were the legislative majority. What will happen now if the Assembly has to convene in the absence of any majority at all? Won't things become (assuming one can imagine it) even worse?

That's one theory. But it isn't the only one. Legislatures have a way of surprising us, and one of the most interesting ways is this: When Democrats and Republicans stumble into a situation in which the only alternative to cooperation is outright disaster, they manage, against every expectation, to behave.

Three times in the past decade, an electoral accident has thrown a state legislative body into the deadlock of an exact numerical tie—an equal number of Democrats and Republicans, no way to break it, and the prospects of a session in which no genuine majority could be said to exist at all. In every such case, the initial forecast has been disaster. And sometimes it has begun that way. In the Indiana House, in 1989, the 50 Democrats and 50 Republicans started out by throwing pencils at each other in the legislative chamber and refusing to budge an inch on who the speaker would be. But that didn't last. Within a few weeks, they had agreed to rotate the speakership on what amounted to a daily basis ("Stereo

Speakers," the press called it), split the committee chairmanships and give individual members of both parties the right to manage their own legislation on the floor. Not only were the two parties civil to each other but the whole process looked a good deal more orderly than it had in previous years when one party or another was running the show.

Two years later, faced with a similar predicament, the Michigan House made a different choice: It opted to switch leaders on a monthly basis. At the end of each month, the presiding speaker of one party turned the gavel over to his counterpart in the other, and the committee chairmen did the same. The result was a legislative biennium that shocked everyone by producing more genuine accomplishment than the legislature had seen in years: an overhaul of the school finance system, a new auto insurance law, medical malpractice reform and progress toward restructured criminal sentencing guidelines.

While the Michigan House was operating on the speaker-of-the-month plan, the Florida Senate, deadlocked at 20-20, was trying yet another approach. It voted to place Republicans in control one year and Democrats the next. Here too, the results are instructive. Things worked best the first year, as the Republican Senate president gave the Democrats several key committee chairmanships to assuage their anxieties about minority status. In the second year, the Democratic leadership took some of the chairmanships back and ran legislative business in a generally more partisan way, and the spirit of comity unraveled a bit. Still, the overall verdict at the end was that the quality of legislation and government hadn't declined as a result of the stalemate: If anything, it had improved.

YOU DON'T HAVE TO BE A PARLIAMENTARY genius to learn some lessons from all this. One is that when you leave people no alternative but to share power, even the most battle-hardened and adversarial legislative antagonists do it with a skill and grace that surprises not only their critics but themselves. The other lesson is that the more often you force them to exchange power, the better they tend to do. Just as, in the words of Samuel Johnson, the prospect of being hanged "concentrates the mind wonderfully," the prospect of an imminent return to minority status serves to keep a legislative leader from forgetting the precepts of the Golden Rule.

I don't think the Florida Republicans treated Democrats in a more gentle way during their year in control because they are nicer people; I think it was because they saw the clock ticking and didn't want to be run over when they fell out of power at the end of the year. The Democrats, taking over in the second part of the biennium and at the start of an election campaign, could entertain the hope that voters would give them an absolute majority in the fall and thus render them immune to the consequences of partisan overreaching. (Alas for them, it didn't happen. Republicans won a majority in the Florida Senate on November 8 and can now run it pretty much as they like.)

On the basis of these three experiences, it's tempting to argue that what the voters should do is contrive to throw every legislature into deadlock every two years, and then demand that the two parties exchange control on an hourly basis, with the speaker from one party steering through as much legislation as possible during his 60-minute majority, then ducking out for a sandwich while the other side gets a chance. When he returns, all of his members would get up and move across the aisle, like a volleyball team rotating when it regains the serve. Not only would this provide an absorbing ritual to spectators in the gallery, it would provide badly needed exercise to members who get very little of it during a conventional legislative term.

The more I think about this, the more convinced I am that it is the one sensible version of term limits. Let them stay in office forever; just don't let them keep the same seat for more than an hour at a time.

THERE IS, SADLY, A PRACTICAL REASON WHY MY "hour-of-power" legislative reform proposal stands little chance of being adopted. It would be very difficult for voters to know whom to support in their individual districts in order to throw the entire legislative body into a tie. The only way to manage it would be to resort to vote fraud on a scale that seems to me excessive, even under the circumstances.

But if the idea of turning legislators into quick-change artists is a joke, the concept of shared power is not a joke. Our three little experiments suggest not only that it is possible but that this is a good time to start giving it some thought. Now

that we know our two major parties can govern well by accident, we should try to find out if they can do it on purpose.

What Indiana, Michigan and Florida stumbled on in their throes of stalemate, albeit briefly, was genuine shared government: a situation in which both parties have a role in the decisions, a piece of the responsibility, and a personal and political stake in having a result that will look good to the voters.

Unfortunately, shared power is an extremely rare commodity. How many situations have there been in recent state politics, other than brief crises, in which governors or legislators, without the prodding of partisan numerical deadlock, cut the political sparring, agreed to share the credit and the responsibility, and governed across partisan lines? You can conduct your own search if you want to. I don't think you will come up with very many. And so it is reasonable enough to assume there won't be much in the way of shared power in the next couple of years, either. But if there ever was a moment when the electorate seemed to want it, that moment is right now, as the 1995 legislative sessions begin all over the country. The voters expressed a good many complaints at the polls in November, but one of them surely was a complaint against partisan bickering and smash-mouth politics.

Maine may provide the best single example. No state endured a more excruciating brand of partisanship than Maine did over the past eight years, with Democratic House Speaker John Martin and Republican Governor John McKernan not only calling each other names but staking out rigid bargaining positions that made it painfully difficult for the state to deal realistically with its severe budgetary problems.

The Maine voters reacted to all that partisanship in November by doing several interesting things. They turned the House Democrats out of power; they elected a legislature with 87 freshmen—nearly half the entire membership; and they selected an independent governor, Angus King, whose most conspicuous platform plank called for an end to petty partisanship.

Some of those who survived the wars of the past decade emerged from the election predicting that the time for shared power in Maine was finally at hand. "There will be no hardball politics," the non-partisan House clerk flatly declared. "No one has the stomach for it."

The best we can do is hope against all the weight of accumulated experience that he might be right. Nothing would be more welcome at this moment in American politics than some evidence that it is possible for two political parties to share power without a fluke of arithmetic forcing them to do it.

Term Limits Change Ohio's Landscape: Groans About 'Dead-End' Jobs, Cheers for Looser System

Paul M. Barrett

Staff Reporter of The Wall Street Journal

COLUMBUS, Ohio—The Buckeye State doesn't have to wait to find out how term limits for politicians will work. Term limits are already here and having an impact.

GOP state Sen. Gary Suhadolnik, fretting about job prospects in "the real world," has gone back to school for a master's in business administration. Patrick Sweeney, a senior Democrat in the state House, fumes that term limits have eroded party discipline and made it harder to recruit new candidates. Brooke Hill, an active Democrat from Cincinnati, turned down an invitation to run for a house seat this year. "You get in there, you're learning the ropes," says Ms. Hill, "and then just when you're getting seniority, you're out the door."

All of which is exactly what advocates of term limits say they hoped for. "The system is more anarchical, more freewheeling," says GOP Rep. Rick Hodges, who is running for his second two-year term. "There will be more opportunity for the citizen-legislator as opposed to the career politician."

In Ohio, eight-year limits on service in the state House and Senate took effect in 1992, so the rules won't officially force any lawmakers to leave office until the year 2000. But the state already is a living laboratory to observe the early practical, and sometimes surprising, implications of a critical element in the anti-incumbent movement sweeping the nation.

In a new Wall Street Journal/NBC News poll, 80% of registered voters support limiting the terms of members of Congress. Voters in 17 states already have restricted the tenure of their state or federal representatives, and eight more have put term-limit proposals on next month's ballot. House GOP candidates have pledged in their Contract with America to bring term limits to a vote.

Congressional term limits imposed by states have been challenged as unconstitutional and haven't been put into effect. In late November, the U.S. Supreme Court will hear oral arguments on the constitutionality of the congressional curbs, but limits on state legislators don't raise the same legal questions and aren't at issue before the high court.

DESTABILIZING THE STATUS QUO

The destabilizing impact of the rules was amplified here when longtime Democratic House Speaker Vernal Riffe announced last January that he would retire after this year. Mr. Sweeney would probably succeed Mr. Riffe as speaker if the Democrats retain control of the House, but he complains about trying to supervise "young members who campaigned on term limits . . . [and] who give you a hard time because [their attitude is], 'Hey, I'm going to be somewhere else in six or eight years.' "

There are similar stirrings on the other side of the state. With Republicans given a good chance of winning a majority of House seats next month, junior members of the GOP caucus are discussing a radical proposal to rotate the speakership and key committee chairs every two years.

Some younger politicians welcome the new fluidity and air of competitiveness. "We don't have the luxury to wait, so we're moving more quickly than the old seniority system would have allowed to introduce legislation, to make our mark," says 32-year-old Rep. Michael Wise, who is running for his second term this fall. As a freshman, the conservative Republican introduced bills to limit welfare benefits and block proposals to shift local property tax revenue from wealthier districts to pay for improved schools in poorer areas. The legislation didn't pass, but Mr. Wise believes his aggressive start will make him a player on these issues if he is re-elected.

'A DEAD-END JOB'

But the flux makes many older politicians anxious. "For the first time in my life, I'm in a dead-end job," grouses Mr. Suhadolnik, the GOP senator. He fears being trampled in a mass exodus of lawmakers in 2000. That's why the 14-year incumbent is working toward an M.B.A. at Cleveland State University and leaning toward leaving the Senate when his current term ends in 1996. "I'll be 50 in 2000," he says, "and that doesn't sound too exciting to me in terms of starting over with a new job."

The state's term limits won't cut off all political careers as much as it seems on the surface. The fact that the eight-year clock starts over if a lawmaker moves to the other house has accelerated movement up the political ladder. For example, Democratic Rep. Mark Guthrie, who for 13 years has represented a district east of Columbus, says that term limits were one among several reasons he decided to run for a state Senate seat this fall.

But the weakening grip of party leadership has produced some results that have surprised even foes of term limits. The legislature last session passed an ethics-reform measure that went much further than top Democrats wanted in limiting gifts and other perks for lawmakers. "Term limits established a kind of public-interest momentum" that carried over to the ethics debate, says Janet Lewis, executive director of the Ohio branch of Common Cause, a liberal political-reform group that opposed term limits in the state.

Some opponents of term limits in Ohio and elsewhere have argued that by forcing continual turnover, the rules will strengthen well-heeled lobbyists. These critics argue that veteran lobbyists' institutional memory and tactical knowhow will become more valuable in the ab-

sence of the traditional seniority structure. It's too early to make definitive pronouncements on this score, but there are some indications that term limits have had another effect: Corporate lobbyists in Columbus are courting a wider range of legislators, because persuading a few party leaders isn't enough any more.

Robert Klaffky of the Republican lobbying firm Van Meter, Ashbrook & Associates confirms that strategies are changing drastically. Representing a horse-track operator who favored a bill to allow off-track betting, Mr. Klaffky says that his initial instructions were to deal with just top party leaders and then to approach ranking members of key committees. When that didn't seem to work,

though, he ended up "going around, member by member," trying to make his case. The bill passed this year after a struggle.

More generally, lobbyist Paul Tipps, a former state Democratic chairman, says that if the demise of the seniority system causes the General Assembly to bog down on passing controversial legislation, voters will be quicker to mount ballot initiatives like the one that brought term limits. In fact, activists who pushed term limits in Ohio have now joined with term-limit opponent Common Cause to press for a popular referendum on campaign-finance reform.

Says Mr. Tipps: "The message is that voters are unhappy, and the whole political system better respond."

Reviewing Political Science on a Local School Board

Gerald M. Pomper, *Rutgers University*

Gerald M. Pomper is professor of political science at the Eagleton Institute of Politics, Rutgers University. After a sabbatical at Australian National University, he will return to his small town in New Jersey, deliberately unidentified in this essay.

For eight years, I have been a member of my local Board of Education, including two years as its president. While doing what I could to improve the education of 1,500 students annually, I have also broadened my awareness of the relevance of political science to the practical work of government.

My colleagues did not always appreciate my academic specialty. On one occasion, when I made a particularly unrealistic suggestion, the board president (ironically, also a Ph.D. in the field) commented, "There speaks a true political scientist." Yet sometimes the discipline proved helpful to them. For example, we wrestled one evening past midnight with the proposed promotion of a mediocre but highly popular athletic coach. I convinced myself, and some others, to support the appointment by invoking Max Weber's "ethics of responsibil-

ity"—surely one of the most arcane considerations ever used in making local educational decisions.

In this informal report, I want to stress the relationships between my limited experience to more general aspects of democracy. School boards, to a great extent, emphasize that strand of democratic thought, exemplified by the ancient Greeks and Rousseau, that focuses on the importance of the community. In these theories of what Jane Mansbridge calls "unitary democracy," citizens voluntarily assume office, repress any private interests, and promote a discoverable common good.

This is the official doctrine, but the surprising reality is that school board behavior largely fits the ideal. Of the twenty board members with whom I served, only one had an unsheathed ax to grind. And he (or, respecting confidentiality, she) gained

neither victory nor respect. Board members receive neither pay nor perquisites more attractive than free tickets to chilly football games. They typically will spend one to two evenings a week on school business, slighting their families and careers, earning the unpleasant rewards of complaints over everything from taxes to crayons. Still, they come each week, to consider the carpeting in the high school library, or the price of grilled cheese sandwiches, or —too rarely—the goals of education.

School board members believe in the doctrine of the common good. In practice, however, they must deal with a more familiar strand of democratic thought. This strand, well represented in our founding political philosophers such as Locke and Madison, focuses on the competition of interests, in conflict and its resolu-

From *PS: Political Science & Politics*, June 1991, pp. 223-225. © 1991 by the American Political Science Association. Reprinted by permission.

tion, and on the winning of immediate victories.

Being Americans, school board members are attracted to this competitive form of politics. In statewide training sessions of newly elected board members, for example, the most lively discussion in the corridors will be about campaign strategies, not the scheduled topics of parliamentary procedure or curriculum development. There are many reasons for this preference. Election campaigns are exciting, satisfying to the ego (if you win), and clear in the results. In contrast, governing the schools involves considerable tedium, constantly reminds you of the limitations on your "power," and produces few clear results. Having won their seats, school board members often echo Robert Redford's closing line in *The Candidate*: "What do we do now?"

The difference between electioneering and governing is a familiar problem for office-holders, most recently illustrated by President George Bush's surgery to remove the lips that promised "No new taxes." I believe it is a particular problem for school board members, who are not professional politicians and are therefore less likely to be able to find the appropriate middle way between two opposite temptations. One temptation is to concentrate on winning and holding office, a course sometimes pursued by legislators who overemphasize "the electoral connection." Since there are few extrinsic rewards, this course is less likely to attract boards of education.

The greater peril for these officials is that they will concentrate too much on governing and neglect their constituents. The anthropologist must beware of "going native," and becoming overly identified with his or her host society. Similarly, a board member must beware of "going professional," and becoming overly identified with the school district's permanent administrators.

It surely is tempting. The voters pay little attention to the schools, unless their children or their wallets are affected; the professionals sincerely devote their lives. The voters are factually uninformed; the professionals know the literature. The

voters collectively speak to the board only once a year, when the budget is presented; the professionals talk to the board weekly, sometimes daily. The voters have only one, if powerful, sanction over the board, its potential defeat in the next election (although many will not run for a new term); the professionals have multiple sanctions, from teacher resistance to personal disapproval.

Moreover, the institutional framework fosters this identification. Virtually everything that happens in the schools is the legal responsibility of the board, from the selection of textbooks to the electricity bills. Yet a sensible board will want its teachers to choose texts and its business manager to order lightbulbs. Having intelligently delegated responsibility, the board then is inevitably in the position of defending decisions that it did not, in fact, make.

A successful school board will be political, in the best sense of the word. It will go beyond the clearly desirable goals undoubtedly held by its members to develop a strategic sense on ways to accomplish these ends. This strategic sense will begin with Harry Truman's doctrine, that effective government basically means "trying to persuade people to do the things they ought to have sense enough to do without persuading them."

The board on which I served was as intelligent and devoted a group as one could find. Almost all were professionals, and usually five of nine members had doctorates. We were genuinely devoted to educational excellence and enthusiastically endorsed the national agenda for change that followed publication of *A Nation at Risk*. In seeking change, we learned some lessons, or at least realized some obvious truths, illustrated here by admittedly idiosyncratic and unreliable case anecdotes.

The first lesson is that good intentions and good policies are not enough. Boards of education, like other political bodies, must go further, working to develop supporting coalitions. We neglected this dictum when we were faced by declining enrollment in foreign language classes. Essentially, we faced a choice between continuing three languages

(French, Spanish, and German) with limited opportunity for advanced instruction, or cutting the least popular language, German, in order to provide more years of advanced classes in French and Spanish.

We opted, as I preferred, to emphasize depth over breadth, but we did so suddenly, with too little explanation, and with inadequate provision for those students who had already completed the first year of German. The result was a raucous public meeting at which we were accused of everything from causing the national trade deficit to ethnocentrism. The political result was to spur opposition to our budget and to board members running for reelection, contributing to the defeat of both.

The first lesson is that good intentions and good policies are not enough.

Another tough decision provides a contrast. Declining enrollment had led to the closing of a neighborhood elementary school that was now rented, without profit to the board. Located in the most desirable area of town, it was economically attractive to potential developers, and sentimentally attractive to its neighborhood alumni. By selling it, the board could gain a large amount of capital funds for necessary major repairs to the remaining school buildings. Opponents of a sale, mostly those near the school, argued that it should be "stockpiled" against the possibility of future increases in enrollment. One of these residents, another academic, began a vigorous campaign against both the sale and my reelection.

The "facts" favored a sale: enrollment projections indicated a stable or declining student population, and the building, even if reopened, would be very expensive to renovate. More important than the bare facts, however, was convincing the public. We held a series of public meetings, circularized the neighborhood residents, and commissioned outside experts.

Following Schattschneider, we broadened the "scope of conflict" by showing how a sale would benefit taxpayers beyond the immediate area and how the proposed sale to a private school for special education would benefit handicapped children. Our final, decisive point was the price: $2 million for a facility originally appraised at a quarter of that value. Announcing the sale two weeks before the board election also, and not coincidentally, aided my own reelection effort.

To win support, a second rule is Lyndon Johnson's: "you gotta dance with the fella who brung you." To effectuate democratic control, a school board must remind itself that

To effectuate democratic control, a school board must remind itself that it is the representative voice of the voters, not the public organ of the school professionals.

If war is too important to be left to generals, schools are too important to be left to educators.

it is the representative voice of the voters, not the public organ of the school professionals. It should trust its own sense of values and priorities. Its governmental model should be the idealized Congress, providing direction, oversight, a healthy skepticism, and only conditional support in regard to the executive branch. It should avoid the closed if cozy relationships of a British cabinet or the "iron triangles" of congressional committees, lobbyists, and federal regulatory agencies. If war is too important to be left to generals, schools are too important to be left to educators.

On infrequent occasions, I and other board members forgot this rule. Sympathetic to the problems of dedicated professionals, we sometimes were too sympathetic. An important instance came when the school system went through its periodic state assessment. Although generally evaluated highly, the district failed to meet some of the state's standards. The most important of these was inadequate performance in mathematics by sixth-grade pupils. That failure was actually due to poor supervision by an administrator, but the board accepted the blame. It was noble to protect the administrator, but a political mistake.

Mathematics instruction also provides a contrasting example. Responding to parental complaints, the board was unhappy with the level of instruction for high-achieving elementary students and with test scores of low-achieving high schoolers. We were offered various rationalizations: algebra would be harmful to the health of twelve-year-olds, geometry shouldn't be taught before the tenth grade, even though tested by the state in ninth grade. Aided by new administrators sharing its goals, the board acted. It set specific goals for improved performance in math and insisted that the professionals find ways to achieve these goals. Given a clear mandate, teachers and administrators overcame the alleged problems and met the board mandate.

Changing the schools requires more than this kind of occasional intervention. Board members are amateurs, busy people, and transitory officials. My third rule is that successful boards of education must institutionalize change within the professional establishment itself. Educators themselves recognize this principle. They emphasize that programs should be "proactive" and that the staff must "buy in" to change (cliches as irritating as political science's jargon).

Yet in education, the structural imperatives (not to coin a phrase) are largely opposed to change. The people who choose careers in teaching are generally more concerned with personal security than with innovation. The environment of schools is

generally hierarchical and non-participatory, isolating teachers from one another. Career advancement depends largely on years of service, rather than originality. Administrators are mostly recruited from the inside and, in New Jersey, given tenure in their executive positions after three years. There is little direct competition, and few market tests of success. The inertial forces are so great that even the brightest flames are prone to early burnout.

Seeking change within these severe limits, my board futilely exchanged the positions held by its tenured administrators. An ineffective superintendent became an inefficient business administrator. Two mediocre

. . . successful boards of education must institutionalize change within the professional establishment itself.

elementary school principals were switched. One became a colossal failure in the new school; the other became an embarrassing insubordinate. Eventually, all were persuaded to retire, not without significant financial cost.

Other strategies have been more effective. By creating a new assistant superintendent for curriculum, we have established line responsibility for instructional change. Individual grants to teachers have encouraged classroom innovation. Hiring outside evaluators of specific programs have provided more objective measures of success while making the district's teachers more aware of current research findings. Giving parents power to override some school decisions, e.g., on placement of their children in reading levels, has provided a check on the professionals.

There are other measures that are now discussed and may prove useful, in this district and nationally, but none are a panacea for the evident ills of American education. School-based management may free teachers to use their talents more fully, but it may also become only a means to protect teachers from parents or to advantage the children of the few participating parents. Market competition among schools may free parents from the strictures of the "one best system" that dominates our schools, but it may also add to the disadvantages of our most needy children. Budget limitations may force administrators to re-examine their priorities, but it may also mean that we only buy inexpensive pencils when we need costly computers. Limitations of terms of office will lessen the risk of "capture" of board members, but may leave professionals less subject to informed oversight.

Ultimately, the proximate solutions to these insoluble problems are simple to state and difficult to achieve. Hire the best people you can find, provide necessary but limited resources, watch them carefully, stick to a few programs over the long haul, and emphasize implementation over policy declarations.

As I leave my colleagues, I remain hopeful because I have experienced the dedication of these democratic activists and the devotion characteristic of most school professionals. I urge political scientists, and other citizens, to take up public office, to serve, and to learn. But, in so doing, they must remember Weber's caution: "Only he has the calling for politics who is sure that he shall not crumble when the world from his point of view is too stupid or too base for what he wants to offer."

Wisconsin's 'quirky' veto power

Wisconsin legislators, outraged by the governor's veto power, plan to fight their battle in the U.S. Supreme Court.

Michael H. McCabe

Michael H. McCabe is assistant director of CSG's Midwestern office.

Chalk up another victory for Wisconsin Gov. Tommy G. Thompson in an ongoing battle with Democratic lawmakers over the scope of his authority to veto spending bills.

Thanks to a recent decision by a federal court of appeals, the Republican governor remains free to exercise one of the most unusual veto powers in the nation—at least for now.

At issue is a provision in the Wisconsin Constitution that empowers Thompson to approve or veto any appropriations bill "in whole or in part." Like similar measures in other states, this provision enables the governor to remove individual line items from a large spending bill without resorting to a full veto.

The result is a revised bill that automatically becomes law unless the governor's action is overridden by a two-thirds vote of the Legislature. There's nothing unusual about that, but in practice, Wisconsin's "partial veto" has been used in ways unimaginable in other states.

Thanks to the silence of the state constitution on this point, Wisconsin's governors have, over the years, taken it upon themselves to define the scope of their partial veto authority. Not surprisingly, they have taken full advantage of this license by vetoing whole sections of spending plans as well as individual sentences, words, parts of words, single letters, digits, spaces and even the drafting symbols that appear in enrolled bills.

In 1987, the governor used the partial veto power to substitute the Legislature's language that certain juveniles could be detained for "not more than 48 hours," with language that said they could not be detained for more than "10 days."

Equally unsurprising is the fact that the creative use of this power doesn't always sit well with the Legislature. By stringing together the remnants of a partially vetoed bill, the governor can effectively create new language, sometimes thwarting the express intent of the General Assembly.

Though lawmakers retain the power to override such measures, the constitutional requirement of a two-thirds majority to do so can leave smaller legislative majorities frustrated. Here again, Wisconsin is not alone.

Override provisions requiring super majorities are fairly common and serve to magnify the voting power of legislative minorities in any state. The difference is that a creative partial veto combined with a legislative failure to override can result in the enactment of a law that has never been approved by a legislative majority.

In this respect, Wisconsin is unique.

Disgruntled lawmakers have repeatedly challenged the governor's creative use of the partial veto, claiming it infringes upon their legislative authority. But state courts in Wisconsin have consistently sided with the governor.

The Wisconsin Supreme Court has acknowledged that the partial veto originally was intended to curb the General Assembly's habit of attaching controversial substantive measures to omnibus spending bills to secure their passage. But the court has specifically rejected the contention that the partial veto only may be used to eliminate rather than create language. In fact, the only judicially-imposed limitation on the governor is that the result of a partial veto must be a complete and workable law that is germane to the subject of the original bill.

In the spring of 1990, Wisconsin voters narrowed the governor's power by approving a constitutional amendment that prohibited the rejection of individual letters to create new words in a bill. But according to Senate President Fred Risser, the so-called "Vanna White veto"

Governors' Powers to Veto Appropriations Bills

State or other jurisdiction	May Veto Amount	May Veto Language	State or other jurisdiction	May Veto Amount	May Veto Language
Alabama	Y	Y	New Hampshire	N	N
Alaska	Y(a)	N	New Jersey	Y(a)	N
Arizona	Y	N	New Mexico	Y	N
Arkansas	Y	N	New York	Y	N
California	Y(a)	N	North Carolina	N	N
Colorado	Y	Y	North Dakota	Y	Y
Connecticut	Y	N	Ohio	Y	Y
Delaware	Y	N	Oklahoma	Y	N
Florida	Y	Y	Oregon	Y	Y
Georgia	Y	N	Pennsylvania	Y(a)	N
Hawaii	Y(a)	N	Rhode Island	N	N
Idaho	Y	N	South Carolina	Y	Y
Illinois	Y(a)	N	South Dakota	Y	Y
Indiana	N	N	Tennessee	Y(a)	N
Iowa	Y	Y	Texas	Y	N
Kansas	Y	N	Utah	Y	N
Kentucky	Y	N	Vermont	N	N
Louisiana	Y	Y	Virginia	Y	Y
Maine	N	N	Washington	Y	Y
Maryland	Y	N	West Virginia	Y(a)	Y
Massachusetts	Y(a)	Y	Wisconsin	Y	Y
Michigan	Y	Y	Wyoming	Y	N
Minnesota	Y	N	American Samoa	Y	N
Mississippi-	Y	Y	Guam	Y(a)	N
Missouri	Y	N	No. Mariana Islands	Y	N
Montana	Y	Y	Puerto Rico	Y(a)	Y
Nebraska	Y(b)	N	U.S. Virgin Islands	Y	Y
Nevada	N	N			

Y — Yes   N — No

(a) Governor also can reduce amounts in appropriations bill. In Hawaii, governor can reduce items in executive appropriations measures, but cannot reduce nor item veto amounts appropriated for the judicial or legislative branches.

(b) No appropriation can be made in excess of the recommendations contained in the governor's budget except by a 2/3 vote. The excess is not subject to veto by the governor.

The Book of the States, 1990-91 Edition, published by The Council of State Governments

was only "the most outrageous form of partial veto," because individual letters can be changed. Even without it, a creative governor can subvert legislative intent by crafting new provisions within a bill.

Risser continues to spearhead efforts to limit the partial veto. Last year, he and Assembly Majority Leader David Travis took the Legislature's case into federal court. There the two Democrats alleged that Republican Gov. Thompson's exercise of the partial veto in 20 recent instances violated federal constitutional safeguards. But in June 1990, District Court Judge John C. Shabaz, a former Republican leader in the Wisconsin Assembly, ruled in favor of Thompson.

The plaintiffs appealed, but to no avail. Last April, the 7th Circuit Court of Appeals affirmed the district court's decision, leaving little room for the plaintiffs to maneuver. In an opinion written by Circuit Judge Richard Posner, the court held that Wisconsin's partial veto provision was not unconstitutional because, "the federal Constitution does not fix the balance of power between branches of state government."

In denying the lawmakers' charges, the court noted the availability of a political remedy for their grievance — "amend the Wisconsin Constitution" — and concluded that there is "no need to involve the federal courts in this affair and no legal basis for doing so."

"A modest shift of power among elected officials is not a denial of republican government or even a reduction in the amount of democracy."

— Wisconsin 7th Circuit Court

The plaintiffs, according to Travis, remained "absolutely convinced of the righteousness of our cause" and quickly petitioned the court for a rehearing. That request was denied in May, but by mid-June, the lawmakers were preparing to take their case to the U.S. Supreme Court.

Risser believes the 7th Circuit failed to address the plaintiffs' main point — namely, that "laws should only be made by a majority." Risser contends that when a new law is created by partial veto, the fundamental principles of republican government are undermined.

Although the plaintiffs are pursuing their case, the Circuit Court's opinion offers little hope for success.

W hile conceding that Wisconsin's partial veto may well alter the balance of power in favor of the governor, the court concluded that "a modest shift of power among elected officials is not a denial of republican government or even a reduction in the amount of democracy." That the partial veto is "unusual, even quirky, does not make it unconstitutional."

To make matters worse, from the plaintiffs' perspective, the appellate court noted that lawmakers' grievances were compounded by their own actions, since the partial veto power is limited to appropriations bills. While the governor has partially vetoed non-appropriations items, it is only because legislators continue to attach substantive provisions to spending bills.

While the governor is reportedly pleased with the court's decision, the plaintiffs remain unconvinced — and undaunted. Travis "felt all along that the issue would have to be decided one way or another by the U.S. Supreme Court."

Risser agrees and was unmoved by the Circuit Court's admonishment that legislators upset with the governor's veto power should change the state constitution. "There's a political remedy to just about every issue the Supreme Court deals with," said Risser. "The courts should act to protect the basic philosophies at stake in this case."

Failing a reversal by the Supreme Court, lawmakers may be forced to reconsider their options. A constitutional amendment is possible, but the amendment process in Wisconsin is a lengthy one requiring legislative consent to any proposed language in two consecutive sessions of the General Assembly. Then the voters have the final say.

In the meantime, the governor's "quirky" power remains safe.

The Lure of the
Strong Mayor

ROB GURWITT

Sometime during the next few years, there is a good chance that Dallas will do the unthinkable: discard its city manager form of government. For the field of local administration, that would be a bit like England deciding to scrap Parliament. And it would be something more: a sign that the age of municipal reform, as it has been practiced in America for the better part of this century, is coming to an end. For Dallas is an emblem of sorts.

For years—until San Diego passed it in size—Dallas was the largest city in the country with a so-called "council-manager" form of government, in which an elected council sets broad policy guidelines but an appointed manager actually runs the city day-to-day. For decades, Dallas has been a thumb in the eye to those doubters who argued that the manager system might be fine for medium-sized, uncomplicated cities, but that large cities need the firm hand of a mayor with power. Dallas has routinely ranked among the best-run cities in the country, zealously guarding its triple-A bond rating and setting a national example for the businesslike way it has managed its affairs.

So why, all of a sudden, is there talk of change? For exactly the reason you'd expect: politics.

Dallas has changed radically since it first adopted the city manager plan in 1931. For years, the city was essentially run by its business community, the political leadership drawn exclusively

Cities have been turning to professional managers for the past 80 years to try to get the politics out of local government. Now a few of them are wondering whether it is time to put some politics back in.

from the prosperous white neighborhoods of north Dallas. The manager was essentially the instrument of that leadership.

These days, though, power has splintered. Many of the city's top business executives now work for out-of-town corporations or have moved themselves to the suburbs; meanwhile, the city's Hispanic and African-American communities are starting to come into their own at City Hall and are finding they don't always like the established ways of conducting business. The present mayor—who is elected at-large but has little administrative authority—has been unable to develop a steady working relationship with either the council or the manager. As the entire community struggles to deal with a limping economy and a rising tide of the usual urban troubles, there is a growing feeling that Dallas is adrift without strong leadership.

So the city's hallowed institution of manager government is getting hit from all sides: from business leaders who mourn the loss of the old Chamber-of-Commerce consensus, and from newly elected black and Hispanic politicians who think their constituents are not getting enough attention. The result is that there is public talk of junking the whole system—quite possibly in favor of a strong-mayor plan.

"There are some who are beginning to appreciate that the great problem in Dallas is no longer how to do those things on which the city leadership has a consensus, but instead is to figure out what to do in the first place," says Royce Hanson, dean of the School of Social Sciences at the University of Texas at Dallas.

It may be that in the end, Dallas will opt to keep its structure intact. If it does, though, it will be for reasons quite different from the good-government reform sentiments that have maintained the city manager system all these years. For what the city's situation makes clear is that the demands of the moment are not for less politics—they are for more.

"The era of municipal reform is clearly over," public administration scholar George Frederickson writes in a recent paper on the subject. The battle over reform, he points out, was fought on such issues as efficiency, economy and ending corruption. "Today," Frederickson argues, "issues of political responsiveness are as important as efficiency and economy."

That is because even in once-homogeneous communities the claimants to power—neighborhoods, minority groups, citizens' associations—are multiplying. It is no longer just the Chicagos and New Yorks of the country that must forge consensus from a cacophony of voices before they can move forward; that is now the task for Dallas and a host of other cities that used to pride themselves on being far less complicated.

So it shouldn't be startling that some communities are looking to reshape how they are governed, and in particular are considering boosting the powers of the mayor. It may not be possible to end poverty, house the homeless, disband gangs, repave corroding streets, find the money to revive a withering economy or put an end to civic squabbling. But one thing citizens clearly can do is refashion local government with the hope that someone—a mayor, an elected county executive—someone—can assemble the political authority to grapple better with those problems.

Which is why Dallas isn't alone in considering change. Dade County, Florida, which includes Miami and has a population of more than 2 million, is hearing a new round of demands for a strong elected executive. On the other side of the same state, St. Petersburg has just decided to jettison 60 years of city manager government in favor of a strong mayor. And in the West, where so-called "reform government" is considered as much a birthright as unlimited access to water, Sacramento is gingerly looking at change. A good 80 years after Dayton, Ohio, became the first major American city to put a manager system in place, the argument over which form of government is best appears ready to heat up again.

To some extent, of course, it never died down. Ever since the reform movement got rolling in the 'teens and '20s, cities have been turning to manager government in an effort to become more businesslike or to rid themselves of corruption.

The strong-mayor system, usually accompanied by intense partisan war-

---

The strong-mayor system, usually accompanied by intense partisan warfare, was seen by the original reform generation as fiscally wasteful and too susceptible to patronage abuses.

---

fare, was seen by the original reform generation as fiscally wasteful and too susceptible to patronage abuses. The main alternative existing at that time—commission government, in which a small number of commissioners serve both as legislators and as the heads of city departments—seemed a poor substitute: It diffused leadership and often produced incompetent administrators. The idea of a professional, non-partisan city manager, administering government while avoiding politics, neatly matched the taste of reformers for reconstituting local government on a professional basis.

As a public policy idea and as a national movement, the city manager system probably reached the peak of its popularity by the 1950s. But cities continued to switch to it long after that. It was only in 1986 that the International City/County Management Association, in its quinquennial "Forms of Municipal Government" survey, found for the first time that manager government had passed the strong mayor form in popularity, holding sway in 53 percent of the cities that responded. That figure dropped to 51 percent in 1991, although the slight shift may have been due to changes in the sample, not to abandonments of the plan.

And over the years, the values that the reform movement advanced have become a permanent part of the civic landscape. The 1991 ICMA survey, in fact, found that the most likely structural change being made by cities—even those with strong mayors and partisan politics—was the addition of a chief administrative officer, a professional appointee who could coordinate the running of the city. Indeed, more than one-third of the strong-mayor cities have hired an administrator. The administrator in a strong-mayor city is sometimes in a rather tenuous position; the mayor can fire him or her virtually at will. Nevertheless the clear trend is for cities without managers to aim for some of the professionalism that cities using the manager system have achieved.

At the same time, though, manager government has itself been evolving. In fact, it is difficult these days to find places that still adhere to the orthodox reform structure. As laid out by Richard Childs, the generally acknowledged father of the city manager movement, a reformed city should have a small (generally five-seat) council whose members are elected at large; the mayor comes from the council, and is little more than a presiding officer and ceremonial presence. The operations of government are the responsibility of the appointed manager.

In city after city, the result of those reforms was a government devoid of the patronage-mongering and political selfishness that had afflicted cities with strong mayors; it was also, however, a city government whose leaders were relatively insulated from the electorate and who, in many communities, were all drawn from the Chamber of Commerce and from a single upper-crust part of town. Those are difficult features to justify in an era when neighborhoods are trying to reassert themselves in the councils of power and Hispanics and African-Americans are taking a place at the table.

And so the manager system has itself adjusted. Either by vote of the people or by judicial fiat, city councils have been expanding in size and abandoning at-large elections for district elections; only one-third of the councils in cities above 100,000 are now elected at-large. Just as important, a full 61 percent of the manager-run cities now have directly elected mayors, a shift designed to give the system a greater measure of political accountability and leadership. These mayors still lack administrative clout—the manager continues to wield that—but they do serve as figures of political accountability to the community at large. "The council-manager plan has been greatly modified, and that has made it more responsive," says George Frederickson. "Like a willow, it has bent with the times." One political scientist, the University of Alaska's Greg Protasel, has in fact suggested that were it not for the council-manager plan's ability to become more politically sensitive, it might have been abandoned in greater numbers.

But there are times when "reforming reformism," as some onlookers have dubbed the process, is simply not enough. Take, as an example, St. Petersburg, a manager city that long ago modified its system by adding both district council elections and a directly elected, although administratively weak, mayor. This spring St. Petersburg decided to go much further—it threw out city manager government altogether.

On the surface, the city's decision to go to a strong mayor seemed mostly to be about personalities. The city manager system had become an issue after an acting manager fired Police Chief Ernest Curtsinger, whom many blacks considered racially insensitive but who was enormously popular with many white retirees. Curtsinger's firing led a group of outraged supporters to push for changing the city's council-manager charter to create a strong-mayor structure; that proposal wound up on the March election ballot, along with the regularly scheduled election for mayor—which, not coincidentally,

featured both Curtsinger and the sitting mayor, David Fischer.

The contrast between the two candidates was striking. Fischer, a longtime consultant on municipal finance with an intellectual, somewhat remote style, drew the bulk of his support from the city's black and affluent white communities: Curtsinger, a smooth politician with a populist bent, took the white middle class. To a remarkable degree, voters' opinions on the charter change paralleled their opinions of the candidates: Where Curtsinger was strong, so was the proposal for a strong mayor; where Fischer drew support, so did opposition to charter change. And yet an odd thing happened on election day: The charter change passed while Curtsinger lost, and Fischer, who had supported keeping his position formally weak, suddenly found himself with new powers.

Even in an election so firmly rooted in the politics of the moment, though, the city's abandonment of the manager system had its origin in a far more basic question than whether Ernest Curtsinger should run the city or not. Over the past decade and more, the city's leaders have been trying to reshape St. Petersburg, to redevelop its downtown and change its image as a sleepy haven for senior citizens. After a major downtown redevelopment project was rejected by voters a decade or so ago, the city council—with the active support of the city manager and much of the downtown business establish-

ment—went ahead on its own and pushed through both a new office/retail development and construction of a new baseball stadium. Both were approved and built without much input from the average citizen.

That might have been all right if the city's neighborhoods felt they had gotten something in return, but they haven't; both major projects, in fact, still

sit unoccupied. So by this year's elections, the neighborhoods had grown restless.

"They feel all their tax dollars have gone downtown to this economic revitalization, their tax rates have gone up because of shortfalls in the projects and money has been reallocated from service areas to pay the debt," says Darryl Paulson, a political scientist at the University of South Florida. "So there's great dissatisfaction, particularly because they were not allowed to publicly participate in whether or not these projects should go ahead." The neighborhoods' vote for a strong mayor was, as a result, not only a vote against particular officials but a protest against the whole idea of a government system that seemed so unaccountable to citizens' desires.

Whether that same participatory impulse ultimately produces a similar result in Dallas remains very much in doubt. It is only in the last couple of years—since the 1991 court-ordered switch from an at-large council to 14 members chosen by district—that the Hispanic and African-American neighborhoods of south Dallas have had real representation at City Hall. Some of the current calls for change come from newly elected black and Hispanic council members, who argue that their communities have been given the short end of the stick by the city's professional man-

The more hands on the tiller, the harder it is to steer. Diversity places a huge burden on the one person elected to perform the task of bringing people together: the mayor.

agers. "We can't prioritize based on community needs," says one of the city's new African-American council members, Don Hicks. "The system is just not responding."

But other blacks and Hispanics, and liberal whites who are allied with them, believe something very different: that it would be foolish to change the system just as the disadvantaged begin to accumulate power within it. Indeed, for some of those who fought to make city government more pluralistic, the talk of moving to a strong mayor looks a lot like a ploy by the Old Guard to shift power away from the newly diverse council.

"Now that minorities are finally at the table, and we have all geographic areas of the city equally represented," asks Lori Palmer, a white council member from south Dallas, "why would there be a suggestion that we transfer power from the council to the mayor? In this city, voting strength is still in north Dallas, with Anglo voters, so for some time I would predict our mayors will be elected by the northern and Anglo side of city. It is suspicious that there would be interest in consolidating power in a mayor's position."

The argument that the city needs the steadying leadership of a strong mayor draws little sympathy from this camp. "We've just gotten into the loop," says Al Lipscomb, who as deputy mayor is the city's highest-ranking black official. "Are you saying that self-determination is cumbersome compared with one ruler?" His answer is straightforward. "Hell no. That's what makes this city thriving, refreshing and full of effervescence."

In fact, there is a strain of thought in Dallas that holds that, like an Eastern European country, the city is adjusting to the realities of democracy brought on by the *perestroika* of district elections. If all the city's politicians learn their roles under the current system, the reasoning goes, the city will get back on track. "What needs to happen is the city manager needs to exercise greater demand for policy decisions to come out of council, and less day-to-day micromanaging," says Jim Buerger, a former council member and one-time mayoral candidate. "And the council needs to establish its role in relation to establishing policy." In the meantime, Buerger and others argue, the mayor, Steve Bartlett, has been trying to act like a strong mayor despite the fact that he is a constitutionally weak one. In a system that demands consultation with the manager and the council, that cannot help but create bruised feelings and political squabbling.

If Dallas ultimately decides to stick with its council-manager form, then, it will be as much an effort to safeguard political diversity as it is to ensure administrative efficiency. The question is whether that sort of decision will produce the leadership the city needs.

That is because "effervescence," as Lipscomb puts it, exacts a price: The more hands there are on the tiller, the harder it is to steer. Diversity places a huge burden on the one person elected to perform the task of bringing people together: the mayor. But in a manager-run city, the mayor has very few tools he can use to accomplish that task.

The best that such a city can hope for is that its mayor will prove adept at what some experts like to call "facilitative" skills. James Svara, who teaches political science at North Carolina State University, argues that the pressures of civic diversity will, in fact, produce just such people. "The facilitative mayor," Svara wrote recently, "leads by empowering others—in particular the council and the manager—rather than seeking power for himself or herself." In this view, the mayor is a kind of information broker, promoting communication among politicians and trying to manage conflict and settle differences.

Interestingly enough, one of the more adept facilitators in office at the moment is the mayor of perhaps the preeminent strong-mayor city in the country—Ed Rendell of Philadelphia. Rendell has put an end to years of discord by carefully sharing both the spotlight and his thinking with other politicians, especially City Council President John Street and members of the city's state legislative delegation. "He recognizes," says Frederick Voigt, who directs a reform-era civic watchdog group known as the Committee of 70, "that while he possesses tremendous power, he has to share it; he has to deal in consensus politics."

At the same time, though, Rendell has been unabashed about using the powers of his office to face down public employee unions and make steep cuts in the city's budget. It has been an extraordinarily difficult task, in large measure because the city's disparate communities take pride in a sort of prickly independence. "It is a city of Balkan states," says Voigt, "and that makes it politically, racially and ethnically combustible. They have had to distribute the pain equally, and that

could not be done without the centrality of power. If you fragmented it, there would be too many discordant voices without anyone in charge."

A similar calculus lies behind the push in Dade County, Florida, to look seriously at moving to an elected chief executive. "It would be very difficult for a weak mayor in Dade County to call upon support from all the diverse elements of the community during a time when some of the decisions are bound to be unpopular," says Tom Fiedler, political editor of the *Miami Herald*. "It's too easy for the rest of the community to disown that person and say, 'Well, that's what Hispanics do,' or 'You can't trust the blacks,' or 'It's just the Anglo good-old-boy system.' There's got to be leadership in which every element of the community is invested in some way."

None of this is to say that it is impossible for manager-run cities to produce leadership of that sort. Several of the more highly respected mayors this country has produced in recent years gained their stature precisely because they were able to implement their visions in communities with appointed managers— among them Henry Cisneros of San Antonio, Pete Wilson of San Diego and, among current mayors, Emanuel Cleaver II of Kansas City, Missouri.

Nor, for that matter, do strong-mayor cities produce winners all the time. "Strong political leadership is a very rare commodity," says Bob Kipp, a former city manager of Kansas City. "It doesn't correlate with one structure or another: It's just difficult to find these little diamonds in the rough who turn out to be effective and courageous political leaders. People say you don't find many strong elective mayors in council-manager cities; the fact is, you don't find many of them anywhere."

That is probably so. Which makes it all the more sobering that in these days of shrinking municipal budgets, economic uncertainty and social decay, mustering the civic will to make gut-wrenching choices requires the deft touch of talented politicians. The most important challenge isn't to write charters for them; it is to nurture them in the first place.

The New Judicial Federalism:

The States' Lead in Rights Protection

A lot of attention is given to the rights afforded American citizens by the Bill of Rights amendments to the U.S. Constitution. But state constitutions are equally important, often expanding upon federal protection. Many times, state courts have interpreted state constitutional guarantees liberally. This trend, sometimes referred to as the new judicial federalism, can serve as an example to developing democracies as a means of protecting and supporting their ethnic diversity.

John Kincaid and Robert F. Williams

John Kincaid is executive director of the U.S. Advisory Commission on Intergovernmental Relations, Washington, D.C. Robert F. Williams is professor of law at Rutgers University, Camden, N.J.

Claus von Bulow, whose trial was popularized in the film *Reversal of Fortune*, might not be a free man today but for the protection afforded individual rights in Rhode Island's Constitution.

Incriminating evidence in his wife's death was thrown out by the state court under the state's exclusionary rule. That decision hinged on the state high court's interpretation of search-and-seizure provisions in Rhode Island's constitution. The U.S. Supreme Court later declined to review the state ruling because the decision was based on independent and adequate state grounds.

Rhode Island is not alone in going farther than the U.S. Supreme Court in protecting individual rights. The emergence since 1970 of many state high courts as assertive protectors of individual rights comes as a surprise to many people. The fact that state courts are expanding protections beyond those guaranteed by the Bill of Rights is even more surprising. This development, called the new judicial federalism, defies traditional theories of American federalism, which saw the states being eclipsed by the federal government in every field.

The new judicial federalism generally refers to the authority of a state court to interpret its state constitution so as to provide broader rights protections than those recognized by U.S. Supreme Court interpretations of the federal Constitution.

As in the von Bulow case, such state decisions are immune from Supreme Court review when they are based on "independent and adequate" state constitutional grounds.

In a 1970 decision, for instance, the Alaska Supreme Court wrote:

> While we must enforce the minimum constitutional standards imposed upon us by the United States Supreme Court's interpretation of the Fourteenth Amendment, we are free, and we are under a duty, to develop additional constitutional rights and privileges under our Alaska Constitution. . . . We need not stand by idly and passively, waiting for constitutional direction from the highest court of the land.

The Power of Interpretation

It is one thing for the Supreme Court to hold that people have certain rights under the federal Constitution. It is quite another for the Court to hold that people do not have certain rights. Because both kinds of decisions come from the "highest court in the land," we tend to believe that both should have the same force in every court, police precinct and state and local office throughout the land. But, just because a government action is not prohibited by the federal Constitution does not mean that it is automatically permitted under a state's constitution. A state constitution is the supreme law of a state, so long as it does not contradict the U.S. Constitution.

The new judicial federalism allows state courts and legislatures to set rights standards that are higher, but not lower, than those established under the U.S. Constitution. States also may recognize rights such as privacy and victims' rights that are not even found, at least not explicitly, in the U.S. Constitution. As such, the new judicial federalism conforms to an old principle of American federalism: that states may act where the U.S. government has elected not to act, so long as state action does not violate the U.S. Constitution or federal law.

Actually, the new judicial federalism is no longer new. Since 1970, state courts have rendered at least 700 decisions providing broader rights than those recognized by the U.S. Supreme Court or new rights not found in the Bill of Rights. Partly in response to this development, the U.S. Advisory Commission on Intergovernmental Relations in 1988 issued *State Constitutional Law: Cases and Materials*, the first textbook of its type ever published.

Examples of new rights protections can be found in Florida whose constitution contains a privacy provision approved by voters in 1980. It reads: "Every natural person has the right to be let alone and free from governmental intrusion into his private life except as otherwise provided herein." Under this rule, the Florida Supreme Court struck down a state law that required minors to obtain parental consent before ending a pregnancy, and it voided a municipal ordinance prohibiting people from sleeping in their automobiles. The Florida court also used the provision to uphold a 1990 law that broadened the "right to die" for citizens of the state.

State vs. Federal

However, most state court decisions under the new judicial federalism involve interpretations of state constitutional provisions that are very similar or identical to provisions in the U.S. Bill of Rights. A state court may interpret its state provision more broadly than the U.S. Supreme Court interprets the companion federal provision. Thus, state courts can choose to follow federal precedent or take a higher road and expand rights protections.

For example, in 1988 the U.S. Supreme Court ruled in *California vs. Greenwood* that police do not need a warrant to search trash put out for collection. In 1990, however, the New Jersey and Washington high courts ruled that their state constitutions do require police to obtain a warrant to search curbside trash. If no warrant is obtained, then evidence gleaned from the search will not be admitted in state court.

However, federal agents operating under U.S. rules need not obtain warrants to search curbside trash in New Jersey and Washington. This revival of dual federalism in the judicial arena raises interesting intergovernmental issues. For example, will federal agents deliver evidence gathered without warrants to state police? Probably. Will such evidence be admitted in state courts? Possibly.

The New Jersey Supreme Court recently held in split decisions that such evidence can be admitted in state court so long as there was no active cooperation "between the officers of the two sovereigns." Thus, after decades of cooperative federalism, during which great emphasis was placed on getting states to cooperate with federal rights laws and rulings, state courts now are talking about "uncooperative federalism," and about the need to protect their citizens' rights against federal action. This development could disturb intergovernmental cooperation in law enforcement.

State constitutions offer opportunities to entrench rights for which there is no national consensus.

Another question is whether states can nullify federal action. If states can set rights standards that are stricter than federal standards, can they apply those standards to federal agents within their borders — despite the supremacy clause of the U.S. Constitution? If states cannot abridge rights protected by the U.S. Constitution, can the federal government come into a state and abridge rights protected by the state constitution? Must the federal government explicitly preempt a state rights protection in order to immunize itself from state nullification?

These kinds of questions were raised by Thomas Jefferson and James Madison against the Alien and Sedition Acts passed by Congress in 1798. Their Virginia and Kentucky Resolutions triggered a debate over state nullification and interposition thought to have been settled by the Civil War.

Until recently, the new judicial federalism generally was viewed as a liberal movement. Indeed, former Justice William J. Brennan Jr. helped spur the movement in a now famous *Harvard Law Review* article in 1977. Critics charge that the new judicial federalism is little more than a reflex liberal reaction to the conservative Burger and Rehnquist Courts. The activism of the Warren Court years (1954-69) is being kept alive by numerous "little Warren courts" in the states.

But conservatives have also had victories in state courts. In 1991, the Pennsylvania Supreme Court produced a conservative ruling based on a liberal reading of the "takings" clause in Pennsylvania's Constitution. The court struck down Philadelphia's historic preservation ordinance on the ground that its application in this case constituted a "taking" of the owner's property without just compensation. The decision sent shock waves through the historic preservation and environmental protection communities because of its constraining implications for government regulation of private property. The decision is being reconsidered, though, because several concurring justices believe the court went overboard.

The U.S. Supreme Court has upheld other preservation and environmental laws against challenges under the "takings" clause of the Fifth Amendment to the U.S. Constitution. However, the court is hearing several new "takings" cases this term.

Looking Ahead

The future of the new judicial federalism is hard to predict. If the U.S. Supreme Court resumes an activist rights role, it may again move ahead of state courts. Also, given that most state high court justices must face the voters periodically, activist justices may be unseated by a disgruntled electorate. In addition, state constitutions can be amended more easily than the U.S. Constitution. In 1982, for instance, Florida voters nailed their supreme court to the federal rights floor by approving a constitutional amendment requiring the court to adhere to the U.S. Supreme Court's view of the exclusionary rule under the Fourth Amendment. By 1982, the Court had narrowed its view of the Fourth Amendment compared to the view of the Warren Court. Thus far, however, voters have expanded rights as much as they have restricted them through state constitutional amendments.

Finally, the new judicial federalism revives some basic questions about rights. If rights are universal, should they not apply equally everywhere? If not, what rights are universal, and what rights can vary among states? Just as women once crossed state lines to obtain abortions, will ambulances carry people across borders to states with more liberal right-to-die laws? Will some ambulances go in the opposite direction, carrying patients away from relatives eager to "pull the plug" under liberal state rules?

Although universal rights may seem to be the natural order, independent state constitutions offer opportunities to entrench certain rights, at least in some places, when the nation or its highest court cannot agree on applying these rights. We have already seen signs of this with regard to privacy, victims' rights, women's rights and environmental rights provisions in some state constitutions. In this way, states can also serve as laboratories for rights experimentation.

The new judicial federalism may have implications for emerging democracies worldwide, as well. Often, ethnic, religious and linguistic hostilities preclude consensus on common rights. However, entrenching even a few common rights in the national constitution is a step in the right direction that can foster the trust needed to break down barriers to the recognition of more universal rights.

View From the Bench: A Judge's Day

Judge Lois G. Forer

Lois G. Forer is a former judge in the Philadelphia Court of Common Pleas.

At 9:30 the court personnel begin to assemble. The crier opens court. "All rise. Oyez, oyez, all persons having business before the Court of Common Pleas Criminal Division come forth and they shall be heard. God save this honorable court. Be seated and stop all conversation. Good morning, Your Honor." The crier calls out the names of the defendants. Most of them are represented by the public defender. He checks his files. One or two names are not on his list. A quick phone call is made to his office to send up the missing files.

On one particular day when I was sitting in criminal motions court, three cases had private counsel. One had been retained by the defendant. The other two had been appointed by the court to represent indigents accused of homicide. Where are these lawyers?

As is customary, the court officer phones each of them and reminds his secretary that he has a case listed and he must appear. Several of the defendants are not present. The prison is called to locate the missing parties. The judge, if he wishes to get through his list, must find the lawyers and litigants and order them to come to court.

Frequently the prosecutor cannot find his files. When he does, he discovers that a necessary witness has not been subpoenaed. The case must be continued to another day. The other witnesses, who are present and have missed a day's work, are sent home. The defendant is returned to jail to await another listing. Often cases are listed five and six times before they can be heard.

On this day there were three extra-ditions. Amos R. is wanted in South Carolina. Seven years ago he had escaped from jail and fled north. Since then he has been living in Philadelphia. He married here and now has two children. His wife and children are in the courtroom. He is employed. Amos has not been in trouble since leaving South Carolina, where 10 years ago he was convicted of stealing a car and sentenced to nine to 20 years in prison. He had no prior record. In Pennsylvania, for the same crime, he would probably have been placed on probation or at most received a maximum sentence of two years.

Now he testifies that he didn't steal the car, he only borrowed it. Moreover, he didn't have a lawyer. When he pleaded guilty he was told he would get six months. This is probably true. Also, he was undoubtedly indicted by a grand jury from which Negroes were systematically excluded. All of these allegations would be grounds for release in a postconviction hearing, for they are serious violations of constitutional rights. But they are irrelevant in extradition hearings. The only issues that the judge may consider before ordering this man to leave his family and shipping him off to serve 18 more years in prison are whether he is in fact the Amos R. named in the warrant and whether the papers are in order. There is little judicial discretion. One is often impelled by the system to be an instrument of injustice.

This is the dilemma of a judge and of many officials in the legal system. Following the rule of law may result in hardship and essential unfairness. Ignoring the law is a violation of one's oath of office, an illegal act, and a destruction of the system. Some choose to ignore the law in the interests of "justice." Others mechanically follow precedent. Neither course is satisfactory. The judge who frees a defendant knows that in most instances the state cannot appeal. Unless there is an election in the offing and the prosecutor chooses to use this case as a political issue, there will be no repercussions. But it is his duty, as it is that of the accused, to obey the law. If the judge is not restrained by the law, who will be? On the other hand, it is unrealistic to say, "Let the defendant appeal." In the long period between the trial judge's ruling and that of the higher court, if it hears the appeal, a human being will be in jail. One does not easily deprive a person of his liberty without very compelling reasons. Almost every day, the guardians of the law are torn between these conflicting pulls.

After hearing the life story of Amos R., as reported by the prosecutor, the young defender said, "Mr. R. wishes to waive a hearing."

I looked at the lawyer. "Mr. R., do you know that you have a right to a hearing?"

"Yes."

"Have you consulted with your attorney about waiving a hearing?"

"My attorney?" R. looks bewildered.

"Your lawyer, the defender," I pointed to the young man.

"Oh, him," R. replies. "Yes, I talked to him."

"How long?"

" 'Bout two minutes."

"Your Honor," says the defender, "I have spoken to the sheriff. There is no question that this is the Amos R. wanted. The papers are in order."

I search through the official-looking sheaf of documents with gold seals and red seals and the signatures of two governors, hoping to find a defect, a critical omission. At last I discover that Amos R. was arrested in New Jersey on a Friday night. He was not taken to Pennsylvania until the following Monday. It is 89 days that he has been in jail in Pennsylvania. The extradition hearing must by statute be held within 90 days of arrest. By adding on the three days he was in custody in New Jersey, I

First published in *The Washington Monthly,* February 1975. Adapted from *The Death of the Law* by Judge Lois G. Forer. © 1975 by Judge Lois G. Forer. Reprinted by permission of Curtis Brown Literary Agency, Ltd.

conclude that the 90-day time limit has not been met. Amos R. is once again a free man. This happy ending is unusual. Bureaucratic inefficiencies seldom redound to the benefit of the individual.

Prisoners of Bureaucracy

The next four matters are bail applications. All the defendants fit the stereotype. They are black males under the age of 30. Only one is in the courtroom. The others are in the detention center. It is too much trouble and too expensive to transport them to court for a bail hearing. I must decide whether to set free or keep locked up men whom I cannot see or talk to. If I don't release them, they may be in jail for as long as a year awaiting trial. The law presumes that they are innocent. I look at the applications. This is not the first arrest for any of them. For one there are records going back to age nine, when he was incarcerated for truancy.

"The defendant's juvenile record may not be used against him in adult court," I remind the prosecuting attorney.

"I know, Your Honor," he replies apologetically, "but the computer prints out all the arrests."

"How many convictions?"

The computer does not give the answer to that question.

One man is accused of rape. The record shows that his prior offenses were larceny of an automobile and, as a child, running away from home. The police report indicates that when the police arrived the defendant was in the complainant's apartment with his clothes off. He left so quickly that he abandoned his shoes and socks. The complainant admitted knowing him and gave his name and address to the police. No weapon was involved.

My usual rule of thumb is a simple one: "If he had time to take off his shoes, it wasn't rape."

Before releasing an alleged rapist from jail, possibly to prey on other victims, I want to speak with the accused. Although Lombroso's theory that one can tell a criminal by his physical appearance is out of fashion, I still want to see him, but he is not in the courtroom. Perhaps his lawyer, the defender, can give some helpful information. The defender, however, has never seen the accused. Someone else interviewed him on a routine prison visit. No one knows whether he has a family, a job, a home.

"Please have this defendant brought to court tomorrow and get me some information on him," I tell the defender.

He replies, "I'm sorry, Your Honor. I'll be working in a different courtroom tomorrow. There is no way I can find out about this man."

"We're dealing with human beings, not pieces of paper," I expostulate. "You are his lawyer. You should know him."

The young defender sadly shakes his head. "Your Honor, I work for a bureaucracy."

So do I, I remind myself, as I look at the clock and see that it is past 11:00 and there are 14 more matters to be heard today.

Four Up, Four Down

I refuse bail for a 14-year-old accused of slaying another child in a gang rumble. Will he be safer in jail than on the street, where the rival gang is lying in wait for him? I do not know. The boy is small and slender. The warden will put him in the wing with the feminine homosexuals to save him from assault. I mark on the commitment sheet that the boy is to attend school while in prison awaiting trial. But if the warden does not honor my order, I will not know.

A 23-year-old heroin addict tells me that there is no drug treatment program in prison. "It's just like the street. Nothin' but drugs," he says. I try to move his case ahead so that he can plead guilty at an early date and be transferred to the federal drug treatment center. He, like so many others up for robbery and burglary, is a Vietnam veteran. He acquired his habit overseas and now must steal in order to pay for his daily fix.

The next matter is a petition to suppress a confession. Court appointed counsel alleges that the defendant did not make a knowing and intelligent waiver of his rights when he confessed three murders to the police. Cornelius takes the stand and describes his life. His history is typical. He was sent to a disciplinary school at 11, ran away at 12, and spent a year in juvenile jail. At 17, there was a conviction for larceny and another period of incarceration. He is married, two children, separated from his wife. He is vague about the ages of the children. Cornelius works as an orderly in a hospital earning $80 a week take-home pay. At the end of each week he divides his money in two parts: $40 for living expenses and $40 for methadrine, which costs $20 a spoon.

Where does he buy it? On any corner in the ghetto. He steals the syringes from the hospital. His expenses are minimal except for the precious methadrine. He is riddled with V.D. He seldom eats.

While on a high, he shot and killed three strangers. Why did he do it?

"There are these voices I hear. They're fightin'. One tells me to kill; the other tells me not to. Sometimes I get so scared I run out into the street. That's when I'm in a low. But when I'm in a high, I feel I can walk in the rain without getting wet. I don't feel sad, I ain't lonely. When I'm comin' down from a high, I got to get another shot."

Now he is in a low—sad, soft-spoken, withdrawn, disinterested in his own fate. I see his skinny brown arms pocked with little needle scars. The psychiatrist says that when Cornelius is on drugs he cannot gauge reality. He could not understand the meaning of the privilege against self-incrimination and make a knowing and intelligent waiver of his rights.

The earnest psychiatrist explains patiently. I watch Cornelius, wraith-thin, sitting in withdrawn disinterest, lost in some dream of flight. Is he mad or are we—the prosecutor, the defense lawyer, the psychiatrist, and the judge? After five hours of testimony, I rule that the confession must be suppressed. There are dozens of eye-witnesses. The confession is not necessary to convict Cornelius. After this hearing, and before trial, a psychiatrist for the defense will testify that Cornelius is not mentally competent to stand trial; he cannot cooperate with his lawyer in preparing his defense. A psychiatrist for the prosecution will testify that when Cornelius has withdrawn from drugs he will be able to participate intelligently in his defense. The motion to defer trial will probably be denied. At the trial itself, one psychiatrist will testify that at the time of the shootings Cornelius did not know the difference between right and wrong and the nature and quality of his act. Another will testify that he did. Neither psychiatrist saw Cornelius at the time of the crimes. Both of them examined him in prison months later. They are certain of their opinions.

A middle-aged, white, epicenely soft man is next on the list. His face is a pasty gray. He mutters under his breath. He is accused of committing sodomy on three teenaged boys. Most of his meager salary he spent on these boys, and now they have turned on him. I order a psychiatric examination simply because I don't know what else to do. A month later the report is sent to me. It follows a standard format: facts (gleaned from the accused), background, diagnostic formulation and summary, and recommendation. This report states: "Probable latent schizophrenia. We recommend a full examination 60-day commitment." At the end of 60 days and the expenditure of hundreds of dollars, the doctors will decide that he is or is not schizophrenic, possibly sociopathic. A long period in a "structured environment" will be recommended. But what will the judge do? There are only two choices: prison, where he will be tormented and perhaps beaten by strong young thugs, or the street.

Lost in the Jailhouse

Most of the prisoners brought before me are young—under 30. I also see children who are charged with homicide. They are denied even the nominal protections of the juvenile court and are "processed" as adults. The 14-year-old accused of slaying another child in a gang rumble; the 16-year-old dope addict who, surprised while burglarizing a house, panicked and shot the unwary owner; the girl lookout for the gang, who is accused of conspiracy and murder. Many of these children are themselves parents. Can they be turned back to the streets? I refuse bail for an illiterate 15-year-old accused of murder and note on the bill of indictment that he be required to attend school while in detention. I ask the court-appointed lawyer to check with the warden and see that the boy is sent to class. But is there a class in remedial reading at the detention center? Who would pay for it? Not the overburdened public schools or the understaffed prisons. It is not a project likely to find a foundation grant.

A perplexed lawyer petitions for a second psychiatric examination for his client. The court psychiatrist has found him competent to stand trial but the lawyer tells me his client cannot discuss the case with him. Randolph, who is accused of assault with intent to kill, attacked a stranger in a bar and strangled the man, almost killing him. Fortunately, bystanders dragged Randolph away. I ask to speak with Randolph. A big, neatly dressed Negro steps up to the bar of the court. He speaks softly, "Judge," he says, "I'm afraid. I need help."

Randolph is out on bail. This is his first offense. He has a good work record. He is married, has two children, and lives with his family. It is Friday morning. I fear what may happen to him over the weekend. The court psychiatric unit is called.

"We've got people backed up for a

month," the doctor tells me. "Even if I took Randolph out of turn I couldn't see him until next week." When he does see Randolph it will be a 45-minute examination. A voluntary hospital commitment seems to be the only safeguard. But at least he will be watched for ten days. Gratefully, Randolph promises to go at once to the mental health clinic. What will happen to him after the ten-day period?

There is no time to wonder. The next case is waiting.

It is a sultry day. When the ancient air conditioner is turned on we cannot hear the testimony. When it is turned off the room is unbearable. At 4:45 p. m., I ask hopefully, "Have we finished the list?" But no, there is an application for a continuance on an extradition warrant. The papers from the demanding state have not arrived. It is a routine, daily occurrence.

I look around the courtroom. By this hour only the court personnel and a few policemen and detectives are present. "Where is the defendant?" I inquire. The prosecutor does not know. He is not responsible for producing him. The defender does not have him on his list. "Is he in custody?" I ask. We all search the records and discover that he was arrested more than five months ago. There is no notation that bail has ever been set. No private counsel has entered an appearance. A deputy sheriff checks and reports that he has not been brought up from the prison. The computerized records show that this man has never had a hearing. Hardened as we are, the prosecutor, the defender and I are horrified that someone should be sitting in jail all this time without ever having had an opportunity to say a word. Is he, in fact, the person wanted for an offense allegedly committed years ago and hundreds of miles away? Was he ever there? Is he a stable member of society? Has he a family, a job, a home? Is he a drug addict? No one knows. The papers do not indicate. No one in the courtroom has ever seen him. Each of us makes a note to check on this forgotten prisoner whom the computer may or may not print out for appearance on some other day in some other courtroom.

Nobody Waived Good-bye

The scene in criminal trial court is similar. Most of the cases are "waivers" and guilty pleas. The accused may waive his constitutional right to be tried by a jury of his peers and be tried by a judge alone. Fewer than five per cent of all cases are tried

by jury. In most cases, the accused not only waives his right to a jury trial but also to any trial and pleads guilty. Before accepting a waiver or a plea, the accused is asked the routine questions. Day after day defense counsel recites the following formula to poor, semiliterate defendants, some of whom are old and infirm, others young and innocent. Read this quickly:

"Do you know that you are accused of [the statutory crimes are read to him from the indictment]?

"Do you know that you have a right to a trial by jury in which the state must prove by evidence beyond a reasonable doubt that you committed the offenses and that if one juror disagrees you will not be found guilty?

"Do you know that by pleading guilty you are giving up your right to appeal the decision of this court except for an appeal based on the jurisdiction of the court, the legality of the sentence and the voluntariness of your plea of guilty? [The accused is not told that by the asking and answering of these questions in open court he has for all practical purposes also given up this ground for appeal.]

"Do you know that the judge is not bound by the recommendation of the District Attorney as to sentence but can sentence you up to –– years and impose a fine of ––– dollars? [The aggregate penalty is read to him. Judges may and often do give a heavier penalty than was recommended. They rarely give a lighter sentence.]

"Can you read and write the English language?

"Have you ever been in a mental hospital or under the care of a psychiatrist for a mental illness?

"Are you now under the influence of alcohol, drugs, or undergoing withdrawal symptoms?

"Have you been threatened, coerced, or promised anything for entering the plea of guilty other than the recommendation of sentence by the District Attorney?

"Are you satisfied with my representation?"

All this is asked quickly, routinely, as the prisoner stands before the bar of the court. He answers "Yes" to each question.

The final question is: "Are you pleading guilty because you are guilty?" The defendant looks at the defender, uncertainly.

"Have you consulted with your lawyer?" I inquire.

"Right now. 'Bout five minutes."

"We'll pass this case until afternoon. At the lunch recess, will you please confer with your client," I direct the defender.

In the afternoon, the accused, having talked with the lawyer for another ten minutes, again waives his right to a trial. He has been in jail more than eight months. The eight months in jail are applied to his sentence. He will be out by the end of the year—sooner than if he demanded a trial and was acquitted.

The plea has been negotiated by the assistant defender and the assistant prosecutor. The defendant says he was not promised anything other than a recommendation of sentence in return for the guilty plea. But the judge does not know what else the defendant has been told, whether his family and friends are willing to come and testify for him, whether his counsel has investigated the facts of the case to see whether indeed he does have a defense. The magic formula has been pronounced. The judge does not know what the facts are. Did the man really commit the offense? Even if there were a full-scale trial, truth might not emerge. Many of the witnesses have long since disappeared. How reliable will their memories be? The policeman will say he did not strike the accused. The accused will say that he did. Friends and relatives will say that the accused was with them at the time of the alleged crime. The victim, if he appears, will swear that this is the person whom he saw once briefly on a dark night eight months ago.

The lawyers are in almost equal ignorance. The prosecutor has the police report. The defender has only the vague and confused story of the accused. The judge is under pressure to "dispose" of the case. There is a score card for each judge kept by the computer. The judges have batting averages. Woe betide those who fail to keep pace in getting rid of cases. A long trial to determine guilt or innocence will put the judge at the bottom of the list. The prosecutors and public defenders also have their score cards of cases disposed of. Private defense counsel—whether paid by the accused or appointed by the court and paid by the public—has his own type of score card. For the fee paid, he can give only so many hours to the preparation and trial of this case. He must pay his rent, secretary and overhead. All of the persons involved in the justice system are bound by the iron laws of economics. What can the defendant afford for bail, counsel fees, witness fees, investigative expenses? All of these questions will inexorably determine the case that is presented to the court.

The National Conference on Criminal Justice, convened in January 1973 by Attorney General Kleindienst, recommends that plea bargaining be abolished within five years. What will replace it?

At the end of a day in which as a judge I have taken actions affecting for good or ill the lives of perhaps 15 or 20 litigants and their families, I am drained. I walk out of the stale-smelling, dusty courtroom into the fresh sunshine of a late spring day and feel as if I were released from prison. I breathe the soft air, but in my nostrils is the stench of the stifling cell blocks and detention rooms. While I sip my cool drink in the quiet of my garden, I cannot forget the prisoners, with their dry bologna sandwiches and only a drink of water provided at the pleasure of the hot and harried guards.

Was Cottle really guilty? I will never know. Fred made bail. Will he attack someone tonight or tomorrow? One reads the morning paper with apprehension. It is safer for the judge to keep them all locked up. There will be an outcry over the one prisoner released who commits a subsequent offense. Who will know or care about the scores of possibly innocent prisoners held in jail?

This is only one day in a diary. Replicate this by 260 times a year, at least 15,000 courts, and 10 or 20 or 30 years in the past. Can one doubt that the operation of the legal system is slowly but surely strangling the law?

I must sit only three and a half more weeks in criminal court. But there is a holiday. So with relief I realize that it is really only 17 more days that I must sit there this term. Next year I shall again have to take my turn.

I am reminded of Ivan Denisovich. Solzhenitsyn describes Ivan's bedtime thoughts in a Soviet prison. "Ivan Denisovich went to sleep content. He had been fortunate in many ways that day—and he hadn't fallen ill. He'd got over it. There were 3,653 days like this in his sentence. From the moment he woke to the moment he slept. The three extra days were for leap years."

WATCHING THE BENCH

Justice by Numbers

Mandatory sentencing drove me from the bench

Lois G. Forer

Lois G. Forer, a former judge of the Court of Common Pleas of Philadelphia, is the author, most recently, of Unequal Protection: Women, Children, and the Elderly in Court.

Michael S. would have been one of the more than 600,000 incarcerated persons in the United States. He would have been a statistic, yet another addition to a clogged criminal justice system. But he's not—in part because to me Michael was a human being: a slight 24-year-old with a young wife and small daughter. Not that I freed him; I tried him and found him guilty. He is free now only because he is a fugitive. I have not seen him since the day of his sentencing in 1984, yet since that day our lives have been inextricably connected. Because of his case I retired from the bench.

Michael's case appeared routine. He was a typical offender: young, black, and male, a high-school dropout without a job. The charge was an insignificant holdup that occasioned no comment in the press. And the trial itself was, in the busy life of a judge, a run-of-the-mill event.

The year before, Michael, brandishing a toy gun, held up a taxi and took $50 from the driver and the passenger, harming neither. This was Michael's first offense. Although he had dropped out of school to marry his pregnant girlfriend, Michael later obtained a high school equivalency diploma. He had been stead-ily employed, earning enough to send his daughter to parochial school—a considerable sacrifice for him and his wife. Shortly before the holdup, Michael had lost his job. Despondent because he could not support his family, he went out on a Saturday night, had more than a few drinks, and then robbed the taxi.

There was no doubt that Michael was guilty. But the penalty posed problems. To me, a robbery in a taxi is not an intrinsically graver offense than a robbery in an alley, but to the Pennsylvania legislature, it is. Because the holdup occurred on public transportation, it fell within the ambit of the state's mandatory sentencing law—which required a minimum sentence of five years in the state penitentiary. In Pennsylvania, a prosecutor may decide not to demand imposition of that law, but Michael's prosecuting attorney wanted the five-year sentence.

One might argue that a five-year sentence for a $50 robbery is excessive or even immoral, but to a judge, those arguments are necessarily irrelevant. He or she has agreed to enforce the law, no matter how ill-advised, unless the law is unconstitutional.

I believed the mandatory sentencing law was, and like many of my colleagues I had held it unconstitutional in several other cases for several reasons. We agreed that it violates the constitutional principle of separation of powers because it can be invoked by the prosecutor, and not by the judge. In addition, the act is arbitrary and capricious in its application. Robbery, which is often a simple purse snatching, is covered, but not child molestation or incest, two of society's most damaging offenses. Nor can a defendant's previous record or mental state be considered. A hardened repeat offender receives the same sentence as a retarded man who steals out of hunger. Those facts violate the fundamental Anglo-American legal principles of individualized sentencing and proportionality of the penalty to the crime.

Thus in Michael's case, I again held the statute to be unconstitutional and turned to the sentencing guidelines—a state statute designed to give uniform sentences to offenders who commit similar crimes. The minimum sentence prescribed by the guidelines was 24 months.

A judge can deviate from the prescribed sentence if he or she writes an opinion explaining the reasons for the deviation. While this sounds reasonable in theory, "downwardly departing" from the guidelines is extremely difficult. The mitigating circumstances that influence most judges are not included in the limited list of factors on which "presumptive" sentence is based—that an offender is a caretaker of small children; that the offender is mentally retarded; or that the offender, like Michael, is emotionally distraught.

So I decided to deviate from the guidelines, sentencing Michael to 11-and-a-half months in the county jail and permitting him to work outside the prison during the day to support his family. I also imposed a sentence of two years' probation following his imprisonment conditioned upon repayment of the $50. My rationale for the lesser penalty, outlined in my lengthy opinion, was that this was a first offense, no one was harmed, Michael acted under the pressures of unemployment and need, and he seemed truly contrite. He had never committed a violent act and posed no danger to the public. A sentence of close to a year seemed adequate to convince Michael of the seriousness of his crime. Nevertheless, the prosecutor appealed.

Michael returned to his family, obtained steady employment, and repaid the victims of his crime. I thought no more about Michael until 1986, when the state supreme court upheld the appeal and ordered me to resentence him to a minimum of five years in the state penitentiary. By this time Michael had successfully completed his term of imprisonment and probation, including payment of restitution. I checked Michael's record. He had not been rearrested.

I was faced with a legal and moral dilemma. As a judge I had sworn to uphold the law, and I could find no legal grounds for violating an order of the supreme court. Yet five years' imprisonment was grossly disproportionate to the offense. The usual grounds for imprisonment are retribution, deterrence, and rehabilitation. Michael had paid his retribution by a short term of imprisonment and by making restitution to the victims. He had been effectively deterred from committing future crimes. And by any measurable standard he had been rehabilitated. There was no social or criminological justification for sending him back to prison. Given the choice between defying a court order or my conscience, I decided to leave the bench where I had sat for 16 years.

That didn't help Michael, of course; he was resentenced by another judge to serve the balance of the five years: four years and 15 days. Faced with this prospect, he disappeared. A bench warrant was issued, but given the hundreds of fugitives—including dangerous ones—loose in Philadelphia, I doubt that anyone is seriously looking for him.

But any day he may be stopped for a routine traffic violation; he may apply for a job or a license; he may even be the victim of a crime—and if so, the ubiquitous computer will be alerted and he will be returned to prison to serve the balance of his sentence, plus additional time for being a fugitive. It is not a happy prospect for him and his family—nor for America, which is saddled with a punishment system that operates like a computer—crime in, points tallied, sentence out—utterly disregarding the differences among the human beings involved.

The mandatory sentencing laws and guidelines that exist today in every state were designed to smooth out the inequities in the American judiciary, and were couched in terms of fairness to criminals—they would stop the racist judge from sentencing black robbers to be hanged, or the crusading judge from imprisoning pot smokers for life. Guidelines make sense, for that very reason. But they have had an ugly and unintended result—an increase in the number of American prisoners and an increase in the length of the sentences they serve. Meanwhile, the laws have effectively neutralized judges who prefer sentencing the nonviolent to alternative programs or attempt to keep mothers with young children out of jail.

Have the laws made justice fairer—the central objective of the law? I say no, and a recent report by the Federal Sentencing Commission concurs. It found that, even under mandatory sentencing laws, black males served 83.4 months to white males' 53.7 months for the same offenses. (Prosecutors are more likely to demand imposition of the mandatory laws for blacks than for whites.)

Most important, however, as mandatory sentencing packs our prisons and busts our budgets, it doesn't prevent crime very effectively. For certain kinds of criminals, alternative sentencing is the most effective type of punishment. That, by the way, is a cold, hard statistic—rather like Michael will be when they find him.

Sentenced to death

In the past two decades, all 50 state legislatures have enacted mandatory sentencing laws, sentencing guideline statutes, or both. The result: In 1975 there were 263,291 inmates in federal and state prisons. Today there are over 600,000—more than in any other nation—the bill for which comes to $20.3 billion a year. Yet incarceration has not reduced the crime rate or made our streets and communities safer. The number of known crimes committed in the U.S. has increased 10 percent in the last five years.

How did we get into this no-win situation? Like most legislative reforms, it started with good intentions. In 1970, after the turmoil of the sixties, legislators were bombarded with pleas for "law and order." A young, eager, newly appointed federal judge, Marvin Frankel, had an idea.

Before his appointment, Frankel had experienced little personal contact with the criminal justice system. Yet his slim book, *Fair and Certain Punishment*, offered a system of guidelines to determine the length of various sentences. Each crime was given a certain number of points. The offender was also given a number of points depending upon his or her prior record, use of a weapon, and a few other variables. The judge merely needed to add up the points to calculate the length of imprisonment.

The book was widely read and lauded for two main reasons. First, it got tough on criminals and made justice "certain." A potential offender would know in advance the penalty he would face and thus be deterred. (Of course, a large proportion of street crimes are not premeditated, but that fact was ignored.) And second, it got tough on the "bleeding heart" judges. All offenders similarly situated would be treated the same.

The plan sounded so fair and politically promising that many states rushed to implement it in the seventies. In Pennsylvania, members of the legislature admonished judges not to oppose the guidelines because the alternative would be even worse: mandatory sentences. In fact, within a few years almost every jurisdiction had both sentencing guidelines and mandatory sentencing laws. Since then, Congress has enacted some 60 mandatory sentencing laws on the federal level.

As for unfairnesses in sentencing—for instance, the fact that the robber with his finger in his jacket gets the same sentence as the guy with a semiautomatic—these could have been rectified by giving appellate courts jurisdiction to review sentences, as is the law in Canada. This was not done on either the state or federal level. Thus what influential criminologist James Q. Wilson had argued during the height of the battle had become the law of the land: The legal system should "most definitely stop pretending that the judges know any better than the rest of us how to provide 'individualized justice.' "

Hardening time

I'm not sure I knew better than the rest of you, but I knew a few things about Michael and the correctional system I would be throwing him into. At the time of Michael's sentencing, both the city of Philadelphia and the commonwealth of Pennsylvania were, like many cities and states, in such poor fiscal shape that they did not have money for schools and health care, let alone new prisons, and the ones they did have were overflowing. The city was under a federal order to reduce the prison population; untried persons accused of dangerous crimes were being released, as were offenders who had not completed their sentences.

As for Michael, his problems and those of his family were very real to me. Unlike appellate judges who never see the individuals whose lives and property they dispose of, a trial judge sees living men and women. I had seen Michael and his wife and daughter. I had heard him express remorse. I had favorable reports about him from the prison and his parole officer. Moreover, Michael, like many offenders who appeared before me, had written to me several times. I felt I knew him.

Of course, I could have been wrong. As Wilson says, judges are not infallible—and most of them know that. But they have heard the evidence, seen the offender, and been furnished with presentence reports and psychiatric evaluations. They are in a better position to evaluate the individual and devise an appropriate sentence than anyone else in the criminal justice system.

Yet under mandatory sentencing laws, the complexities of each crime and criminal are ignored. And seldom do we ask what was once a legitimate question in criminal justice: What are the benefits of incarceration? The offenders are off the streets for the period of the sentence, but once released, most will soon be rearrested. (Many crimes are committed in prison, including murder, rape, robbery, and drug dealing.) They have not been "incapacitated," another of the theoretical justifications for imprisonment. More likely, they have simply been hardened.

Sentence structure

Is there another way to sentence criminals without endangering the public? I believe there is. During my tenure on the bench, I treated imprisonment as the penalty of last resort, not the penalty of choice. And my examination of 16 years' worth of cases suggests my inclination was well founded. While a recent Justice Department study found that two thirds of all prisoners are arrested for other offenses within three years of release, more than two thirds of the 1,000-plus offenders I sentenced to probation conditioned upon payment of reparations to victims successfully completed their sentences and were not rearrested. I am not a statistician, so I had my records analyzed and verified by Elmer Weitekamp, then a doctoral candidate in criminology at the Wharton School of the University of Pennsylvania. He confirmed my findings.

The offenders who appeared before me were mostly poor people, poor enough to qualify for representation by a public defender. I did not see any Ivan Boeskys or Leona Helmsleys, and although there was a powerful mafia in Philadelphia, I did not see any dons, either. Approximately three fourths of these defendants were nonwhite. Almost 80 percent were high school dropouts. Many were functionally illiterate. Almost a third had some history of mental problems, were retarded, or had been in special schools. One dreary day my court reporter said plaintively, "Judge, why can't we get a better class of criminal?"

Not all of these offenders were sentenced to probation, obviously. But I had my own criteria or guidelines—very different from those established by most states and the federal government—for deciding on a punishment. My primary concern was public safety. The most important question I asked myself was whether the offender could be deterred from committing other crimes. No one can predict with certainty who will or will not commit a crime, but there are indicators most sensible people recognize as danger signals.

First, was this an irrational crime? If an arsonist sets a fire to collect insurance, that is a crime but also a rational act. Such a person can be deterred by being made to pay for the harm done and the costs to the fire department. However, if the arsonist sets fires just because he likes to see them, it is highly unlikely that he can be stopped from setting others, no matter how high the fine. Imprisonment is advisable even though it may be a first offense.

Second, was there wanton cruelty? If a robber maims or slashes the victim, there is little likelihood that he can safely be left in the community. If a robber simply displays a gun but does not fire it or harm the victim, then one should consider his life history, provocation, and other circumstances in deciding whether probation is appropriate.

Third, is this a hostile person? Was his crime one of hatred, and does he show any genuine remorse? Most rapes are acts of hostility, and the vast majority of rapists have a record of numerous sexual assaults. I remember one man who raped his mother. I gave him the maximum sentence under the law—20 years—but with good behavior, he got out fairly quickly. He immediately raped another elderly woman. Clearly, few rapists can safely be left in the community, and in my tenure, I incarcerated every one.

Yet gang rape, although a brutal and horrifying crime, is more complicated. The leader is clearly hostile and should be punished severely. Yet the followers can't be so neatly categorized. Some may act largely out of cowardice and peer pressure.

Fourth, is this a person who knows he is doing wrong but cannot control himself? Typical of such offenders are pedophiles. One child abuser who appeared before me had already been convicted of abusing his first wife's child. I got him on the second wife's child and sentenced him to the maximum. Still, he'll get out with good behavior, and I shudder to think about the children around him when he does. This is one case in which justice is not tough enough.

By contrast, some people who have committed homicide present very little danger of further violence—although many more do. Once a young man came before me because he had taken aim at a person half a block away and then shot him in the back, killing him. Why did he do it? "I wanted to get me a body." He should never get out. But the mandatory codes don't make great distinctions between him and another murderer who came before me, a woman who shot and killed a boy after he and his friends brutally gang-raped her teenage daughter.

I found this woman guilty of first-degree murder, but I found no reason to incarcerate her. She had four young children to support who would have become wards of the welfare department and probably would have spent their childhoods in a series of foster homes. I placed her on probation—a decision few judges now have the discretion to impose. She had not been arrested before. She has not been arrested since.

Of course, the vast majority of men, women, and children in custody in the United States are not killers, rapists, or arsonists. They're in prison for some type of theft—a purse snatching, burglary, or embezzlement. Many of these criminals can be punished without incarceration. If you force a first-time white-collar criminal to pay heavily for his crimes —perhaps three times the value of the money or property taken—he'll get the message that crime does not pay. As for poor people, stealing is not always a sign that the individual is an unreasonable risk to the community. It's often a sign that they want something—a car, Air Jordans—that they are too poor to buy themselves. Many of them, if they are not violent, can also be made to make some restitution and learn that crime doesn't pay.

Of course, to most of us, the idea of a nonprison sentence is tantamount to exoneration; a criminal sentenced to probation has effectively "gotten off." And there's a reason for that impression: Unless the probationer is required by the sentencing judge to perform specific tasks, probation is a charade. The probationer meets with the probation officer, briefly, perhaps once a month—making the procedure a waste of time for both. The officer duly records the meeting and the two go their separate ways until the probationer is arrested for another offense.

When I made the decision not to send a criminal to prison, I wanted to make sure that the probation system I sent them into had teeth. So I set firm conditions. If the offender was functionally illiterate, he was unemployable and would probably steal or engage in some other illegal activity once released. Thus in my sentencing, I sent him to school and ordered the probation officer to see that he went. (I use the masculine pronoun deliberately for I have never seen an illiterate female offender under the age of 60.) I ordered school dropouts to get their high school equivalency certificates and find jobs. All offenders were ordered to pay restitution or reparations within their means or earning capacity to their victims. Sometimes it was as little as $5 a week. Offenders simply could not return to their old, feckless lifestyles without paying some financial penalty for their wrongdoing.

Monitoring probation wasn't easy for me, or the probation officers with whom I worked. Every day I'd come into my office, look at my calendar, and notice that, say, 30 days had passed since Elliott was let out. So I'd call the probation office. Has Elliott made his payment? Is he going to his GED class? And so on. If the answer was no, I'd hold a violation hearing with the threat of incarceration if the conditions were not met within 30 days. After I returned a few people to jail for noncompliance, both my offenders and their probation officers knew I meant business. (Few probation officers protested my demands; their jobs were more meaningful and satisfying, they said.)

Of course, probation that required education and work and payment plans meant real work for criminals, too. But there was a payoff both the probation officers and I could see: As offenders worked and learned and made restitution, their attitudes often changed dramatically.

Time and punishment

My rules of sentencing don't make judgeship easier; relying on mandatory sentencing is a far better way to guarantee a leisurely, controversy-free career on the bench. But my rules are, I believe, both effective and transferable: an application of common sense that any reasonable person could follow to similar ends. What prevents Americans from adopting practical measures like these is an atavistic belief in the sanctity of punishment. Even persons who have never heard of Emmanuel Kant or the categorical imperative to punish believe that violation of law must be followed by the infliction of pain.

If we Americans treated crime more practically— as socially unacceptable behavior that should be curbed for the good of the community—we might begin to take a rational approach to the development of alternatives to prison. We might start thinking in terms not of punishment but of public safety, deterrence, and rehabilitation. Penalties like fines, work, and payment of restitution protect the public better and more cheaply than imprisonment in many cases.

Mind you, sentencing guidelines are not inherently evil. Intelligent guidelines would keep some judges from returning repeat offenders to the streets and others from putting the occasional cocaine user away for 10 years. Yet those guidelines must allow more latitude for the judge and the person who comes before him. While some states' sentencing laws include provisions that allow judges to override the mandatory sentences in some cases, the laws are

for the most part inflexible—they deny judges the freedom to discriminate between the hardened criminal and the Michael. Richard H. Girgenti, the criminal justice director of New York state, has long proposed that the legislature give judges more discretion to impose shorter sentences for nonviolent and noncoercive felonies. This common-sense proposal has not been acted on in New York or any other state with mandatory sentencing laws.

Current laws are predicated on the belief that there must be punishment for every offense in terms of prison time rather than alternative sentences. But when it comes to determining the fate of a human being, there must be room for judgment. To make that room, we must stop acting as if mathematic calculations are superior to human thought. We must abolish mandatory sentencing laws and change the criteria on which sentencing guidelines are based.

Why not permit judges more freedom in making their decisions, provided that they give legitimate reasons? (If a judge doesn't have a good reason for deviating—if he's a reactionary or a fool—his sentencing decision will be overturned.) And why not revise the guidelines to consider dangerousness rather than the nomenclature of the offense? If we made simple reforms like these, thousands of nonthreatening, nonhabitual offenders would be allowed to recompense their victims and society in a far less expensive and far more productive way.

You may be wondering, after all this, if I have a Willie Horton in my closet—a criminal whose actions after release privately haunt me. I do. I sentenced him to 10 to 20 years in prison—the maximum the law allowed—for forcible rape. He was released after eight years and promptly raped another woman. I could foresee what would happen but was powerless to impose a longer sentence.

And then there are the other cases that keep me up nights: those of men and women I might have let out, but didn't. And those of people like Michael, for whom justice shouldn't have been a mathematical equation.

IN SEARCH OF THE TOUGHEST STATE ETHICS LAW

Just how far can states go in restricting activities of public officials in the name of ethics?

JOYCE BULLOCK

Joyce Bullock is a senior policy analyst with CSG in Lexington, Ky.

But weaker efforts can drag out recovery after a scandal. One example is Alabama, which in September 1993 became the fourth state in as many years to call a special session on ethics reform. Meeting in the wake of its governor's conviction of ethics violations, the Legislature hammered out what seemed to be a solid ethics measure. But the state's new governor vetoed the bill under media pressure and claims by critics that it would, among other things, weaken the State Ethics Commission's investigatory authority.

That leaves many in government wondering what is solid ethics legislation, and how feasible it is to construct a tough law. And how can we evaluate laws when they vary so much from state to state? Each year, The Council of State Governments receives hundreds of ethics inquiries from legislators, staff, ethics agencies and reporters. Most are in search of the "toughest" state ethics law. But what are the common assumptions of toughness in ethics reform? Here's what to look for when evaluating an ethics law:

Telling all

Disclosure regulations are becoming synonymous with openness and accountability in government. Currently, 40 states require public employees to file financial disclosure reports at least annually. What must be reported varies from specific dollar amounts to narrow or broad categories for assets, income, financial transactions, loans and gifts.

For example, the Connecticut State Ethics Commission reviews more than 1,000 reports each year from state legislators and employees who are in key decision-making positions or earn more than $60,000 annually. The reports contain information on sources of assets, loans and outside business interests. Selected portions of the reports, such as the sources of credit indebtedness and business interests of immediate family members are confidential. The remaining contents are open to the public.

A 1993 Iowa law calls for disclosure reports from upper-level executive branch departments and agency heads and employees. The law requires disclosure of sources, as opposed to amounts, of compensation to identify or avoid potential conflicts of interests.

Reporters who examine such state reports alert the public to questionable activities. Just the thought of how an activity or gift might appear if splashed across the front page of a newspaper is enough to make officials think twice before accepting favors.

"State officials are finding that perks, such as fact-finding trips paid for by lobbyists, are falling by the

Since 1990, 15 states have passed major ethics reform measures - many of them toughening up existing laws. The more sweeping reform measures have followed big scandals - among them Arizona, Kentucky and South Carolina. While the passage of a strong new ethics law may not restore public confidence, it helps clear the table for other issues.

wayside due to media scrutiny and open records," said Dan Mollway, executive director of the Hawaii State Ethics Commission.

To make disclosure information more easily available to the public, many states are experimenting with electronic means, while others remain bogged down in the paper flow of thousands of completed forms. Many states are copying and modifying the Washington Public Disclosure Commission's reporting software to improve filing and access. In most states, it is up to the media to delve through the completed forms, and most media searches are limited to the constitutional officers and legislative leadership.

In the meantime, the issue of confidential records is becoming obsolete. "There is no such thing as confidential disclosure records," said Mollway. "Not all of Hawaii's records are open, however any entity with subpoena power such as the FBI or the local prosecutors' office can still obtain them." In Hawaii's case, disclosure information includes financial information on spouses, which also can be subpoenaed.

Potent agencies

Tougher laws provide for an enforcement structure that is authorized to issue subpoenas, initiate an investigation on its own volition, conduct administrative hearings, file independent court actions, impose administrative fines or penalties, and issue declaratory rulings. Thirty-nine states empower ethics agencies to conduct investigations on their own volition, and 42 states authorize them to issue advisory opinions, declaratory rulings or interpretive statements. Recent major scandals in Arizona, Kentucky and South Carolina have resulted in this type of authority for their state agencies, while West Virginia became the first to provide for a special prosecutor in 1989.

"Codes of conduct, disclosure mechanisms and compliance authority are meaningless without an aggressive commission to follow

through," said John Contino, director of the Pennsylvania Ethics Commission. He said the enforcement authority must be an independent commission or risk losing public confidence in the process. If a state agency or legislative committee investigating a scandal just refers it to the governor's office or legislative chambers for action, the public can question whether the process is impartial.

"The independent commission process safeguards against such questions," said Contino.

One such long-standing agency is the Massachusetts Ethics Commission, which was established in 1978. The commission can levy civil fines or bring civil action against individuals failing to comply with the state's conflict-of-interest and disclosure laws, and refers cases or investigates cases with the Massachu-

Why Wisconsin is tough

Nearly everyone mentions Wisconsin when asked about tough ethics legislation. While some states' provisions may be stricter, the Wisconsin package is a force to be reckoned with.

General guidelines. A Wisconsin official may not accept a meal, travel or gift offered because of the official's public position. Lobbyists and their employers are prohibited from furnishing anything of value to any state official or employee unless it is furnished to the general public under like circumstances.

Standards of conduct. The code forbids a state official from using public position to obtain anything of more than insignificant value for the private benefit of the official, the official's family or the official's business. An official is prohibited from representing a client before a state agency. There is a one-year revolving door restriction during which time an official can't return to lobby.

Financial disclosure. All officials and candidates file statements of economic interest for public inspection at the time they enter the public arena and update them annually. Creditors, investments, real estate and names of commercial clients are identified, but amounts are not. The board has reported a 100 percent compliance rate on filed reports for several years.

Lobbying registrations and reporting. Lobbyists and their employers must register once during the Legislature's two-year term. Every six months the lobbyist's employer files a report containing the time and resources used to influence legislation, a gubernatorial veto or an administrative rule. The report identifies by number and subject each bill and rule on which the organization hoped to influence action and accounts for all lobbying expenditures, including costs of research, studies and compilation of statistics, costs of encouraging citizens to communicate views to state officials and compensation paid to lobbyists.

Jurisdiction. The standards of conduct apply to officials in all three branches. The ethics code applies to all key state policy-makers and executives, a group comprising officials chosen in statewide elections, legislators, judges, and all of the governor's appointees including members of citizen boards and agency executives. Local officials also are covered.

Board member qualifications. By statute, a member of the State Ethics Board may not be a member of a political party or be affiliated with a partisan club or organization. A member may not hold any other office or employment in either state or local government.

Source: Wisconsin Ethics Board

setts Attorney General's Office or district attorneys.

A newer agency with similar authority is the Iowa Ethics and Campaign Disclosure Board, which was established in 1993. The board replaces the Iowa Campaign Finance Disclosure Commission and has the authority to initiate investigations, whereas the former commission could investigate only the filing of a formal complaint. The new board also has power to issue both informal and formal advisory opinions and has jurisdiction over lobbyists who lobby executive branch agencies.

Conflict of interest

The purpose of a conflict-of-interest statute is to prevent public officials from abusing or appearing to abuse their status and power for private gain. During the early 1980s, the following six areas were identified as core elements of outlawing such conflicts. Most states restrict or ban officials from: (1) abusing an official position for personal gain, (2) providing benefits to influence official actions, (3) using confidential government information, (4) taking part in outside business activities that conflict with public service responsibilities, (5) nepotism, and (6) giving government contracts to their own companies or to friends or relatives.

While those elements are enshrined in most state ethics laws, states are going even further.

"There is a movement towards zero tolerance with regard to conflict-of-interest standards at the state level. It's happening provision by provision," said Mollway.

Newer provisions address post-employment or the "revolving door" of former public officials lobbying the legislative bodies or agencies on which they served. Many states require at least a one- or two-year wait. (See "Ethics fact sheet" table)

The toughest conflict-of-interest laws ban officials from accepting even token benefits that might be construed as influencing them. South Carolina joined Wisconsin in enacting a "no-cup-of-coffee" pro-

vision (nothing of value even if it is as inexpensive as a cup of coffee).

Iowa now bans all gifts to officials except food and drink valued at $3 or less and consumed in one sitting. Twenty-two states set limits ranging from $10 to $100 per official per year and couple the restraints with disclosure requirements.

"These new provisions are also part of a movement to remove a double standard that legislators are not subject to the same ethics restrictions as other public employees," said Mollway, referring to similar

limits that have long applied to executive branch officials in many states.

Further crackdowns on lobbying

Increased restrictions of lobbyists' contributions to elected officials and increased itemization of their expenditures support Mollway's statement. Colorado, Kentucky, South Carolina and Vermont now completely ban lobbyists from contributing to officials' or candidates' campaigns. An additional 22

Ethics fact sheet

- **Term limits** — Since 1990, voters in 17 states have passed term limit restrictions on state legislators and/or members of Congress: Arizona, Arkansas, California, Colorado, Florida, Maine, Michigan, Missouri, Montana, Nebraska, North Dakota, Ohio, Oklahoma, Oregon, South Dakota, Washington and Wyoming. Maine's action applies to state executives as well.
- **No contributions from lobbyists** — Four states completely ban lobbyists from contributing to campaigns at any time: Colorado, Kentucky, South Carolina and Vermont.
- **No contributions from lobbyists during legislative sessions** — Twenty-two states prohibit lobbyists from making contributions during a legislative session: Alabama, Alaska, Arizona, Arkansas, Colorado, Connecticut, Georgia, Iowa, Kansas, Kentucky, Louisiana, Minnesota (also applies to caucuses), Nevada, New Mexico, North Carolina, Oregon, South Carolina, Texas, Utah, Vermont, Washington and Wisconsin.
- **Post-employment restrictions** — Thirty-five states have set post-government employment restrictions, many of which have been passed since 1988. Seventeen of these restrictions are for one or two years following employment.
- **Gifts and lobbyists expenditures limitations** — Thirty-nine states restrict the monetary value of gifts a public employee may receive. Five states also hold lobbyists accountable for not making gifts in excess of the following thresholds to state officials: California ($10 per month per official), Connecticut ($50 per gift per year, $150 for food/drink per year), Michigan ($37 per month per official), South Carolina (nothing of value) and Wisconsin (nothing of value). Seven states also restrict the dollar amounts lobbyists may spend per official per year: Iowa ($3/day), Kansas ($40), Kentucky ($100), Nevada ($100), South Carolina (nothing of value), Texas ($500) and Wisconsin (nothing of value).
- **Investigatory authority** — Agencies that may initiate an investigation on their own volition result in 10 times the number of investigations per year as those which may only investigate in response to a formal complaint.

(*Sources:* The Book of the States, 1994-95 *(available July 1994) and the* COGEL Bluebook *(1993). Both books are published by The Council of State Governments.)*

states prohibit such contributions during a legislative session. Most states have passed these provisions since 1988.

Since 1990, 10 states extended lobbyists reporting requirements to include itemization of expenditures over a certain amount. Lobbyists, too, must report on their lobby-related expenditures in 40 states.

Walking the talk

Most states require commissions to publish reports or handbooks that explain their jurisdictions' ethics code. Florida, Hawaii, Illinois, Indiana and South Carolina have developed videos to explain their codes. As ethics laws become more complex, public officials will need more guidance and informal chan-

nels to seek answers to gray-area concerns. California, Kentucky and Wisconsin now mandate ethics training for public officials. Arizona instituted annual training for legislators after its scandal. In Wisconsin, lobbyists are required to attend ethics training sessions.

Which state is toughest? Ten state ethics administrators who have each tracked changing ethics provisions for many years were polled to identify the toughest state ethics law. Responses were mixed, but Wisconsin emerged as the winner due to its well-known, strong lobbying provisions. The respondents also mentioned Connecticut, Kentucky, Massachusetts, Pennsylvania, South Carolina and Texas.

Three administrators recommend watching Oklahoma and Rhode Island as potential up-and-

comers. Both states' independent ethics commissions have constitutional authority to develop the code of conduct for public servants in their states, although Oklahoma's is subject to legislative review. Both commissions have faced and won challenges to their authority at the state supreme court level since 1990.

Looking ahead, the media and interest groups will continue to press for new reforms in keeping with the movement toward zero tolerance and no double standards. Experts conservatively estimate that each year five states will pass major ethics reform measures. And if Rhode Island and Oklahoma are successful in setting the future standard of toughness in ethics reform, we can expect to see media pressure for such authority in states with an initiative process.

The Buddy System

Political patronage, nepotism, favoritism, conflict of interest. Do vendors and contractors still win government contracts based on who they know rather than what they know?

Patrick Rains, Associate Editor

"To the victor belongs the spoils of the enemy," exclaimed New York Senator William Marcy in 1832. The senator's popular slogan was coined during the first presidential administration of his friend and colleague, Andrew Jackson. The use of public offices and contracts as rewards for party loyalty and services, also known as the spoils system, is believed to have formed during Jackson's eight-year tenure as president when he replaced nearly 2,000 of the government's 11,000 employees with more "deserving" candidates. Translation: You scratch my back, I'll scratch yours.

Has the "good ol' boy" system actually changed that much since Jackson's time? On the local levels, consultants are hired by firms to lobby public officials and contractors contribute to campaign funds. Do these actions represent real ethics problems or are they just part of running local government?

Cleaning Up

The Department of Sanitation in Newark, N.J., does more than just clean up the city; some workers have been cleaning up at the bank as well. Nine people, including alleged members of organized crime and the manager of Newark's Division of Sanitation, were recently charged with bilking the city of anywhere from $800,000 to as much as $3 million for falsified and overcharged municipal services.

Samuel Verderese, the 60-year-old manager, was indicted on charges that he billed the city for services that were not delivered. Bogus payments for snow removal, automotive maintenance, waste disposal and recycling

services allegedly netted Verderese $600,000. Mayor Sharpe James immediately suspended Verderese without pay pending the outcome of the investigation.

Just how the money was taken remains a mystery. All the numbers check out on paper, according to the mayor. Even after an auditor and investigator have thoroughly researched the case, the city is still no closer to discovering how the system was circumvented. Other municipal employees are believed to have colluded with the racketeering activities since no one person handles the vouchers. "Someone had to look the other way or have a suspicion," says James. "It should have been brought to our attention. The fraud may be more extensive than we anticipated.

"We're seeing corruption at the worst level because it was fraud against the city of Newark as well as the citizens," laments James. "It undermines the whole professional system of civil service where a 30-year career employee can rise from picking up cans to being administrator. It hurts a little more because you don't choose those individuals; they get to where they are by merit and rising to the top."

The city is quickly taking action to correct its contracting problems by terminating all current and future contracts with those companies indicted; instructing the Director of Engineering to conduct a detailed study of all procedures currently in place, and; appointing a Division of Investigation that includes full-time auditors, an investigator, law officer and an administrative person who will be a watchdog on every city department whether or

not there is actual suspicion or complaints.

James also promises to hire a professional administrator to oversee the Sanitation Department. "This goes against the Civil Service edict but I believe that department requires a professional with a background in accounting and managerial skill to be on top of and accountable for the millions of dollars that flows through that department," he says.

Prevention has always been part of the mayor's plan. A municipal code of ethics was implemented when James took office and once a year each employee is required to watch a video on the signs and consequences of fraud.

"I don't know if this is an indictment of the concept of privatization," says Michael Chertoff, the state's chief federal prosecutor, in a recent *New York Times* article, "but it suggests that no method of delivering municipal services should escape the need for diligent supervision. There will always be a small minority of people seeking to enrich themselves."

Just Between Friends

Fiscal morass is how most economic observers define New Orleans' deficit-ridden budget of $15 million. To combat the problem, Louisiana Governor Edwin Edwards and New Orleans Mayor Sidney Barthelemy proposed what many consider the city's last and best hope for a economic revival — a land-based casino on the Rivergate site near downtown.

During the next 30 years, the payoff for city government may be as much as $2.5 billion and may create nearly 15,000 new and permanent jobs. The project is worth $400 million with staggering future earnings for the winning bidder, so it's little wonder that companies vying to operate New Orleans' casino attempt to gain the upper hand with public officials, some say by hiring their friends as consultants or, rather, as personal lobbyists.

After all, it's the governor who selects the state casino board that selects the casino operator. And since the city owns the land that will be home to the project, it's the mayor who selects the developer of the site.

Former New Orleans state senator Hank Braden IV was hired by Caesars World as a consultant on casino licensing and gaming. Braden just happens to be Barthelemy's closest confidante. Although not on the city's payroll, critics claim that Braden has so much influence with the mayor that he is known as the "shadow mayor." Caesars also hired Bob d'Hemmcourt, a friend of Governor Edwards.

And other developers countered by snatching up former acquaintances. Billy Broadhurst, another associate of

Edwards, was hired by developer Christopher Hemmeter of Hemmeter-Woodmont.

Hemmeter even hosted the mayor and his wife as well as several political leaders and their spouses at his Hawaiian resorts to demonstrate what he could do for New Orleans. The mayor says there is nothing unusual in the trips; in fact, he visited other resort developments to study their quality.

To the surprise of very few, Hemmeter and Caesars unveiled a joint proposal prompting some competitors to conclude the alliance's combined political influence would be impossible to overcome. And, yes, it was the Hemmeter/Caesars group that eventually won the bid.

Barthelemy says the contract was awarded based on a thorough study of the proposals rather than any lobbying efforts. "My campaign manager was on another group, several of my supporters were on a local group. In public office, we try to get the best people around us that have expertise and resources and they usually get involved

in all kinds of business in the community."

"It's ludicrous to think that we hire people to get special favors from public officials," says Daniel Robinowitz, president of Hemmeter-Woodmont. "If they are the best person for the job, we're not going to hold it against someone that they're the friend of the governor or mayor."

The Buck Stops Here

Indianapolis Mayor Stephen Goldsmith is considered an ambitious public official who is positioned for a future run at Indiana's gubernatorial seat. He is a strong proponent of reinventing government by streamlining departments to the bare essentials and out sourcing work to the private sector. But, according to Priscilla Neale, a former associate engineer with the Indianapolis Department of Public Works, this brand of out sourcing of government contracts can raise some sticky ethical questions.

One such example is Marty Mann, a former city engineer, who left the Department of Public Works to join the engineering/design consulting firm of Paul I. Cripe as a consultant. However, the firm not only has an on-call contract with the city that allows Mann to come back and work for the city in a similar capacity to his former city position. Mann was even scheduled to supervise city employees until those in the department complained.

Barry Baer, director of Public Works, says that Cripe does in fact have an on-call contract with the city, but he is unaware of Mann working on any city contracts and adds that there is not a conflict if Cripe has Mann working city contracts. "That's up to them to assign him. I have no say about that."

According to Neale, this kind of consulting is common practice throughout city government. "Individuals have made money working for the city, then go out to work at a consulting firm and come back to work for the city making substantially more money as a consultant than they could have ever dreamed of making as a city employee." The city does not carry them as personnel, so the mayor can boast of trimming the fat off city government.

Beulah Coughenour, city-county councillor and chairman of the public works committee has heard these same allegations from other sources as well. She has received anonymous letters and held conversations with current and former city employees who claim that vendors must pay a $25 fee to be

Court Rules Sludge Contract Valid

In New Jersey, an effort by 11 Essex and Union County towns to void their construction contract for the $20 million Decker sludge dewatering plant has been thwarted in State Superior Court.

Judge Edward Beglin dismissed with prejudice the towns' efforts to nullify the contract. He also ordered the municipalities to arbitrate their dispute with Cris Tec Associates Inc., of Whitehouse, N.J., the plant's builder.

Attorney Steven Brawer, of Mandelbaum, Salsburg, Gold, Lazris, Discenza & Steinberg in West Orange — representing the company and its principals, Michael and Ernest Renda — notes that the court's use of the term, "with prejudice," permanently bars the towns from seeking to void the terms of their contracts.

The municipalities contracted for the construction of a plant they needed to comply with federal and state consent decrees, under which the towns agreed to stop dumping sewage sludge in the ocean by March 17, 1991. To meet the deadline, the towns — organized as the Joint Meeting of Essex and Union Counties — awarded a contract on Dec. 22, 1989, for the construction of the

sludge plant to Cris Tec. Towns participating in the project are East Orange, Hillside, Irvington Maplewood, Millburn, Newark, Roselle Park, South Orange, Summit, Union and West Orange.

Brawer says the Joint Meeting refused to address the more than $12 million in claims that the company had against them. As a result, it sought to arbitrate its claims under contract terms specified by the Joint Meeting. At that point, when the plant was 90 percent completed, the Joint Meeting moved to nullify the contract. The group filed charges that the company broke the law by misrepresenting and unlawfully substituting subcontractors employed on the job.

In his ruling, Judge Beglin noted the company kept the Joint Meeting aware of changes in subcontractors in a timely fashion. "And more importantly," the Judge concluded, the Joint Meeting did not complain until "the project was over 90 percent completed." He also noted that in substituting a contractor in one field, cited by the Joint Meeting, Cris Tec did so, "so that the schedule could be met," and that the change "did not include any taking of undue advantage nor in making any harm."

on a preferred list to do business with the city and those who don't pay don't win contracts. "I have no problem charging for a service that is a convenience, but I don't think it should prohibit any vendor from getting information on what projects are going to be bid," says Coughenour.

Other states have started similar programs and the state of Florida was even involved in a messy lawsuit, but Ande Gregg, administrator for central purchasing says the so-called list is nothing more than a registration list that the city implemented to offset mailing costs. "Each bid that the city does costs $343. We were spending a whole lot of money to a lot of people who never respond." So, the city actually has a $25 registration list that is intended to save costs and prompt only those vendors actually interested in bidding for contracts.

"They're not even clever about it," says a city insider who has witnessed "the favored and contributors getting most everything [contracts]." Any vendor can supposedly still conduct business with the city because all bids are required by law to be advertised, "but 75 percent of city purchases are not bid; they're done through quotes, open market purchasing after bids have been considered invalid or straight purchasing." Those are not advertised in the paper, according to the insider. In fact, many quotes are not even mailed out unless they have a lot of detail specifications. Quotes are received over the telephone or through the fax machine and then posted. "Every one of those requisitions is kicked back, and only those vendors registered with the city are to be used. Thus, the city does not receive the competitive pricing and quality work it needs."

In or Out?

Is privatization of government services really to the advantage of the city, and is it conducted ethically? Not according to Frederick Thayer, professor of public and international affairs at the University of Pittsburgh. He says contracting out services or public/private partnerships is akin to conspiracies to loot the public treasury. "If a firm feels it must pay out large amounts of money in the form of bribes and payoffs to inspectors and government officials to ensure that it will gain the contracts it needs, this 'sunk cost' is likely to prevent that firm from doing an efficient job," he says. "If the officials pocketing handouts are in a position to spend enough public funds on the contract to guarantee first-class

performance, of course, the costs associated with the contract will be much higher than they should."

Michael Messina, a labor economist with the American Federation of State, County and Municipal Employees, says that contracting out services is just a crutch for government officials trying to find easy solutions to service problems. "The alternative is to look within. They have a talented pool of workers who do the work and know where there are problems and commit the resources to providing better service," he says.

"The bottom line to me is excellence," says Joyce Bullock, staff director of the Council of Governmental Ethics Laws. "As long as the safeguards and regulations are in place, and the supervisory capacity is there to ensure there are no abuses to the system then why not privatize?"

'You can't just look up contracting in a cookbook and then go out and do it.'

Constance Cushman

Bullock believes privatization contracting will continue regardless of the ethics issue. The state of the economy will dictate that those who provide quality services at lower prices will win the contracts everytime.

"You can have all sorts of procedures to guard against corruption in it [contracting], but then you start to eliminate the economies of privatizing," says June Beittel, project manager with the International City/County Management Association. "Police checks, citizen panels and high performance bonds guarantee against corruption but they also increase contracting costs. The best insurance against fraud is the open bid process."

What to Do?

From 1987 to 1990, the New York State Commission on Government Integrity, an investigative panel born

from a series of corruption scandals involving officials on all levels of government, made numerous proposals on the measures the city needs to take to reduce corruption in local government, many of which were subsequently enacted by the city. The Commission proposed several reform measures to address the city's contracting abuses:

• Streamlining government: In 1979, the American Bar Association's *Model Procurement Code for State and Local Governments* recommended that cities implement a central procurement policy body to oversee citywide contracting. Instead of each city agency developing its own contracting policies and documentation, one central authority would be responsible for a city's day-to-day purchasing.

"The reflex response to scandal is overcontrol by 'paperwork police,' without the basic structural changes that are required for effective management," says Commission Chairman John Feerick. "But this simply does not do the job. In fact, it may make the problem worse."

"Government can over-regulate which tends to stifle," agrees Constance Cushman, a former member of the Commission and currently on the New York City Procurement Policy Board. "Some vendors are reluctant to bid on city work due to inordinate delays, as well as inconsistent rules and procedures." To remedy the problem, the Board started a comprehensive program that makes each agency more responsive, from approval to payment.

Across the country, contracting departments are buried in layers of review and approvals processes that tend to paralyze the system. Although well-intentioned, not all vendors have the time nor the financial resources to endure a city's time-consuming, expensive approval and payment process.

Also a lack of standardized language on contracts forces many smaller vendors to seek legal aid, an expensive proposition most cannot afford. Thus, opportunities for corruption abound when a small group of firms are the only bidders for city work. Not surprisingly, the Commission reports less competition has a chilling effect on the open-bid system which inevitably leads to bid-rigging and collusive behavior among vendors and officials.

• Training programs: Many municipalities suffer from a serious lack of experienced contracting personnel. New York City spends $6.5 billion on contracts on a variety of supplies and services. Proper training and tools should be supplied for those city work-

Contract Contacts

Contracting and Volunteerism in Local Government: A Self-Help Guide uses worksheets, case studies and sample forms to help local officials follow a step-by-step approach for exploring the use of contracting and volunteers. It lists resources for communities considering contracting out and organizations that provide information on effective volunteer management.

Appendices provide two sample services contracts and detailed informa-tion on two volunteer programs. The guide list for $30. ICMA, 777 North Capitol St, NE, #500, Washington, D.C., 20002

The **Guardian** is a bimonthly pub-lication on recent governmental ethics, campaign finance, freedom of information and lobby law activities.

Each issue features summaries of developments at the state and feder-al level in the United States and Canada. A one year subscription is $54. The Council on Governmental Ethics Laws, c/o The Council of State Governments, Iron Works Pike, P.O. Box 11910, Lexington, Ky., 40578-1910.

The American Federation of State, County and Municipal Employees provides ethics information and gov-ernment contracting case studies in two booklets: **Government For $ale: An Examination of the Contract-ing of State and Local Govern-ment Services** and **The Privatiza-tion/Contracting Out Debate**. To order, write: AFSCME, 1625 L Street, N.W., Washington, D.C., 20036.

---

ers entrusted with billions of taxpayer dollars.

"It's a mistake to think that you can do contracting the same way you would approach cooking," says Cushman. "You can't just look up contracting in a cookbook and then go out and do it. Public contracting requires more so-phistication, judgment and expertise."

Training programs not only help con-tracting personnel do a better job, but alerts them to the warning signs of possible contracting abuses in the sys-tem.

New York City has implemented an ambitious Procurement Training In-stitute that takes workers weeks of classwork and on the job training to complete. Coursework ranges from pro-posals, specification, negotiations as well as ethics.

• Policing systems: The Commission reports that instead of trying to police each contract before it is awarded, cities need to develop a system for re-viewing contract decisions after the fact, on a selective post-audit basis, to make certain that contracts are being awarded in accordance within city's procedures and for the best value.

Computerized monitoring is impor-tant to aid in the quick analysis of post-award review. Cities should invest in computerized monitoring systems to look for suspect trends in contracting procedure.

Cushman agrees that post-auditing is very important, but she also stress-es the need for "effective pre-bid con-ferences to clear up any problems with specifications; protest mechanisms so the competition can essentially police the system and have public disclosure so the competition has access to the information they need to police the sys-tem."

However, no matter how many safe-guards are implemented, the real bur-den rests with those elected and hired to serve the public good. "Anytime two people get together there's always a chance for misconduct," says Mayor James. "We're not in the business of legislating morality. Sometimes you can only hope that people will do the right thing."

If the working poor can't get to edge-city jobs, many politicians argue that jobs should be lured back to the city through programs like enterprise zones, with generous tax breaks for firms locating in poor neighborhoods. Unfortunately, they have never been shown to generate many new jobs in impoverished communities. A related solution was pioneered by Portland, Ore., which in 1973 limited sprawl by drawing a boundary at the edge of the suburbs. The path of development thus moved back toward the city. However, such growth controls can boost land costs and hurt the poor.

More housing. Another solution is to build more low-cost housing in the growing suburbs. Children who have been through the Gautreaux Project, which relocates Chicago welfare families to private apartments in suburbs like Hoffman Estates, are twice as likely to go on to college and land good jobs as their peers who stay behind. But building affordable apartments in affluent suburbs, even for working families, is extremely difficult because of local opposition.

Some say a more sensible reform is for states to make it illegal for municipalities to stop homeowners from fixing up their basements and garages and rent-ing them. Legalizing "granny flats" could open up millions of relatively low-cost rental units, at no taxpayer cost, throughout existing suburbs. It might also allow people with modest incomes who otherwise could not afford "nicer" suburbs the chance to subsidize their mortgages with rental income, the way generations of immigrants built wealth by owning three-flat apartments.

A number of urban geographers see the decline of older working-class suburbs as a benign and natural part of the succession of cities that is useful in providing somewhat better neighborhoods for city refugees. What these experts don't see is the suffering of those refugees, many of them black, who have sunk retirement nest eggs into suburban homes, only to watch their investments wither and their neighborhoods decline. Nor do they see the damage that increasing class isolation may be doing to the national character. "The less citizens of different classes mix in neighborhoods and schools, the greater the chance that a snobbish European class structure will take hold," argues author Mickey Kaus in "The End of Equality." To many, that doesn't seem very American.

BY PAUL GLASTRIS WITH DORIAN FRIEDMAN

Indianapolis and the Republican Future

ROB GURWITT

Mayor Steve Goldsmith is convinced a big city can be governed from the ideological right. If he succeeds, he may end up changing politics in many places besides his own.

Over the course of the last year or so, the city of Indianapolis has become something of a wayside shrine for conservative pilgrims. Richard Riordan passed through shortly after winning the mayoralty of Los Angeles. Bret Schundler—the young Jersey City mayor who has been setting Republican hearts aflutter—was so taken with it that he extended a short trip in order to study it more fully. The Heritage Foundation has singled it out as a model for its disciples. The Los Angeles-based Reason Foundation, a libertarian think tank, has been acting as though it were under contract to the city's convention and visitors bureau.

What has them all excited is Republican mayor Stephen Goldsmith and his insistence on treating seriously the universal campaign cliché about running city government like a business. In the two years since he took office, Goldsmith has taken paring government to an extreme that few other mayors in this country have even considered. He has privatized a long list of city services, forced city employees to compete with the private sector for service contracts, slashed hundreds of middle-management positions and injected private-sector standards of cost-effectiveness into City Hall operations. All of this has made him a hero to the libertarian right. To a solid core of conservative Republicans around the country, Steve Goldsmith is coming to represent the future of urban Republicanism.

Privatization is what all the conservative visitors want to know about, and the mayor and his staff are eager to talk about it. But it is not the most radical part of his agenda, or the one with the highest stakes in the long run. The most important ideological experiment in Indianapolis is the one Steve Goldsmith is conducting on inner-city redevelopment. He has tried, with varying degrees of success, to hand responsibility for community issues over to neighborhood groups and use them to find a way of creating the conditions for capital to begin flowing back into poor neighborhoods.

This is not an endeavor in which the GOP has shown much interest in recent years, anywhere in the country; the party's attention has generally been aimed at its base in the vote-rich suburbs. The last high-profile effort to develop momentum on poverty issues in Republican circles was Jack Kemp's, when he was President Bush's housing secretary, and it was stopped cold by White House indifference. Yet what is becoming clear in Indianapolis is not only that Republican mayors can have something to say about rebuilding fraying neighborhoods but that if the GOP wants to rewrite the basic equations of urban politics, they must.

A year ago, of course, the notion that Republicans had anything more than a limited future in American urban life seemed implausible at best. Other than Indianapolis and Columbus, Ohio, the cities governed by Republicans were for the most part small or, as with Dallas and San Diego, confined to the Sun Belt. But then the

GOP presence in city government gained dramatic reinforcement with the election of Riordan in Los Angeles and Rudolph Giuliani in New York, and with Schundler's election to a full term in Jersey City. It was, in many respects, a mold-shattering set of elections: When Schundler first became mayor after a special election late in 1992, his city hadn't been led by a Republican for 75 years; Los Angeles had been under Democratic control for 36 consecutive years when Riordan took office; and Giuliani is New York's first Republican mayor since John Lindsay left the GOP in 1971.

There is no doubt that the Democrats handed all three of them an opportunity. Each ran against a Democratic opponent who, to an electorate tired of crime, taxes and large municipal bureaucracies, represented more of the same. But the elections were less a referendum on party label than on efficacy, as the current popularity of such pragmatic reformers as Cleveland's Michael White, Milwaukee's John Norquist and Philadelphia's Ed Rendell—all of them Democrats—suggests.

Indeed, if their examples are any indication, the current era of fiscal scarcity has to some degree made party label irrelevant. White has won tighter work rules and budget cuts from the police union; Norquist not only has cut property tax rates but is pressuring department managers to end inefficient practices by holding them accountable for achieving detailed objectives; Rendell has won huge wage concessions from the municipal unions, has created a private-sector task force aimed at streamlining government and is putting city services out to competitive bid.

Even so, there is no question that as a party, the GOP now has an opportunity to shake up the political landscape. In the 1992 presidential election, Democrats showed that they had learned how to appeal to suburban voters, following the cues of governors and state legislators who used the 1980s to forge a winning Democratic profile in what had been traditional Republican territory. Now it appears that the current crop of Republican mayors will give the GOP a core of politicians who can articulate an urban agenda for the party and may, in the long run, teach it how to win votes in the cities.

"This is really an opportunity for the party to rebuild," says Donald Haider, a professor of public management at Northwestern University and a one-time Republican candidate for mayor of Chicago. "Just as the Democrats played on Republican turf in the suburbs, now Republicans have a chance to play on their turf. This gives them a wonderful opportunity to sell what Jack Kemp could never sell during the Bush administration."

What Kemp could never sell, of course, was the notion that Republicans have more to say on urban affairs than that they are tough on crime. To do that, though, GOP mayors will have to prove not only that they are adept at cutting bureaucracy—a talent that current Democratic mayors obviously possess as well—but that they also have a viable approach to dealing with such ills as inner-city disinvestment and the spread of blight. Even more important, they will have to show that they have the ability to turn their theories on those matters into actual progress. Steve Goldsmith's experience in Indianapolis suggests that will not be easy.

There is no question that Goldsmith, 47, has had an extraordinary impact on Indianapolis city government in a short time. He arrived in 1992, after spending 12 years in local government as the Marion County prosecutor and in the wake of two mayors of enormous stature: Richard Lugar, who successfully fought to create the "Unigov" structure under which the city and its Marion County suburbs were joined, and William Hudnut, whose focus on downtown revitalization transformed the city's skyline, got the massive Hoosierdome built and turned Indianapolis into "the amateur sports capital of the world," as it now likes to call itself.

Both of those men, also Republicans, were politicians of the first rank. They were tireless promoters of the city both within and beyond its bounds and forceful in articulating a broad vision for its citizens. Hudnut, for his part, was unquenchable when he worked a crowd. He seemed to revel in such mayoral duties as wearing a leprechaun suit at the St. Patrick's Day parade.

It is hard, if not impossible, to imagine Goldsmith in a leprechaun suit. His personality is more distant than his predecessors', and he has little patience for political etiquette. It took him six months in office before he sat down with the president or the majority leader of the city/county council, both of them Republicans who had worked closely with Hudnut. His relations with the council, whose Republican majority is split into loose pro- and anti-Goldsmith factions, remain formal at best.

Instead, Goldsmith is—there is no delicate way to put this—a management wonk. He still teaches a course on public management at Indiana University in Bloomington and has a voracious appetite both for reading and talking about the subject. He inundates his staff—mostly young people drawn from the private sector—with the latest works on both public and business management, and expects them to become conversant. A joke that ran through the city press corps at the time of his 1991 campaign against Democrat Louis Mahern was that Mahern was running for mayor, while Goldsmith was running for city manager.

And yet in two years Goldsmith has put as marked an imprint on Indianapolis as any politician could hope for. He has done it, more than anything else, by his single-minded insistence on infusing city government with the principle of competition. In fact, the competitive idea underlies not only Goldsmith's management style but all the things he wants to accomplish in the city's neighborhoods and especially in its poorer communities.

When he began, Goldsmith seemed convinced that privatization was the only legitimate path for Indianapolis city government to take. He doesn't think that anymore. "I was increasingly impressed," he says now, "with the inherent ability of our own employees to perform better when the system allowed them to; I underestimated what they could do if we unloaded the bureaucracy off the top of their heads." The result was that Goldsmith evolved from believing in "privatization at all costs," as he puts it, to competition as "the core strategy." So while the municipal golf course has been unloaded, and such functions as sewer billing, microfilming and road contract monitoring simply contracted out, garbage delivery and some road maintenance tasks were opened up to competitive bidding and then won by city crews that had found ways to cut their costs.

The changes have been popular among citizens as a whole but are controversial in political circles, since they have cost the city some talented managers and some government functions that critics believe should remain with the city. "If you cut back on your regulatory agencies, it doesn't show up right away; it shows up ten years down the road," says Hudnut, whose relations with Goldsmith are frosty at best, but who nonetheless endorses the drive toward smaller government.

What has motivated Goldsmith to remake city government top to bottom is a conviction that Indianapolis is in a struggle with its neighbors for both residents and businesses, and that it simply does not have the option of raising taxes in order to continue paying for services. Instead, he harbors a fundamental belief that market forces and competition will ultimately serve citizens better than what he and his staff routinely call the government "monopoly."

Both of those interests—keeping taxes low and introducing market forces into arenas once the sole domain of government—undergird his attention to the inner city. Finding ways to bring private capital back into poor communities, he argues, is crucial if cities want to keep the tax burden on businesses and the middle class from becoming overwhelming. "We've tolerated the disintegration both of the family and the neighborhood, and then have tried to ameliorate that by the transfer of wealth from the suburbs or people with money," he says. "That's pretty short-sighted, because cities don't have that much wealth. Economic opportunity, as opposed to income redistribution, will be the key to a city's success. We have to bring up one group without bringing down the other."

It is, Goldsmith argues, a quintessentially Republican approach. "You have to be committed to changing the marketplace, which I view as a Republican strategy," he says. "We want to create the opportunity for private capital, including jobs, to flow back into those communities."

The heart of Goldsmith's strategy is a form of decentralization that turns over substantial governmental power to such bodies as neighborhood improvement associations and community development corporations. In Goldsmith's view, this "municipal federalism" would extend to such activities as park maintenance—with neighborhood associations doing their own contracting for services—and even road repair.

That basic concept has not been met with uniform excitement. "You can tell a neighborhood association you want to let them cut their own grass and fix their own streets," says Stephan Fantauzzo, director of the state's AFSCME Council 62, "but the fact is people would rather pay taxes and have the city cut the grass and fix the streets."

In the case of neighborhood redevelopment, however, Goldsmith's plans have drawn considerable support. The city's role would essentially be to pave the way for community groups to put together the financing packages and hire the developers needed to rebuild housing or revitalize a commercial strip. "We're not builders of homes or bankers ourselves," says Nancy Silvers, Goldsmith's deputy mayor for neighborhoods, "but we should be brokering those kinds of activities. The city has to be a player in housing and economic development: It has to pull the people to the table and get the resources in line."

Toward that end, Goldsmith has redirected the city's own development agenda away from the downtown focus of the Hudnut years and toward the communities that encircle the city's core. He has more than doubled the amount of funding set aside for community development corporations out of the city's federal Community Development Block Grant money, and amended the reimbursement process so that the neighborhood groups have enough cash early in the development process to keep projects moving. He also is steering a substantial chunk of a $500 million infrastructure improvement bond to repairing streets, building sidewalks and upgrading commercial thoroughfares in central-city communities.

At the same time, Goldsmith is trying to reconfigure the city's development bureaucracy to be more responsive to particular neighborhood concerns. "The way government is shaped now, it is functionally divided and bureaucratic," he says. "Instead, it ought to be ten people's job to restore our toughest neighborhood—to figure out how to do the houses, how to do the streets, how to make the park work, how to deliver the social services. Instead of a planning department and a housing department and just on and on, what we ought to have is the Department of Near West Side Indianapolis."

All of that is attractive in theory, and it has given Goldsmith a solid base of support in neighborhoods and among political activists who don't usually line up behind Republican politicians—even "populist" Republicans, as Goldsmith likes to call himself. Even so, turning these notions into reality has been an uneven process at best.

For one thing, Goldsmith's shift of attention has not only been away from downtown but it has also been away from affluent suburban neighborhoods that enjoyed close working relations with city officials in the 1980s. Some outlying neighborhood leaders are clearly resentful. "There's millions of dollars going into seven inner-city neighborhoods," says one. "Our position is, why can't you do something for both the suburbs and the inner city? Their position is, it's either-or."

Goldsmith dismisses such criticism as the griping of privileged communities that had grown accustomed to receiving the lion's share of attention from City Hall. To some extent, he is right. But it is also true that in his haste to reinvent the city's machinery, Goldsmith lost the people who could have made the transition smoother—mid-level managers familiar with the communities involved who might have been able to translate the concerns of the city to its citizens, and vice versa.

If the only neighborhoods affected by that had been suburban ones, where needs are less dire than in the inner city, it would be one thing. But it hasn't always been clear that Goldsmith or the relative newcomers who run his administration fully understand what is entailed in working closely with poor neighborhoods. This is, after all, a new departure for a staff whose experience is overwhelmingly drawn from the business world, not the streets. "He has surrounded himself with bright, talented people who have never squashed a grape," says Susan Williams, a Democrat on the city/county council who represents a majority-black district on the edge of downtown. "These are very progressive concepts the mayor has, but the implementation has fallen flat."

Some unsuccessful experiences,

such as a controversial and ultimately abortive attempt to privatize the management of two high-rise public housing developments, have been hard lessons in how difficult it can be to translate the entrepreneurial mindset that Goldsmith has fostered into the language of neighborhood participation. "We have a lot of people here filled with missionary zeal and imbued with only the best motives, and sometimes what our staff feels is self-evident is very much not," says Anne Shane, Goldsmith's chief of staff. "Sometimes they fail to understand that it takes time to rebuild a trust relationship when the constituents you're dealing with haven't historically had a good experience with city government."

The issue of trust is a crucial one for Goldsmith, because he is essentially asking the city's neighborhoods to take on responsibilities they haven't had to shoulder before, and there is no small amount of cynicism to overcome. "They're dealing with a lot of apathy," says Keith Broadnax, a program officer at the Indianapolis office of the Local Initiatives Support Corporation, "because everyone's been coming in and promising a lot of things for 25 years and never delivered."

So the ultimate test for Goldsmith's plans will be how well the new order delivers tangible achievements. And on that score, there have been some successes. Despite some turmoil at the upper ranks of the Department of Metropolitan Development, which oversees both downtown and neighborhood development, the city's planners have made themselves easily accessible to neighborhood groups, and the results have begun showing up in new sidewalks and redeveloped housing. The city has created neighborhood "code compliance committees" designed to allow community residents to identify their priorities for cleaning up dilapidated or abandoned

If it works in Indianapolis, will it work in New York or L.A.? Nobody knows.

housing, and has begun acting on their requests to tear down drug houses.

Perhaps most important, there are a lot of neighborhood activists, at least in the central city, who see Goldsmith as the first high-level politician in a long time who seems genuinely interested in giving them a say over where their communities go. "We don't want a welfare mentality, just for the city to come to us as a partner," says Olgen Williams, a foreman at Marathon Oil and chairman of Westco, an umbrella organization that brings together several mostly black West-Side neighborhoods. "And Mayor Goldsmith has come to us and said, 'I can't do it alone.'"

There remains, to be sure, a fair degree of skepticism. Some neighborhoods, though they have worked with the city for more than a year in drawing up plans for redevelopment, have yet to see any tangible change. As Dorothy Burse, director of a neighborhood association on the Near East Side, says, "All the plans we draw are not worth a dime until the dollars that take them off the paper and make them a reality are available." And there is considerable concern that some neighborhoods, simply by virtue of being better organized or endowed with more capable leadership, will wind up in better shape than others. The city is opening a "Neighborhood Resource Center" explicitly to train community leaders, but Goldsmith admits it should have been done sooner. "We were so busy trying to develop our capacity that

we missed the time to develop their capacity," he says.

Even so, there is no question that, in just two years, Goldsmith has turned Indianapolis into the first major test case of a Republican approach to cities that has until now existed solely in the "empowerment" rhetoric of Jack Kemp and his followers. In the process, he has raised the possibility that Republicans can turn conventional politics on its head by making allies of people to whom pulling the Democratic lever is as natural as breathing.

Whether Riordan, Giuliani and Schundler will follow suit isn't clear yet. They have all talked about urban revitalization at one time or another, and Schundler in particular has laid out a general push for welfare reform and the creation of development zones in the city; none of the three, though, has limned out a detailed strategy for making community development a reality. Even so, what the new Republican mayoral club represents more than anything else is a chance to demonstrate the workability of such ideas as decentralization and shifting power—and responsibility—away from government and to the community at large. To be sure, it's unlikely that a Giuliani or a Riordan could adopt anything that looks just like Goldsmith's program. Indianapolis is uniquely well-designed to be a laboratory, in large part because both its geography and its problems are of a manageable size. New York and L.A. are different animals altogether.

It would be ironic if the party that for years has played to suburban fears of the city and what it represents were to find its future in the knotty issues of urban governance. Yet for a GOP that has been wracked by division over social issues and unable to articulate a coherent vision of what it stands for, the cities may prove to be a lifesaver.

Block Watch

Not in Your Backyard, Say Community Panels In Suburban Enclaves

Associations Call the Shots On Fences, Parking, Pets As Homeowners Fume

That Satellite Dish Has to Go

Mitchell Pacelle

Staff Reporter of The Wall Street Journal

ROCKVILLE, Md.—Good fences make good neighbors, Allen Warshaw figured, after he was cracked over the head with a log by a neighbor he had accused of stealing firewood. So he decided to enclose his backyard with one six feet high.

Forget it, said the neighbors. Rules of the community association in the 330-home enclave limit fences to four feet. Complaining of arbitrary enforcement, Mr. Warshaw hired a lawyer and fought, eventually spending $14,000 on legal fees before giving up and ordering a four-foot fence.

But the association's architectural control committee wasn't satisfied; the $1,600 fence, though it had four-foot boards, actually topped out at more than 48 inches above the ground, it told him. And besides the spacing between the boards wasn't right. Fix it or it goes, the committee demanded.

SUBURBAN SPRAWL

In many parts of the country, buyers of new houses can no longer call their homes their castles. About 100,000 of the roughly 300,000 dwelling units in Montgomery County, an affluent expanse of suburban Washington that includes Rock-

ville, are ruled by community associations, including nearly all newly built homes. In Mr. Warshaw's neighborhood, Derwood Station South, his yard and home are very much the business of the association, a private, government-like body that enforces strict rules about everything from paint and storm doors to sandboxes and birdhouses.

Nationwide, there are about 150,000 such communities, housing nearly 32 million people, or one in eight Americans, according to the Community Associations Institute in Alexandria, Va. That is up from 20,000 communities in 1975.

Why people buy in the communities is a matter of some dispute. People in the real-estate industry say buyers often are attracted by the strict standards, believing they enhance quality of life and preserve values. But homeowner advocates contend that many people accept the rules because there is little or no other affordable new housing available. Subdivision developers form the community associations to manage and levy fees for common facilities and obligations such as road maintenance.

UTOPIAN NIGHTMARES

Many homeowners, of course, are willing to relinquish some freedom in exchange for the form of suburban utopia the associations aim to create. But the

hoped-for serenity of these tightly controlled environments is increasingly being shattered by emotional disputes over rules. Homeowners like Mr. Warshaw, who has lived in his Rockville neighborhood for about nine years, complain that their communities have fallen under the control of small-minded, heavy handed neighbors. You have a better chance of winning a fight against city hall, they say, than your community association.

"People move into these places, and they discover that the dream of owning their own castle isn't so shining," says Lawrence Holzman, a Rockville lawyer representing the fledgling Maryland Homeowners Association, a grass-roots organization dedicated to helping people like Mr. Warshaw. Dorothy Sager, a 78-year-old former school teacher who founded the group, complains that community associations are "a minigovernment without checks and balances without oversight and without an enforcement agency."

SUBSTANCE OF CONTROL

Many homeowners like the controls. "When you live in a town, you never know when you're going to get purple shutters across the street," says Pat Newman, owner of a townhouse in a planned community in Barrington, Ill. And association managers and lawyers say the restrictions are no secret to buyers, since the rules are spelled out in sales documents. "In theory, people know what they're buying into, and they should live with it," says Beverly Hills lawyer Leonard Siegel, who won a landmark California Supreme Court case this month upholding a Culver City condominium association's pet ban. But he concedes that "this kind of issue is an emotional issue."

That may be an understatement, given the intensity of disputes over architectural restrictions and bans on such things as window air conditioners, curbside auto repairs and basketball hoops. Of associations surveyed in 1991 by the Community Associations Institute, 90% reported reprimanding residents in letters, 25% had been involved in arbitrations and 18% had been embroiled in litigation.

It is cats and dogs that really have them fighting. In the Culver City case, entertainment manager Natore Nahrstedt ran up a $35,000 legal bill after her condominium complex's managers spied Boo-Boo, Tulip and Dockers through her window and ordered her to evict the cats. She argued that since they didn't leave her apartment, make noise or smell, the ban was unenforceable under a California law invalidating "unreasonable" restrictions. She lost.

Architectural restrictions can turn simple remodeling into an exercise in frustration. Caroline Stelle, a clerical worker who took advantage of a federal affordable-housing program to buy a 1,600-square-foot townhouse in a planned community in Silver Spring, Md., spent $7,000 last year adding a bay window. But the size at which it was built differed from that in the community-approved plan, prompting a lawsuit from the board to force her to rebuild. Ms. Stelle says she can't afford to make the changes, nor to hire a lawyer. "I feel totally helpless," she says.

Then there is the matter of parking. In Twin Rivers N.J., horseback-riding instructor Betty Stiles is fuming over a rule barring trucks. When she bought her home in the planned community last year, she says, her lawyer said her Ford Ranger pickup wouldn't be a problem because it was small and wasn't commercial. He was wrong. Her choices now: getting ticketed or towed by the commu-

nity's security force or parking as far as a mile away.

"It's asinine. This is America, not Russia," Ms. Stiles says. "If I were a wealthy person, I'd fight the hell out of them." Instead, she is trying to sell her pickup. But she is also supporting a neighbor's efforts to mount a class-action lawsuit against community restrictions.

Satellite dishes, considered an eyesore by many boards, result in some of the most bizarre disputes. Association lawyer James Curry of Orlando, Fla., cites pending litigation involving a man trying to get around a ban by disguising his satellite dish as a patio umbrella. Another case was resolved by a homeowner carving a giant divot into his backyard to conceal his television receiver.

A few rebellious homeowners have bested their associations. A San Diego man beat a truck ban by convincing a court that his small pickup was no more unsightly or disruptive than a car. But for the most part, courts have been unsympathetic to homeowners looking to buck the rules, many of whom admittedly failed to read the fine print of their purchase contracts.

"If the board of directors is not being arbitrary, and [X rule] doesn't violate public policy, then the court is likely to say its enforceable," says Denver lawyer Edward Burns Jr., head of the lawyers committee of the Community Associations Institute.

Since courts won't tolerate restrictions that run afoul of broad public policy—discriminatory rules, for instance—litigious homeowners often try to "sidle up to some constitutional issue," Mr. Burns adds. Satellite-dish owners have argued, to no avail, that the First Amendment guarantees their right to receive broadcasts.

Ever since the 1960s, when some of the nation's first huge planned communities went up in Virginia and Maryland, community planners and lawyers have been grappling with the question of whether they are private businesses or de facto governments.

"We started making the argument to judges, 'This is like a government,' so we can do things like assess fees," recalls David Mercer, a lawyer in Alexandria who

has been representing community groups for 15 years. "Then people started reverberating back, 'If you're a government, I must have rights.'" Management then started asserting the need to run like a business, he says. "It's an issue that's not going to be resolved."

Many Americans first heard about homeowners' associations during the housing boom after World War II, when some developers and real-estate agents used them as tools of exclusion, to build neighborhoods segregated by class or race.

But in recent years, the business exigencies of home development account for the growth of community associations. Because of the dwindling supply and rising cost of land around major cities, developers need to pack more homes on smaller plots. Putting playgrounds, pools and tennis courts on commonly owned land eases the crunch.

In addition, many cash-strapped towns and cities don't have the money to supply services to large new developments. Builders who are willing to take responsibility for road maintenance, garbage pickup and other services commonly handled by municipalities may get speedy approval. These developers, in turn, form community associations to act as governing bodies and "tax" residents to cover costs. In the process, the developers typically codify how the homes and yards must look.

"It's like a tacit conspiracy between developers and public officials to privatize development of public services without admitting they're doing it," says Evan McKenzie, a University of Illinois political-science professor and author of "Privatopia," a history of community groups. "This takes the step of suburbanization one step further. To some extent, they're seceding from urban and suburban America."

Developers typically turn over governance of the communities to an elected, all-volunteer board of directors, which must enforce the rules. Not surprisingly, only a small minority of residents get involved, and those who do tend to be the ones most concerned about maintaining standards.

5. CITIES AND SUBURBS

On enforcement matters, board members often rely on the advice of the management firms and lawyers that handle their communities' business affairs. Often, their advice is to be unbending in enforcement.

"That's balderdash," says Robert Diamond, a Falls Church, Va., lawyer who represents both associations and homeowners. "The board can make exceptions for good cause anytime it wants."

After informing Mr. Warshaw by letter that his fence had to be rebuilt, his association wrote to all of his neighbors: "If we do not enforce the rules with this individual, then we will not be able to enforce them later in other cases."

Jeffrey Van Grack, a Rockville lawyer for the association, concedes that "personalities came into play" in the standoff. Several days after fielding a reporter's questions, Mr. Van Grack said the association no longer had a problem with Mr. Warshaw's fence as it was built.

Homeowner advocates say few owners have the energy or financial wherewithal to battle their boards. But Ralph White, a government auditor living in an affluent neighborhood of Silver Spring, Md., had both. Even though Mr. White's plans for a driveway extension had been approved, a community-board official told laborers to stop work, complaining that the drive was several inches too close to the property line. Mr. White threatened board members with arrest if they set foot on his property again. Both sides hired lawyers.

"The board was just trying to comply with its covenants," says one member, who declines to be identified. "It turned into the most vicious campaign. I've never seen a community get so worked up." Mr. Van Grack, who represented the association in the early going, calls it "a personality dispute that got blown out of proportion." Homeowners eventually elected a new board, which dropped the objections and issued a statement of regret over "the significant time, expense and turmoil" the Whites endured.

Proponents of community-association living cringe over such tales, contending most boards are reasonable. Others say the disputes, however limited, send a troubling message about the changing nature of the American neighborhood.

Mr. Holzman, the lawyer, wonders: "When you're raising your children in a neighborhood where the local government can take great liberties in restricting how you express yourself, without the constitutional protection that we have come to expect, what is the next generation going to grow up to expect from their *real* government?"

The Sweet Smell Of Secession

Disgruntled neighborhoods around the country have found a new way to get city hall's attention: file for divorce.

ELIZABETH NIENDORF

Elizabeth Niendorf is a GOVERNING *editorial assistant.*

Last July, the town of Long Island, Maine, celebrated Independence Day as never before. There weren't just the traditional fireworks and cookouts—there was genuine independence. The 160 permanent residents of Long Island, a quiet fishing village 45 minutes off the Maine coast, had proclaimed themselves free at last of the city of Portland, to which they had belonged for 207 years.

Why they did it was simple enough. "Our property taxes went up five times in one assessment," said Long Islander Cynthia Steeves. "What they did was start everyone thinking if we could figure out what the city of Portland was taking in tax dollars and what we could do." It turned out that, on average, Portland received $300,000 more in property taxes every year from Long Island than it paid back to the island in services.

Once it set the course for rebellion, Long Island never turned back. After

winning the approval of the Maine legislature to hold a formal referendum on breaking away, Long Island residents voted overwhelmingly in November of 1992 to go it alone. Last July, they became a government unto themselves. "We're electing regular people," says the enthusiastic planning board chairman, Robert Jordan.

The start-up money for the new government of Long Island came from about $10,000 in T-shirt sales and private contributions. Even the building for the town hall was donated. "All of the town has been working for nothing. No one has been collecting on phone bills or postage," says Nancy Jordan, Robert Jordan's wife and the head of the board that now runs the island's one school, which has 19 students.

The only drawback is that what the islanders set out for in the first place, a large tax reduction, is not what they got. Their taxes for 1993 are $22.38 per thou-

sand dollars of assessed property, only $2.27 lower than those in Portland. Five dollars of that money goes to pay off a share of Portland's debt.

Notwithstanding that one small fiscal detail, it has all been worthwhile, the secessionists claim. Nevertheless, Long Island offers a small cautionary tale for the surprisingly many villages and neighborhoods that are currently considering exactly the move the islanders chose to make. The consequences can be difficult to predict.

There is no doubt that secession is, if not a national craze, at least a growing issue. In the past couple of years, the communities of Oak Cliff and Coconut Grove have considered seceding from Dallas and Miami, respectively. There have been secession campaigns in two Boston neighborhoods, South Boston and Roxbury. A collection of rural counties in western Kansas and a chunk of northern California have made breakaway noises.

Many of these small-scale rebellions, perhaps most of them, will never come to anything. Still, there are certain to be more of them in the next several years, fueled by tax increases, feelings of underrepresentation in city or state decision making, and complaints of chronically poor service in areas far from the seat of government.

THE ISSUE WILL BE ESPECIALLY visible next month, when the borough of Staten Island holds a referendum on whether to secede from New York City.

People joke that Staten Island, home to the infamous Fresh Kills landfill, is New York's garbage dump. Actually, it is the city's most uniformly prosperous borough as well as the smallest, a mid-

The vote in Staten Island next month could be a catalyst for secession efforts across the country.

dle-class residential enclave of 380,000 people. Closer to the Union County courthouse in Elizabeth, New Jersey, than to City Hall in lower Manhattan, Staten Islanders have always seen themselves a community apart. They will become a city apart if they vote for secession and manage to persuade the New York legislature to go along with it.

The current secession drive began four years ago, when a court decision abolished the New York City Board of Estimate, on which all five boroughs, regardless of size, had the same voting strength. Staten Island's interests in the city are now represented by three seats on a city council with 51 members in all. "It's proving to be ineffective to address Staten

Island issues in the larger council," argues Mark F. Muscaro, president of Staten Island's Chamber of Commerce. The chamber came out for secession in June.

Moreover, the Board of Estimate issue turned out to be a trigger for all sorts of complicated feelings of neglect and indifference on the part of the city. "People on Staten Island got to saying, 'We don't have anything: no identity, no services,'" says Dan Singletary, an early leader in the secessionist movement. Cynics like to add that there are other things Staten Island does not have, does not want and does not wish to pay for—notably a sizable minority or low-income population and the social services such a population requires.

In 1990, 83 percent of Staten Islanders voted to begin the secession process. With the support of their state legislators and Governor Mario M. Cuomo, the New York State Charter Commission for Staten Island was established to draft a city charter for the island and study the implications of secession. The commission membership, critics said, titled toward independence.

As expected, the commission found that Staten Island had the resources to make it on its own. Yet even with a strong revenue base, the island currently contributes $170 million less to New York than it receives in services. The administration of Mayor David N. Dinkins used that figure to argue that independence would be the equivalent of a $170 million property tax hike for an independent Staten Island.

The commission has responded that the $170 million gap likely would not exist if the island were a separate entity. "New York has an enormous service budget and bureaucracy unlike any other local government," says Joseph P. Viteritti, the charter commission's executive director and head of the Center for Management at New York University's Wagner School of Public Service. "Staten Island, given its size, won't have to maintain all those services. And instead of having a separate department for highways, sanitation and transportation, it might have a public works department all in one structure."

In fact, the whole issue of the tax gap appears to make little difference to many of the Staten Island residents, including the business community. Last April, in an informal Chamber of Commerce poll of its members, most respondents said they would support secession even if they

knew taxes would climb higher as a result. Although Borough President Guy V. Molinari and some residents insist that secession will mean much higher property taxes for Staten Island, there is good reason to believe that the referendum will pass.

If that does happen next month, the number of secession campaigns around the country is likely to increase. Some of the rebels will learn, however, that Staten Island, landmark case though it may be, doesn't begin to cover all the possible complications. It is, to begin with, an island. Its boundaries, just like those of Long Island, Maine, are clear. In most other situations, the problem of defining borders is troublesome enough to frustrate even the most ardent secessionists.*

Take Oak Cliff, for example. In 1990, leaders in this south Dallas community threatened secession when a redistricting plan temporarily eliminated the area's traditional council district and split Oak Cliff among five constituencies. Seizing upon the remap issue to stir up long-simmering feelings of neglect by City Hall, residents joined together to support a bill in the Texas legislature to allow Oak Cliff to secede. The question was, however: What is Oak Cliff?

"What you call Oak Cliff is a matter of dispute," says Royce Hanson, dean of the School of Social Sciences at the University of Texas at Dallas. "The secessionists included about one-third of Dallas in Oak Cliff, but it is traditionally substantially smaller than that."

The real issue was that Oak Cliff is a pocket of white middle-class homeowners located within the poorer minority part of town, south of the Trinity River. What the secessionists had sought to do was carve out a territory for themselves big enough to be fiscally healthy. But without skipping across the river to include affluent areas further north, that would be hard to do. In the end, the legislature did not pass the bill.

IN FACT, THOUGH, SECESSIONists don't always have to win actual separation to accomplish much of what they set out to get. Last March, in Florida, Dade County voters defeated a measure that would have allowed communities with 5,000 or more registered voters to consider seceding from Miami and would have let unincorporated areas of the county incorporate themselves into new cities. But despite the outcome of that vote, some of the separatists say they have been treated with considerably more respect in its aftermath. "There has been an increased awareness in the halls of government in Dade County and in the city of Miami," says Jose Rojas, whose community of Kendall had considered incorporating to free itself of county jurisdiction. Previously, Rojas says, the Dade government was "big, fat and unresponsive." Now, in his opinion, "those that represent Kendall do tend to be a little more responsive and accessible."

Guillermo Olmedillo, the chief planner for Dade County and a former Miami city official, concedes that Rojas has a point. Miami, Olmedillo says, would be "affected very deeply" if affluent communities such as Coconut Grove were to break away, taking tax dollars with them. "Now there is a sense of urgency there," he says. "It was a failed attempt, but it was a serious attempt."

How far will the secession fad go? You can make the case that much of it amounts to posturing and political maneuvering; some campaigns, such as the ones at the state level in California and Kansas, are difficult to take seriously at all, while others, as in Oak Cliff, are unlikely to make it past the legal complications and legislative obstacles.

On the other hand, there is Staten Island, which may very well pull it off.

And there is the inescapable fact that secessions are taking place all over the world, as states and provinces separate from nations and form new political jurisdictions that seemed unthinkable only a matter of months ago. That is not going to happen here, but it is bound to give people ideas. And some of the ideas are going to turn into headaches for those whose job it is to keep larger communities together.

[*In the November 2, 1993 elections, residents of Staten Island, N.Y., voted for secession by a 2-to-1 margin. The secession issue was then placed in the hands of the governor and State Legislature. *Editor.*]

Finances and Economic Development

- Revenues (Articles 43–51)
- Economic Development (Articles 52–56)

Like all governments, state and local governments need financial resources to carry out their activities. State and local governments rely on a variety of revenue sources, including sales taxes, income taxes, and property taxes; user charges (for example, motor vehicle registration fees and college tuition); lotteries; and grants of money from other levels of government. But despite this diversity of funding sources, the overall financial situation of state and local governments is often far from satisfactory.

Conspicuous attempts to curb spending at all levels of government have been made in recent years. Most prominent among such measures was Proposition 13, passed by California voters in a 1978 referendum. Proposition 13 put ceilings on local government property taxes and, in turn, affected the programs that local governments in California could offer. The Proposition 13 tax revolt soon spread to other states. By now, measures designed to limit government spending have come into effect in states and localities across the country. At the national level, a constitutional amendment has been proposed and legislation has been passed in attempts to make it difficult for Congress to pass an unbalanced budget.

Unlike the national government, state and local governments get a sizable portion of their revenues from intergovernmental grants. The national government gives money to state and local governments with various conditions attached. Money can be given with virtually no accompanying strings or with considerable limitations on how it can be spent. Similarly, states provide state aid to local governments under varying sets of conditions. Governments providing financial grants, of course, exercise control over the amount of funds available and the conditions attached to such funds. This, in turn, can cause considerable uncertainty for governments relying on grant money. As should be apparent, intergovernmental relations and state and local finances are areas that overlap considerably.

The financial situation of state and local governments differs from that of the national government in other important respects. The national government has considerable ability to affect the national economy by controlling the money supply and by budgetary deficits or, at least in theory, budgetary surpluses. By contrast, most state and local governments are legally required to balance their budgets. For those not required to have balanced budgets, it is difficult to borrow money for large and persistent budget deficits. The fiscal crises of New York City and other local governments during the 1970s showed that lenders will go only so far in providing money for state and local governments whose expenditures are consistently greater than their revenues. The declaration of bankruptcy by Orange County, California, in late 1994 reveals how tempting it is for local governments to pursue risky, although potentially very profitable, investment strategies, especially in difficult financial times.

Both the national government and state and local governments seek to promote economic development. New industries employ workers who pay taxes and, thus, increase government revenues. What is new on the state and local scene is the energy and persistence with which states and localities compete with one another to attract industries to their areas.

Finances are a complicated but critical aspect of state and local government. The first section of this unit treats taxes, lotteries, and related revenue-raising matters. The second section focuses on activities of state and local governments related to economic development.

Looking Ahead: Challenge Questions

Approximately how much money do you (or your parents, if you are not a full-time wage earner) annually pay to local, state, and national governments, respectively? Is this an easy question to answer? Why or why not?

Property tax, a tax on the value of real estate and buildings, is a primary source of revenue for local governments. Do you think people who live in rented apartments or houses avoid property taxes? Why or why not?

Why do you think that the national government has assumed more and more of the burden for raising revenues for all three levels of government?

What do you think is the best means for state and local governments to raise revenues: property taxes, income taxes, sales taxes, lotteries, user charges, or something else?

After reading Ronald Snell's article, "The Tax the Public Loves to Hate," do you think that measures such as Proposition 13 in California and Proposition 2 1/2 in Massachusetts are desirable? Why or why not?

Revenue-Raising Partners

State and local governments, closest to home, provide the services most visible and most important to taxpayers.

James Edwin Kee and John Shannon

James Kee, associate professor of public administration at George Washington University, is a visiting scholar at The Urban Institute. John Shannon, former director of the U.S. Advisory Commission on Intergovernmental Relations, is a senior fellow at The Urban Institute.

What is the most significant feature of American Federalism? After 200 years, state governments and their local government partners remain vibrant domestic policy leaders in the federal system. This remarkable achievement can be traced largely to one overarching truth: During peacetime, the 50 state-local systems of government possess inherent political advantages over the national government when competing for taxpayer support.

After 50 years of apparent federal government centralization, the nation has entered a new period we call "competitive federalism," where leadership in domestic policy will flow to whichever level of government can persuade its voters to provide the tax revenue for necessary government services.

Most political scientists and economists, as well as the general public, assume that the national government enjoys an enormous competitive advantage in raising money. However, the history of the last 50 years points in just the opposite direction. Since World War II, Washington, D.C., has gradually pulled back, and state and local governments have steadily advanced on the general revenue front. In 1944, the federal government raised nearly five times as much general revenue, excluding Social Security, as state and local governments. Now they are essentially equal.

When raising general revenue, the 50 state-local systems have at least six political advantages over the national government.

 The close-to-home advantage. Even during periods of severe national crisis, state and local officials never lose control of "core" domestic programs—police, education, land use, local and regional transportation, economic development, public health and public amenities (parks, museums and libraries).

State and local officials are closer to the people in the sense that they operate programs perceived to have the most direct benefit for the greatest number of citizens—a situation that tends both to lessen taxpayer resistance and to generate public support for additional funding.

By sharp contrast, primary responsibility for many of the nation's necessary but highly controversial domestic tasks now rests with Washington: income redistribution, environmental protection, affirmative action and occupational safety. In addition, federal financing of a wide variety of special interest chores, such as subsidies for small business, hospitals for veterans and price supports for farmers, is not perceived to affect a large number of people and tends to generate taxpayer resistance to higher federal taxes for general government purposes.

Only in the special trust fund areas, such as Social Security and Medicare, has Washington repeatedly pushed through major peacetime tax increases. Why? Because in these areas there is a close connection between the dedicated tax paid and the benefit received.

 The balance-or-else advantage. There is an iron law that governs the financing of democratic governments: There can be no major tax rate hike *for general government* purposes without a major crisis. Because they must operate with balanced budgets, states and localities frequently confront crisis. Regional and national recessions, judicial mandates and acute demographic pressures (like the baby boom) are stressful but generate consensus that prompts or forces state and local officials to vote major tax increases that would be politically suicidal without a crisis. The higher taxes usually linger on once the crisis has passed—the upward ratchet effect.

Federal policymakers have a natural revenue-raising advantage only during a major war. In the last 50 years, Congress has enacted a general income tax rate hike on only three occasions, World War II, the Korean War and the war in Vietnam. Once the war is over, conservative demands for tax cuts and liberal urgings to spend the peace dividend on domestic needs create an anti-crisis, a polarizing situation that leads first to a gradual reduction in general federal taxes and then to an enormous run-up of the federal debt.

3 The divide-and-conquer advantage. More than 80,000 units of government making decisions about revenues and expenditures have been created by the states, all competing for public support. This central feature of the American federal system allows states to match more closely the pain of taxation with the rewards of specific benefits and services. In addition, as the state and local tax load increases, state legislators become willing to give local officials more tax rope.

Required to tax uniformly across the nation, the federal government lacks the crucial ability to disperse decision making to these thousands of local governing units.

The "big four" advantage. Driven by budgetary realities and competitive concerns, most of our 50 systems now make fairly balanced use of the big four revenue sources: income, sales and property taxes and user fees. For example, when Connecticut was faced with a large deficit, it couldn't further hike its sales tax and corporate income tax rates for fear of damaging its competitive position with neighboring states. Thus, it was forced to enact a broad-based individual income tax.

In addition, states especially have a wide variety of miscellaneous levies– "sin" taxes, lotteries and regulatory fees–to bridge smaller budgetary gaps. Diversification is the incrementalist's dream, allowing state and local governments to make a series of light surgical probes on the taxpayers' pockets. In contrast, raising the federal income tax is akin to amputation.

The follow-thy-neighbor advantage. Unlike the federal government, states and local governments are constantly forced to upgrade services to keep up with their neighboring jurisdictions. Often unusual allies— liberal reformers and conservative business leaders—come together to argue for greater taxes for education and better roads.

However, in an increasingly competitive world market, the federal government will also find that it too will come under increasing pressure to keep up with its foreign trading partners in education, the environment and fiscal discipline.

The less-to-lose advantage. State and local officials tend to be less risk-averse than their Washington counterparts. Most are "citizen legislators"; their office is not their whole life and career. If they vote for an unpopular tax increase and are defeated in the next election, it is not the end of the world.

With the decline of political parties,

Revenue as a Percentage of Gross National Product

Year	State & Local General Revenue	Federal General Revenue	Total General Revenue	Federal Social Insurance Revenue	Total Government Revenue
1940	9.1	5.7	14.8	.8	15.6
1944	4.9	23.5	28.4	1.3	29.7
1954	7.1	18.3	25.4	1.6	27.0
1964	9.3	15.6	24.9	2.9	27.8
1974	11.7	14.8	26.5	5.1	31.6
1984	12.1	13.7	25.8	6.1	31.9
est. 1990	13.2	13.7	26.9	6.8	33.7

Source: Bureau of the Census data, selected years. State-local general revenue excludes federal aid, employee pension payments and utility and liquor store receipts. Federal general revenue excludes postal receipts; Social Insurance Revenue includes Social Security, Medicare and certain other federal insurance trust fund receipts.

the rise of PAC funding and the emergence of the independent "political entrepreneur," members of Congress have become increasingly risk-averse. Higher congressional salaries and generous perks of office make federal elected officials ever more fearful of political defeat.

Some of the advantages of raising revenue locally (close-to-home, balance-or-else and divide-and-conquer) are inherent in the current political structure of American federalism. The other three advantages (big four, follow-thy-neighbor and less-to-lose) reinforce the first three, but are more susceptible to political change.

What is the big message for state-local relations? When competition for general revenue is viewed broadly, we have only two basic contestants: Washington, D.C., and the 50 state-local revenue systems. Why? Because local governments are the essential offspring and partners of state government in financ-

ing and delivering most domestic public goods and services; they're not standalone units of government.

Over the past several decades, the great advances made in strengthening state revenue systems were driven largely by the need to respond to local concerns, such as property tax relief and school finance reform. The growing diversification of revenue at the local level and the creation of myriad special districts provide convincing evidence that state government recognizes the advantage of using local government to gain political accountability for the financing of specific expenditure demands.

In *The Federalist Papers*, Madison argued that if the states did not exist, the central government would be forced to create them. It is equally true that if local governments did not exist, the states would have had to create them—as their indispensable partners and allies in a highly competitive federal system.

Our Outmoded Tax Systems

State tax systems were invented in a different age for a different set of circumstances. The fit between the systems and the realities becomes more imperfect every day.

Ronald K. Snell

Ronald K. Snell is director of NCSL's fiscal affairs program.

Now that state tax collections have improved, Medicaid cost increases are no longer burning like a prairie fire through state budgets, and sustained economic growth seems likely, can legislators put tax issues out of their minds?

If state finances are improving, why even raise the issue? "If it ain't broke, don't fix it." Why should state officials subject themselves to the stress and misery of talking about taxes, let alone the fundamental reconsideration of state tax policy?

> *It is time to consider more fundamental questions of how well state tax systems in the 1990s reflect the American economy of the 1990s.*

States' tax policy may not be *broken*. But it's chugging along like a '39 Studebaker on a 1990s expressway: getting somewhere, in a manner of speaking, but not efficiently, not reliably, not in a very satisfactory way.

From 1989 through 1993, budget shortfalls and tax increases dominated legislative sessions. Legislators debated countless changes designed to give larger shares of shrinking resources to corrections, education and health care while revenue growth stalled. Time and again, unhappy legislators voted to increase taxes to sustain state spending while constituents' incomes were stagnant or shrinking. Legislators, governors and taxpayers alike are ready to put the subject of taxes aside—except for the possibility of tax cuts, which occupied many legislatures in 1994.

But the time to stop thinking about taxes has not yet come. The issue that needs attention, however, is not revenue raising in the short term. For now, most states appear to be in solid fiscal health—with the exception of northern New England and California, places where the recession of 1990 has never ended.

It's Time to Remodel

It is time to consider more fundamental questions of how well state tax systems in the 1990s reflect the American economy of the 1990s. That is the subject of the book *Financing State Government in the 1990s*, published jointly by the National Conference of State Legislatures and the National Governors' Association. Three other formidable 50-state policy associations—the Federation of Tax Administrators, the Multistate Tax Commission and the National Association of State Budget Officers—provided much of the policy discussion in the book. The result, according to Hal Hovey of State Policy Research Inc., is "the new conventional wisdom among state officials." Conventional wisdom or not, the book asks legislators and governors to consider remodeling a structure of state taxation that has developed haphazardly for over half a century.

To see why this is necessary, consider the general nature of state tax policy—the kind of taxes state governments rely upon, what they tax and how the taxes operate. Then consider how America has changed since the foundations of current state tax policy were laid.

States Tax Alike

It's possible to talk about tax systems in terms of the 50 states, despite the great differences in individual policies, because states have tended to make their policies resemble those of their neighbors. The 50 state governments have two major sources of tax revenue—the general sales tax and the personal income tax. The third state tax source is the corporate income tax, which in terms of revenue is far less important than either of the two mainstays. And all 50 states mandate that local governments impose property taxes, usually to finance a substantial chunk of elementary and secondary education as well as to pay for local administrative expenses.

Every state, except New Hampshire and Alaska, has either a general sales tax or a broad-based personal income tax and most have both. Only five states (Alaska, Delaware, Montana, New Hampshire and Oregon) do not impose a general sales tax. Seven states (Alaska, Florida, Nevada, South Dakota, Texas, Washington and Wyoming) have no personal income tax, and two more (New Hampshire and Tennessee) tax only investment income.

States rely heavily on sales and personal income taxes. In FY 1992 state governments collected $328 billion in taxes (not including any local government taxes). Of that amount, $108 billion or 33 percent came from the general sales tax and $104 billion or 32 percent from personal income taxes. The corporate income tax (collected by 45 states) produced $21.5 billion, a little under 7 percent of total state tax collections.

Local property taxes produce more revenue than any state tax. Figures for

> *The way Americans generate wealth and the way they spend their income has changed dramatically since the 1930s.*

FY 1992 are not yet available, but in the year before, local property tax collections were more than half as large as total state tax collections. For that reason, any substantial reduction in local property taxes, such as the one the Michigan Legislature approved in 1993 or the one Oregon voters approved in 1990, forces major revisions in finances if state government makes up for the revenue forgone.

This basic picture of heavy reliance upon general sales taxes and personal income taxes, supplemented by a corporate income tax at the state level and by property taxes at the local level, has characterized state government since 1971. From 1961 through 1971, income taxes were enacted in 10 states and sales taxes in 10 states (for 19 states in all—Nebraska double-dipped). Only two states have added either tax since 1971, so that the general outline of state tax systems has been stable for 20 years. But the roots of the current tax systems go back much further, to the years of the Great Depression.

Replacing State Property Taxes

The current system was invented in the 1930s to replace old state property taxes. As late as 1932, state governments collected more revenue from property taxes than from their sales, personal income and corporate income taxes combined. During the Depression, the failure of property taxes to produce revenue and their potential for destroying the assets of farmers and homeowners led 16 states to adopt individual income taxes from 1931 to 1937. Even more

states—23 from 1933 to 1938—followed Mississippi's lead in trying out the newly invented general sales tax. Although the nation's economy has enjoyed a sea change since the dismal 1930s, these taxes remain much as they were designed to be in the days of dust bowls and Hoovervilles.

The state adoption of sales and income taxes in the 1930s represented modernization. Basing state taxes on wages, salaries and consumption instead of real estate recognized that the United

States had become a nation of factory and office workers instead of farmers. That was, of course, a belated discovery for state policymakers in the 1930s—in 1929, nonfarm personal income was 10 times as great as farm income in the United States. It took an economic crisis of previously unknown proportions to bring the discovery home.

System Outmoded Again

Over the past 50 years, economic changes of similar magnitude have again outmoded state tax systems. The economy of smokestack industries they were designed for no longer exists. The way Americans generate wealth and the way they spend their income has changed dramatically since the 1930s.

Manufacturing is in decline relative to other areas of the economy. In the

1930s, services accounted for about one-third of GNP; the share fell briefly because of wartime manufacturing growth, but has grown steadily since the late 1940s. The share of GNP attributable to the production of goods has declined steadily since the mid-1940s. In 1975, the production of services became a larger share of GNP than that of goods, and the services sector has continued to grow in relative as well as absolute terms.

An equally important change has occurred in how Americans spend their money. We eat at MacDonald's instead of buying groceries, and we rent videos instead of buying books. Consumers in 1990 spent smaller proportions of their money on durable and nondurable goods than in 1960, much less on groceries and about the same share on housing. But expenditures on services (which include restaurant and take-out meals and explain how Americans manage to eat) grew from 25 percent to 42 percent of consumer expenditures.

The trend toward producing and consuming more services and fewer manufactured goods is likely to continue. The services sector is the fastest-growing and healthiest part of the economy. In the 1980s, the goods-producing sector of the economy grew at a rate of 0.2 percent a year while services grew at 3.8 percent a year.

Two other kinds of changes deserve notice because they are also significant in the structure of state tax policy. Americans are growing older. In 1940, less than 7 percent of Americans were over age 65. By 1990, their share had grown to 12.5 percent. The share of the

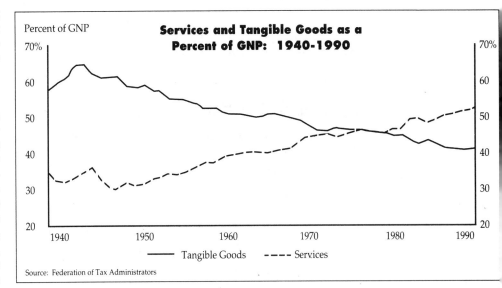

Percent of GNP

Services and Tangible Goods as a Percent of GNP: 1940-1990

—— Tangible Goods   - - - - Services

Source: Federation of Tax Administrators

population that has reached what we consider to be retirement age will continue to grow for the next 50 years.

Finally, not only has the nature of business production changed, but so has the scope. The most dramatic signs have been the rapidity with which the latest round of the General Agreement on Tariffs and Trade (GATT) followed the North American Free Trade Agreement—international business is more and more a visible, everyday fact. Exports of goods and services grew from 5.6 percent of gross national product in 1970 to 10.5 percent in 1991; imports have grown even faster.

Within the United States, a steadily increasing share of business transactions crosses state lines. Millions of homeowners send their mortgage payments to a bank in another state. Mail-order catalog sales have grown enormously. More and more businesses operate in more than one state. The local department store may exist in name, but it is likely to belong to a national conglomerate. National franchises have replaced mom-and-pop operations.

So far this is a familiar story. Its relevance for state tax policy is this: All three of the most important state taxes—the general sales tax, the personal income tax and the corporate income tax—have, to some extent, been made obsolete by economic and demographic change. States have tended to overlook the need for fundamental tax reform while the national economy has changed. State tax systems have been revised, updated and reformed to an extent that would be admirable if the

American economy were still what it was in 1972. But tax policy has fallen behind the times.

What a Good System Is

It matters because the fundamental changes just described have distorted the workings of state taxes so that they no longer comport with reasonable expectations of what ought to characterize a state tax system:

• *Equity*—Taxpayers who are in similar circumstances should be treated similarly, and dissimilar treatment should be reserved for taxpayers whose situations are dissimilar.

• *Promoting economic efficiency*—As a rule, it is desirable to design taxes to have as little impact on individual and business decisions as possible. When taxes are intended to discourage or encourage specific behavior, they should be carefully targeted to their intended purpose.

• *Broad bases*—Broad bases help to distribute tax burdens, and, by contributing to low rates, minimize the effect of taxation on the private sector's economic decisions.

• *Productivity*—How much revenue a government should collect is a political issue, but whatever the decision is, a tax system should predictably produce that amount in order to prevent frequent changes to bases and rates to preserve the revenue stream.

The economic and demographic changes listed above have had specific consequences for state taxes.

State Sales Taxes

Sales taxes are a good example of how states have failed to adapt their tax systems to changes in the economy. In almost every state, sales tax bases remain, as they were in the 1930s, focused on tangible goods; in most states, they exclude most services. The shift toward production and consumption of services and away from manufactured goods has prevented the sales tax base from growing in proportion to the national economy, requiring rate increases to maintain the relative productivity of the tax. Purchases of services are favored over purchases of goods, since goods are taxed and services are not. The tax is less stable and more regressive than a broader based sales tax would be.

Because more than half of the states enacted their current sales tax statutes during the 1930s, the tax base reflects the U.S. economy during the Great Depression. Most personal consumption at that time consisted of purchases of tangible property. Such services as existed (other than housing, education and utilities) were generally from manual labor. As a result, most sales tax systems became taxes on retail sales of tangible property, and they mostly excluded purchases of services.

Despite recent attempts in some states to broaden the sales tax base, service transactions still are generally untaxed. Because a growing share of consumer money is spent on services, this explains the fact that sales tax collections fail to grow in proportion to the economy. The average state sales tax rate grew from 3.54 percent in 1970 to 5.07 percent in 1992. Yet due to the narrowing of the tax base through enacted exemptions and increased service consumption, the substantial rate increase succeeded only in holding collections at a constant share of GNP. State sales tax collections were 2.7 percent of GNP in 1970, and they remained at 2.7 percent in 1990.

Excluding services from state and local sales and use tax bases raises policy issues beyond that of revenue productivity. Exclusion affects the neutrality of the tax by treating similar transactions in dissimilar fashion. A system that taxes the purchase of new items, but does not tax repairs, favors repairs over purchases. Exclusion of services also affects the stability of the tax during the economic cycle. A tax structure that includes only purchases of tangible personal property (especially one that

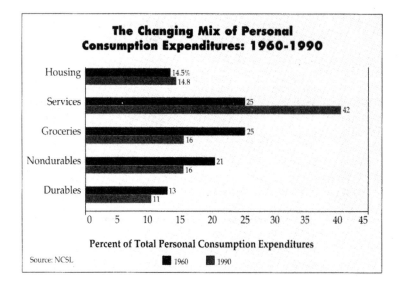

The Changing Mix of Personal Consumption Expenditures: 1960-1990

Housing — 14.5%, 14.8
Services — 25, 42
Groceries — 25, 16
Nondurables — 21, 16
Durables — 13, 11

Percent of Total Personal Consumption Expenditures

Source: NCSL   ■ 1960   ■ 1990

exempts food for home consumption) is more sensitive to downturns in the economy than a more broadly based tax. Finally, the expansion of a sales tax to services can make the sales tax less regressive.

Personal Income Taxes

Changes in the U.S. economy and demographic patterns pose growing problems for the base and equity of the state personal income tax as well as its responsiveness to personal income growth. A growing proportion of personal income goes untaxed because of specific federal and state decisions to give it preference.

The same is true of American workers' pay. Untaxed fringe benefits are increasing—health insurance, pre-tax contributions to pension plans, various forms of deferred compensation for retirement savings and flexible spending accounts. Since state income tax bases generally conform to the federal tax base, this income goes largely untaxed at the state level as well.

These benefits affect the equity of the tax because two workers can receive similar total compensation, but substantially different untaxed benefits. They will be treated differently because one worker enjoys more tax-exempt income than the other. Since there is a tendency for higher paid workers to receive more fringe benefits than lower paid workers, the exclusion of fringe benefits from income taxation reduces the progressivity of the income tax.

Exempting fringe benefits from income taxation while more compensation is made in the form of fringe benefits also reduces the responsiveness of income taxes to economic growth in the United States. The reason is that a greater proportion of that growth is used for nontaxable compensation.

In addition, many states provide special tax credits, deductions, exemptions and exclusions for certain kinds of income received by people over 65, often without means testing. Such preferences pose a number of policy problems. Households headed by people over 65 are less likely than any other age group to be below the poverty line; 6.5 percent of such households were below the poverty line in 1992, as opposed to 11.5 percent of all American households.

Age-specific tax breaks, therefore, benefit a relatively prosperous group of people. They also benefit a growing number of people, as the American population ages. Such policies are not only inequitable, if equity requires similar treatment for people whose incomes are similar, but they will also be increasingly expensive as more of the population becomes able to take advantage of them.

In general, the proportion of American personal income subject to taxes is shrinking (although the *dollar* amount continues to grow). Tax-protected income such as social security, pension payments, welfare benefits and untaxed fringe benefits have grown from 14.3 percent of personal income in 1970 to 20.5 percent in 1990. Earnings and investment income have fallen as a percent of national personal income, while the kinds of income that are not so fully taxed have grown as a percentage of national income. Thus, state personal income taxes are being levied on a smaller proportion of total personal income than in the past.

Without changes in tax policy or patterns of compensating workers, the responsiveness of the personal income tax to growth in national personal income will steadily decline.

Taxes on Business

A third area in which change in the economy has outstripped state policy is the taxation of business. Current corporate income taxes were written largely with manufacturers in mind and are not as effective in reaching businesses that produce services. One reason springs from the difficulty of determining where provision of a service can be said to occur for tax purposes. Take an imaginary example: A New York advertising

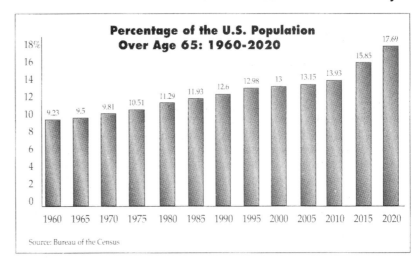

Percentage of the U.S. Population Over Age 65: 1960-2020

Year	Percentage
1960	9.23
1965	9.5
1970	9.81
1975	10.51
1980	11.29
1985	11.93
1990	12.6
1995	12.98
2000	13
2005	13.15
2010	13.93
2015	15.85
2020	17.69

Source: Bureau of the Census

agency develops a TV ad campaign for a company in Chicago. The agency uses data stored in a computer in Massachusetts, and it has a design studio and some offices in Connecticut. As the campaign progresses, presentations sometimes are done by teleconference using a rented satellite uplink studio in Connecticut and sometimes in the client's Chicago office. So diffuse a set of activities was not envisioned in corporate tax law as it exists in most states.

Even for more traditional forms of production, the increase in interstate and international activity has created situations state business tax law was not designed to handle. Inconsistencies among the states allow for loopholes that interstate corporations can legitimately use to protect income from taxation. The rapid growth in interstate and international commerce confronts the states with questions about their authority to tax multi-jurisdictional transactions and businesses, the preservation of tax bases, and the distribution of the tax burden between companies that operate in only one state and those that operate across state lines.

Policies Create Problems

Finally, policies of the federal government and of state governments themselves have created problems. Federal preemption through statutes is one threat, a good example being the way that the Railroad Revitalization and Regulatory Reform Act preempted some aspects of state control of taxation and created a privileged position for railroads vis-a-vis other transportation industries. Federal courts also can limit state freedom to act, as the Supreme

Court did in the *Bellas Hess* case, which limits states' authority to require out-of-state vendors to collect sales tax on items shipped into the state. The possibility exists that GATT may infringe upon state powers of taxation. State governments themselves can damage their tax systems with economic incentive packages that erode tax bases and shift tax burdens, thus raising issues of fairness.

What's To Be Done?

Given all these ways that state tax systems have failed to keep pace with economic change, what will happen? And what will legislators do?

Two things seem likely if states fail to modernize their taxes. Tax bases will become even less equitable, as the winds of change benefit some groups in the population and some kinds of business. Equity matters; taxpayers notice unfairness and have never been very patient with it.

Second, with tax bases becoming narrower, taxes will not grow in proportion to economic growth without repeated rate increases. State expenditures in recent years have tended to grow as fast as the economy or faster, driven by education and health spending. Proponents of higher education, welfare reform and more aid to local governments are likely to exert pressure for greater state spending and will push for tax increases. Proponents of smaller government could welcome taxes that produce slow revenue growth as a brake on government growth.

If state governments see these issues as problems to be solved, what can be done? Good analysis of state tax policy is the first step, since in some cases the statement of a problem suggests a solution. *Financing State Government* in the 1990s has some general recommendations:

• **Review the ways that changing economic conditions affect a state's tax structure.** The kinds of structural issues discussed in this article have received little attention in state tax reform in recent years, a point made very clear in a recent report by Steven D. Gold and Jennifer McCormick, *State Tax Reform in the Early 1990s*. Although states continue to make personal income taxes somewhat more progressive and sales tax bases a little broader, they have ignored fundamental issues.

• **Consider state tax policy systemically, not as a set of unrelated components.** State and local tax policy are intertwined; the progressivity of one tax can offset regressivity of another; scant use of one tax can require high rates from another.

• **Carefully evaluate the impact of economic development incentives upon state tax policy.** Interstate competition for economic development can force states to grant incentives or shape tax policy in ways that may not be cost effective overall.

• **Cooperate with other states.** States have preferred to go it alone, but the complexities of the modern economy, the pressures to grant economic development incentives and the dangers of federal preemption increase the value of cooperative efforts, state compacts and uniform state laws.

Specific Taxes

Recommendations with regard to specific taxes are harder to make since they have to be adjusted to individual situations in the states, but here are potential courses of action for policymakers to consider:

• **Expand sales taxes to more sales.** Expanding sales tax bases to reflect economic change means expanding them to services. Florida and Massachusetts both did so on a large scale and then repealed most of them. There are a number of objections to extending sales taxes to business services: The sales tax is a tax on consumers and should not be levied on components of production; it could cause "pyramiding" since the taxes would likely be passed on through sales to ultimate consumers; and it could affect interstate competitiveness.

Sales taxes on consumer services are less likely to involve such disadvantages. In many states, substantial numbers of consumer goods have been excluded from sales tax bases over the years, and those exemptions can cost more than they are worth. For example, some tax experts point out that the exclusion of groceries from sales tax is an expensive way to benefit the poor since affluent people receive a greater gain.

• **Expand personal income taxes.** Again, legislators should review exemptions, deductions and exclusions of income, asking whether the advantages offered to some are worth their cost in terms of equity and the higher tax burden that others must bear. Tax breaks for the elderly without adjustment for income levels need reconsideration. They will pose increasingly difficult questions of fairness across age groups as the number of elderly increases, and they will be more and more expensive in terms of lost revenue.

Reform for Reform's Sake

Legislators hardly ever attempt tax reform for its own sake. Reforms are more likely to accompany changes in tax rates because the change in rates conceals the shifting tax incidence that reforms produce. Reform for its own sake has high political costs and few friends. Anyone whose taxes will increase because of reform will doubt its value, and people who are promised tax relief through reform will be skeptical of the promise. A recent study that found some sort of tax reform in 39 states from 1990 through 1993 found only one state in which the reform was intended to be revenue neutral. Change for the sake of improving the system is rarely ventured.

But the accumulated distortions that a generation of structural economic change has caused in state tax systems require such efforts. If policymakers are to avoid continual patching and tinkering with state taxes, they need to look at fundamental issues and assumptions, and make fundamental revisions.

It's Not a Miracle, It's a Mirage

As more and more states legalize gambling, its benefits as a revenue source become more and more dubious.

Steven D. Gold

Steven Gold is the director of the Center for the Study of the States, Nelson A. Rockefeller Institute of Government, State University of New York. A version of this article appeared in *State Fiscal Brief* published by the center.

Casino mania is sweeping the country. Until a few years ago, the only places where intrepid gamblers could legally try their luck at blackjack or slot machines were Nevada and New Jersey. Now at least 10 states (not counting Indian reservations) authorize casinos, and all signs point to a rapid proliferation of gambling palaces from coast to coast.

New forms of state-sponsored gambling—like video poker machines and keno—are popping up. And 37 states offer lotteries.

One of the main reasons for the popularity of legalizing new forms of gambling is the lure of easy money. With legislators struggling to balance state budgets and citizens resisting tax increases, gambling looks like a bonanza—a way to raise revenue painlessly and at the same time spur economic development.

Unfortunately, expectations about the benefits of gambling are wildly inflated because:
• It is unrealistic to expect gambling to generate enough revenue for states to significantly reduce reliance on taxes.
• As casinos open in ever more states, their potential for producing state revenue and stimulating economic development diminishes. Casinos are most beneficial when they attract many resi-

dents from outside states. As more states have casinos, more competition will exist among them, and fewer out-of-state residents will be attracted to any particular state.

People often are confused about the role of gambling in state finances for three reasons:
• Failure to distinguish between gross and net revenue: For example, in 1991 state lottery sales were $19.2 billion. But $10.4 billion was paid out in prizes and $1.2 billion went for administration, leaving $7.6 billion for state coffers. In other words, only 40 percent of lottery sales were available for state programs after paying out prizes and covering administrative costs.
• Not understanding relative magnitudes: $7.6 billion sounds like a lot of money, and it is from many perspectives. But total state tax revenue in 1991 was $311 billion. Lotteries produced less than 2.5 percent as much as taxes; excluding the states that did not have lotteries, the proportion rises to 3.2 percent. Lottery revenue looks like small change compared to the revenue from sales and income taxes.
• Counting revenue gains from newly initiated lotteries: State lottery revenue increased nearly sevenfold between 1980 and 1991. Some of this increase came from expansion of the 13 lotteries that existed at that time. But most of the growth is attributable to new lotteries, which sprang up in 19 additional states.

Composition of Gambling Revenue

The biggest contributor to gambling revenue in most states is the lottery. In

1991 lotteries generated $7.6 billion in net revenue. By 1993, this had risen to approximately $9.3 billion.

These figures include not only traditional lotteries (scratch cards, lotto games, etc.) but also so-called video lotteries, which are often nothing more than video poker games. Although these games are essentially a form of the slot machine, they are called video lotteries because the state lottery organization oversees them or the euphemism apparently makes them more morally and politically acceptable.

Lotteries look enormous compared to the revenue states receive from pari-mutuel taxes (mostly from bets on horse races but also from dog tracks and jai alai). In 1991, revenue from that source was only $635 million. This was 3.5 percent less than the year before, which in turn was 1.2 percent less than revenue in 1989. In fact, pari-mutuel taxes are the slowest growing source of state tax revenue. In 1991, they produced less for states than they did in 1980 when they raised $731 million.

Pari-mutuel tax revenue has been hurt by competition from lotteries and by the waning popularity of horse racing. In response to the economic problems of racetracks, many states have reduced their taxes on the industry. Thus, although betting at tracks has grown slowly, revenue has actually decreased.

What about casinos? Nevada's gambling and casino entertainment taxes in 1991 produced $348 million, along with another $57 million from licenses for slot machines and other games. These taxes brought in about 24 percent of

Nevada's tax revenue. When other business taxes and the tourism it produces are counted, the gaming industry accounts for about half of Nevada's state tax revenue. But Nevada is unique. It combines a population of less than 1.5 million with a huge gambling industry. Gambling could not have nearly as much impact on state finances in a more populous state.

Consider, for example, New Jersey, population nearly 8 million, where the state's take in 1991 was $246 million in casino gross revenue taxes, along with another $50 million from licenses for casinos and slot machines. New Jersey's total state tax revenue was $11.6 billion, so these taxes and license fees were only about 2.5 percent of that total. Even if the taxes paid indirectly through spending at hotels, restaurants and other establishments are included, gambling accounts for less than 4 percent of state taxes.

A Closer Look at Lottery Revenue

The table on this page shows lottery revenue available for state programs in 1991 in relation to population and total tax revenue. Massachusetts had the highest lottery revenue per capita, $78. The lottery produced more than $50 per capita in eight other states (Connecticut, Florida, Illinois, Maryland, New Jersey, New York, Ohio and Pennsylvania). In general, per capita revenue tends to be considerably higher in urban than rural states.

Lottery revenue is a small factor in state revenue systems. Lotteries in 1991 raised only 3.2 percent as much as taxes (counting only the states where lotteries existed).

Compared to other states, lottery revenue is the highest proportion of total state tax revenue in Florida (6.1 percent) and in South Dakota (5.6 percent). Both of these states have relatively low tax revenue, in part because they are among the nine states that do not impose a personal income tax. Florida benefits from lottery purchases by tourists while South Dakota was the national pioneer in allowing widespread video lotteries.

South Dakota's video lottery revenue continued to shoot up after 1991, primarily due to higher tax rates. The state raised the tax rate from 20 percent to 25 percent in January 1991 and then to 35 percent. Recently it went up to 36 percent. Per capita net revenue to the state from video lotteries was about $68 in FY 1993, far higher than any other state.

Oregon, which has the second most successful video lottery operation, projects per capita revenue of $32 in FY 1994.

Lottery revenue has grown surprisingly slowly if one excludes expansion due to adoption by additional states. Between 1985 and 1991, lottery revenue rose more slowly than other tax revenue, falling from 3.7 percent to 3.2 percent of total revenue in states with lotteries. To some extent, this drop occurred because lotteries were not very productive in many of the states where they started after 1985. But the growth of lottery revenue also lagged behind that of tax revenue in several states with well established lotteries, including Maryland, New Jersey, Illinois, Pennsylvania, Michigan and Rhode Island.

State Tax and Lottery Revenue Per $100 of Personal Income, 1980 and 1991

Tax	1980	1991
Total	*$6.79*	*$6.70*
General sales	2.14	2.23
Personal income	1.84	2.14
Motor fuel	0.48	0.45
Corporate income	0.66	0.44
Motor vehicle licenses	0.24	0.22
Other licenses	0.12	0.13
Insurance	0.15	0.13
Public utilities	0.17	0.12
Tobacco	0.19	0.09
Property	0.14	0.07
Severance	0.21	0.07
Death and gift	0.10	0.04
Alcoholic beverages	0.12	0.01
Corporation licenses	0.07	0.11
Document transfers	0.04	0.04
Pari-mutuels	**0.04**	**0.01**
Other	0.08	0.11
Lotteries	**0.05**	**0.18**

Note: Personal income excludes District of Columbia.

Source: U.S. Census Bureau, *State Government Finances;* personal income provided by U.S. Bureau of Economic Analysis, estimates as of Sept. 2, 1992.

Lotteries differ from other sources of revenue in several respects, one of which is that they need substantial marketing effort to produce increased money for the state. Much of the growth of revenue has been attributable to introduction of new games, and lotteries have to be advertised extensively to maintain interest.

By the late 1980s, many state lotteries had already adopted the features that have been successful in stimulating interest and increasing participation. Future growth probably depends heavily on nontraditional games like video lotteries and club keno.

Cannibalism

The figures cited for state revenue produced by gambling do not consider negative effects on tax revenue. If people buy lottery tickets or lose money at a casino, they have less income available to spend on goods and services subject to the sales tax or excise taxes, like gasoline, alcoholic beverages and cigarettes.

Relatively little research is available on the extent of such cannibalism. According to Mary Borg and associates, who issued a report, *The Economic Consequences of State Lotteries*, the magnitude of the tax loss depends on whether a state relies heavily on sales and excise taxes or whether it imposes a substantial personal income tax. The impact is larger in states that rely more on consumption taxes. They generalize that the loss of tax revenue is usually less than 15 percent of lottery revenue, although it can go as high as 23 percent.

For casinos, the impact on tax revenue depends not only on the state tax system but also on the extent to which casinos attract gamblers from out of

---

Gambling Is No Panacea

- Lotteries, casinos and other forms of gambling cannot generally produce enough state tax revenue to significantly reduce reliance on other taxes or to solve a serious state fiscal problem.
- As ever more states allow casinos, the potential economic development and tax benefits diminish greatly.
- Lotteries produced $7.6 billion for state programs in 1991, which represented only 3.2 percent of tax revenue in the states that had lotteries.
- Pari-mutuel taxes were the slowest growing source of state tax revenue between 1980 and 1991.

State Lottery Revenues
Fiscal Years 1985 and 1991

State	Per Capita				Percent of Tax Revenue	
	1991	Rank	1985	Rank	1991	1985
National Average	$40.74		$34.99		3.16%	3.51%
Massachusetts	78.46	1	40.51	4	4.86	3.60
Maryland	68.98	2	59.74	1	5.24	6.10
New Jersey	67.83	3	51.31	2	4.52	5.03
Florida	64.34	4			6.21	
Connecticut	60.10	5	39.99	5	3.97	3.66
Ohio	58.10	6			5.50	
New York	52.31	7	32.15	7	3.34	2.76
Illinois	50.59	8	45.11	3	4.39	5.57
Pennsylvania	50.30	9			4.62	
Michigan	45.81	10	39.57	6	3.87	4.14
South Dakota	41.80	11			5.56	
Virginia	41.18	12			3.78	
Delaware	37.15	13	22.48	8	2.17	1.70
New Hampshire	30.67	14	4.21	13	5.43	0.97
Maine	27.85	15	3.77	14	2.21	0.44
Indiana	26.95	16			2.45	
California	25.50	17			1.73	
Rhode Island	24.75	18	18.32	9	1.98	2.06
Wisconsin	24.42	19			1.72	
Arizona	22.92	20	7.15	12	1.82	0.77
Vermont	22.25	21	1.74	15	1.84	0.20
Washington	19.67	22	10.69	10	1.24	1.03
Colorado	16.67	23	9.02	11	1.75	1.27
Idaho	15.57	24			1.34	
Minnesota	14.88	25			0.94	
Kentucky	14.65	26			1.08	
West Virginia	13.76	27			1.06	
Iowa	13.69	28			1.11	
Missouri	12.68	29			1.31	
Oregon	12.41	30			1.20	
Kansas	8.87	31			0.79	
Montana	5.52	32			0.55	

Note: Revenue excludes prizes and administrative costs.
Source: U.S. Census Bureau, *State Government Finances*, [year].

state. It is more positive if the casino is part of a destination resort rather than being patronized heavily by day-trippers.

Economic Development Benefits

In addition to the revenue that states receive directly from taxes on casinos and places like racetracks, they also benefit indirectly from the employment created there and at businesses like hotels and restaurants that serve their patrons.

Once again, the magnitude of this economic benefit depends on the extent to which patrons live in or out of state. If they are in-state residents, their spending on gambling takes away from their outlays on lotteries and products subject to the sales tax.

As casinos spread across the landscape, their economic development potential diminishes because it becomes increasingly difficult to attract a high proportion of out-of-staters. Except in Nevada, the gaming industry is not large enough to make a big difference in a state's economy.

Magnitude Not as Great as Thought

The point of this analysis is not that gambling fails to add to state revenue. It does. Because of gambling, states can increase their spending and provide more service. But the magnitude of this effect is not as great as people often think. The potential revenue from gambling is relatively limited when viewed in the overall context of a state budget.

The benefits of gambling need to be weighed against its regressivity and the social costs that are often associated with it:

• Easier access increases the prevalence of compulsive gambling. Few if any states have established effective programs to deal with that.

• Casinos require substantial investments in public infrastructure and increases in services like police protection. Their costs should be subtracted when considering the net benefits from gambling. (This point applies to any job-creating activity, not just casinos.)

• Gambling tends to undermine the work ethic. It is particularly questionable for a state government to spend heavily on advertising that encourages "get rich quick" dreams when the odds are heavy that playing a lottery will make one poorer, not richer.

We appear to be on the threshold of an unprecedented situation. In the past, casinos in the United States and Europe have usually been located in remote vacation settings. If in a large city, they usually catered to a limited, elite clientele. Now for the first time we are likely to have large casinos in big cities open to the masses. The social consequences could be more serious than we have seen in the past.

The momentum toward widespread availability of casinos and games of chance like video lotteries and keno appears irresistible. If it were just a matter of providing people with new forms of entertainment—that would be one thing. But as a painless way to solve the fiscal problems of state government, gambling is a mirage.

The Tax the Public Loves to Hate

Although sometimes called unfair, the property tax stabilizes local finances and allows local governments to control their own affairs.

Ronald K. Snell

Ronald K. Snell is director of NCSL's fiscal affairs program.

When the president of the United States said he doesn't like broccoli, broccoli-haters everywhere took heart. Most Americans' attitude toward property taxes is about like President Bush's toward broccoli—best considered as compost. But the hard fact is that property taxes, like broccoli, are good for us. And while we can find substitutes for broccoli—the ever delightful brussels sprouts, cauliflower and spinach—there doesn't seem to be a substitute that will do the job of the property tax.

The property tax has two irreplaceable roles in America public affairs. First, it offsets the instability of the two other major state and local taxes—personal income and sales taxes. Income and sales tax collections wax and wane with the economy; the property tax's sluggish response to changing economic conditions helps maintain an even revenue flow. And second, in much of the United States, local governments' revenue from property taxes allows local citizens and local governments a degree of control over their own affairs that cannot exist otherwise.

Despite those roles, the public generally has considered the local property tax the "Worst Tax Except for the Federal Income Tax." When the Advisory Commission on Intergovernmental Relations began its annual survey of public attitudes about taxes in 1972, a whopping 45 percent of participants declared that the local property tax was the worst tax of the possible choices—federal income, state income, state sales and local property. Reconsideration in 1973 brought the public around to the opinion it has held ever since: Except for the federal income tax, the local property tax is the least fair tax in the United States.

People who value fairness in taxation criticize property taxes because they bear no relation to people's ability to pay (ability to pay is usually considered a criterion of a good tax). The value of people's property, especially residential property, is not a key to their income, and elderly people especially can find that property taxes take a growing proportion of their income over time. Some people think it's just plain wrong to tax the unproductive bricks and boards that make up their houses.

Assessment practices and the length of time between assessments can make the tax unfair. Assessment is difficult, especially for properties that in any way are unusual. Market value is something that can only be guessed at until a property is sold. In addition, everyone has heard of assessors who manipulate values for reasons of their own. Elected assessors are said to be especially prone to do so, in order to stay in office.

Even with the fairest and least ambitious of assessors, problems can occur when years go by between assessments. Property values can grow slowly over the years, but the assessment reflects that growth only occasionally, so that property owners are hit periodically by large and apparently arbitrary jumps in the taxable value of their property.

Differences between property taxes in different communities can undermine equity, fairness and hopes for economic development. When communities are forced to rely heavily on property taxes, communities with little taxable property suffer either from worse roads and schools than their neighbors or higher taxes or both. Such fiscal disparities are one of the major problems with the property tax, according to former St. Paul mayor George Latimer, now dean of the Hamline University School of Law: "Location ought not to control the level of social services." Reduction of such disparities is one reason for state aid to local governments or state assumption of former local services.

Every elected official is familiar with the disadvantages of the property tax, and all homeowners have felt the disadvantages at one time or another. But what can be said on the other side? Are there any reasons to preserve the traditional role of property taxes in state and local finance despite their bad press?

There are reasons to value the property tax. Some of them are fiscal, but the important ones are political—that is, they have to do with public policy. It is the political reasons that make the property tax truly irreplaceable in state and local government.

First, the fiscal reasons. Property taxes make up such a large part of state and local tax collections—over 30 percent—that any substantial reduction in property taxes takes either large reduc-

From *State Legislatures*, December 1991, pp. 37-39. © 1991 by the National Conference of State Legislatures. Reprinted by permission.

tions in government operations or large increases in other taxes. Where do those other taxes come from? The other taxes generally come from state government, which means that the blame for tax increases moves from local officials to state legislators and governors.

Nebraska, for example, has had two rounds of state tax increases in 1990 and 1991 in order to reduce residential and utility property taxes and to improve equity across the state. In 1990 the state increased state income taxes 17.5 percent and sales taxes 25 percent in order to provide 10 percent relief for property taxes. In 1991 the Legislature had to raise about $100 million in new state taxes to replace revenue lost because of a court decision requiring lower assessments of pipeline property. The state invented one new business tax—a surcharge of 2 percent on depreciation claimed on federal income tax returns— and raised other business taxes to make up the loss. So far the impact on business is unknown. Nebraska is a stark example of the magnitude of state tax increases it takes to cover significant property tax relief.

Nebraska faced the issue head on and raised state taxes to cover the lost local revenue that property tax reductions would mean. By contrast, California and Massachusetts over the years have discovered what happens if you reduce reliance on local property taxes without replacing the revenue.

In 1978 Californians amended their state constitution with Proposition 13, which capped property taxes at 1 percent of market value and limited increases to 2 percent a year until the property changed owners. The *California Journal* says that Prop 13 saves California homeowners and commercial property owners $15 billion a year—big money even in California.

But at what cost? Before Proposition 13 passed, counties spent about 30 percent of their budgets on "discretionary" items like libraries, parks and roads. The county supervisors' association reported that the percentage fell below 5 percent by 1988, because the counties' revenue had to meet obligations for law enforcement and public welfare. And over 10 years, property taxes fell from covering 52 percent of school district expenses to 19 percent. The state's share of school district funding rose from less than half to nearly three-quarters. The need for the state to replace property

taxes with general funds helped force the Legislature to increase various taxes by $7.3 billion in 1991. County governments and schools will get 75 percent of the increase ($3.5 billion more for schools than the year before, and over $2 billion more for county governments).

Massachusetts is another state where a local property tax limit has shifted the job of raising money from local governments to the legislature. In 1980 the voters used the initiative to pass a law capping the property tax, usually referred to as Prop 2-1/2. It has worked as intended to reduce the burden of property taxes. Local property taxes fell from $5.80 for every $100 of personal income in 1979 to $3.34 in 1989. Taxpayers were saving $2.8 billion a year by 1989, assuming that without Prop 2-1/2, property taxes would have claimed the same share of personal income in 1989 as in 1979.

Like California, Massachusetts achieved this miracle in part by shifting revenue raising from local governments to the state. State aid to local governments nearly tripled from 1979 to 1989, costing taxpayers $2.6 billion a year more in 1989 than in 1979. The tax burden shifted, almost dollar for dollar, from local property taxes to state sales and income taxes.

Some people might welcome that change, reasoning that state sales and income taxes show more growth than property taxes do and that many people consider sales and income taxes to be fairer than property taxes. But there's a downside too: The state governments that turn on the spigot of state aid can turn it right off again as well.

That's one of the ways state budgets got balanced in Massachusetts and New York in 1991—by cuts in aid to local government. Cities, counties, towns and school districts in those and other states see their fortunes rise and fall along with the vicissitudes of the state budget.

It's the same in California, where the governor and Legislature increased state sales and income taxes sharply to provide more aid to local governments. County officials in California think not enough was done, and they may be right. But in making that argument they are repeating a hard fact of life for California counties: They are at the mercy of state government finances. If California's fiscal crisis continues, state officials

might have to reconsider the decisions made in 1991.

And that's the real point about the irreplaceability of the property tax. Property taxes traditionally have protected the continuity of the basic services local governments provide—law enforcement and fire fighting, health and building codes, libraries, streets, parks and schools—the basic protections and structures of American community life. Senator Bob Jauch of Wisconsin says, "Locals can't depend on state and federal governments—they'll protect their own purses. Communities need their own sources of money." Representative Kitty Gurnsey of Idaho emphasizes how dependent local services are on property taxes. If a new property tax limit passes in Idaho, she predicts "there'll be a hue and cry for the state to take over senior citizens centers and youth programs and support to libraries."

Property taxes are ideal for funding basic services because property taxes are a stable revenue source—one that's there in bad years and good, not subject to rapid fluctuations because of a year's economic change. Richard Mattoon, an economist at the Federal Reserve Bank in Chicago, says that for Midwestern states the "relative stability of the property tax has proven to be an advantage during the recent recession."

A lot of the fiscal problems states have had in 1990 and 1991 have been due to the way personal income taxes, sales taxes and corporation income taxes respond to a recession. Collections fall fast. As soon as corporate profits decline, corporation income taxes go into freefall. Income tax collections drop as people are laid off or incomes are cut. Thrifty buying reduces sales tax collections.

Property taxes hold up better, providing, as Mattoon says, a "steady, sluggish revenue source for local governments." Even if property prices drop, there's a delay before property taxes reflect decreased market values. The property tax is unrivaled as the source of a steady revenue stream that can float local government services through good and lean times.

As a tax that belongs almost entirely to local government, it can provide independence for local governments as well as security. State and federal governments are suspect to many Americans. Mayor James Howaniec of Lewiston, Maine, says, "It seems that the further one gets from local government, the less accountable are the elected officials." Boston Mayor Raymond Flynn told Congress in February, "It's a lot different in the neighborhoods listening to the people than it is sitting in the statehouse listening to elected officials." Last winter when the White House floated a proposal to replace $15 billion in local government grants with new state block grants, New Orleans Mayor Sidney Barthelmy, president of the National League of Cities, responded that the proposal was unacceptable: "States' distribution of revenue does not meet the needs of municipalities and is often delayed before being allocated to us."

The frustration behind such mayoral remarks is at least partly due to the mayors' dependence on state and federal funding. That in turn is partly due to local governments' lack of taxing power, and that in turn to reduced reliance on property taxes. Maybe it's time to return responsibility for services and taxes to local governments through greater use of locally levied property taxes. That may be the best single way to make government responsive and answerable to the voters, and to make voters understand that services cost someone money.

This is not a suggestion that we go back to the days of 1902, when 86 cents out of every dollar state and local governments collected came from property taxes. That's plainly inappropriate in a post-industrial society where much wealth is intangible, where knowledge is as important a source of income as a broccoli farm or a two-family house.

Senator Jauch suggests an appropriate role for property taxes in today's system of state and local finance: It ought to be the foundation of the local revenue system, augmented by other kinds of taxes and state aid, but still the underpinning for necessary local services. George Latimer agrees; he points out the key is not to rely on the property tax so much that it creates serious fiscal disparities among communities.

Senator Jauch and former Mayor Latimer speak from experience in Wisconsin and Minnesota, where state governments have elaborate programs to limit the regressivity of property taxes. Minnesota refunds property tax payments to individual taxpayers based on their incomes, up to a maximum of $1,100. Wisconsin has an effective program for low-income taxpayers, although, Jauch notes, the property tax burden consequently is shifted to middle- and upper-income taxpayers. And, according to Jauch, the property tax credits have no political effect: "All people look at is their bill, not their credits."

I t's pointless to hope that the property tax will ever be a popular tax, no matter how much is done to relieve burdens on low-income and elderly people; all that matters is that taxpayers tolerate it. It's important that they continue to do that.

The practice of decreasing local reliance on property taxes has meant more than relief to homeowners. It has imposed giant costs on state fiscal and political systems.

Reduced reliance on local property taxes increases the relative importance of state taxes that are just not as reliable a source of revenue when times get rough. That can mean tremendous threats for local governments if state budgets have to be cut.

Lawmakers at least should remember that every dollar they agree to send as a subsidy to local governments increases the likelihood of another tax vote in the legislature.

People who are concerned about the balance of authority among federal, state and local governments should remember that the power to tax is not just the power to destroy, as Justice John Marshall commented. The power to tax is also the power to create. Shifting the tax stream from local governments to state and federal governments shifts authority as well. Without a steady, reliable, strong flow of revenue, local governments cannot govern. And the best possible source of that power to govern is the property tax.

The Quagmire of Education Finance

**Decades of litigation and reform
haven't made schools equal.
Could holding them to standards of
'adequacy' be a better idea?**

Charles Mahtesian

The schools have never been very good in Lincoln County, West Virginia, one of the poorest pockets of Appalachia, but a decade or so ago, people there were nurturing hopes that their children might yet have a chance to succeed the way the area's most famous son succeeded.

Chuck Yeager had overcome a meager Lincoln County education to become a test pilot, fly faster than the speed of sound, and eventually win national celebrity. The state Supreme Court had just ruled, in effect, that the county's children should not have to break quite so many barriers as Yeager did. In 1979, in the case of *Pauley vs. Bailey,* the court agreed with a group of local parents and students who complained that Lincoln County schools were simply not providing the "thorough" and "efficient" education mandated by the state constitution. Lincoln's schools, it said, were "woefully inadequate."

Few could quarrel with that. In Lincoln County, virtually every aspect of a child's educational experience was deficient. The physical plant was in tatters. Library, medical and counseling services scarcely existed. The county leadership itself seemed almost indifferent to the problem. There was widespread talk of property tax shenanigans that kept appraisals artificially low and, as a result, school district coffers dry.

In defining what kind of education a child should receive, the high court said West Virginia schools should prepare kids for "useful and happy occupations, recreation and citizenship." A lower court then directed the legislature to devise a plan addressing those recommendations for Lincoln and all the other counties in the state whose schools were found to be inadequate.

The final product of that effort, ambitiously titled the Master Plan for Education, came out in 1983. In addition to calling for greater funding equity between school districts, it established a whole range of education quality standards. It called for more teachers, higher salaries for teachers, new buildings and equipment. The Master Plan was a ray of hope for Lincoln and all the poor counties of West Virginia that were in essentially the same boat.

A decade later, though, the unfortunate truth is that the court case and the Master Plan accomplished very little. "Our case had all sorts of wonderful language in it," says West Virginia Supreme Court Justice Richard Neely, "but it didn't amount to a bowl of whiz."

A state school accreditation panel recently recommended probation status for 18 of Lincoln County's 19 elementary and secondary schools. The 19th was rated "seriously impaired." In one elementary school, a single instructor teaches the 4th, 5th and 6th grades together. The situation is not too much different in other parts of rural West Virginia. "You can safely say we're not anywhere near meeting the criteria set in *Pauley vs. Bailey,*" says William McGinley, general counsel for the West Virginia Education Association. "I'm not sure it's even considered an attainable goal." In the years since the master plan was issued, a handful of other school finance-related suits have been filed in different parts of the state, all charging in one way or another that the state was not living up to its end of the bargain.

West Virginia now has a great deal of company. In the past decade, and especially in the past three years, states all over the country have endured the same cycle of litigation, court decision, attempted legislative remedy, and further litigation. When state courts struck down school financing systems in Montana, Texas, New Jersey and Kentucky in 1989, they sparked a boomlet of lawsuits that currently involve about half the states in the country. The overriding issue in nearly all these places has been dollars—spending disparities per pupil between rich and poor districts.

In Texas, inequities between the 50 highest- and lowest-spending districts has forced the entire state into a legal black hole. The state Supreme Court ruled the school funding system unconstitutional in 1989, then rejected the

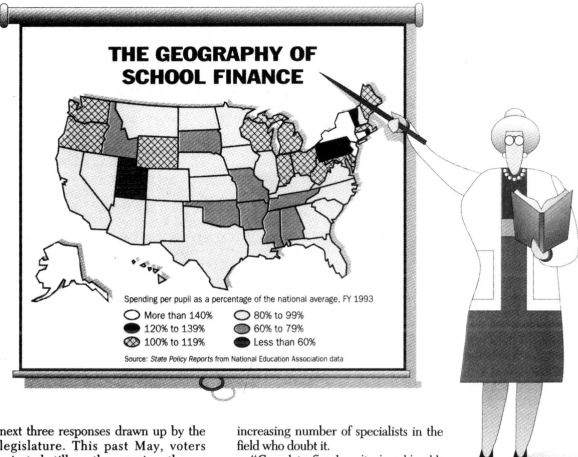

THE GEOGRAPHY OF SCHOOL FINANCE

Spending per pupil as a percentage of the national average, FY 1993

○ More than 140%   ○ 80% to 99%
● 120% to 139%   ● 60% to 79%
⊗ 100% to 119%   ● Less than 60%

Source: *State Policy Reports* from National Education Association data

next three responses drawn up by the legislature. This past May, voters rejected still another version, the so-called "Robin Hood" plan, named that by opponents because it allegedly stole property taxes from rich districts to give to poor ones. Legislators finally passed a new plan, just prior to a court-imposed June 1 deadline, but even that system is going to be challenged in court.

Where this will all end is a puzzling and frustrating question. The only road to equity that seems remotely practical in most states from a fiscal point of view involves capping the expenditures of the wealthier districts—promoting mediocrity by "leveling down." And monied districts are just as quick as poor ones to seek legal redress when their interests are threatened.

At the same time, the parade of court cases and legislative arguments have provoked larger doubts about whether trying to achieve equity by tinkering with the spending formulas is anything more than a mirage in the first place. Even if a state sees to it that per pupil expenditures are the same in every one of its counties, does that mean real equity? Would it give children from the poorest district in south Texas an education equal to one received by kids in wealthy suburban Dallas? There are an

increasing number of specialists in the field who doubt it.

"Complete fiscal parity is achievable only in theory," says David Franklin, a specialist in school finance law at the Center for Study of Educational Finance at Illinois State University. "In practice, it will never be done. It is not possible in the real world. The fiscal demands of different districts means it's a goal never to be achieved." For if the laws of demographic change do not render existing financing systems obsolete, the costly and resource-draining sociological problems of an increasing number of students will. Establishing strict mathematical equality among the counties or districts in a state does nothing to take into account the special needs of troubled urban areas and depressed rural districts like Lincoln County.

The clearer these realities become, the more legislators and courts begin looking for other solutions to the problem, ones that avoid the quagmire of dollars-per-pupil. And as they do that, some of them are returning to arguments the West Virginia court outlined more than a decade ago in the *Pauley vs. Bailey* case—arguments related not only to equity but also to adequacy. By looking beyond funding formulas—and requiring the state to

consider quality of education—West Virginia's high court helped lay the groundwork for the newly emerging adequacy movement. The strictures were not met—but the logic is gaining more adherents all the time.

Adequacy moves away from an emphasis on dollar inputs—or how much it will cost to bring poorer districts to fiscal parity with their wealthier counterparts—toward a closer scrutiny of the things education dollars are supposed to buy—teachers, facilities, curricula, test scores. The adequacy movement is part of the larger push in education toward linking funding to outcomes, in accordance with national education standards and goals.

Under the rubric of adequacy, the whole question returns to where it was in Lincoln county more than a decade ago: Are kids receiving an education that gives them the skills necessary for a productive life? Under this broad definition, quantity of aid is replaced by quality of education provided.

"There's a general view in the school finance field that equity suits are not as sophisticated or up-to-date as adequacy," says Michael Kirst, a professor of education at Stanford University and the former president of the California Board of Education. "You have two powerful forces converging around adequacy. Number one is the push toward national standards and goals. It shifts adequacy toward outcomes. Number two is the realization that equalization of spending has not led to pupil achievement gains."

The movement to adequacy is gaining steam despite the fact that even its enthusiasts are unclear as to precisely what the term means. Mary Fulton, a policy analyst at the Education Commission of the States, joins a chorus of other education experts when she says there is no consensus over how to define it. "You can produce a lot of data to show inequities exist. You can show that pretty easily. Adequacy is a little messier."

Messy or not, there is no question that adequacy has sufficient meaning and seems to promise sufficient benefits to attract the attention of poor counties and districts all over the country that have gained little from the years of argument over funding formulas. It was the adequacy concept that buttressed the crucial decision of the year so far in school finance, the decision of an Alabama Circuit Court that the state's educational system was below minimal standards and therefore unconstitutional. "Our goal was to make sure children have the resources and opportunities that they need to succeed," says Helen Hershkoff of the American Civil Liberties Union, which represented the plaintiffs in Alabama and is involved in similar suits in Connecticut and Louisiana."In Alabama," Hershkoff says, "it was clear that fiscal equity was not the solution."

Circuit Court Judge Eugene Reese agreed with that assessment in April, when he declared that the Alabama education system was not meeting its own standards. Not only was the school system broken, said Reese, but there were specific ways to fix it—not simply by reallocating tax dollars, but by taking seriously the mission to provide skills necessary for a productive and successful life.

Reese went so far as to specify nine basic outcomes for an adequate education. Among them were skills in oral and written communication, math and science; sufficient understanding of gov-ernmental processes and of basic civil institutions to enable citizens to understand issues that affect the community; sufficient understanding of the arts so they can appreciate their cultural heritage; sufficient levels of academic or vocational training to enable them to compete in the state, nation and world; and sufficient support and guidance so that each student feels a sense of self-worth and ability to achieve. He gave state officials until October to prepare a response to his decision.

In some important ways, the Reese decision was simply a logical extension of the 1989 Kentucky Supreme Court ruling that Kirst calls "the mother of all adequacy suits." The Kentucky court in effect burned down the state's education system in order to save it. In ruling the system inadequate as well as inequitable, it threw out virtually everything—the mechanism for funding education and all the laws creating school districts, school boards and the state education department. All regulations regarding teacher certification and school construction were declared unconstitutional as well. The legislature responded the following year by enacting a massive education reform law whose implementation was estimated to cost well over a billion dollars over a period of several years.

Judge Reese said little in the Alabama case this year that had not been said in Kentucky earlier. But his ruling came at a point when school reform advocates throughout the country were three years further down the path of marathon equity cases and no meaningful improvement. Within a few weeks, the Massachusetts Supreme Court invoked arguments similar to Reese's in ruling that that state's schools were inadequate as well as inequitable. Three days after that ruling, Governor William F. Weld signed a $1.7 billion school reform bill requiring uniform curriculum and testing policies statewide and enhancing the powers of school principals in an effort to boost overall quality as well as equity.

But the real test could come in Oklahoma, where plaintiffs in a pending case are seeking to invalidate the state's school finance system based solely on arguments of adequacy. There, a coalition of poor districts charges that there is inadequate funding to pay for the standards put forth under the state's comprehensive school reform measure, enacted in 1990.

"We're not talking about reading, writing and arithmetic," says Mark Grossman, attorney for the Fair School Finance Council. "We're talking about what you need to know about today, not some general standard that existed a long time ago."

What children need to know to live productive lives is at the heart of adequacy, and yet is also its greatest stumbling block. Without any societal consensus about just what adequacy entails—or what it might cost—there is the strong possibility that it might lead to a trail of contradictory litigation as debilitating as the one that followed in the wake of the early equity decisions. "From our point of view, we're not sure what it means," says Guy Hurst of the Oklahoma attorney general's office, which is charged with defending the case. "In our interrogatories, someone mentioned they needed an administration testing building. A lot of people said they wanted computer system-type stuff."

In other states as well, defining adequacy promises to be as problematic as defining equity. Some activists relish the prospect of inner-city schools being declared inadequate, thereby forcing officials to allow school choice or vouchers for private schools. Others fear minimum adequacy standards will only perpetuate the gap between poor and wealthy schools. They say abandoning the equity approach now would be a terrible mistake. "The more immediate problem is these wide inequities," says Kern Alexander, a school finance specialist at Virginia Tech. "The state constitutions do not permit them."

But for poorer states such as Oklahoma and Alabama, states that have traditionally funded their schools at low levels, successful adequacy arguments are bound to seem a legitimate route to better funding. In Alabama, the wealthiest district in the state still spends less than the national average per pupil. In such places, it is more plausible to argue for raising overall funding levels than to

In the long run, would adequacy be a cheaper solution than fiscal equity? Probably not.

insist on redistributing the existing scarcity from one county to another. In wealthier areas though, arguments based on adequacy may be much harder to sell. "There's more of a chance of it coming up in poor states," says Mary Fulton, at the Education Commission of the States. "Some people would have a hard time understanding how a district in New Jersey could be spending $9,000 per pupil and be inadequate."

It also depends on the language in the state constitution. Education clauses vary enormously, some vaguely citing a "thorough and efficient" system, some calling for a "uniform" system of schools. Massachusetts' constitution calls for the Commonwealth to "cherish the interests of literatures and sciences." In Indiana, the constitution calls on the legislature to "encourage, by all suitable means, moral, intellectual, scientific and agricultural improvement."

The vaguer the constitutional language, the harder it is to win a case on adequacy alone. That could turn out to be a problem in Oklahoma. "We don't have the provisions in our constitution that Kentucky does," says Hurst. "Ours just says a system of free education. It does not have a qualifier."

There is always the possibility, of course, of changing the constitution. In the past, Illinois courts found that the state's financing system was indeed inequitable, but not unconstitutional. To strengthen their state's education clause,

school reform activists placed an amendment on last November's ballot making education a fundamental right, rather than a "goal." One purpose of the proposal was to strengthen the hand of equity forces, but it would have made adequacy cases much easier to win as well. In the end, though, voters were frightened away by estimates of the possible long-run costs of the change, which ranged from $1.8 billion to over $3 billion. So the amendment was rejected. If it had passed, says James Ward, a school finance specialist at the University of Illinois, who helped draft it, "the legislature would have had a gun to its head" to adequately fund education.

As Illinois voters indicated, adequacy's daunting price tag is a troublesome issue. When the Alabama case was first filed, then-Governor Guy Hunt called it an attempt to force a $1 billion tax increase. Hunt's assessment may have been extreme, but as David Franklin points out, virtually any push toward adequacy will be costly. "For the vast majority of states," he says, "the fiscal condition is not one that would allow them—of their own volition—to bring school districts to a level of adequacy. And it does not matter what that level is."

The cost of adequacy is also likely to vary widely from state to state. Urban schools, for example, have long insisted they need more funds because of aging facilities and large numbers of impoverished students and immigrant children

with social service needs. The New Jersey Supreme Court agreed in an equity case in 1989, calling for additional funds to meet the special needs of inner city schools. Rural schools have their own unique needs, such as finding the money for transportation over long distances.

But even in the absence of a clear and resolute idea of what adequacy means or what it costs, it seems destined to grow in importance in the next few years as a method of linking resources to existing educational standards. "Ultimately, as outcomes become tied to funding, it will be apparent that a definition of adequacy will play a bigger role," says John Myers, a Denver-based school finance consultant. The development of national goals and the Clinton administration's Goals 2000 program can only give added impetus to the adequacy movement

Adequacy is not going to solve the dilemma of school finance anytime soon; it may in the end be responsible for as much litigation and delay as the equity argument has over the past decade. But it does offer activists a chance to plead their case for reform without having to turn education finance into a zero-sum game, in which the only way poor schools can win is if rich schools lose. For that reason alone, more and more of them are going to be willing to take a chance on it. Given the current situation, adequate schools don't sound like such a bad bargain at all.

Balancing the Budget with Billboards & Souvenirs

PENELOPE LEMOV

For five dollars, the Los Angeles County coroner's office sells toe tags just like the ones it uses to identify corpses at the county morgue. Its regular customers aren't other coroners, or organizations that stock disaster supplies. They are ordinary consumers who want the tags to carry around as key chains. And the product is being snapped up by local residents, curious tourists and international shoppers from as far away as Nigeria who hear about them through the coroner's mail order catalog, *Skeletons in the Closet.*

The catalog carries other best-selling items as well—beach towels designed with the police-chalk outline of a body, boxer shorts emblazoned with the word "undertaker," mugs with the drawing of—what else?—a skeleton on the front. Marilyn Lewis, who runs the marketing effort for the coroner's office, admits that sales are helped by the L.A. location: Celebrity cases capture the media's attention, and that, Lewis admits, "gives us an edge." It's an edge that's been grossing $20,000 a month since the sales effort got under way a year ago.

But you don't have to be Los Angeles to find something that people will buy as an offbeat governmental souvenir. Chicago is doing it, as is Phoenix, and even such nondescript smaller places as West Covina, California, just outside L.A. itself. They will operate stores that hawk mugs, banners, T-shirts and other merchandise inscribed with their place name and sometimes a picture or a slogan. The American people may not like government, they may think it wastes money, they certainly resist giving it any more

There are more ways of making people subsidize government than you ever dreamed of.

County of Los Angeles Department of Coroner

taxes—but offer them a toe tag from the morgue or a coffee mug with the official country seal, and they seem to have a hard time resisting.

Souvenirs aren't the only things governments are learning to peddle in ways they never considered before. Public transit departments, which have long sold advertising space on buses that ply their city or county streets, have a new option for those sales—the full body wrap. Public buses and light rail cars in such places as Tampa and Portland, Oregon, now offer advertisers the giant canvas of the entire vehicle—from tip to tail and roof to road—to display their message. By eliminating traditional restrictions on the size of legally permitted display ads, many transit agencies are raking in twice as much advertising revenue as they did just a couple of years ago.

Sometimes they go a little too far. When Pleasant Hills, Pennsylvania, needed a new pumper truck for its volunteer firefighters, they decided they would pay for it by turning it into a commercial product. In exchange for the $300,000 cost of the truck, they were willing not only to run the sponsoring company's corporate logo on the side, but to have firefighters appear at public functions, in full uniform, handing out samples of the company's products. But even though the firefighters hired an advertising company to peddle the idea, there were no serious takers.

Every year of the 1990s seems to bring an expanded definition of the idea of marketing government. Be it the sale of goods or services, of advertising space on public property, of licenses to produce merchandise for a copyrighted logo or any number of other unusual deals, localities are searching out ways to woo private citizens and businesses into using their personal cash to help pay government bills.

It's an idea whose time was pushed forward by the prolonged recession and by the tight budgeting reality that continues to prevail, particularly at the local level. While the recession has eased nationally, and state governments—with some exceptions—are raking in ample revenue, many localities, and particularly counties, face ongoing spending pressure that continues to cause budgetary stress. Two of the basic areas of service for which counties carry enormous responsibilities—corrections and social services—are increasing at a rate that exceeds growth in revenues. Nowhere is that more true than in California, where the counties and the state itself are still laboring under the drag of a recession.

It's no wonder, then, that many of the more creative marketing strategies are originating in the Golden State—even in relatively conservative cities and counties where the local governments are traditionally averse to flashy end-runs around taxpayers. "Until the fiscal crisis really hit, most localities were pretty cool toward marketing," says Dusty Brogan, marketing specialist for Los

Angeles County's Department of Beaches and Harbors. "Now they're starting to look at assets that are marketable and exploit those that have potential."

Entrepreneurial promotion won't exactly fill billion-dollar budget gaps or pay the salaries and benefits of even a small department. But that's not the point. The marketing exercises raise additional money to help fund or expand programs that legislators have either placed on starvation diets or zeroed out entirely. The sale of merchandise through the *Skeletons in the Closet* catalog, for example, supports a coroner's program that sensitizes teenage drivers to the perils of drunk driving.

At the state level, the California Department of Conservation invented a popular Smoky the Bear-like character named Recycle Rex to be the "spokesdinosaur" for the department's efforts to educate young people about recycling. The department has signed a licensing agreement with the Walt Disney Company to develop and market a full line of Recycle Rex merchandise, including apparel, school supplies and toys. The state will be paid royalties on the sale of this merchandise around the world.

In the end, most of the money earned by the promotion will itself be recycled, back into the department's efforts to encourage recycling and the

purchase of recycled products. Some of the Rex merchandise, such as tote bags and mugs, will be fashioned from recycled soda bottles. The educational campaign thus will continue even though the state is no longer willing to subsidize it from its regular revenues.

It isn't just a matter of consumer sales. The L.A. County Information Systems Advisory Body is developing a computer network that will sell access to electronically transmitted justice-related information. It plans to reinvest the fees attorneys and law firms pay for the data in technological improvement. Given the recession in the state, the traditional sources of revenue for such investment have dried up. "We can't give up just because we don't have money," says John Doktor, who heads up the Information Systems Advisory Body for Los Angeles County, of his agency's marketing efforts. "We have to think of new ways to get it."

Elsewhere, local governments are marketing their financial expertise. In Cleveland, the Cuyahoga County treasurer's office is advising 90 other localities on their short-term investment portfolios and executing the trades for them.

The project started as an in-house response to low rates of return on short-term investments. To beef up those returns, county Treasurer Frank Gaul had his staff develop the expertise to actively trade for the county's short-term investment portfolio. Between 1985 and 1991, portfolio earnings soared from $5 million a year to just over $30 million. With a record like that, Gaul had something to sell neighboring jurisdictions. "They pay us a minimal handling fee," Gaul says. "We let them share in the profits."

As with any venture that mimics business, entrepreneurial marketing is not without dangers. At the most mundane level, T-shirts and mugs that don't sell are a drag on profits. Capital is needed for overhead. Counties and cities that go into the retail business need to find ways to protect themselves against business reversal. One way, of course, is to look to the private sector to invest in the development of the stores. That is what Los Angeles County is doing. Despite the success the coroner's office has had running its mail order business with existing administrative staff, the county plans to tap professional expertise in its future marketing ven-

City of Charlotte Department of Transportation

The 'full body wrap' on a city bus in Charlotte, North Carolina. For every inch of space, an inch of advertising.

tures. "If you have people involved in things they are not trained to do," says Bretta Beveridge of the county's marketing department, "you run risks."

There are more than market risks involved. If a government venture competes with private business, that can lead to charges of foul or unfair play. In bringing to market its computer network programs for government information, L.A. County is doing its best to steer clear of competition with the private sector. The county does not provide retail access to the data. Rather, it acts as a wholesaler, selling information to companies that then repackage and resell it to the public.

Recycle™ Rex

© 1992 CA DEPT. OF CONSERVATION

that their tax dollars are sufficient to cover it. This is a special concern for Los Angeles County as it develops a system of privately financed kiosks at supermarkets and other commercial locations. The kiosks will bring government information directly to citizens in more convenient ways than, say, having to go to a courthouse to inquire about the status of a case. The reality, however, is that, in Los Angeles County right now, there are no tax dollars to pay for the implementation of the electronic highway. "Convenient systems wouldn't be there without fees," Doktor says. "We couldn't afford it."

When it comes to the more colorful schemes for marketing government, there frequently are questions of taste. "We don't want to offend citizens by the

tastelessness of an item," says Dusty Brogan. She insists that when companies pay to have their message conveyed via county-owned trash barrels or bike racks at beaches, the department makes an effort to be sensitive to "site blight—doing something so overwhelming that people couldn't enjoy the beach."

Taste has certainly been a dilemma for the L.A. coroner's office. When medical examiners in other cities are asked about the possibility of trying something like *Skeletons in the Closet* in their home towns, they nearly always tell the press they wouldn't do it, that such merchandising doesn't show proper respect for the dead. But even that's redounded to L.A.'s benefit. As soon as such a quote from the coroner in Houston appeared in the paper there, for instance, the Los Angeles coroner's office was flooded with calls from Texas requesting the catalog.

In defense of her office's entrepreneurialism, Lewis insists that the morgue is not capitalizing on a particular person's death or on any well-known case. The mugs and towels with their skeleton drawings or chalked body outlines are supposed to be more whimsical than ghoulish. The toe-tag key rings carry the admonition not to drink and drive. In any case, Lewis says, they "depict what we do. We

When L.A. County's Beach and Harbor Department decided to develop a caller-pay 900 number for surf reports, however, there were complaints that government might be competing with and taking business away from the private sector, which could be forced out of the market as a provider of the information. The service, which has not been fully developed yet, is estimated as potentially a $20 million a year countywide operation. "At that point," marketing specialist Dusty Brogan says, "the private sector might say we are competing. At this point, they're nervous that information and statistics they've gotten for free and reformatted could carry a charge." That said, Brogan also notes that the county charter contains a warning against government competition with private business.

If business is not resentful, the public at large may be. Some taxpayers do not like paying for government information at all, since it seems to them

Los Angeles Department of Beaches and Harbors

Lifeguard as billboard: Speedo provides bathing suits and other gear for all 900 Los Angeles County lifeguards.

have 20,000 cases a year, and 18,000 are homicides."

Pennsylvania's Cameron County confronted a somewhat different dilemma of taste. Cameron, a rural county whose largest town, Emporium, has only one stop light, has gone into the discount divorce business. It processes divorce papers for less than one-third the amount that a big city such as Philadelphia does. The county, which has been marketing divorce for five years now, earned $250,000 last year, only $25,000 less than it took in from real estate taxes. The extra money paid for, among other things, a handicapped access retrofit at the recreation center, a ballot-counting machine, new tiled floors and computers in the courthouse. But boon though it quickly became, the county's newest industry spawned controversy among religious leaders who felt it was unseemly to appear to be condoning and encouraging divorce. Pragmatism eventually won out. So did the argument that the divorces were being filed, whether Cameron County processed them or not.

When a locality gets into heavy-duty marketing, there can be questions of legal authority. It took several state laws to give counties in California the power to become big-time merchandisers. A 1982 law, for instance, gave counties permission to deal in advertising space on real and personal property. A few years later, the state gave local governments the right to license intellectual property. Two years ago, the legislature allowed counties to sell some supplies and services at market value. Before that, the county was only able to sell goods and services at cost. "Now you can see what the market will bear and become a player in that price range," says Brogan.

Her beach department is playing that game for all it is worth. Last year, it raised $1.4 million in hard cash and cost savings from its wide variety of marketing programs. It is hard to find anything the department won't sell. There is advertising not just on the trash barrels and the bike racks but on the beachside chalk boards that tell

swimmers and surfers the water temperature.

There is an agreement between the beach department and Ford Motor Co. that calls for the automaker to donate to the department 40 vehicles—mostly passenger vans and pickups for lifeguard operations. Not only do the vehicles carry Ford's logo on their sides but Ford gets exclusivity: No other vehicle manufacturer can have signage at events on Los Angeles County beaches.

Then there's the Speedo deal. The swimwear company gave the county 900 bathing suits, shirts and caps for its lifeguards to wear. The beach department doesn't have to buy those supplies out of its own budget. All it has to worry about is the occasional startled swimmer, lifted out of the water after a close call, who opens her eyes to find herself staring straight at a rescuer decked out in full Speedo corporate regalia. It may be more than some are prepared for.

A Bankruptcy Peculiar to California

Sallie Hofmeister

Special to The New York Times

LOS ANGELES—Here's one cutting edge California phenomenon that is not likely to make it big elsewhere in the nation: the first major bankruptcy of a local government caused by taking risky bets with taxpayers' money.

The $2 billion investment loss that forced Orange County to declare bankruptcy in December can be traced largely to local recklessness in the face of fiscal and economic pressures that are peculiar to California. Indeed, while a number of municipalities around the country have been plagued by losses from financial derivatives gone bad, the worst troubles are concentrated in this state. Apart from Orange County, for instance, a recent nationwide survey of local governments found that six other California counties stood out as engaging in "significantly more aggressive" investment strategies than was typical.

Unable to raise taxes, Orange County invested.

"Orange County's problem is not a national problem," said Steven Gold, director of the Center for the Study of the States in Albany. "Local governments across the country are strapped, but none has pursued such risky strategies to raise money because no state is as hemmed in by restrictions against raising taxes."

Those restrictions and California's own fiscal distress will also make digging out of the hole that much more difficult. Economists say that Orange County must now undergo a belt tightening it long avoided by relying so heavily on the profits from its investment pool.

"Orange County will do what it already should have, which is to cut services," said Esmail Adibi, director of the Center for Economic Research at Chapman University in the city of Orange.

Just last June, for instance, as employers like GM Hughes Electronics were drastically reducing their work forces in Orange County, the county government added 900 people to its payroll, largely to handle an increase in the welfare caseload. And it spent $1.5 million to acquire land near the John Wayne Airport to build an office building despite vast empty office space in the area left by the recession.

In fact, while the private sector in the county lost 55,000 jobs from 1990 through 1994, the local government and its districts, Mr. Adibi calculates, "managed to add 6,000 people to the payroll, paid for by bond financings and investment returns."

The roots of the problem that erupted with such fury in Orange County in December can be traced back to 1978. That's when California voters overwhelmingly approved Proposition 13, a citizen referendum that rolled back local property taxes to 1 percent of market value and limited increases to no more than 2 percent a year. It took other special circumstances, however, to put so many California counties in such difficult positions.

Shortly after Proposition 13 was adopted, the state government, bolstered by a fat surplus and a cornucopia of tax revenues received in the booming 80's, stepped in to keep local governments afloat by providing them with extra funds to carry out their duties. It also shouldered them with extra responsibilities. But when the state's economy slowed in the late 1980's and then plunged into recession, California's coffers ran dry. The obligations only increased.

Most local governments were squeezed between lower tax revenues and rising costs for education, health care and law enforcement. That pressure was intensified by a slew of additional state mandates and a continuing influx of immigrants, who put extra demands on government services. The state, in response, relaxed even further restrictions on investments so local treasurers could seek higher returns, despite the higher risks.

Robert L. Citron, the Orange County treasurer who resigned just before the county field for bankruptcy, was a key author of the legislation allowing counties to borrow heavily and invest in riskier securities.

A bankruptcy's root: Proposition 13's tax rollback.

Orange County, while clearly the most daring, was not the only place in California to take advantage of the new freedom to speculate with taxpayer money. The risky investment practices that wreaked havoc in Orange County, Moody's Investors Service found, were also pursued actively in six other counties: San Diego, San Bernardino, Monterey, Placer, Solano and Sonoma. Only a scattering of places outside California were so aggressive.

After the bankruptcy, Moody's, a leading Wall Street credit-rating agency, surveyed 1,450 counties, cities, school districts and local agencies across the country. Orange County stood alone in the degree to which it took chancy interest rate bets, relied on borrowed money and allowed municipalities outside the county to join its pool, according to the bond rating agency. (Moody's has now vowed to alter its standards for judging municipal bonds after failing to detect Orange County's troubles in advance.)

"None has the characteristics of Orange County's pool," said David Brodsly, a vice president in Moody's San Francisco office.

But a few others deserve close attention. San Diego, for instance, whose $3.3 billion fund has dropped 11 percent in value, told investors in December that they would share in that loss if they tried to withdraw their money. The action was taken in a bid to prevent a run on its fund similar to the one that led to Orange County's bankruptcy.

Nor is Orange County the only one of California's 58 counties that is on the ropes. Verging on collapse, eight tiny counties asked the Legislature for a $15 million bailout package in the fall. They were turned down.

Merced County is negotiating with the state for $6 million in relief, while Butte received $11 million in the early 1990's, a loan that it has yet to pay back.

Perhaps the biggest blow to these communities came from the state's own hardship, and particularly, from a 1988 voter initiative, Proposition 98, that mandated specific levels of state spending on education. To fulfill that obligation, the state has largely drawn on county resources.

Over the last three fiscal years, according to Terry Brennand, a lobbyist for the California Association of County Treasurers, the state has redirected $4 billion in local property taxes to the schools. That has left counties with less money to pay for libraries, parks and other services not mandated by the state, shaving their discretionary spending, in some cases, to as little as 5 percent from an average 17 percent in the late 80's, according to Dan Wall, an official at the California State Association of Counties.

Some counties managed in part by increasing their reliance on the public markets for financing. Although California makes up about 12 percent of the national economy, it accounted for 16 percent, or $26 billion, of all long-term municipal bonds issued in 1994, according to the Securities Data Company. Merrill Lynch, the biggest municipal underwriter and deeply involved in Orange County's troubles, handled 37 percent of the business.

The squeeze also encouraged exotic local financings—sale leasebacks, special tax assessments and fees—that have made California's tax system among the most cumbersome in the country.

"We now have a system of government," said Jeffrey Chapman, a pro-

fessor of public administration at the University of Southern California, "that is so arcane that only 15 people in the state understand it."

Counties also searched for bigger investment returns, with some following the lead of Mr. Citron, the treasurer of Orange County for more than two decades who emerged as something of a Pied Piper in the state because his investment returns were consistently higher than most municipal treasurers in the country.

But with the risks of Mr. Citron's strategies now abundantly clear, California is moving to tighten investment requirements on local governments. Curt Pringle, an Assemblyman from Garden Grove in Orange County, has introduced a bill that would limit borrowing to 10 percent of a county's portfolio, restrict the use of derivatives to 5 percent, and ban raising money from bonds strictly for investment. A similar measure is expected to be introduced soon in the State Senate, which held hearings in December on Orange County.

Still, municipal bond experts say the state government, by failing to play a more active role in repairing the damage in Orange County, could end up casting a long shadow over California's finances. Other cities on the verge of bankruptcy—New York, Philadelphia and Cleveland among them—relied heavily on their states to back bond offerings and other measures that helped overcome budget squeezes.

"In every other major credit crisis in government in the last 25 years, states have taken a lead role," said J. Chester Johnson, chairman of Government Finance Associates Inc., a financial adviser to state and local governments in New York. "There is an implied moral obligation of states to help their municipalities. Without the leadership and support of California in dealing with this bankruptcy, all state issues will continue to suffer in the market."

Budget Chicken: The Newest High School Sport

Many school districts can no longer afford their athletic programs. Nowadays, supporting the team may mean with money.

CHARLES MAHTESIAN

Last March, the school board in New Castle, Delaware, approved a draconian budget proposal that eliminated all high school extracurricular activities—from the yearbook and band to football and field hockey. For William Penn High—the largest secondary school in the state—books took precedence over basketballs.

As expected, students, parents and faculty members were furious. Many athletes at William Penn lined up transfers to private schools, while others planned to move to another school district. About the only folks pleased by the scenario were rival football players: They welcomed a reprieve from the annual beating administered by the five-time state champion Colonials.

But all the while, unbeknownst to the students, they were being used as dupes. No one really had any intention of pulling the plug on high school sports. Rather, the school board was trying to scare voters into approving a property tax increase on the May ballot. A similar measure had been defeated in the fall of 1992, so the board wanted to give the community an idea of what life might be like without the proposed revenues. It worked. Voters responded in the affirmative.

New Castle's game of budget chicken is becoming a common strategy. When up against balky taxpayers and severe cuts in school budgets, local officials have learned exactly what to do: hold high school athletics hostage. Without an increase in funding, the argument goes, we cannot afford sports. In many sports-crazed communities, where local high school sports is

the only game in town, no other threat holds more shock value.

It can even work in a place as large as Chicago. Each high school athletic department there used to receive $6,700 to cover as many as 23 different boys' and girls' sports. In 1991, the Board of Education decided that for the 1991–92 school year, each school would have to get by with $750, barely enough to pay the referees' fees for a couple of games. A year later, after even deeper budget cuts, the principals of 75 public schools unanimously voted to suspend all winter sports programs, including basketball. Canceling high school hoops in Chicago amounts to heresy, so the ploy ultimately proved successful. Besides attracting national attention, the stunt sparked the startled business community into a fund-raising effort that saved the season.

While school boards rarely carry through with such cuts—only a small number of districts have completely shut down all athletic and extracurricular activities—many are having to find new sources of money to keep their athletic programs intact.

Over the past decade or so, as the number and variety of sports teams was increasing, the funding began to shrink, creating the crisis situations some school districts now face. At first, athletic directors were able to spread the pain, doling out a little to every team. But soon some schools found that it was a struggle to afford any sports at all.

EQUIPPING PLAYERS WITH uniforms, helmets, jock straps, shin

guards and mouthpieces is indeed an expensive undertaking. Then there are bats, balls, sticks, and nets, not to mention the lime, fertilizer and lawn care for the field. For an away game, factor in costs for a bus, a driver and gasoline. For home games, add in fees for umpires or officials.

Traditionally, high schools have picked up the tab for these costs. "Fifteen or twenty years ago, it would have been unheard of in the state of Indiana for a student-athlete to purchase his own shoes for the team," says Gene Cato, commissioner of high school athletics for the Indiana High School Athletic Association. "Now it's commonplace." Some athletic programs are able to supplement their budgets with gate or concessions revenues in high-profile sports like boys' football or basketball. But as a rule, few schools actually make any money off their programs.

Usually, a place on the boys' basketball—or football—team is the safest place to be during a budget-cutting storm. For many communities, the local football and basketball teams are a rallying point, or in some minds, the custodians of a town's prestige. And it is not always the boys' teams that are treated with kid gloves. In Iowa and Indiana, for example, girls' basketball would be considered an untouchable sport. However, individual sports like golf or gymnastics have no hardcore constituencies, thus leaving them vulnerable.

But failing to encourage and support sports like golf or tennis is a mistake, says Jim Loper, assistant director of the New Jersey Interscholastic Athletic Association. "The irony is that they are less expensive," says Loper. "And they are the 'carryover' sports that you play long after you leave school. For 96 percent of football players, high school is the last time they'll wear a helmet. But you can play golf until you're 96."

Elimination of any sport is still the exception. Instead, less drastic measures, such as shrinking coaching staffs, shortening schedules, and canceling freshman and junior varsity sports programs, are usually sufficient. Scrimmages, at any level, are becoming a thing of the past.

Another way schools are coping with meager budgets is by implementing a pay-to-play system, a kind of user fee. "There are more and more schools opting for that kind of arrangement," says Bruce Howard, communications director for the National Federation of State High School Associations. Of course, the very idea of user fees for sports rubs just about everyone the wrong way. Opponents of pay-to-play fees—which range from $30 to $600 per activity—argue that the charges are discriminatory.

The playing field has long been viewed as offering opportunity and equality to all students, regardless of their social and economic backgrounds. The financial burden of user fees may not be a concern in many of the affluent suburban districts that have adopted user fees but it could be unfair to middle- and lower-class students at schools like William Penn in Delaware. "We look at athletics as part of the educational process," says Jack Holloway, athletic director at William Penn. "You don't have to pay for chemistry, do you?" At William Penn, you do not have to pay to play either.

As distasteful as everyone agrees the fees are, a growing number of schools are adopting them, if begrudgingly. "Times being what they are, it's the only option they are left with," says Howard, "and that's better than cutting

The debate over user fees raises the issue of whether athletics are part of a high school education.

the programs altogether." Still, it does not mean people are going to like it. In Tucson, Arizona, participation rates dropped 30 percent after a $105 fee per activity was imposed. The fees were cut in half after numerous complaints from parents and students.

One sure way to sidestep the user fee issue is to emulate highly organized, private fund-raising efforts in places like Fremont, California. There, supporters created the Fremont Athletic Network, a non-profit corporation that milks the business community for money and sponsors various fund-raising events. For their first event alone, organizers raised about $10,000. They surpassed that figure in their next fund-raiser, a celebrity basketball tournament, then raised even more at an event featuring rap star Hammer as honorary chairman.

OF ALL THE OPTIONS AVAILable, attaining corporate sponsorship is one of the most sought after. Until recently, corporate interest was limited to professional and college sports, but it is beginning to trickle down. That may not mean much to the badminton team, but it can be lucrative for popular sports like basketball and football.

In Indiana, for example, Farm Bureau Insurance signed up as a sponsor for the Indiana High School Athletic Association for 10 years at a cost of $2.75 million. IHSAA plans to put the money into an endowment fund that will pay for state tournaments in less-popular and nonrevenue-producing sports. For Indiana high school athletics, the sponsorship has been a boon, says Cato, but he warns others to be cautious. "Nobody is going to give you big dollars for nothing. You have to determine what you have in your state that is worth something to corporate people." What's in it for Farm Bureau Insurance? For starters, the company's name is splashed all over the hallowed Indiana boys' basketball tournament. The televised tournament—which drew over 40,000 fans to the Hoosier Dome for last year's championship final—is an annual event rivaled in statewide popularity only by the Indianapolis 500 car race.

One school system has discovered gold in taxing professional football and baseball gate receipts. In San Francisco, 49ers and Giants fans pay a surcharge on every ticket to a game. The tax, the only one of its kind, levies a 25 cent charge on Giants tickets and 75 cents on a 49ers ticket. Before the tax, the school superintendent suggested eliminating all athletics to make up for a $25 million cut in the general school budget. "Sports were the only thing in the school system that hadn't been gutted," says Supervisor Terence Hallinan, the ticket tax sponsor. "Before I proposed it, I was assured we were at the end of high school sports."

At first, the pro teams balked at the idea, but now they grudgingly support it. So do city residents, who get a $1 million infusion into their high school and middle school athletic programs. "It's a great tax," says Hallinan, "if there is such a thing." For high school athletes in San Francisco, there is.

Taxing Travelers To the Hilt

Lodging taxes have a lot of political appeal. But when they get too high, they can cost more than they bring in.

ELLEN PERLMAN

New Yorkers probably haven't noticed, but lately their streets and sidewalks have been a little less crowded than they might have been. It's not that the hyperkinetic city and its sights have lost their appeal. It's just that, for many convention-goers and other visitors, the price to see them has become too dear.

In 1990, in an effort to reduce the state's budget deficit, the legislature slapped a 5 percent tax on hotel rooms. That brought New York City's total state and local lodging tax to more than 19 percent for rooms costing more than $100.

In pushing the city's room tax to a level several percentage points higher than in any other U.S. city, the state took a gamble, ignoring outcries that the hospitality industry would suffer.

It wasn't long before the impact was being felt. Meeting planners began sending clients elsewhere. Perhaps worse, at least symbolically, the meeting planners themselves decided not to meet in New York. The Professional Convention Management Association, whose 3,500 members book 143,000 meetings a year, informed city officials that it would not consider New York as an option when choosing a site for its annual convention. When a group whose members book 30 million room-nights annually closes the door on a city, state and city revenue officials have to take notice.

"New York was viewed as being over-taxed and uncompetitive," says Salvatore Prividera, spokesman for the New York State Hospitality and Tourism Association. But the problem went beyond image and perception. One study showed that although the state would have collected $463.2 million in tax revenue from the hotel tax between 1990 and 1996, it would have lost $962.8 million in sales and other taxes. More than a dozen major industries, from construction to retail, would suffer from loss of business.

In September, the state backed down and rescinded the 5 percent of deficit-reduction tax. New York City reduced its tax by 1 percent this month, fulfilling a campaign promise of Mayor Rudolph Giuliani's. Now the city's room tax is merely steep, as opposed to exorbitant. But it is more in line with other large U.S. cities, such as Chicago, Houston, Philadelphia and Seattle, whose rates hover in the 13 to 15 percent range.

Still, the travel and tourism industry has not eased up on efforts to hold lodging taxes down. The industry has been circulating a brochure that lists the 50 cities with the top bed-tax rates and the other charges that befall visitors. The media has picked up on it and publicized it in many cities. With the "Campaign to Keep Travel Competitive," the industry is trying to deter states and cities not only from continuing to raise or create hotel taxes but also from slapping on various other "tourism taxes," such as charges on car rentals, restaurants, entertainment and airport use.

To politicians, the attraction of tourism taxes is that for the most part they don't fall on their own constituents. Exporting taxes to visitors would seem to be a relatively painless way to diversify the tax base and increase revenues. In the 1980s, state and local government just about everywhere raised or imposed taxes on hotels, restaurant meals, car rentals and attractions. From 1975 to 1991, tax revenues generated from travel increased from $4.8 billion to $21 billion, according to a report by the federal Advisory Commission on Intergovernmental Relations.

But there is a point at which the law of diminishing returns seems to set in. How high can tourism taxes go before they begin to hurt more than they help? While there's no precise answer, 15 or 16 percent seems to be "the line beyond which people will not go," says Roy Evans, executive vice president of the convention management association. "After that," Evans adds, "cities probably will create problems for themselves."

There is another rule of thumb that's widely agreed upon, one New Yorker learned so painfully: "If you're higher than everybody else, you're too high," says Luke Rich, former director of the New York Senate's tourism committee.

OF COURSE, MANY OTHER COST factors enter into the decision making, including air fares to a city, convenience, facilities and overall daily costs. It seems cities don't necessarily suffer from raising lodging taxes as long as total tourism costs remain competitive.

Columbus, Ohio, for example, upped its room taxes by 4 percent a few years ago to build and operate a new convention center. Its current bed-tax rate of 15¾ percent is the highest in the nation. But the city's convention and meeting business is flourishing, and the new convention center is drawing business beyond projections. One reason: Room rates are relatively low, averaging $55 a night. Meeting planners look at the whole package, not just tax rates, says Seymour Raiz, spokesman for the Greater Columbus Convention and Visitors Bureau.

And when that package is delivered, the tally for a visit drops Columbus to a rank of 41 against other cities, according to a survey by *Corporate Travel* magazine. Columbus can still tout itself as a bargain, Raiz says, despite its position at the top of the room-tax charts. "We wish we did not have the distinction we have," he proffers. But, he adds, "it's not a chilling price tag."

On the other hand, while Chicago's lodging tax, at nearly 15 percent, is in line with its big-city competitors, the city is more expensive overall than most, and officials there have the feeling that the city is on the edge of a tax precipice. The city's lodging tax jumped to the present level nearly three years ago to fund construction of convention facilities, and so far there has been little loss of convention or meeting business. But further tax increases are considered unlikely.

The idea of raising the tax has come up in discussions of funding an Olympics or a political convention but has been shot down right away, says Kate Haymaker, the Chicago Convention and Tourism Bureau's public relations manager. "Under no circumstances can we go above that line. We will start losing business to competitors."

Boston has a relatively low hotel tax, at nearly 10 percent, but it ranks as the third most expensive U.S. destination overall because of its high costs for lodging, meals and car rental, according to the *Corporate Travel* survey. So raising the tax further could cause problems.

Even less-expensive jurisdictions have had to retreat from the 15 percent mark. Prince George's County, Maryland, in the suburbs of Washington, D.C., found that a decision to raise hotel taxes for deficit reduction cost the county business. As soon as the total tax on a hotel room reached 15 percent in 1989, occu-

STICKER SHOCK
Highest combined state and local lodging taxes
(as of December 1, 1994)

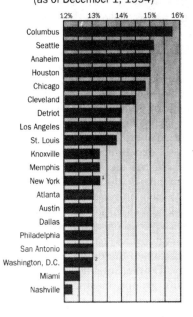

¹ Additional $2 hotel fee.
² Additional $1.50-per-night hotel occupancy tax.

Source: Campaign to Keep Travel Competitive

pancy rates nosedived. The county now is making its way back down the tax charts and eventually will lower the total room tax to 10 percent. And people are coming back to the county to sleep.

DESPITE THE RETREATS ON lodging taxes taking place in Prince George's County and New York City, there's no sign of a general trend toward cutting room taxes. One reason is that, as in Columbus, many jurisdictions locked in those lodging taxes to pay off bonds that were issued to fund convention facilities.

Some local officials even see some growth room left in lodging taxes. Chuck Weber, a city council member in Kansas City, says his city's relatively cheap rate of nearly 12 percent is not wooing travelers from St. Louis, where the rate is close to 14 percent—no matter what the travel industry says. "Peo-

ple didn't come to Kansas City from more expensive cities. I think they're crying wolf here," says Weber.

So, Weber asks, why not charge visitors something to help improve the Kansas City convention area? Despite Weber's arguments, in November the voters rejected an initiative that would have added a $2 hotel room surcharge, so at least for now the city isn't likely to feel the wrath of the travel industry.

And although the fondest hope of the convention and tourism industry is to get visitors riled up about paying high tourism taxes, even industry people concede there is no guarantee the negative press from travel industry campaigns will affect the travel business to a specific destination, particularly when it's the tourism dollar, as opposed to the convention dollar, that's at stake. Although tourists might be aghast at a huge tax surprise on their hotel bill in the morning, they are unlikely to avoid a destination because of it. You don't detour to Honolulu, where the lodging tax is just 9 percent, if what you want to see is the Statue of Liberty.

And as for convention business, there is another factor at work. The meeting planners group, after successfully black-balling New York and getting it to stop using lodging taxes for deficit reduction, is not targeting any other city as a place to avoid, even those in the 16 percent range. That's because the industry doesn't get nearly as incensed by high tax rates when the revenues are plowed back into tourism or convention-related activity, rather than going toward a general fund or deficit reduction.

"If you're going to tax so high on travel services, put it back into tourism, promoting the city, improving the infrastructure or more visitor information booths. Help build up the visitor economy," says Rick Webster, director of tax policy for the Campaign to Keep Travel Competitive. "It's earmarking we're looking for,"

Whether some brave city would like to test the industry's forbearance by raising taxes to the hilt for a new convention center is another question. At a certain point, there is a fragile balance to travel and tourism taxing strategies. What tips that balance may not be felt until a locality goes too far. Ask New York.

The Third Wave of Economic Development

State policymakers are beginning to ask what really matters
in economic development.

Dan Pilcher

Dan Pilcher is NCSL's economic development specialist.

In Wichita, Kan., a shortage of skilled machinists leads 33 aerospace subcontractors, helped by a state grant, to begin an apprenticeship program with area community colleges.

The Iowa Economic Development Department encourages the "clustering" of rural communities to work on economic development. The department helps small towns analyze their needs and solve mutual problems together.

Oregon measures its movement toward its stated economic, social and community goals through a "Benchmark" of more than 150 indicators.

These three examples illustrate principles that some experts say underlie the emerging "Third Wave" in economic development, which, since late 1990, has come to frame a lively debate about the future of state programs for economic growth.

The major strategies of the Third Wave are all long-term investments. Investments in people through education and workforce skills. Investments in distressed communities through help for the people and businesses in those communities. Investments in programs that encourage business and local government to work together.

The dilemma of the states' painful fiscal crunch and their deep worries about global economic competition is leading to the closest examination in more than a decade of what constitutes effective state economic development.

The Third Wave is a label coined by Bob Friedman of the Corporation for Enterprise Development (CFED), a Washington, D.C.-based research and consulting firm. Third Wave principles are also being applied to education,

> If "government is the answer to all problems" is the thesis, and if "government is the source of all problems" is the antithesis, then the Third Wave is the synthesis. It is a rethinking of what government can do and cannot do, and how it can do it more effectively. We've got to get smart.
>
> —R. Scott Fosler, Committee for Economic Development

school-to-work transition (including apprenticeship programs) and workforce training.

For the last decade and a half, when a state went into recession its legislature and governor invariably increased spending for economic development and adopted new programs. This changed in 1991. Legislatures in Illinois, Iowa, Kansas and North Carolina, for example, cut the budgets of economic development agencies and programs. Iowa cut its department by 30 percent. The Illinois legislature reduced the budget of the Department of Commerce and Community Affairs 40 percent, from $90 million to $51 million, resulting in the layoff of 108 staff. And Michigan is considering cutting its Commerce Depart-

ment—and thus its innovative programs—by 75 percent.

In other states, economic development fared better. For example, the Pennsylvania legislature increased program spending 32 percent, from $136 million to $180 million. Oregon is drawing national attention for its steps to reform education and the workforce and for being the first state to embrace explicitly the notion that its economic development effort should assist critical industries to help themselves become more competitive in the global economy.

This new way of looking at economic development concentrates on substance and how programs and services are delivered. It calls for a radical restructuring of state programs that includes the following principles to increase scale, quality and accountability:
• Relying on competition to ensure quality services from different public and private providers instead of relying on government as the sole supplier of services.
• Providing automatic feedback from businesses and communities.

• Providing comprehensive services at the local level.

• Using incentives to encourage clusters of firms to build their competitiveness and capacity to do business.

• Encouraging relationships between service providers and the communities and businesses who need them.

At this point, the Third Wave seems less a solidified theory of economic development and human investment than an emerging set of principles to guide lawmakers and others as they examine how to restructure state government and programs.

Some critics of the Third Wave say it doesn't help distressed rural and urban areas and poor people. The Third Wave focuses on how to deliver economic development programs, says consultant Brandon Roberts, "but—unstated and unquestioned—is the issue of 'to what end?'"

Brian Bosworth, a consultant and former president of the Indiana Economic Development Council, defines the traditional goals of economic development as increasing the standard of living, promoting equity and broadening the distribution of wealth, creating different paths of economic opportunity and choice for different people, and enhancing people's hope of improving their economic future.

In general, the new efforts under way involve a markedly different role for state government than in the past. For example, in Oregon the legislature created a special committee on the wood products industry that met with firms and developed legislation to help the industry help itself become more competitive.

Some states work through intermediary organizations. In Pennsylvania, the state's Manufacturing Innovation Networks program and nine Industrial Resource Centers have nurtured the growth of flexible manufacturing networks in critical industries. Florida and Massachusetts give money to community organizations that provide neighborhood residents with housing, job training and business assistance. The Texas international trade office helped establish more than 20 community offices that promote the export of Texas products.

To keep the state focused on a long-term vision and goals, at least four

This is Third Wave

Examples of economic development programs in both Europe and the United States that appear to deserve the Third Wave label include the following:

• The northern Italian region of Emilia Romagna, once among the poorest of that country, has relied on service centers for specific industries and business networks (machining and textiles, for example) to improve the competitiveness of small firms.

The nine service centers provide small firms and their networks with information and help in product design, marketing and technology transfer. Each non-profit center was created by a consortia of firms with help from ERVET, a quasi-public agency established by the regional government. The result has been that in 30 years Emilia Romagna has jumped from 17th to second in per capita income of Italian regions.

For example, in Modena about a half-dozen small firms work together to produce robots used in the manufacture of automobile engines. One business coordinates production while the individual firms contribute steel fabrication, knowledge of the market and customers' needs, electronic controls and systems design.

• In the United States, at least 50 flexible manufacturing networks now exist in 14 states. A flexible manufacturing network is simply a group of small- or medium-sized firms that decide to cooperate in order to increase their competitiveness by attaining a goal that they cannot reach individually. Collaboration can mean many things, from sharing market information or working jointly on a project to training workers or sharing in the purchase of a new production machine. The industries range from heat treating in Ohio and machine tools in Pennsylvania to defense contracting in Montana and metal working in Arkansas.

• In North Carolina, the Rural Economic Development Center is a private non-profit organization established by the legislature. The center, funded by the legislature with $2 million per year, has raised $2.5 million from the private sector. Its programs include improving the quality of education, venture capital, rural leadership, capital financing for women and minorities, community development corporations, a micro-enterprise loan fund and flexible manufacturing networks.

states—Indiana, Kansas, Oklahoma and Oregon—have placed strategic economic development plans in permanent, quasi-public commissions.

To encourage grassroots action, Iowa, Kansas, North Carolina and Oregon give local communities money and assistance to develop and implement their own plans.

American state policymakers and economic development experts have been studying the success of the regional economies of Baden-Wurttemberg in Germany, Jutland in Denmark, Smaaland in Sweden and Emilia Romagna in Italy for several years.

The secret to the prosperity of these

regions "has been the broad recognition by business that cooperation is essential to competitiveness in an international economy," says C. Richard Hatch of the New Jersey Institute of Technology.

"The key unit of production is no longer the individual company but a decentralized network of companies," Robert Howard, associate editor of the *Harvard Business Review,* wrote recently. "These networks make possible continual innovation through a delicate balance of competition and cooperation, demands and supports." These networks can be found in Japan, Europe and California's Silicon Valley.

To help businessmen create and benefit from such networks, a new institutional context, a new kind of infrastruc-

The First and Second Waves

Bob Friedman and Doug Ross of the Washington, D.C.-based Corporation for Enterprise Development have characterized state economic development efforts as having three waves or phases.

Mississippi started modern state economic development (the First Wave) in 1936 with industrial recruitment, known as smokestack chasing, to lure branch plants down from the industrialized North.

Since then, recruitment has relied on such programs as national advertising, tax incentives, customized job training and subsidized infrastructure. As the economic woes of the United States worsened in the late 1970s, recruitment spread to states outside the South.

In the last decade, for a variety of reasons, recruitment has become perhaps the most widely debated part of state economic development. Critics have long questioned the effectiveness of recruitment programs and incentive packages because, according to several studies, state incentives are far down the list of what is most important to a business when deciding on a site.

Recruitment, though, is still alive and well, especially in the case of facilities that employ large numbers of people. State and local governments in 11 states, including Colorado, Indiana, Kentucky and Oklahoma, assembled incentive packages that run into the hundreds of millions of dollars to try to land a new $1 billion United Airlines maintenance facility.

Beginning in the late '70s and early '80s, a growing number of legislators and governors realized that most new jobs—80 percent to 90 percent—come from existing and new businesses.

Meanwhile, by 1980, 70 percent of U.S. products faced foreign competition within the nation's borders. Technology, workforce quality, capital, global market knowledge and customer service were the new factors in competitive advantage, as Japan and West Germany vividly demonstrated.

This led states to the "Second Wave": concentrating efforts on business activity within their borders. This label is applied to state programs in such areas as exporting, capital finance, managerial and technical assistance, workforce training, entrepreneurial development, technology innovation and deployment, product development and so forth across most major areas of business activity.

By fiscal 1988, the states were spending more than $1 billion on a bewildering array of programs, according to the National Association of State Development Agencies. About two-thirds of state economic development agencies were spending more on bolstering indigenous firms than on recruiting outside ones. Ross, a former Michigan Commerce Department director, likens the array of state programs offered to businesses to the offerings on a restaurant menu: "Please take one."

States found themselves under almost irresistible political pressure to adopt new programs if other states—especially those nearby—had adopted them.

Moreover, in the early and mid-1980s, most states undertook major investment and reforms in education, infrastructure, environment, taxes, workers' compensation and regulations. Motivated by worries over changes in the structure of the American economy and the effects of international competition, governors and legislators aimed these systemic efforts not at individual firms but at the state's economic foundation.

Second Wave initiatives sought to fill perceived market gaps and imperfections through government programs that directly provided economic development services to individual businesses. These services, however, were scattered across state departments and among divisions within departments, and they often operated independently from each other. In addition, they were usually based in the state capital, thus not easily accessible to firms across the state.

By the late 1980s, a number of states, legislators, program evaluation staff and others were increasingly troubled not only by sticky problems of how to measure the results of economic development programs but the inability of these efforts to make a real difference in the state's economy.

The most important criticism of Second Wave programs is that even if they work well, they may have only a marginal impact on a state's economic base because they lack sufficient scale to transform a state's economy substantially.

"On average, a state's economic development effort will affect only about 1 percent of the firms within the state," said Brian Bosworth, former president of the Indiana Economic Development Council.

"The states have a wealth of economic development models," said Bill Nothdurft, a public policy consultant, "but none of them is funded sufficiently to really make a difference."

---

ture is needed, according to Howard. State government, trade associations, labor unions, and other groups can play a role in creating this new infrastructure.

Helping communities and firms organize to help themselves by helping each other will not be easy for state policymakers. Competition, not cooperation, has long been the hallmark of relations among localities and businesses.

"The biggest [U.S.] institutional limitation—compared to our international competitors—is the weakness of trade associations, which view themselves as lobbyists rather than service providers to their member firms," said Anne Heald, program officer for the German Marshall Fund of the United States. The National Tooling and Machining Association, for instance, which has helped 20 of its 50 local chapters develop flexible manufacturing networks, is one of the few national trade groups that promote networking. Trade associations in Japan and Europe are more apt to provide services such as market information, sharing of technology and workforce training, to their members to improve their global competitiveness.

Beyond the issue of helping those

who will help themselves lies the question for state policymakers of political and financial accountability of Third Wave programs.

In the past, lawmakers exerted control over public spending by placing programs within state agencies. For legislators and governors, political accountability—in the sense of claiming credit for creating programs, appropriating funds and controlling the money and the programs—was inherent in most early economic development.

How to evaluate the tax money spent on Third Wave programs and private or quasi-public organizations is a thorny issue. Political control over the new round of efforts will likely be tenuous for governors and legislators.

Some legislators will be concerned that surrendering control of the purse strings for even a quasi-public organization may invite misuse of the funds. In many states, however, legislators serve on the boards of these agencies and can thus exert their influence on behalf of public policy and accountability. The legislature still holds the power of the purse if the agency depends on a regular appropriation.

In short, legislators and governors will have to confront the choice of relinquishing direct administrative and financial control if they want to reap the possible benefits of Third Wave programs. In theory at least, the new way of looking at economic development holds the potential for a greater political constituency to support it if groups of communities and key industries can be mobilized to help themselves.

In state after state, there is a growing consensus that improving the quality of the state's workforce will improve its competitiveness in the long run. "The challenge of economic competitiveness is the challenge of competence," says Bill Nothdurft, a public policy consultant who has studied European education and workforce training systems. "To the extent that there is a secret weapon in Europe's rise in international competitiveness, it is that they are continuing to produce a steady stream of highly skilled, motivated, educated and competent workers."

Friedman of CFED says that one goal of the Third Wave should be to offer people incentives and resources to

Oregon Looks to Europe for a Model

Oregon is gaining national attention for undertaking a new approach to economic development that encourages small businesses in the same industry to work together to become competitive in the global market.

Oregon's economy, based heavily on timber and agriculture, faces significant declines because of concern for the environment, which includes protecting endangered species such as the spotted owl and the native salmon. The future of Oregon's economy, therefore, depends on its ability to add value to a limited or even declining resource base.

With help from the German Marshall Fund of the United States and the Northwest Policy Center at the University of Washington, a group of Oregon and Washington legislators, economic development officials and business leaders in September 1989 examined Western European programs. The Oregon team paid particular attention to Italy, where flexible manufacturing networks—groups of small firms cooperating to compete effectively in global markets—have driven the economic resurgence of several regions.

Denmark also provided a model for Oregon's plan. The Danes have made small business networks the centerpiece of their national strategy to compete in the 1992 single market of the European Community.

"In Denmark, we saw an impressive program to make small businesses internationally competitive by encouraging cooperation in international marketing," said Senator Wayne Fawbush, co-chair of the legislature's Joint Trade and Economic Development Committee. Denmark established a program of network brokers, who bring together firms to define and solve common problems and offer feasibility grants of up to $10,000 to groups of three firms.

The American delegation noted that the best European programs:
• Emphasize individual industries, not individual businesses.
• Focus on services such as market information and new technologies that improve the competitiveness of firms, instead of government subsidies.
• Encourage businesses to manage and finance these services.

During the 1991 session, the Oregon legislature, using some of these ideas, created a wood products competitiveness corporation to encourage businesses in the timber industry to work together. The corporation, composed of industry representatives, will receive $2.25 million from the state to encourage small groups of firms (networks) to solve mutual problems. Firms in the network might share the cost of acquiring a new production process or training their workforce, the cost of common services such as marketing and accounting, and work together to produce a product.

"The legislature," says Fawbush, "expects this independent quasi-public corporation to fashion a strategy for competitiveness that addresses the industry's needs and gets wide participation from firms throughout the state."

support themselves and their families through jobs or their own businesses.

"Think of the policies in American history that have generated significant, widespread, long-term economic growth," says Friedman. "They are policies like the GI Bill and the Homestead Act—democratic investments in the common genius of the American people." The Third Wave must have modern versions of such policies, he says.

Is the Third Wave a breakthrough in economic thinking, or just a new way of looking at old economic development techniques?

Whatever the answer, one thing is clear: The field is in lively ferment and accepted approaches are being challenged. The model that emerges will probably define in large measure state economic development for the 1990s and into the 21st century.

Romancing *the* Smokestack

There's no end in sight to the competition for industry. But a few places are starting to think the game should have some rules.

Charles Mahtesian

I f there's a politician these days who seems to understand the futility of smokestack chasing, it is Illinois Governor Jim Edgar. Since his election in 1990, he has lectured his colleagues on the folly of making extravagant offers to lure businesses or to keep them from leaving. He even convened a private Washington, D.C., summit between governors and corporate leaders to talk the matter over. In August 1993, Edgar was the architect of a truce adopted by the National Governors' Association that, among other things, urged states not to use public resources merely to influence the location of private investment.

But before Edgar left Springfield to announce the treaty, he took care of some of his own business—okaying the use of public resources to influence the location of a wavering in-state company. The deal gave Tootsie Roll Industries $20 million in loans, $1.4

million in state and local tax exemptions and $200,000 in job training funds. Then, when Edgar returned, he signed off on a tax incentive package amounting to nearly $30 million, plus $700,000 in job training funds, for a Nabisco plant producing Fig Newtons and Oreos.

Edgar's ambivalent approach to the prevailing economic development strategy is hardly unique among public officials. In 1991, three years after hammering his election opponent for lavishing incentives on a foreign carmaker, Indiana Governor Evan Bayh muscled out nine other finalists with a $291 million incentive offer for a United Airlines maintenance facility.

While virtually every governor, legislator and development official laments the zero-sum nature of the contest, the industrial recruitment wars continue with no end in sight. As with the Cold War arms race, no state or city is willing

to disengage unilaterally. And the bidding game is by no means played only by industrial giants such as Illinois and Indiana.

Since statehood in 1889, North Dakota governors have seen fit to call only nine special legislative sessions. Usually they have dealt with emergency or war-related measures. The 10th and latest special session, however, concerned a less lofty subject—luring a $245 million corn processing plant to the state. These days, the prospect of attracting a new industrial facility passes for both an emergency and a war.

In order to compete with rivals Minnesota and South Dakota, North Dakota Governor Ed Schafer felt the state's tax code needed some adjustment. So over three days this past summer, the legislature, almost without opposition, carved out various tax exemptions to make their state a more attractive place to process corn. They won't know just how attractive they've made it until sometime next year, when the Northern Corn Processors Cooperative makes its decision.

As economic development battles go, these governors got off lightly. None had to appear on the Phil Donahue show, as seven others did when General Motors' Saturn auto plant was up for grabs in the mid-1980s. The Tootsie Roll logo will not have to appear on top of the scoreboard at University of Illinois football contests, as the Mercedes-Benz insignia did at a Crimson Tide game last year when Alabama was seeking the company's new sports-utility vehicle plant.

And Nabisco never bargained with an "ideal incentive matrix," a 104-item wish list that the Intel Corp. issued in 1992 to those interested in landing two new computer chip factories. In addition to tax breaks, the company sought incentives such as immediate resident status for its employees and their dependents (so that they could receive lower, in-state college tuition), discounts on moving expenses and mortgage costs, and other assorted goodies.

While Intel's wish list might sound outrageous, in the current incentives war between the states, it is fast becoming the norm. The company actually found two Southwestern states—Arizona and New Mexico—that acquiesced to many of its demands.

But there is a positive side to nightmares like the incentive matrix: The more brazen and costly relocation demands become, the more state and local officials find themselves reexamining their industrial strategies. Ever so slowly, they are starting to distribute incentives more judiciously, implement accountability measures and demand remuneration if companies fail to deliver on their promises.

Smokestack chasing is not a new phenomenon, just more publicized—and more costly—than ever before. The most recent round dates back to the early 1980s, when Tennessee put together an incentives package that paid roughly the equivalent of $11,000 per job for a Nissan automobile manufacturing plant. Five years later, the Volunteer State also won the Saturn circus after a 30-state winnowing process. By then, the per-job costs had more than doubled to $26,000.

Not to be outdone, Kentucky offered an estimated $150 million in incentives in its successful 1985 effort to bring a Toyota plant to Georgetown. Broken down by the job, it comes out to about $50,000 each.

But it was Alabama's 1993 deal with Mercedes-Benz that heated up the smoldering debate over smokestack-chasing mania. When the dust settled after a 35-state, 100-site battle royal for the sports-utility vehicle plant, Alabama was left standing with an incentives package estimated at about $300 million—or somewhere in the neighborhood of $200,000 for each of the 1,500 expected jobs.

Early on, company executives told inquiring state officials they would not be moved by a bidding war. But once states began offering tax abatements, Mercedes willingly played auctioneer. Unsuccessful competitors for the plant groused that the company played states off each other to get the best possible deal. Judging from the final agreement, it is hard to conclude otherwise.

In the end, Alabama had committed to building a $5 million welcome center for visitors to the plant, purchasing a fleet of the new vehicles and paying workers' wages while they are in training. Almost $80 million in state money will go to infrastructure improvements and close to $100 million will pay for site development.

Governor Jim Folsom argued that, at least for his state, the Mercedes deal was a steal, if for nothing other than its symbolism—that is, to break through old stereotypes and announce to the corporate world that Alabama is open for business. There is certainly some precedent. Kentucky's mad scramble for industry has left little doubt in business circles as to its hospitality toward industry and commerce.

But critics of the Mercedes deal think it stands for something more ominous: The state's willingness to give huge tax breaks to healthy firms while, at the same time, it is under a judicial mandate to spend hundreds of millions of dollars to fix up its inadequate public school system.

"Many of the states are in the position they are in because they failed to invest in basic infrastructure over the years—the infrastructure of education, the road system, technology systems, financial systems," says Brian Dabson, president of the Corporation for Enter-

prise Development and co-author of a 1994 report, *Bidding for Business: Are Cities and States Selling Themselves Short?* "Those building blocks of economic development are simply not well enough developed for them to compete. We are talking about decades of neglect, so they can ill afford to chase companies."

The traditionally underdeveloped southeastern region has garnered much of the industrial recruitment notoriety, but it is clearly not a regional fad. On the West Coast, for example, California is weathering not only a crippling recession but an invasion of economic development pirates seeking to persuade businesses to relocate out of state.

More than 20 state and local offices are scattered across Southern California, staffed by individuals who make a living by trying to induce California business executives to move their operations out of state.

The height of ignominy may have come last year, when 65 state and local economic development organizations from across the country held a business relocation expo in Anaheim, designed to lure away Golden State businesses.

Even truces and treaties have been unable to stop the practice of interstate raiding. Anyone who doubts that needs only to look toward the East Coast, where poaching characterizes the relationships among New York, New Jersey and Connecticut.

In 1991, the last time the three states agreed to a non-aggression pact, New Jersey Governor James Florio broke it within months. Worse yet, he rubbed New York's face in it by creating a recruitment fund paid for out of revenues from the World Trade Center—jointly owned by both states.

Actually, it's not difficult to understand why Florio did what he did. If nothing else, the politics of smokestack chasing are simply too enticing. Any job-creation venture—even those with dubious claims—translates into great press. And if the deal turns out to be a bomb, the evidence likely will not filter out until long after an administration is out of power—if it surfaces at all.

"Industrial recruitment remains so tempting that a lot of states are going to continue, primarily for political reasons," says Peter Eisinger, director of the LaFollette School of Public Policy in Wisconsin and an authority on economic development strategy. "Unfortunately, governors have found it to be an easier strategy than saying, 'I put $15 million in a high-tech consortium that in 15 years will employ 5,000 people, but right now employs 15 people in little white lab coats.'"

Part of the problem is that there is generally very little pressure on officials to refuse to compete for such potentially lucrative prizes. Although a few existing firms occasionally squawk about the fairness of subsidizing newcomers, for the most part the business community has been an implicit co-conspirator in the incentives war. For example, local business leaders have been known to snipe at governors such as Edgar in Illinois or John Engler in Michigan for their failures to romance wayward industry.

In a recent report, the National Governors' Association pointedly asked business leaders to stand by state officials when one company is seeking unreasonable incentives at the expense of other businesses or the state. "In some cases, we laid cover for governors who didn't want to get involved in bidding wars," says Jay Kayne, policy director for NGA. "It was tough for some governors to say, 'I'm not going to go after Mercedes-Benz or Toyota.'"

One reason state chambers of commerce have been reluctant to lead the charge against incentives is because their members are generally divided over the issue. After all, the reasoning goes, some may have the opportunity to cash in sometime down the road.

Oddly enough, small business has not been heard from either, despite the fact that most of the goodies are going to bigger firms. "In terms of lighting torches, taking up pitchforks and marching on the capitol, that's not what's happening," says Jim Wiedman of the National Federation of Independent Business. "It doesn't affect anyone directly."

Perhaps they should be taking up their pitchforks. In essence, incentives mean that existing business is subsidizing new business. The money for related development—such as schools, roads and other services—has to come from somewhere. Given the corporate tax, excise tax, inventory tax, raw materials tax, sales tax and other assorted tax exemptions freely distributed these

Quantifying the economic impact of incentives and subsidies is an inexact science.

days, that money is certainly not coming from the new businesses.

"If you are going to allow a new company to get away with not paying any taxes for 10 years, somebody else has to offset that," says Dabson. "Those costs are borne by existing companies. So basically what you're creating is an inequitable tax system where existing companies are paying taxes on behalf of new ones."

But rather than agree to halt the bidding game, many existing firms have simply upped the ante. This past summer, New York City officials found themselves forced to cough up millions in concessions to a company that publicly admitted it had no intention of moving away but thought it ought to get in on the action.

To understand what happened, it is necessary to go back to 1989, when the NBC television network threatened to bolt the city for New Jersey. In return for staying put, the city offered $100 million in tax breaks and other concessions. Four years later, rival network CBS recieved a $50 million payoff. So, naturally, ABC came knocking at city hall. It came away with $26 million in sales tax abatements and electricity cost concessions by promising to create 185 jobs.

Was it worth it? It's almost impossible to tell for sure. As with most other incentive packages, there's a pretty good chance that no one will ever know. "Nobody in the press does a cost-benefit analysis. Nobody ever

looks to see if the jobs promised materialized. Nobody ever looks to see whether the new plant sparks associated growth," says Eisinger. "There are, however, banner headlines saying, 'South Carolina Beats Out Dozens of Other States for BMW Plant.'"

Economists themselves are divided over the effect incentives have on relocation decisions. Surveys of business executives and relocation consultants indicate incentives are merely one of many factors taken into consideration. But quantifying the incentives and subsidies is also an inexact science. And the economic impact of a new or upgraded facility is unclear because so much depends on the economic forecasting model or multipliers used.

"Even if costs and effects of incentives were known, it is hard to quantify how much the resulting development contributes to public revenues and public costs," notes Hal Hovey in *State Policy Reports*, "not to mention benefits and costs that don't find their way into state and local budgets."

But it doesn't always take an economist to figure out which of the most recent deals have disaster written all over them. And that may be the best news of all in the incentive wars. Because the more deals disappoint, the more closely both lawmakers and the public will scrutinize incentives. In fact, the recent shuffle steps toward holding companies accountable are based not necessarily on a desire for better public policy but on the fear of being burnt on a bad deal.

The debacle in Pennsylvania, where Volkswagen opened the first foreign auto plant in America in 1978, is among the most notorious. It took a $71 million incentives package to win the bidding battle with Ohio, but a giddy Governor Milton Shapp promised the plant could one day produce as many as 20,000 jobs. It never came close. Within five years, half of its 6,000 workers were laid off. Within a decade, it had closed down for good.

Plenty of other deals went sour in the 1980s—including a Playskool toy factory in Chicago and an Anchor Hocking glassmaking plant in West Virginia. In both cases, the companies took state or local incentives, then attempted to move away. After bitter court battles, Chicago and West Virginia were able to extract settlements.

More recently, Minnesota's arrangement with Northwest Airlines has attracted attention. In 1992, the state agreed on an $840 million loan, grant and tax-break package for the St. Paul-based company to site two repair facilities in the state's economically depressed Iron Range region. Within months, the airline was teetering near bankruptcy. Northwest still went ahead and accepted part of the deal—a $270 million loan—then announced that the facilities were "on hold." The state is reluctant to pursue any action which could push Northwest over the brink.

Those ultimately unsatisfying results have underscored the need to make companies uphold their end of the bargain. Among the recent mechanisms: "right-to-know" laws that require estimates of jobs created or destroyed, sophisticated cost-benefit analyses and incentives targeted at specific industries. Most are manifestations of deals gone sour or unkept promises. "The laws are reactions to horror stories or are in lieu of litigation," says Greg LeRoy, a policy consultant to the Federation for Industrial Retention and Renewal, an advocacy group that calls for increased accountability measures. "It's a city or state's attempt to say, 'No one will do that to us again.'"

In response to a recent industrial recruitment uptick—and its accompanying tax breaks—the Arizona legislature tightened state statutes this year to dissuade in-state business poaching, to target key industrial "clusters," such as high technology, and to require a cost-benefit analysis for large-scale incentive packages.

Still, the legislation is loaded with potential loopholes, such as ways to get around the cost-benefit analysis, notes Mary Jo Waits, author of an 1993 economic incentives study for the University of Arizona's Morrison Institute for Public Policy. "It's not totally 100 percent wonderful," she says. "But it's a step in the right direction."

Yet none of the new measures can guarantee that the promised benefits of a new company will ever materialize. For that reason, a growing number of places—including Arizona—are exploring a mechanism widely used in Western Europe, known as the "claw-

Clawbacks require firms to repay subsidies if they fail to deliver on their promises.

back." Under a clawback provision, firms must repay all or part of subsidies if they fail to deliver, under-perform or over-promise.

The township of Ypsilanti, Michigan, could have used such a measure back in 1992 when it sued General Motors for closing its 4,500-worker Willow Run plant. Local officials insisted that 17 years of tax abatements—which they said totaled $1.3 billion—had included job-security pledges by GM. In a closely watched case, the township won an injunction at the circuit court level, but saw the decision overturned in 1993 by the state Court of Appeals.

The city that won the GM bidding war, Arlington, Texas, did not make the same mistake. If the GM agreement is breached, the city not only gets back taxes but penalties and interest as well.

There are limits, however, to the effectiveness of clawbacks. For starters, development officials are less than enamored of them, if only because relocating companies dislike them. Besides, enforcement is, and is likely to remain, uneven mostly because public officials are reluctant to penalize already financially troubled companies.

"Clawbacks certainly are increasing," says the University of Wiscon-

sin's Eisinger. "But the jury is out on how effective they are going to be. There are a lot of loopholes for firms. They are imperfect devices."

That's what worries critics of Indianapolis' agreement with United Airlines. While the contract includes clawback provisions, its terms allow maximum wiggle room when it comes to the definition of jobs created. "It's starting to percolate out just how insane the United Airlines thing is," says Bill Styring, president of the Indiana Policy Review Foundation, a conservative think tank.

A federal role in smokestack chasing may also be brewing, much to the consternation of virtually everyone involved in the industrial recruitment battles. In one case, Wisconsin's congressional delegation drafted protective legislation in August after Milwaukee employer Briggs & Stratton announced it would shift local jobs to Missouri and Kentucky—a move partly subsidized by federal block grant funds.

The outcry for federal involvement, though, is mainly coming from advocacy groups that are on the outside looking in. There is about as much chance that governors and legislators will join the call for the feds as there is that the governor of Alabama will be seen driving a Yugo.

"It would be a disaster," warns Phil Burgess, president of the Center for the New West, a Denver-based think tank. "The last thing we need is the federal government ruling on whether a state could entice business. What authority does the federal government have to say anything about a state's industrial policy or lack of one?"

For the time being, the answer is none. Which means in all likelihood states and localities will continue their hot pursuit of industry and jobs. And in the end, it may take an economic development disaster, not regulation by the feds or any other body, for them to fully recognize the risks of indiscriminate smokestack chasing.

"The change will come not because we put a gun to their heads," says the NGA's Jay Kayne, "but because it represents good public policy."

Or because, in the long run, wooing businesses too extravagantly would be bad public relations.

The Strange Career of Enterprise Zones

Conceived a decade ago as a libertarian economic experiment, they have been reborn as a descendant of the Great Society.

WILLIAM FULTON AND MORRIS NEWMAN

William Fulton is editor of California Planning & Development Report, *a monthly newsletter. Morris Newman is senior editor of* CP&DR.

Like everything else in Southern California, the Watts Enterprise Zone is low-scale, sprawling, and seemingly endless. Stretching almost eight miles north to south and five miles east to west, it encompasses an entire world, from the broad residential boulevards of L.A.'s historically black neighborhoods to the city's main industrial corridor, picking up portions of four other small cities along the way. This is the rough urban landscape made legendary by "Boyz N the Hood" and a hundred violent rap videos, and transformed into a metaphor for decaying urban America by the 1992 Los Angeles riots. Against an image that powerful, a mere enterprise zone seems no more than a puny weapon.

And the fact is that in its nine-year history, the Watts zone, with its tax breaks and employment credits for business, has enjoyed no more than modest success. By the city's own count, only 2,500 non-retail businesses exist inside the 20 or so square miles of the zone located within the L.A. city boundaries, and most of them were there before the enterprise zone was created. Many of them are furniture manufacturers, sheet metal companies and recycling firms located in a slightly run-down but still vibrant industrial area near Florence and Central, 30 blocks north of Watts. Tom Hawkins, a former car dealer who serves as L.A.'s zone manager, uses direct-mail promotion methods to try to sign the businesses up for his limited arsenal of enterprise zone benefits—mostly state wage credits and local utility price breaks.

Like enterprise zone managers around the country, however, Hawkins and his L.A. colleagues have essentially spent the past decade waiting for "the big fish"—a federal enterprise zone program that would provide large tax breaks for businesses, creating truly powerful financial incentives for locating in depressed areas.

Now L.A. has its big fish on the line. The Clinton administration has made it clear that the Watts zone—or at least a large chunk of it—will be selected as one of nine "empowerment zones" nationwide. Along with tax breaks for businesses within the zone will come an onslaught of focused federal help, including special attention from the Small Business Administration, relaxed inner-city lending requirements under the Community Reinvestment Act and new programs to provide billions of dollars in capital for housing. The sum total of direct federal largess may reach $100 million in aid for the Watts zone all by itself.

After a decade as the subject of Washington cocktail-party discussion, enterprise zones are about to become a cornerstone of federal urban policy.

The fish that Hawkins and his cohorts are about to land, however, is not exactly the one they started out casting for. In giving enterprise zones a central role for the first time, President Clinton has transformed the concept almost beyond recognition.

As championed by Republican theoreticians of the 1980s—Stuart Butler, the British-born economist generally regarded as the creator of the idea, and Jack Kemp, the former HUD secretary—enterprise zones were a libertarian approach to urban problems. Government was to award tax incentives and clear away government red-tape in inner-city areas, stimulating a revival led by the private sector.

Clinton's idea doesn't look much like that at all. Under the terms of the budget bill passed last September, the nine empowerment zones—six urban and three rural—will receive not only tax breaks but also a wide range of traditional programs for social service, community development and crime prevention. "The whole idea of the enterprise zones is not only to bring tax credits, but to do truly innovative things, such as bringing together different federal agencies on the same problem," says HUD Secretary Henry Cisneros.

The more that local officials hear about the social programs, the better they seem to like the new Clinton concept. "Tax incentives alone are not going to get you very far," says Marilyn Lurie, L.A.'s director of commercial and industrial development. "The problems that affect businesses are really complex, and are not all dealt with by tax incentives—crime, drugs, security, insurance costs."

The most determined opponents of this new program are the conservatives who have been promoting the enterprise zone idea for the past decade. They are convinced Clinton has perverted it—that his plan is nothing more than a Great Society wolf disguised in the clothing of a supply-side sheep. "The Clinton plan abandons the entrepreneurial spirit which characterized earlier enterprise zone proposals," Kemp charged recently, arguing that it focuses too much on hiring incentives and not enough on capital formation.

The response from the Clinton administration is a simple one. Their idea, they insist, isn't so much a reflection of any liberal ideology as a response to the experiences of zones like the one in L.A. during a decade of trial and error.

The debate over enterprise zones is no longer just a matter of theory. In the early 1980s, when a federal enterprise zone program seemed imminent, states and localities began positioning themselves for it by launching programs of their own. In the past decade, 37 states have designated more than 3,000 enterprise zones all over the country. While the big federal enchilada never came, enterprise zones now have a state and local history that can serve as the basis for launching any new expansion of the idea at the federal level.

Most of the enterprise zone programs have featured at least some tax incentives of the sort originally envisioned. These usually start with state income tax credits, but often go much further. In Ohio, localities were authorized to provide a local property tax abatement of up to 100 percent to zone businesses. In New Jersey, retail sales taxes were cut in half inside the zones. Businesses in the Watts zone can qualify for a 25 percent discount from the L.A. water and power utility.

All of those initiatives fit well within the basic conservative framework. But many of the zones around the country did not choose to stop there. Over the course of the 1980s, the leadership of the enterprise zone movement in America quietly changed hands. As the federal enterprise zone bills languished in Congress, conservative theoreticians moved on to privatization and other attractive new economic crusades. Actual management of the zones shifted to state and local officials, few of them infused with Kemp's libertarian ideology. These officials were willing enough to administer the tax incentives provided by law; they were less enthusiastic about regulatory relief for business, especially in health and safety.

What these managers gradually realized, however, was that once a zone was in place, it could be used for many things beyond its original purpose. Wary at first of a conservative idea, they learned to adapt it to their own goals. "State and local policy makers, as well as administrators, slowly warmed to enterprise zones as more than a tax incentive program," says Richard Cowden, executive director of the American Association of Enterprise Zones. "They found the zones to be a useful targeting mechanism for a wide variety of economic development measures."

The state of New Jersey not only cut its sales tax from 6 percent to 3 percent in all retail establishments inside its enterprise zones but earmarked the resulting revenues for in-zone improvements such as fire trucks and storefront rehabilitation. In Norwalk, Connecticut, the city pledged virtually all of its federal block-grant funds for three years to construction of a bridge connecting its depressed inner-city enterprise zone to Interstate 95—a targeting of resources that had little in common with the original concept of a tax abatement and deregulation program.

But other zones went considerably further—in the direction of the traditional social programs Kemp and his fellow theorists disdain. The enterprise zone in Elkhart, Indiana, has sponsored a job training program for zone residents that concentrates on helping chronically unemployed people learn work skills. So far, 40 zone residents have "graduated" to jobs such as restaurant manager trainee and nurse's aid. In nearby South Bend, a job training program for the chronically unemployed has included transportation and child care services designed to facilitate employment for zone residents.

"We are more of a catalyst to make things happen—a change-maker," says Mark Brinson, program director for the Elkhart Urban Enterprise Association. In his view, an enterprise zone brings together a variety of solutions that might be called "liberal"—but does so with the goal of business and job growth, rather than social services alone. It allows resources to be targeted into particular areas, rather than having them spread thinly to obtain political support, as is more commonly the practice. And it unites business, local government and neighborhood activists together in pursuit of the same goals—a modest achievement, and difficult to measure in dollars and cents, but perhaps the single most important thing enterprise zones have done around the country so far.

"The money was not the important thing in Elkhart," says Arthur Banks, the Indiana state enterprise zone director. "It was the process of doing the strategic planning and involving local people from local areas to help their own direction. That in itself was a powerful thing—to realize that they themselves were the government and could determine their own direction."

There is little question that enterprise zones have quietly strayed far beyond their original mission, and that it is the newer, broader concept that served as the engine for the Clinton proposal. But how much have they accomplished? What does the record of the past decade tell us?

There are some grandiose claims being made. One set of figures released by HUD suggests that state programs have generated 600,000 jobs and more than $40 billion in business investment in depressed areas. Illinois alone claims more than $5 billion in investment and 262,000 jobs created in the zones.

But even enterprise zone advocates generally concede that these figures are little more than fantasy. State enterprise zones do not operate in isolation—they are invariably part of a much larger economic development landscape that includes a variety of programs in addition to the ones specifically authorized by the enterprise zone legislation. Jobs created "in" a zone are not necessarily jobs created "by" the zone—they might well have happened whether the zone existed or not. It is never easy to tell just how much change the zone itself has been responsible for.

And some states have clearly had problems. In California—where a political stalemate in the legislature resulted in two zone programs, a Democratic one and a Republican one—even the HUD survey showed an investment of only $380 million and creation of just 7,000 jobs, a modest performance compared to that claimed by other large states. California has had some notable successes, such as the construction of the first textile mill on the West Coast, which was built by a Japanese company in a depressed part of Fresno. At the same time, however, many zones there have struggled, both statistically and on the ground.

Ohio, which has permitted total property-tax abatements for zone businesses, boasts some of the most impressive numbers in the country—$13 billion in investment and 124,500 jobs, according to the HUD survey. Yet the law didn't set very strict criteria for designating zones—some of them included large tracts of vacant land in rural areas. Anybody who built a factory on this land was granted a tax break and then counted as an enterprise zone success—even though the connection with reviving depressed neighborhoods was negligible. At the end of last year, a political impasse in the legislature caused the entire Ohio law to lapse.

Even in the more successful zones, the initial goal of creating jobs for local residents has proven elusive; rarely do more than a small percentage of new employees live in the zones. Some states have tried to encourage hiring by offering a wage credit for those living inside—or even by mandating that a certain percentage of workers be from the zone. California requires that participating businesses hire 20 percent of their workers from within the zone. But these mandates are a blunt instrument at best. In Brisbane, a small industrial town south of San Francisco, city officials have lobbied to change the hiring mandate because too few locals are qualified for the jobs the zone is attracting.

It is not the failure stories, however, that the Clinton administration seized upon in creating its new program for the

1990s. It is the success stories such as those from Elkhart and South Bend, where the broader idea of enterprise zone as catalyst seems to have translated into some real signs of progress. And the lesson from those places is that the zones work best when the decisions are made at the neighborhood level.

Paul Dimond, the White House aide in charge of creating the Clinton program, insists that it will emphasize "bottom-up rebirth and revitalization," rather than top-down control. "If a few communities can demonstrate how to end the isolation of workers in distressed communities from jobs throughout the labor market," says Dimond, "we can end the incredible unemployment that has ravaged so many distressed communities for too long."

At the offices of the Los Angeles Community Development Department—a block from Skid Row in downtown Los Angeles and 10 miles north of Watts—the city's zone managers are already at work trying to figure out how to draw the boundaries of the L.A. empowerment zone, which can be up to 20 square miles in size. Though no formal commitments have been made, no one has ever really doubted that Watts would form the basis for one of the nine areas to be chosen nationally under the Clinton program. Since the riots two years ago, Watts and South-Central Los Angeles have been the au courant symbol of urban decay, as the South Bronx was in the 1970s. "Our two top priorities are the District of Columbia and Los Angeles," says HUD Secretary Cisneros. "When the enterprise zone legislation was drafted, Los Angeles was very much in mind."

Yet the sheer scale of the task is daunting. Urban poverty and economic isolation stretch across more than 100 square miles of Los Angeles' south side. Even the current, state-designated Watts zone is 30 square miles—50 percent larger than the federal empowerment zone will allow. Among other things, L.A. has a gerrymandering problem in determining which industrial districts and which residential neighborhoods will be included in the proposed new zone.

There are some signs of renewed life in South-Central; new investment by supermarket chains, marketing of a large industrial site owned by the state and construction of a new civic center on 103rd Street, epicenter of the 1965 riots. But most of these efforts started outside the enterprise zone program and probably would have gone forward after the 1992 riots, zone or no zone. And they're still just a drop in the bucket given the vast social and economic problems of the area. The whole situation raises the question of just what the designation as a federal zone will do to help South-Central.

City Hall is glad to offer a blunt answer to that question. "Money," says Marilyn Lurie, the city's industrial development director. "A hundred million dollars over two years." Yet even Lurie and her colleagues are a little cynical about how much the money will do, especially given the federal government's requirement that the money be spent in a two-year period. "Spending $100 million in two years and expecting that to have a lasting impact on changing communities is not realistic," Lurie says. She also fears that Washington might try to control the program too tightly, hogtying the empowerment zones with more regulation, rather than less.

But if the Clinton administration does it the way Paul Dimond promises to do it—from the ground up—there is reason to be at least moderately hopeful. For all the extravagant claims, and the metamorphosis of the entire idea beyond the original Kemp-Butler vision, enterprise zones have shown in Indiana and other places that they can help communities by formalizing the relationship between human development and business development. They can handle social goals with decent success so long as they don't define themselves as entitlement programs—so long as business and job growth remain their highest priorities.

Enterprise zones are never going to create Hong Kong in Watts or the South Bronx. But anytime they serve as a catalyst for bringing human development and business growth together in new combinations, they are doing a job that needs to be done if inner cities are going to be revived at all.

Wild About Convention Centers

Hundreds of cities expect that their new convention centers will bring economic benefits and urban regeneration. Most cities will be left with underused facilities and decades of debt

Lawrence Tabak

Lawrence Tabak is a freelance writer who has written on such varied subjects as tennis, the travel industry, and prairie ecology.

The towers of Kansas City's new convention center rise like the masts of a world-class suspension bridge, spanning Interstate 70. When it is completed, this fall, the massive exhibition hall will join a number of other new facilities around the country which are vying for major conventions. These multimillion-dollar convention centers are built in the expectation that hordes of free-spending conventioneers will bolster local economies and revitalize downtowns. Kansas City officials, like their counterparts around the country, are confident that their dazzling center will pay for itself and then some.

With so much pressure on city budgets, how have cities found the funds to build these megastructures? Is the meeting and convention business so active that more than 300 cities can fill and pay for their municipally funded convention centers? The answers that come from Kansas City are the same ones that echo, however hollowly, across the country.

A slump in convention business in Kansas City in the mid-1980s was especially painful for city officials. Kansas City had been a convention overachiever, surpassing cities two or three times its

size. The loss of business was not particularly mysterious: the number of cities owning and marketing convention facilities tripled from about 100 in 1977 to more than 300 in 1987. Competing cities had newer centers, and many had more attractive downtowns, better climates, and —a critical factor for meeting planners— more hotel rooms near their centers.

The loss of downtown hotels is symptomatic of the declining fortunes of Kansas City's urban center. In the early 1970s conventions could book more than 2,000 downtown hotel rooms; today the number is 1,500. Downtown hotels continue to struggle, and boarded-up buildings remain an eyesore. Visitors will find just a handful of restaurants, no major department stores, no movie theaters, and no night life.

Like other convention-center backers throughout the country, Kansas City officials saw their project primarily as a catalyst for downtown revitalization. The convention-center expansion began with a plan unveiled by a private developer in 1987; he eventually promised to include a twenty-five-story World Trade Center and a flashy 800-room convention hotel along with the expanded convention center. To city officials, the beautiful architectural sketches were like a full banquet set before the starving.

A second developer's proposal had the

convention center expanding in a different direction (away from the first developer's property, and toward property owned by the second). This proposal was ultimately rejected. City-council members recall little if any discussion of underlying merit or ultimate cost. A number of council members toured larger and newer facilities around the country and came back convinced that Kansas City was losing its competitive advantage. Even some cynicism regarding feasibility studies failed to dampen enthusiasm for the project, which was, admittedly, driven as much by emotion and intuition as by facts and figures. Since the bulk of the costs of the project would be paid by the state and by new hotel and food and beverage taxes, worries about finances were soon superseded by the debate over the specifics of the project.

"Lead, follow, or get the heck out of the way" was the way a *Kansas City Star* columnist characterized the prevailing spirit. A feasibility study supplied the necessary endorsement for construction. The cry was taken up by construction interests and unions, and by the city's Convention and Visitors Bureau, an independent body charged with marketing the convention center and tourism. When, in 1989, the city successfully lobbied the Missouri state legislature to contribute $2 million a year, the deal was virtually done.

The convention trade is widely seen as a civic windfall, with thousands of expense-account-laden visitors dropping millions of dollars into the local economy.

The chairman of the Convention and Visitors Bureau echoed the general optimism, suggesting that it was "worth a gamble" that convention-center construction would spark the kind of development exemplified by the promised trade center and convention hotel. A few voices, quickly drowned out, warned that the city should get the promises for affiliated construction in writing.

Many cities have discovered that their residents are not eager convention-center supporters—especially if they get a whiff of tax increases. Heywood Sanders, a professor in the Department of Urban Administration at Trinity University, in San Antonio, has documented that most of the nation's new convention centers are being built without referenda, typically by establishing separate convention authorities empowered to issue bonds without voter approval.

In Kansas City, however, a referendum was called on whether to increase hotel-motel and restaurant taxes so as to pay off the convention-center costs. In early 1990 developers, hospitality-industry members, and construction concerns mounted a $300,000 advertising campaign, assuring voters that the expanded convention center would create jobs, encourage the construction of a new hotel, and revitalize the economy. Best of all, "two-thirds of the funds raised will come from those who live outside the city." (The ads didn't mention that the residents' one third would amount to some $7 million a year, or that the projected jobs had an average annual salary of $14,000—about the poverty level for a family of four.) The convention-center tax initiative passed by a landslide.

Like other new convention centers, Kansas City's will never cover its operating costs and debt expenses with rental revenues—not in the buyers' market created by dozens of competing centers. Income from the new center is projected to reach $3 million a year. Operating costs will be around $6.5 million, marketing will add some $2 million, and annual debt service will be $13 million. Some $18 million a year will be needed to cover the overall losses.

Although cities across the country have developed creative sources of income to recover such losses (horse racing in Orange County, California, for example, and the sale of air rights in Springfield, Illinois), travelers and tourists are the primary candidates to cover costs. Kansas City, like many municipalities, has raised the hotel-motel tax to help cover convention-center costs, to the tune of some $7 million a year. But the biggest new source of income is a citywide 1.75 percent food and beverage tax, which generates more than $9 million a year.

Virtually all cities need to subsidize their new convention centers, but this is not to say that the convention business isn't profitable—for show sponsors (largely associations of one sort or another). Although Kansas City will have to pay some $400,000 a week in total costs (operation, debt service, and marketing) for its center, any given convention will be able to book into the center for up to $40,000, which will provide for three to four days of exhibits and a day or two for setup and takedown. Some of the largest and most attractive conventions will get the use of the entire building free. And even when they're paying rates at the high end of the range (more than a dollar a square foot), sponsors can turn a neat profit by renting the same space to commercial booths, for an average of $15 a square foot. Convention sponsors can make an enormous profit from a three-day show, thanks largely to public subsidies.

IF convention centers cannot come close to breaking even, why do so many cities want them? One factor is civic pride and boosterism. Kansas City officials perceived the new center not only as a source of visitor spending but also as an enhancer of the city's image. Convention centers trigger the natural competitiveness of city officials. When other cities start building centers, officials feel they have no choice if they want to stay in the game.

In the end, convention centers have a dangerous allure. The convention trade is widely seen as a civic windfall, with thousands of expense-account-laden visitors dropping millions of dollars into the local economy without demanding that the city educate their children or guard their houses. A governing assumption is that convention centers will automatically make up their operating losses from taxes on visitors and from the overall economic benefits of visitor spending.

In other words, convention centers are the equivalent of a discount store's weekly loss leaders. Their purpose is not to make money directly but to attract customers. Once convention tourists are in town, they will spend their money in local hotels, restaurants, and stores. Naturally, the biggest boosters for convention centers are nearby hoteliers, restaurateurs, and retailers, and the construction companies and unions that thrive on large capital projects.

A more universal economic benefit is outlined in the feasibility studies that cities invariably commission, for $50,000 or more, to provide a basis for their decisions. These reports, through sheer bulk and impressive-looking tables and charts, are clearly designed to impress the public officials who order them. What they don't do is withstand any sort of intensive scrutiny. "The benefits are invariably less than promised," says Heywood Sanders, of Trinity.

"A public-relations job," is the way Dennis Judd, a co-author of *City Politics, Private Power and Public Policy* and a professor of political science at the University of Missouri at St. Louis, characterizes the key Kansas City study, citing a number of shaky assumptions. For instance, the rosy projections that drove the decision-making assumed construction of a major convention hotel. Yet hospitality experts concur that even the heaviest convention traffic cannot alone support a major hotel, and there was plenty of evidence to suggest that existing downtown hotels were already troubled. These problems were conveniently ignored, and as the convention center rises, no new hotel is in sight. The latest proposal for one, costing $100 million, has the developer putting up $3 million and using the city's creditworthiness to obtain bond financing. A coalition of local business leaders says that the deal "puts the community in jeopardy." Kansas City would not be the first city so desperate for a downtown hotel that it went into the convention-center-hotel business: Tampa, Florida, is a step ahead of Kansas City in its efforts to finance a 900-room hotel with $137 million in city bonds.

The Kansas City feasibility study also projected steady growth in the convention business, slighted the impact of other new convention centers, and used a handy device called an economic multiplier.

Economic multipliers suggest that a dollar spent in the local economy is more than a dollar gained. One dollar spent by a tourist is tracked as it travels through the city. It adds to the bellhop's income, which allows him to rent an apartment and buy groceries, both of which are activities involving other employees. One dollar is thus claimed to be worth two or three or even six or eight as it circulates —and is taxed over and over again.

"Multipliers are grossly misused," Judd says. "They're real, but they're often less than two, and they are usually based on inadequate study of the local economy." Even when multipliers have been adjusted for locale, feasibility studies typically don't adjust them for industry. Work by Marc Levine, the director of the Center for Economic Development at the University of Wisconsin at Milwaukee, has demonstrated that no given multiplier is appropriate across the board— in Milwaukee impact varies by industry from a multiplier of three for the auto-parts industry to one of 1.7 for tourism. "You can always find an economist who'll give you a sufficient multiplier," admits David Arnold, a hospitality consultant based in Philadelphia.

In the key Kansas City study, which was conducted by the now-defunct consulting firm of Laventhal and Horwarth, each dollar spent by conventioneers was considered to multiply to $3.30 for the county and to $4.50 for the state of Missouri, with plenty left over for neighbor-

ing Kansas. A report prepared after the city council's decision, by the Mid-America Regional Council, the quasi-autonomous regional planning authority for Kansas City, reduced the multiplier to a more realistic 1.8.

Levine is one of the few academic researchers who have focused on the economic impact of tourism. His work, including an extensive case study of Baltimore, indicates that overall economic development from tourism has been "dramatically overrated." Instead of sparking an economic revival, it produces a limited number of low-income and part-time jobs. Whereas feasibility reports look at possible futures, Levine suggests looking

The feasibility studies, with their impressive tables and charts, are clearly designed to impress the officials who order them. They don't withstand scrutiny.

at case studies. He mentions in particular Third World countries, whose tourism-based economies have not brought wealth to their populations in general, and New Orleans, which he describes as one of the most successful tourism centers in America but also one of the poorest cities.

Finally, convention-center feasibility studies readily admit (if you translate the technical language) that they make no claim to study comparative merit. Could the same $100 million or $200 million bring in new industries with high-paying jobs? What could this money do to rejuvenate neighborhoods, repair streets, improve schools, or reduce infant mortality? Not only will you not find the answers in these studies; you can't even find the questions.

It is typically argued that convention-center funding comes from travel taxes—

primarily hotel and motel surcharges. The assumption here, as is made quite plain by the hospitality industry, is that taxing visitors is okay, but only if the proceeds are used to recruit more visitors. Increasingly, though, hotel taxes can't cover the cost of lavish new centers, and creative new taxes are being employed.

Center boosters would like to pretend that these levies are the equivalent of user taxes, but Kansas City is quite typical in that 95 percent of hotel taxes come from the pockets of ordinary business and pleasure travelers, and only some five percent from conventioneers. And the food and beverage tax is fundamentally a tax on residents.

Hospitality interests cry foul if a suggestion is made that these taxes might be used for purposes other than bringing in the occasional horde of conventioneers. But tax revenue is tax revenue, and sooner or later cities are going to look longingly at the millions that are being gathered at hotels and restaurants, transported through potholed and crime-infested streets, and sunk into once state-of-the-art (if frequently vacant) downtown convention centers.

IN spite of growing evidence that the benefits of convention centers have been greatly exaggerated, expansions and new construction continue. Open for business late last year, the $500 million Los Angeles Convention Center has been described as the largest public-works project in Los Angeles history. St. Louis's $380 million center will be completed in October of 1995. Charlotte, North Carolina, is a new competitor for major convention business with its $141 million center, to open early in 1995, as is Columbus, Ohio, with its new $94 million center. A $700 million domed stadium and convention-center complex is the focus of hot debate in Boston. New centers are under way or recently opened in San Antonio, Austin, Mobile, Philadelphia, and Providence. Centers in Atlanta, Dallas, Las Vegas, San Francisco, and Chicago either have recently been expanded or are undergoing renovation. A 1993 Trade Show Bureau survey of cities with existing centers showed that 55 percent were planning expansions or new facilities.

The expansions suggest a booming industry, yet demand for space has shown essentially no growth over the past two years, and no available evidence suggests that the situation will improve anytime soon. An American Society of Association Executives forum recently assessed at 40 percent the probability that the trade-show industry would experience a disastrous downward spiral into the early part of the next century.

Projections from those who manage convention centers are hardly rosier. John Swinburn, the executive director of the International Association of Auditorium Managers, wrote in the summer of 1992, "I believe there may be a severe shake-out in the not-too-distant future that may rock the entire business of conventions, consumer shows, and trade shows." Unless centers start paying their way, he predicted, city officials may simply get out of the convention business and convert their centers into enormous community centers.

The convention business is not likely to be helped by the latest changes in the federal tax code. Reductions in the deductibility of entertainment expenses and spousal travel are being described as severe negatives for the convention industry.

Will some communities prosper even if demand remains flat? In fact a few convention centers do seem to be the economic engines that are widely promised. Large convention centers surrounded by hotels, in cities with innate appeal, will always attract the biggest shows and conventions. But for those cities, like Las Vegas, Anaheim, and Orlando, convention-center business is just the icing on the cake of an already large number of visitors.

Jealous cities commonly overlook this,

The desire for showplace convention centers is inflamed by special interests, civic pride, and the sort of mob mentality that leads to gold rushes and bank runs.

imagining that a gorgeous convention center can substitute for a vibrant city, vacation amenities, or a wonderful climate. Even the generous arithmetic of a feasibility expert admits the possibility of trouble. David Petersen, of Price Waterhouse, the dean of the feasibility business, called convention centers "a barometer of center city health" in a 1992 article for *Urban Land* magazine. What Petersen meant is that locations without strong "destination appeal" will have unprofitable convention centers, no matter how enthusiastically the numbers are tweaked. A convention center can be a worthwhile bonus to an area that is already rich in visitors and hotels, but a hotel-poor downtown in Kansas City or Los Angeles cannot expect fluctuating convention traffic to justify construction of a single large hotel, let alone revitalize the city.

John Swinburn, of the facility managers' association, thinks that rental fees must more nearly cover costs, and that centers will have to run their own shows,

collecting the huge profits available to show sponsors. Convention centers are moving cautiously in this direction by absorbing some peripheral profit centers, such as catering and other services. The model for profit-generating convention centers exists in Europe, where community-sponsored exhibition halls operate their own shows and reap the rewards. But, as Swinburn admits, this possibility becomes more and more remote with each new convention-center ribbon cutting.

The desire for showplace convention centers continues, inflamed largely by special interests, civic pride, and the sort of mob mentality that leads to gold rushes and bank runs. Every city is afraid of being left behind, and seems undisturbed by the prospect of twenty-five years of multimillion-dollar debt. Taxes on business and pleasure travelers—who make up the vast majority of hotel users—continue to subsidize convention centers, creating a situation in which traveling Americans support one another's economic recklessness.

Once the investment is made, a city has little choice but to remain in the bidding wars to attract major conventions. For a few days a year the hospitality industry in cities like Kansas City and Providence will glory in the convention business as "city-wides" (conventions large enough to match the hospitality capacities of the host city) fill hotels and restaurants. But all this activity will not correct the basic flaws in the convention-center logic—flaws that mean unending tax support will be needed and urban development will be consistently disappointing.

We will all be paying the price for many years to come. Just check the surcharge on your next hotel bill.

Carla Nielsen

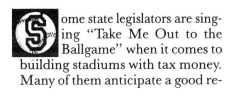ome state legislators are singing "Take Me Out to the Ballgame" when it comes to building stadiums with tax money. Many of them anticipate a good re-

States are entering the high-price arena of athletics by financing stadiums, but . . . are they getting their money's worth?

turn on the state's investment. But other voices are singing a different tune. Economists and other politicians often are saying those lawmakers are way off base. Perhaps the song they're singing — at least when it comes to economic projections — is Lovin Spoonful's "Do You Believe in Magic?"

Across the country, states are opening up their coffers to finance athletic facilities, but the benefits they receive in return are debatable. Sports teams' contributions to the economy are minimal, and often the deal the state works out is too generous, according to opponents. They

say legislators should not get caught up in the glamour of professional sports and throw sound judgment out the window. Lawmakers should take a critical look at whether the investment is a wise one.

Taking different paths

Six stadiums for baseball have been constructed since 1980 in the United States. Only Joe Robbie Stadium in Miami, which initially was used only for football, was built solely with private funds. However, the packages that states have given different sports facilities vary as greatly as the reaction to the plans. Here's a look at how a few states handled the deal:

• Maryland

An old-fashioned looking, red brick warehouse greets out-of-state fans who arrive by train at Oriole Park at Camden Yards' doorstep. Baltimore's ballpark, which opened in 1992, is a leader in giving new stadiums the charm of Wrigley Field in Chicago or Fenway Park in Boston. And by all accounts, the fans like what they see. In 1992, 3.56 million people came to the ballpark; and in 1993, 3.64 million attended games. Nearly 1.6 million out-of-town fans traveled to Baltimore to see the Orioles. That was double the number for the 1991 season, the last

year the Orioles played in Memorial Stadium.

Because the new park is centrally located in the Inner Harbor, instead of the more residential location of the previous park, more revenue is being pumped into downtown Baltimore, stadium advocates say.

"It's an absolute plus for the city of Baltimore," said Maryland Sen. George Della, whose district includes Camden Yards.

The Baltimore Department of Planning estimates that about 35 percent of all fans combined their trip to the ballpark with other activities in the downtown area, which generated about $12.5 million in 1992. Parking revenues raised this figure to $14 million. The Maryland Stadium Authority said state tax receipts, including revenues from retail sales and personal income taxes, totaled $9.4 million; and local tax receipts, revenues from personal income surtax, hotel occupancy tax, admission tax and parking taxes, were about $6.4 million for that year.

Total statewide impact of visiting teams and fan expenditures totaled more than $226 million in annual gross sales, $77 million in employee income and more than 2,340 full-time equivalent jobs in 1992.

However, since the Orioles and a stadium already were located in Baltimore, not all of the figures are

Jacobs Field, which opened in downtown Cleveland this year, helped the Indians sell more tickets before opening day than all last year, when they played at Cleveland Stadium. Photo courtesy of Gateway Economic Development Corp.

new growth. And not everyone is thrilled about the investment in the stadium.

"We're building playpens for sports people," said Maryland Sen. Charles Smelser, D-Annapolis. "I certainly think that what they pay for teams and players, they should be able to pay for their stadiums.

"When we get people to come downtown for games, we get spin-off from hotel rooms and restaurants. But we paid for the whole thing. That's my objection."

The total cost reached $214 million — $100 million for the land and $114 million for stadium construction. (The state also is hoping to lure

When this 21,000-seat arena opens for the 1994-95 basketball season, the Cleveland Cavaliers will move back downtown from suburban Richfield. Photo courtesy of the Gateway Economic Development Corp.

an NFL team to the site, which has room for a football stadium.) The money for Camden Yards is backed by four new rub-off lottery games. The lottery money will pay the debt service for the bonds issued to build the stadium, which is about $13.6 million a year.

• Ohio

In Cleveland, the Gateway Complex is more of a public/private partnership. The complex consists of Jacobs Field, home of the Cleveland Indians, and a basketball arena that will bring the National Basketball Association's Cleveland Cavaliers back downtown after spending several years in suburban Richfield. A major source of funding for the $362 million complex is almost $86 million from a luxury tax on alcohol and tobacco approved by Cuyahoga County voters. In addition, the state will kick in between $29 million and $41 million, which is 8 percent to 11 percent of the total cost of the complex. Private investors will pay about 50 percent.

"It's a huge economic development project for Cleveland," said Michael Dawson, press secretary for Gov. George Voinovich. "It's the largest urban renewal project we know of without federal money. It's very connected to the entire city. There's no doubt this will be a catalyst for renewal."

The Indians, who started their first season at Jacobs Field this year, sold more tickets before opening day than all of 1993 when they played at Cleveland Stadium, a dreary ballpark that was meant for football near Lake Erie. The new site followed Camden Yards' lead and combines the character of an old park with the modern amenities fans expect. The Cavaliers return to downtown is set for the 1994-95 season.

The Gateway Economic Development Corp., a nonprofit organization that oversees the Gateway Complex, will track its economic influence on the city. Dave Goss, vice president of economic development for the group, said the Indians have hired 1,600 part-time employees, which aren't all new jobs because the Indians were already in Cleveland. However, the arena staff will be a true gain of 1,400 to 1,700 jobs, Goss said. The two facilities will be open a total of 250 days a year and are projected to bring about $5 million to the Cleveland economy.

"We have, in relocating the stadium, changed the character entirely," said Rep. Patrick Sweeney, D-Cleveland. "There was no economic development around the old stadium.

"States have the obligation to urban areas for this kind of thing. Cities can't do it alone. But, other cities have problems. When you do for one, you damn well better do it for another. The Cincinnati Bengals want improvements. The Reds want improvements. The example of Cleveland Gateway stimulates people to saying the states will help."

- **Minnesota**

While facilities in Baltimore and Cleveland were funded at least partially with public money, the Target Center in Minneapolis was built by Harvey Ratner and Marv Wolfenson, the millionaire owners of the Minnesota Timberwolves. Ratner and Wolfenson are threatening to move their NBA franchise if someone doesn't take the arena off their hands. The state is looking into a buyout of the six-year-old facility to avoid having Minneapolis lose its second professional team this de-

cade after the National Hockey League's North Stars moved to Dallas. The bill, sponsored by Rep. Richard Jefferson (DFL-Minneapolis), passed by one vote in the House and Senate, and was awaiting the governor's signature at press time. Jefferson's bill proposes that the Metropolitan Council issue bonds. Fees associated with the Target Center — a 10 percent ticket tax and a $1 surcharge on tickets — would pay the debt service. If that doesn't do it, an unspecified hospitality tax would kick in. According to Jefferson, the buyout will cost the state a total of less than $12 million.

Although skeptical about a report that claims the Target Center has a $57 million impact on the state, Jefferson said the investment is still wise because:

- People associated with the team pay $1.5 million in state income tax each year;
- For the approximately 40 events held yearly, the sales tax totals nearly $2 million;
- Department of Revenue data suggest that for the $750,000 the state will pay each year for the lease, it will get four times that in revenue; and
- The Target Center employs 700 part-time workers.

Strategic Defense Initiative (Stadium Wars)

Besides the fighting over stadium funding inside the capitols, states

are doing battle with each other to lure athletic teams. And the conflict becomes a civil war as cities within a state compete for a team, and fellow legislators argue the merits of using public funds to build a new stadium. Mark Rosentraub, associate dean for the School of Public and Environmental Affairs at Indiana University, said the issue is a clear-cut one. The state simply needs to stick to its economic development game plan.

Rosentraub, who has testified before state legislatures about sports facilities, said although the projected economic impact of the stadiums may be high, only 15 to 25 percent of that will be new growth. Most of the money people spend on leisure is being spent in other forms already. It would just be transferred to sports, he said.

"Sports as a component of the economy of any region is very small. It's highly unlikely that it is a stimulus to change things. If they (states) want to buy prestige . . . maybe," Rosentraub said.

Many economists say that legislatures and economic development studies overestimate the impact sports has on a region. Most of the jobs created are either temporary (construction) or seasonal, low-wage employment (concessions, ushers). Robert Baade, Vail professor of economics at Lake Forest College in Illinois, said legislators fail to look at the opportunity costs. State money could be better spent trying to lure companies that pay higher wages.

"In almost all instances, sport is a benign development tool," said Baade, whose new study on sports and economic development was published by the Heartland Institute, headquartered in Chicago. Of the 32 cities where there was a change in the number of athletic teams, 30 cities showed no significant relationship between the presence of the teams and real per capita personal income growth.

However, sports is not merely an economic issue. Civic pride and quality of life should count in the mix, but they are difficult to quantify. The fears of losing a team to an-

"We're building playpens for sports people," said Maryland Sen. Charles Smelser, D-Annapolis. "I certainly think that what they pay for teams and players, they should be able to pay for their stadiums. When we get people to come downtown for games, we get spin-off from hotel rooms and restaurants. But we paid for the whole thing. That's my objection."

other city also contribute to states' willingness to up the ante.

"There is an incredible emotional involvement, with real political implications," Baade said. "If a city loses a franchise, it suggests — or is thought to suggest — that the city is in decline."

However, Rosentraub of Indiana University said that even though owners threaten to move their teams, cities often hold the trump card but don't realize it. According to him, ticket revenues pay only 25 percent of the teams' payrolls. The real money is made through mass media — corporate advertisers and television contracts — so teams would not leave a larger TV market to go to a smaller one. It just wouldn't make sense financially.

Take Indianapolis, for example. When its minor league baseball team, the Indians, threatened to leave if a new baseball field wasn't built, Rosentraub argued that the team was bluffing. It wouldn't leave because Indianapolis has the largest media market in the country for a city with a minor league baseball team. Rosentraub was right. The city now will get a new stadium for its Triple-A ballclub, but no tax revenues will be needed.

Indianapolis also was the only city where sports teams had a measurable, positive impact on the economy. It followed a complex strategy of successfully pursuing professional football in addition to having an NBA team and working to make itself the nation's amateur sports capital. The amateur events brought people from outside the state and country into Indianapolis, so new growth and new tax money were captured.

Although many economists are skeptical of sports' influence on an economy, there are some factors that may increase chances for success:

• There will be more impact if the location is not already the region's recreational center. Less competition will mean greater attendance;

• The location has great potential to bring new money to the state because it is drawing out-of-state tourists;

Sports impact insignificant

This table shows the impact of new stadiums and professional sports teams on real, trend-adjusted, per capita personal income growth for selected U.S. cities from 1958-1987. "Statistically significant" means the probability is 5 percent or less that the correlation is the result of random events.

City	Team presence statistically significant	New stadium presence statistically significant
Atlanta	no	no
Baltimore	yes — negative	n.a.
Boston	n.a.	no
Buffalo, N.Y.	no	no
Charlotte, N.C.*	no	n.a.
Chicago	no	n.a.
Cincinnati	no	no
Cleveland	no	no
Dallas	no	no
Denver	no	no
Detroit	n.a.	no
Green Bay, Wis.	n.a.	no
Hartford, Conn.	no	no
Houston	no	no
Indianapolis	yes — positive	no
Kansas City, Mo.	no	no
Los Angeles	no	no
Miami	no	no
Milwaukee	no	no
Minneapolis	no	no
New Orleans	no	no
New York	no	no
Orlando, Fla.	no	n.a.
Philadelphia	no	no
Phoenix	no	no
Pittsburgh	no	no
Portland, Ore.	can't match data with teams, stadiums	
Sacramento, Calif.	no	no
St. Louis	no	yes — negative
Salt Lake City	no	n.a.
San Antonio	no	no
San Diego	no	no
San Francisco-Oakland	no	yes — negative
Seattle	no	no
Tampa Bay, Fla.	no	no
Washington, D.C.	no	yes — negative

*The Charlotte Hornets and their stadium came on-line together in 1988. Only the team is considered in the model because the model cannot separate the economic impact of the team and the stadium when the two are introduced simultaneously.

No change in the number of teams or new facilities during the sample period is signified by "n.a." The model looks at stadiums 10 years old or less because research has suggested that stadiums will have less effect on sports spending as the stadiums become older.

Source: Robert Baade, Heartland Institute study

"It's a fantastic stadium. Since it first opened, people were in awe," said Maryland Sen. George Della about Camden Yards. "Other cities are looking at the same type of facility. We no longer have smokestack industry for the most part. Sports can't fill the whole gap but will help bring in money."

• The facility is located where fans will patronize other businesses, which will increase indirect expenditures; and

• The facility can house many events.

The trend has been to seek public funds, but cities facing other fiscal problems are becoming less likely to open their coffers. In their place, public/private partnerships are gaining favor.

Some critics wonder why teams worth more than $100 million need public money for stadiums.

"On the demagogic side, you could say why spend money on a shortstop that gets $2 million a year . . . when there is unemployment and poverty. It's hard to get support," said Ohio's Sweeney. "People say, 'The schools are getting screwed,' the farm guy says he's not getting anything . . . .. But in the macro, we have the obligation to do this. Cities don't have the wherewithal to do it."

Baade of Lake Forest College said he hopes legislators will take a more critical look at this emotional issue.

"Maybe it's more appropriate as a psychological issue than as an economic issue," he said. "People use economics because it's a political lubricant and expedient. You tell the public they will get $3 back for every $1 spent, and it will gain acceptance. My concern is to tell the right story. They should question whether sport provides a stream of funds."

While many economists are skeptical of sports' ability to spur the economy, many legislators believe the favorable studies on economic impact, or they at least think it's better than no development at all.

"It's a fantastic stadium. Since it first opened, people were in awe," Della, the Maryland senator, said of Camden Yards. "Other cities are looking at the same type of facility.

"We no longer have smokestack industry for the most part. Sports can't fill the whole gap but will help bring in money."

So maybe legislators aren't looking to hit a home run. Maybe they're just trying to advance the runner — and that, according to stadium proponents, is progress, too.

Service Delivery and Policy Issues

- Service Delivery Issues (Articles 57 and 58)
- Policy Issues (Articles 59–67)

One only has to look through a daily newspaper to realize the multiple and diverse activities in which state and local governments engage. Indeed, it would be an unusual American who, in a typical day, does not have numerous encounters with state and local government programs, services, and regulations.

State and local governments are involved in providing roads, sidewalks, streetlights, fire and police protection, schools, colleges, day-care centers, health clinics, job training programs, public transportation, consumer protection agencies, museums, libraries, parks, sewerage systems, and water. They regulate telephone services, gambling, sanitation in restaurants and supermarkets, land use, building standards, automobile emissions, noise levels, air pollution, hunting and fishing, and consumption of alcohol. They are involved in licensing or certifying undertakers, teachers, electricians, social workers, child-care agencies, nurses, doctors, lawyers, pharmacists, and others. As these incomplete listings should make clear, state and local governments affect many, many aspects of everyday life.

Among the most prominent state and local government functions is schooling. For the most part, public elementary and secondary schools operate under the immediate authority of local school districts. Typically headed by elected school boards, these districts are collectively responsible for spending more than 200 billion dollars a year and have no direct counterparts in any other country in the world. State governments regulate and supervise numerous aspects of elementary and secondary schooling, and school districts must operate within the constraints imposed by their state government. In addition, most states have fairly extensive systems of higher education. Tuition charges are higher at private colleges than at state institutions, and taxpayers make up the difference between what students pay and actual costs of operating state colleges. While the national government provides some aid to elementary, secondary, and higher education and involves itself in some areas of education policies, state and local governments remain the dominant policy-makers in the field of public education.

Crime control and order maintenance make up another primary state and local government function. Criminal statutes, police forces, prisons, traffic laws (including drunk driving laws and penalties), juvenile detention centers, and courts are all part and parcel of state and local government activities in the area of public safety. Presidential candidates sometimes talk about crime in the streets and what to do about it, but the reality is that state and local governments have far more direct involvement with this policy area than the national government does.

Singling out education and public safety in the preceding two paragraphs is not meant to slight the many other important policy areas in which state and local governments are involved: planning and zoning, roads and public transport, fire protection, provision of health care facilities, licensing and job training programs, and environmental protection, to mention just a few. Selections in this unit should provide greater familiarity with various activities of state and local governments.

The first section of this unit focuses on the issue of service delivery. It is important to distinguish between *provision* and *production* of goods and services by state and local governments. For example, a local government may be responsible for *providing* garbage collection for residents and might meet that responsibility by paying a private firm or a neighboring unit of local government to *produce* the service. Similarly, a state government may be responsible for providing penal institutions to house certain kinds of criminal offenders, but it might meet that responsibility by paying a private concern or another state government to *produce* (plan, build, organize, and operate) a prison where offenders will be suitably confined. In recent years, the concept of privatization has figured prominently in discussions and decisions about the best ways for state and local governments to deliver services.

The second section of this unit treats issues facing state and local governments in various policy areas. Interactions among national, state, and local governments frequently play important roles in shaping such policy issues.

Topics in this unit of the book can be viewed as the consequences of topics treated in earlier units. Intergovernmental relations and finances, elections, political parties, interest groups, and governmental institutions all shape the responses of state and local governments to policy issues. In turn, policies that are adopted interact with other components of state and local politics and modify them accordingly. Thus, the subject matter of unit 7 is an appropriate way to conclude the book.

Looking Ahead: Challenge Questions

List all the occasions in a typical day in which you come into contact with state and local government services,

programs, regulations, and the like. Compare your list with a similar list of daily encounters with the national government.

Identify some policies pursued by your state government or one of your local governments that you consider undesirable. Identify some desirable policies, too.

What do you think about the pros and cons of state and local governments contracting with others to produce goods and render services such as garbage collection, fire protection, school maintenance, prisons, and so forth? What does *privatization* mean to you and how do you feel about it? Do you think that the private sector can generally do a better job in producing goods and services than the public sector can? Why or why not?

Do you think it is fair that parents who send their children to private or parochial schools still have to pay property taxes to support public schools in their school district? What about people without any children? Should they have to pay taxes to support public education? Why or why not?

Do you think that your state's system of higher education is satisfactory? Why or why not? Do you think that students attending state colleges should have to pay tuition? Or should state colleges be free in the way that public elementary and secondary schools are?

Is it right for state and local land-use regulations to restrict how private citizens can use property that they own? Do you approve of the power of state and local governments to take property away from citizens through *eminent domain*?

What do you think is the single most important service that state governments are primarily responsible for providing? Local governments? The national government?

If you were an elected state government official, on what policy areas would you concentrate your efforts? If you were an elected local government official?

THE TRICKY PATH TO GOING PRIVATE

In the race to cut costs and improve efficiency, states are teaming up with the private sector.

Linda Wagar

From prison construction to highway maintenance, a growing number of states are letting the private sector take over tasks that once were the exclusive domain of public employees.

Insight into how states are dealing with what is commonly called privatization is given in a report by The Council of State Governments. The *State Trends & Forecasts* report is based on the results of a 50-state survey and a two-day brainstorming session of public- and private-sector officials and union representatives.

Among the findings is that more states are hiring private companies to handle such tasks as revenue collections, printing, custodial and information services. In addition, traditional functions of state transportation departments, such as the maintenance and construction of highways, roads and bridges, are increasingly likely to be handled by the private sector.

The other popular candidates for privatization have been in the area of mental health and retardation, social services and corrections.

Of the 39 states that responded to at least a portion of the survey, the majority cite cost savings and the ability to hire experts in a particular field as the primary motivation behind turning to the private sector. Other benefits of privatization include a private company's ability to get a job done more quickly because it can bypass the red tape and bureaucratic inflexibility that slows down government jobs.

Stanley Brown, deputy director of the Missouri Department of Corrections, says a private company built a maximum security prison in his state about six months faster than it would have taken the state. Brown says time is saved using private companies because they don't need to advertise projects for bid.

In addition, site selection, prison design and construction plans don't need to wait for agency approval. Private firms also are not bound by state laws requiring them to use in-state companies for parts and services.

But Brown says states can sometimes pay a high price for greater efficiency. He estimates Missouri will pay two to three times more for the prison by the time the 20-year lease-purchase agreement has expired than if it had built the prison itself for a cost of about $50 million.

Brown says, however, that the state hopes to save money by privatizing another function in the corrections department: medical care. For the last 18 months, Missouri has contracted with a private firm to provide the doctors, nurses and other health-care workers needed by prisoners.

Using private companies to provide prison medical services is a growing trend in corrections nationwide, says Brown. He says states can no longer afford to pay the kind of salaries to attract or keep health-care workers on staff. In addition, private companies assume all liability.

Privatization has become particularly widespread in state mental health and mental retardation agencies. According to the report, three out of four state mental health and mental retardation officials who responded to the CSG survey say their privatization activities have increased in the past five years.

About one-third of the mental health agencies who responded are using private companies for services such as medical and psychiatric care, specialized foster care, therapy and transportation. In addition, states including Kentucky, Massachusetts, Michigan, South Carolina, Virginia and West Virginia, have privately managed mental health or mental retardation facilities.

Half of the state mental health and mental retardation agencies that responded say using private companies has saved them less than 5 percent over the past five years. Others reported savings in ranges between 5 and 30 percent. Missouri and New Hampshire reported savings of more than 30 percent.

William Charbonneau, assistant director of the bureau of regional support for the New York Office of Mental Health, says using private companies has cut costs by 20 percent to 30 percent. Charbonneau says the number of patients admitted to state psychiatric centers has dropped 34 percent as private programs have expanded, both in hospitals and residential facilities.

As private mental health services have grown, the state has shut down entire buildings that once housed patients. Charbonneau says the private facilities that have replaced them are cheaper to operate and allow patients to live closer to their families.

But not every state has good news to report about the venture into privatization. From education to transportation, stories abound about how services deteriorated once in private hands; how private companies were less responsive to citizen needs; and how costs skyrocketed once the initial contract with the private contractor expired.

The Wisconsin Department of Health and Social Services says efforts to use two private companies to handle the adoption of hard-to-place children was considered a failure after two years. Officials say the private adoption agencies took significantly longer to place children and charged the state more for fewer services.

In New Jersey, state efforts to contract with a large city health department for the diagnosis, treatment, education and prevention of tuberculosis and sexually transmitted diseases "resulted in a complete deterioration of services [because of] critical infrastructure weaknesses" in the city's health department, says Clifford Freund, director of communicable disease control service for the New Jersey Department of Health.

Meanwhile, the Kansas Department of Transportation found that contracting field surveys to private companies delayed numerous projects and increased costs. State officials blame the problems on a lack of skill and poor quality by the private companies.

While the CSG report doesn't address the specific problems these and other states have faced with privatization, it provides general advice on what states should look for before giving a government job to a private company.

The report warns, for example, that as states rely on private companies for services, they could face criticism from employee unions, citizen groups and others. Among the most common complaints of opponents is that services will deteriorate and that privatization is an attempt to break state employee unions by replacing well-paid public-sector workers with low-paid private-sector ones.

The report recommends that officials seek the advice of state employees and the public to find out how a service could be improved before deciding whether to contract the service to a private company.

In addition, the report says that private companies can sometimes accomplish a job for less than the public sector because they have greater authority to fire poor workers and reward good ones. They also require greater accountability from their workers and employ less middle management. The report recommends that states consider adopting similar procedures.

But if a private company is the best choice, the report tells states to develop clear standards and a monitoring procedure to ensure services don't deteriorate once they have been placed in private hands.

One way of countering critics of privatization is to let state workers compete with private companies when jobs go out to bid. A few states have adopted this approach and say it has made state agencies more competitive.

The report concludes that despite the benefits, efforts to privatize can go too far. With this in mind, states should consider placing limits on privatization. In Iowa, for example, privatization is prohibited in a variety of areas, including those responsible for making laws, establishing government procedures, granting licenses, making arrests or disbursing revenue.

Overall, the message is that privatization is no panacea for government ills, but can — if used carefully — help states become more efficient and save money.

To order a copy of the *State Trends & Forecasts* report on privatization: Call 1-800-800-1910, fax (606) 231-1858 or write: The Council of State Governments, Order Department, 3560 Iron Works Pike, P.O. Box 11910, Lexington, KY 40578-1910.

The Wisconsin Department of Health and Social Services says efforts to use two private companies to handle the adoption of hard-to-place children was considered a failure after two years.

Private Firm to Run Schools in Hartford

Malcolm Gladwell

Washington Post Staff Writer

The Hartford Board of Education has agreed to turn over the day-to-day operation of the city's 32 schools to a Minneapolis-based contractor, making Hartford the first community in the country to completely privatize its public school system.

The decision follows years of frustration among parents and educators in Hartford with the performance of the city's schools, which, with 24,000 students, represent the largest school district in Connecticut. Hartford spends $8,450 per pupil per year, substantially more than the state and national average, yet it turns out students who rank academically among the worst in the state.

Hartford school officials and education experts predicted yesterday that the city's arrangement with Educational Alternatives Inc. would be the beginning of dramatic changes in the management of school systems around the country, particularly in troubled areas facing predicaments similar to Hartford's.

"I have no doubt about what we have done," said Ted Carroll, one of the school board members who pushed most strongly for the plan. "It's a paradigm shift. We basically are saying that the old model for delivering education wasn't working in Hartford and, frankly, it isn't working that well in any other urban school district either. It is a structural problem. We have good people man-aging our schools, but they are not people who are necessarily trained as managers. They are well-intentioned and they are smart, but their only experience is with public schools which do not work. We want to team them up with people who have experience with organizations that have worked."

Under the agreement, Hartford will give Educational Alternatives responsibility for the city's entire $171 million education budget, with the understanding that the firm will make a $20 million investment of its money in new computers and renovations, improve financial reporting and facilities management and upgrade training and curriculum. The company will be allowed to keep as profit half of whatever money out of the overall budget it manages to save.

"Big city schools are disaster zones," said Paul Peterson, a professor of government at Harvard University. "Nobody knows how to manage a big city school system effectively and school boards are under tremendous pressure to find alternatives to what we have now. Chicago has tried decentralization. Milwaukee has a choice plan. In Massachusetts we have charter schools, and now we have this in Connecticut."

The deal between the school board and EAI, however, is highly controversial. The teachers union has not endorsed it and the Hartford City Council is also opposed to the plan. Council members said yesterday they consider the deal in violation of the city charter and plan to take the school board to court in a bid to overturn it.

"In laymen's terms, it's an illegal act," said council Majority Leader John O'Connell. O'Connell said that he and others on the council thought that the contract did not force EAI to meet stringent enough goals for academic performance.

The company at the center of the Hartford experiment is an 8-year-old firm that runs two private schools, a public elementary school in Miami Beach and nine public schools in Baltimore, which gave EAI a $26.8 million contract.

Earlier this year, the District of Columbia, with 80,000 students, considered and rejected a request by Education Alternatives to operate 15 schools in the face of grass-roots and teacher opposition.

The Hartford deal, however, dwarfs all previous contracts awarded to EAI and represents the first time that a private contractor has been given control of an entire school district. EAI will essentially take over the operation of every school in the district, including participating in the hiring and firing of employees and assuming control over such things as buying school supplies and designing a new curriculum. If the company spends more than the $171 million given to it by the board, it has to come up with the money. Half of every dollar it spends less than that it gets to keep.

The company will have corporate partners to assist in its tasks, including a facilities management company to cut maintenance and building costs, the accounting firm Peat Marwick to develop sophisticated financial controls and a computer company to aid in designing school-based computer networks.

"They believe they can do things like improve our heating system in ways that can save us money right away and redirect those dollars to be used for specific educational materials and supplies," Carroll said. "We have a group here that is putting both its money and its reputation on the line, and we believe that will trigger a sense of accountability."

The plan, however, faces hurdles before it can go forward, the most serious of which is that the City Council has refused to sign the contract. The board, O'Connell said, has no authority to delegate that kind of responsibility to an outside firm. When the board presents EAI's first bills to the city, he said, the city won't pay them.

School board officials respond that they are not bound by the city's charter, but rather by the laws of the state, which permit this kind of contracting.

The other remaining question is whether EAI can actually do what it has set out to do, namely resurrect a troubled school system and save money at the same time.

"I believe that we have to try different alternatives, but I have no idea which of these alternatives is going to work," Peterson said. "Some of them won't work at all. But, Hartford is doing the nation a service by attempting this . . . we are going to learn from this."

Special correspondents Eleanor Randolph in New York and Rachel E. Stassen-Berger in Hartford contributed to this report.

SCHOOL CHOICE
AND
REALITY

The free market may yet revitalize your public school system. But be prepared for some pain along the way.

Kathleen Sylvester

Hiatt Middle School is a friendly old brick school in a slightly run-down neighborhood of Des Moines. Its student body is what most urban districts would label comfortably diverse: Of the school's 500 sixth, seventh and eighth graders, about one-third are African American or Asian or Hispanic. About half are poor enough to qualify for federal free or reduced-price lunch programs.

But the school itself is not impoverished. There is a sparkling $1.8 million addition with an impressive gymnasium and a labyrinth of high-tech music rooms. There is a new library and media center. Classes are small—just 22 or 23 students per teacher—and a multitude of programs are aimed at the gifted as well as the needy.

And it is not a frightening place. Hiatt's students are mostly cheerful and well behaved. They don't smoke in the bathrooms or deface lockers with graffiti. "You're not going to see guns or knives or drugs or any of that here," says Principal Gary Eyerly. Still, he concedes wearily, "We're an inner-city school."

What Eyerly means is that there are parents in Des Moines who think of Hiatt as an inner-city school. And taking advantage of Iowa's three-year-old open enrollment law, they have opted not to send their children there. It is a program of public school choice, and that is the choice they have made.

About three dozen children, most from a predominantly white and middle-class Des Moines neighborhood called Pleasant Hill, will go to school next year in Southeast Polk, a white suburban school district. Some Pleasant Hill parents cite the proximity of Southeast Polk to their neighborhood; others prefer an arrangement that assigns sixth graders to an elementary school rather than a middle school. And some say rather bluntly that they don't like sending their children to a "nonsuburban" school.

Allowing those families to make such a decision—whatever their reasons—seems harmless enough. They represent only a tiny fraction of the school district's 31,000 students. It is the free market at work—just what choice is supposed to be all about. It will make school more appealing for a group of parents and students who have strong opinions about what education ought to be like. Who would argue with that?

The Des Moines school board. By a 6-1 vote last November, the board rejected the petitions of 122 white students who wanted to use the choice program to leave Des Moines public schools. The board explained its controversial decision by saying it wanted to stem "white flight." Since then, the decision has been largely overruled by the state board of education, and most of the students will be allowed to transfer.

But the issue has generated a controversy that is not going to go away anytime soon. The state's larger cities, Des Moines included, fear that a white-flight exodus carried out under the umbrella of choice may deprive them of many talented students and ultimately resegregate their classrooms.

Meanwhile, in rural Iowa, smaller school districts are struggling with an even more fundamental issue: survival. They worry that Iowa's open enrollment plan may eventually rob them of so many students that they will be unable to keep their doors open.

Iowa, in its third year of open enrollment, has run smack up against some of the unintended consequences of one of the most politically appealing and heavily promoted education reform movements in recent memory. In state upon state this year, governors and legislators are embracing school choice in one form or another as the solution to most of the ills of public education. Indeed, a recent study by the Carnegie Foundation for the Advancement of Teaching says this: "The decade-long struggle to reform American education seems suddenly to hang on a single word: 'choice.'"

But as choice becomes the answer, it raises a new series of questions. And first among them, as in Iowa, is how to manage the unintended consequences of a promising idea.

In its most radical version, choice allows children to use tax dollars to attend any school—public or private. There is just one place where this option is currently being implemented. In Milwaukee, about 1,000 disadvantaged students are being allowed to attend private, nonsectarian schools, with the tax dollars that would have funded their public education used as vouchers for their private education.

But that idea is not spreading. Its popularity generally fades when opponents argue that vouchers would encourage a significant exodus of money and students from the public school system, perhaps weakening the system beyond improvement. More than a dozen state legislatures have debated a Milwaukee-style private school choice plan, but no such scheme has passed. Last November, Colorado voters defeated a ballot initiative to create a statewide voucher plan. This spring, Wisconsin voters rejected a candidate for state education superintendent who supported vouchers.

So except for the Milwaukee experiment, all the choice schemes currently in operation involve public schools only. Minnesota passed the first statewide choice legislation in 1988, allowing students to attend any public school in the state that could accommodate them. Iowa passed similar legislation the following year. Since then, about a dozen other states have given parents the right to choose schools outside their own district. A dozen more are considering it.

Choice within a particular school district is much older: It began 20 years ago with New York City's District 4 in East Harlem, and hundreds of school districts across the country now operate similar programs. Des Moines is one of these. It has long offered a fairly sophisticated open enrollment program, with special schools emphasizing fine arts or science or computers; there are vocational schools and alternative schools and schools for the gifted and talented.

But two years ago, when Des Moines was first included under the state's choice program and the city's parents had another option, some chose to take their children out of the Des Moines schools altogether. About 400 students left in the first year, another 300 the next. In a system that is 20 percent minority, most of those who left in the first two years were white.

So when 128 more students declared their intention to move out of district next year, 122 of them white, the school board turned them down. Board members said they were justified because the transfers were sought for racial rather than educa-

tional reasons. "Not one said they were leaving because the Des Moines public schools could not educate their child," says board member Jacqueline Easley. "So if choice is truly an issue about better education and the free-market approach to choosing better schools, why was that not the issue?"

The way Easley sees it, open enrollment is not only robbing urban schools of white students, it is draining money from an urban school system that has the burden of educating many children with special needs and can ill afford to lose the funds.

That is because Iowa's plan, like those in other states—including Massachusetts, California and Utah—requires local and state tax dollars to follow a student to the new district. When a Des Moines student opts for a suburban school, that student's state aid and proportional property tax contribution leave the city system. This year, that amounts to about $3,400 per student. While a smaller number of students have transferred *into* the district, the Des Moines schools may suffer a net loss of as much as $1.3 million this year.

"I don't like this," says Cathy Talcott, president of the Des Moines PTA Council and mother of four in the city's public schools. "In the long run, it will create schools for the haves and schools for the have-nots.... I don't think leaving a school is the answer. If a school isn't good enough for my child, then quite frankly it isn't good enough for anybody else's child."

The idea behind choice, of course, was that anybody else's child would be able to leave too. Choice is frequently billed as the ticket that allows children from less affluent families the same freedom that the affluent have always had. And indeed, Iowa education officials expected that some less-advantaged children from urban school districts would opt for neighboring suburban schools.

But when they surveyed minority parents in Des Moines, they learned that many couldn't afford transportation to other districts, and some feared their children wouldn't be accepted in suburban schools. While experts have long cautioned that choice

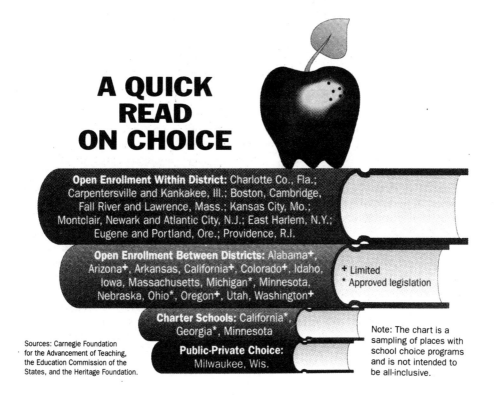

A QUICK READ ON CHOICE

Open Enrollment Within District: Charlotte Co., Fla.; Carpentersville and Kankakee, Ill.; Boston, Cambridge, Fall River and Lawrence, Mass.; Kansas City, Mo.; Montclair, Newark and Atlantic City, N.J.; East Harlem, N.Y.; Eugene and Portland, Ore.; Providence, R.I.

Open Enrollment Between Districts: Alabama+, Arizona+, Arkansas, California+, Colorado+, Idaho, Iowa, Massachusetts, Michigan*, Minnesota, Nebraska, Ohio*, Oregon+, Utah, Washington+

+ Limited
* Approved legislation

Charter Schools: California*, Georgia*, Minnesota

Public-Private Choice: Milwaukee, Wis.

Sources: Carnegie Foundation for the Advancement of Teaching, the Education Commission of the States, and the Heritage Foundation.

Note: The chart is a sampling of places with school choice programs and is not intended to be all-inclusive.

THE CHARTER SCHOOL EXPERIMENT

Specialists who have watched school choice programs evolve over the past few years have become convinced that if they are to work on any large scale—if any of the state efforts are to become more than symbolic—they must not only encourage selectivity but press for innovations in the schools themselves.

"Choice alone doesn't have a lot of effect," says Ted Kolderie of the University of Minnesota, "and innovations alone don't have a lot of effect. Together, they have a catalytic effect."

That notion may be unproven, but it is driving the newest form of choice: charter schools. These schools inject a competitive element into public education because they take away the exclusive franchise of local school boards to operate public schools. Charter schools are public schools, funded by tax dollars, but run by panels of parents and teachers. Richard Elmore of Harvard calls these schools "the managed competition of the education reform movement." They imbue those involved with the idea that schools have customers and clients.

There are just two charter schools operating now, both in Minnesota. But that state has approved a half-dozen more, and the legislature may approve more charter school experiments. California and Georgia have passed charter school legislation, and the Education Commission of the States reports that a number of legislatures—including those in Alaska, Arizona, Colorado, Connecticut, New Jersey, New Mexico, Pennsylvania, Vermont, Wisconsin and Wyoming—have been debating charter schools this year.

In Minnesota, licensed teachers can open charter schools with the sponsorship of the local school district and the approval of the state board of education. The per-pupil state aid then goes to the charter school. Like the experimental schools of District 4 in New York City, such schools have great flexibility. They can set their own hours and design curriculums. They are judged on outcomes, and the state requires only that they provide equal access, don't discriminate, don't offer religious instruction and don't charge tuition.

Milo Cutter, one of the teachers who designed Minnesota's first charter school, the City Academy of St. Paul, says her school is designed to attract 16-to-21-year-old dropouts. Many have had problems with drugs; some have been in jail. The school has just 30 students, runs year-round and offers courses that include experiences outside the classroom.

The City Academy of St. Paul has some very distinct advantages that make the idea of replicating it on a large scale unlikely. It has a pupil-teacher ratio of just four or five students per teacher. And in addition to the state's contribution of $3,800 per pupil, the school receives funding from the local utility, Northern States Power Co., and other outside sources.

Those advantages will make any positive results appear suspect to many observers. Still, the charter school model, like District 4, may offer a clue to how the best schools will be configured in the future—tailored to the individual needs of students and bolstered by community support.

In any event, it is already clear that Minnesota's charter schools are creating pressure on the existing system. In the town of Forest Lake, for example, a group of parents who wanted a Montessori school had been turned down by the school board. But when the parents announced their intention to apply for a charter, the school board reversed its position and found a way to offer a Montessori program. "That speaks to legislators," says Kolderie. "They get the point right away."

—*K.S.*

can't really work . . . without aggressive outreach and transportation programs, Iowa's plan offers little of that sort of help.

In other ways, though, Iowa's choice program is producing the kind of change that its proponents hoped for. One important idea, there as elsewhere, is to use the power of market forces to compel school systems to try to do things differently. That is beginning to happen in the small towns of rural Iowa.

In the northwest part of the state, a cluster of rural communities is collaborating on a series of magnet schools called the Galaxy Project—with each specializing in something it can do well. In Baxter, a village of less than 1,000 people an hour outside Des Moines, citizens were worried that parents who worked in larger neighboring towns would ultimately send their children to school in those towns. That might put the Baxter school system out of business. So Baxter quintupled the size of its school library—and built a child care center at the school. Business is booming at the day care center.

That is one rural success story. But there are other places where statewide choice has brought on a crisis that will be difficult to resolve happily. In tiny Exira, in the western part of the state, business is not booming. The Exira school district now has about 350 students after losing roughly 50 to a more affluent neighboring district in Audubon, 10 miles up the road. That means it has lost about $160,000 of a $2 million budget, and the school district is struggling to stay in business.

While this is a painful struggle, it is precisely the kind of struggle Iowa legislators intended to foster in a state that just a few years ago had 435 school districts, some as small as 87 students. State Senator Larry Murphy, one of the main proponents of choice in the legislature, says that in the pre-choice era, young farm families across the state were trapped in districts with school boards dominated by older citizens with no children in school. Many of those boards had little desire to spend more money on schools. So choice was adopted as a pragmatic solution: It would allow those families to send their children to neighboring districts, or force school systems to consider consolidation.

It has done just that. School consolidations have increased dramatically, and about half of the state's rural schools now are turning to whole-grade sharing—a system that allows districts to combine resources by eliminating some grades and assuming responsibility for neighboring districts' students in the others. One small town may choose to operate first, second and third grade classes; the adjoining town may host grades four, five and six. Both schools are able to stay open.

Exira and Audubon considered such an arrangement several years ago. And most people agreed that the logical thing to do was to send all high school students to Audubon, where there is a bigger and better-equipped school with more course offerings. Exira's high school would then be turned into a junior high for both towns. But that turned out to be too painful a decision for the people of Exira. Exira Superintendent Otto Faaborg says simply that Exira's high school "was the main thing in town" and some citizens wouldn't give it up. After months of negotiation about a whole-grade sharing plan, Exira's school board rejected the idea at a bitter meeting three years ago.

In the mean time, however, statewide choice had passed the legislature. So Exira parents who supported the plan had an alternative. They could send their children to Audubon anyway. And many did.

Exira responded. Voters passed a tax levy to increase funds for school support by 10 percent; the local booster club launched a fundraising effort, and Exira has gone to court, charging that sending its local tax dollars to Audubon amounts to taxation without representation. A lower court ruled against Exira, and the case now is pending in the Iowa Supreme Court.

William Lepley, Iowa's director of education, supports open enrollment. But he also complains that in the legislature's haste to implement it, there was little debate about how to manage choice wisely. Lepley thinks the state eventually will have to make a tough decision about open enrollment. "We will have to decide," he says, "whether to try to extend its opportunities and build in more fairness—or abandon the plan and return to institutional control." Right now, says Lepley, "we don't know enough to make a decision."

Underneath all the commotion that choice is causing in Iowa, however, there are some larger points to keep in mind. The first is that Lepley is right: Not enough is known. Beyond the anecdotes, there is little hard data about how choice actually affects the quality of education. The second point is that few students are taking advantage of it—only about 1.5 percent of all the students in the state.

Those same generalities can be made about most statewide choice programs. In Minnesota, where choice has been in place for five years, solid evidence about how it is working is scant.

One thing that is known is that only a small number of students have crossed district lines in Minnesota, about 1.8 percent in the 1991-92 school year. Even if the state's "second chance" option for troubled students and its college-course option for high school juniors and seniors are included, the number still only reaches about 5 percent.

Ted Kolderie, senior fellow at the Center for Policy Studies at the University of Minnesota, says the reason for the low numbers is pretty clear: Minnesota schools are so similar that travel to a neighboring district rarely offers a distinctive option. Ninety percent of school curriculums are the same, designed and coor-dinated by superintendents who work together. "When kids move," says Kolderie, "it's usually for convenience."

Richard Elmore, a Harvard education professor, suggests that Minnesota officials may have little incentive to evaluate the effects of choice on the schools themselves. They can say they were in the vanguard of a reform movement, he argues, and that is enough. "It's tremendous symbolic politics," says Elmore, "and Minnesota has been playing it like a violin for years."

There is at least one place in the country, however, where choice involves much more than symbolism. In New York City's District 4 in East Harlem, a 20-year-old choice plan has been held up as a national model for replacing pedestrian schools with innovative ones, boosting test scores, lowering dropout rates and luring middle-class students into a poor neighborhood. Over the years, it has been the model other school systems have hoped to emulate.

Recently, District 4's reputation has been questioned. There are charges that test score claims were inflated, that the influx of middle-class students into the district has skewed the results, that teachers who ran the innovative schools "creamed" the most talented students and left the less promising behind in poorer schools, and, finally, that a huge influx of federal funds—not choice—made the real difference in achievement.

But while there is much about District 4 that is unclear, there is also much that is indisputable. District 4 energizes large numbers of parents and teachers and frees teachers to devise truly innovative schools. One important result, says Harvard's Elmore, is that District 4's choice program has consistently attracted poor and minority students in proportion to their numbers in the overall population. The options in District 4 have not tilted to the elite. That is an achievement that none of the statewide plans so far seems to have matched.

The schools in District 4 really do provide alternatives to traditional public education. They are smaller and less bureaucratic. Administrators know all of the students under their supervision. The best schools in District 4 function much like private schools, with school heads behaving like headmasters. Parents choose them because of their distinctive qualities—not for convenience or a means of escape. That is a lesson that any government considering choice in the 1990s needs to pay attention to.

Whether the successes of District 4 can ever be replicated on a statewide scale, however, remains to be seen. But back in Iowa, the legislators who adopted choice so quickly three years ago are now asking a more sophisticated set of questions about how can it can be made to work. They are looking at ways to ameliorate some of its unintended consequences. They are waiting for the state education department's report on the first three years of choice, and have appointed a commission of their own to examine the issue. "Des Moines has special problems," acknowledges Senator Murphy, "and we know we have to deal with that problem."

One thing that the controversy over open enrollment has accomplished, says Cathy Talcott of the Des Moines PTA, is that it has called attention to the special burdens of an urban school system. Now, she says, "I would hope it will serve to shine a light of day and make people see that there is a problem."

"The whole issue became political before we had a round-table debate in Iowa," says Jaqueline Easley. "Now, people are ready to have that debate."

Do we need more prisons?

Point ▶▶▶▶▶▶▶▶▶▶▶   ◀◀◀◀◀◀◀ **Counterpoint**

Ann W. Richards

Ann W. Richards is the former governor of Texas.

Anne M. Larrivee

Maine Rep. Anne M. Larrivee serves on the Joint Select Committee on Corrections, the Maine Criminal Justice Commission and is a member of the Campaign for an Effective Crime Policy.

If government's most sacred and fundamental obligation is to protect its citizens, government is failing to meet its obligation. Throughout this nation, crime and the fear of crime have fundamentally altered the way we live. People all over America, Texans included, lack the assurance that the criminal justice system is making their cities safer, their homes more secure, their streets free from violent crime. We read too many newspaper stories, see too many horror stories on the evening news, talk with too many friends and acquaintances who have been crime's victims, to believe that we have made our communities safe places for our families.

Making America a safer, more secure place to live is not an easy task. It requires a comprehensive approach, a battle on numerous fronts. Building more prisons is an absolutely crucial component of this multifront strategy.

If our criminal justice system is to be effective, the perpetrator of a crime must know that punishment will be swift and sure. Violent criminals must know that many years will pass before they walk free again. They must serve the bulk of the sentence assessed. And we must be assured that the criminal comes out of prison a changed human being.

To meet those objectives, we have to build enough prison cells to end the revolving-door system that turns criminals loose after they have served only a fraction of their sentences. Last year in Texas, our prisons admitted more than 46,000 new prisoners, enough to fill almost all the space we have. Obviously, something has to give. Either you let some out, or you don't let new ones in — or you build more space. Other states confront the same dilemma.

We need more prison space. Here in Texas, we have no choice. Our prisons are so crowded that we have had to resort to releasing violent prisoners after they have served a mere fraction of their sentences. Some 17,000 felons are clogging up our county jails, because our prison cells are occupied. Thousands of warrants go unserved because of a lack of space.

Even though we have added thousands of prison beds in the past two years and have nine prisons under construction, the backlog is so great that jail overcrowding will continue. With a backlog larger than the total prison population of 36 states, Texas has to build more prisons.

Building more prisons is not a panacea; we understand that fact. If prisons are mere holding spaces,

We only need more prisons if they're working. So, let's take a critical look at what has happened in the last 10 years. As statistics from the American Correctional Association clearly show, per 100,000 of population we have doubled the number of people behind bars from 1980 to 1990. And in 1992 according to *Americans Behind Bars: One Year Later*, the U.S. rate of incarceration rose 6.8 percent to 455 per 100,000 population, number one in the world. In second place was South Africa, with 311 per 100,000 incarcerated. Their rate declined in 1991 by 6.6 percent. Our incarceration rate has risen more than 100 percent in the last decade and is still going up. If incarceration works to deter crime, ask yourself if you feel 100 percent safer from crime than you did in 1980. Our streets do not feel safer to me. There has been little impact on crime rates in relationship to the tremendous increase in numbers incarcerated. A recent FBI report shows that 1991 was the bloodiest on record with murders up 5.4 percent from the previous year.

There is no disagreement that perpetrators of violent crimes (rape, robbery, assault) must be incapacitated by prison sentences. However, a study by the National Council on Crime and Delinquency found that 80 percent of those going to prison are not serious or violent criminals but are guilty of low-level offenses; minor parole violations; and property, drug and public disorder crimes. Alternatives such as intensive probation, electronic monitoring, restitution and fines for appropriate offenders have shown to be more effective and less costly than incarceration. Warehousing these prisoners at a cost of about $50,000 per bed for construction and $20,000 per year must be rationally analyzed. We must be sure we are not reacting to cries for a popular "get tough" philosophy by simply increasing the number of prisons and the length of the sentences when we can show no better than a negligible effect on crime. If the goals of incarceration are incapacitation, deterrence, punishment and rehabilitation we must scrutinize the effectiveness of our current sentencing structures and building plans. And we must avoid being lured into decisions to satisfy the need for a politically correct voting record.

Most people understand the need to fund prisons, but want to know their investment is working. They want to be assured that they will be safer, criminals will be punished, and that imprisonment will work.

Point

nothing but criminal warehouses, we will never be able to build all that we need.

We must make sure that the right people are occupying prison cells. We must use the prisons to keep violent criminals off the street. We must lock away the people who have no regard for the life or safety of other human beings.

Of course, we cannot look the other way when nonviolent crime occurs. But too often, the hot-check writer or the young first-time burglar ends up occupying prison space that ought to be reserved for murderers and rapists. That's not smart. We need what the professionals call "alternative sentencing" — electronic monitoring, restitution centers, boot camp, intensive supervision probation. We have to make sure that tax money does not become a scholarship to crime school, otherwise known as prison.

Finally, we need to make sure that the prison experience cuts into the cycle of crime, especially into the escalating cycle created by drugs in our society. We know that eight out of 10 people serving time in our state prisons committed crimes that were directly related to their abuse of alcohol and drugs. Six out of 10 prison inmates are rearrested within three years of their release, and drug offenders have a recidivism rate 25 percent higher than other offenders.

Here in Texas, we have set aside 12,000 prison cells for inmates who were put in prison because drugs or alcohol took insidious control of their lives. We are telling them in no uncertain terms that if they want to get out and stay out, they must undergo rigorous treatment and stop alcohol and drug use.

When inmates are forced to confront their addiction and the harm it has done to their lives and the lives of others, three out of four serve their time and never come back. We know we are cutting costs and crime when an inmate leaves prison clean and sober and determined to stay that way. That is what prisons are supposed to do; they are supposed to change people's lives for the better.

We know that building more prisons will not, in and of itself, eliminate crime. But refusing to build them does not work either. Prisons have their place in a carefully designed, comprehensive system of criminal justice. Our job is not only to build them, but to make sure they function effectively.

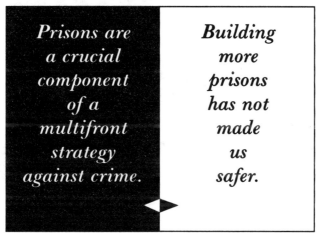

Prisons are a crucial component of a multifront strategy against crime.

Building more prisons has not made us safer.

Counterpoint

I doubt that you could find a handful of voters who think we have crises licked because we now put 100 percent more people behind bars. When informed that from 1982 to 1989 the cost for corrections for the nation per $100 of personal income rose 54 percent while education costs increased only 6 percent, they would wonder how much more good money should be thrown after bad to the detriment of education, health care, early intervention and other methods of building a healthier society.

When we rely on putting people behind bars to decrease crime rates what we fail to recognize is that 98 percent of inmates *will* be out on our streets again. With the trend moving toward incarcerating more and more, funding that could be used for treatment within the prison walls is going to bricks and mortar. The effect is that many inmates are walking out the door with their proverbial new suit and $3 in their pocket with the same problems they brought in, with the same behaviors intact and most likely, new ones learned behind bars. If certain of those inmates had escaped two weeks prior to release, we would have put out APB's, started the manhunts and advised citizens to lock their doors. Ask your corrections officials who's due to be released in the next year from your prisons and if they would feel safe having those inmates in their neighborhoods. Simply building more capacity has not worked.

The answer to the question "Do we need more prisons?" must be no. No, because prison terms are not working; and no, because we are not safer. When the only tool you have is a hammer, every problem looks like a nail. Justice does not mean prisons and only prisons. In an era of scarce resources, we must use more tools, cheaper tools and more effective tools than simply "locking them up," which is costing taxpayers dearly while doing precious little to insure their safety.

Let's look deeper.

Abortion: The Never Ending Controversy

The *Casey* decision, which pleased nobody, changed the terms of the abortion debate and the focus of state legislation.

Jeanne Mejeur

Jeanne Mejeur tracks abortion issues for NCSL.

In the year and a half since the U.S. Supreme Court's latest ruling on a major abortion case, *Planned Parenthood of Southeastern Pennsylvania vs. Casey,* the debate on abortion has grown no less heated, but it's no longer simply a matter of pro-life vs. pro-choice.

In the battle over abortion, the focus has changed from whether or not abortion will be allowed to what kinds of restrictions are permissible.

The *Casey* ruling pleased no one. After months of speculation, pro-life forces were surprised and disappointed that *Roe vs. Wade* hadn't been overturned and abortion outlawed; pro-choice supporters said *Roe* had been decimated.

In its opinion, the Court made it clear that *Roe vs. Wade* was still the law of the land, and that states did not have the power to ban abortion prior to viability. But the Court gave the states a stronger hand in imposing restrictions on access to abortion by upholding almost all of the limits of Pennsylvania's statute.

Whether or not one agrees with the *Casey* decision, it was part of a trend in recent rulings on abortion cases that have continued to support a woman's right to privacy under the 14th Amendment, but have given greater latitude to the states in limiting that right.

The *Casey* decision questioned any "undue burden" placed by state restrictions. The Pennsylvania statute required that a woman be given specific information so that her consent to an abortion would be informed; that she wait 24 hours after being given that information before the procedure could be per-formed; that if married, she notify her husband; and that if a minor, she obtain the informed consent of one parent.

The Court upheld the informed consent, waiting period and parental consent provisions, ruling that they did not place an undue burden on a woman seeking an abortion.

The husband notification provision was rejected as unconstitutional based largely on equal protection rather than on the right to privacy. To have upheld spousal notification requirements would have given husbands legal authority over their wives and "precluded women's full and independent legal status under the Constitution."

In the flurry of legislative activity since the *Casey* decision, several trends have become evident. For the most part, states have stopped trying to ban abortion,

A Retrospective of Significant Cases

1973
Roe vs. Wade
In a landmark decision, the U.S. Supreme Court ruled that states have no compelling interest in regulating abortions during the first trimester of pregnancy. The Court held that "the right to privacy, whether it be founded in the 14th Amendment's concept of personal liberty and restrictions upon state action or in the Ninth Amendment's reservation of rights to the people, is broad enough to encompass a woman's decision whether or not to terminate her pregnancy."

1983
City of Akron vs. Akron Center for Reproductive Health
The Supreme Court ruled that states cannot impose fixed waiting periods on women seeking abortions or require that they be given specific information regarding fetal development and alternatives to abortion. The ruling also struck down parental consent requirements for minors over age 15.

1989
Webster vs. Reproductive Health Services
The Supreme Court upheld a Missouri statute prohibiting the use of public facilities and employees to perform abortions or public funds to counsel women regarding abortion, and upheld fetal viability testing. The Court abandoned the use of trimesters in determining when abortion is permissible, referring for the first time to the state's "compelling interest" in protecting potential human life throughout pregnancy, a concept that had been rejected in *Roe*.

1990
Hodgson vs. Minnesota
and
Ohio vs. Akron Center for Reproductive Health
The Supreme Court upheld a Minnesota statute requiring that both parents be notified 48 hours before an abortion on a minor and an Ohio law requiring 24-hour notification of one parent. In both opinions, the Court departed from earlier references to abortion as a fundamental right, and instead, called it a "liberty interest."

1992
Planned Parenthood of Southeastern Pennsylvania vs. Casey
Although reaffirming *Roe vs. Wade* as the law of the land, the Supreme Court upheld the constitutionality of restrictions on abortion, including mandatory waiting periods, informed consent, parental consent for minors seeking abortion and abortion reporting requirements. The only provision ruled unconstitutional was a requirement that a married woman inform her husband before obtaining an abortion.

since such laws would be unconstitutional based on *Casey*. But there have been a multitude of bills introduced that support alternatives to abortion or call on Congress to reject the proposed Freedom of Choice Act, which would guarantee a woman's right to choose abortion. Though fewer in number, there have also been a significant number of resolutions asking Congress to enact the Freedom of Choice Act and support a woman's right to privacy in personal decisions.

The largest trend is to place limitations on abortion. Certain that limits that go no further than the Pennsylvania law will be constitutional, states have been quick to introduce bills requiring that information be provided before an abortion is performed and that waiting periods be imposed. Almost 100 bills dealing with informed consent and waiting periods were introduced during the 1992 and 1993 sessions. Laws passed in Nebraska, Michigan and Wisconsin.

More than 70 bills concerning parental consent and notice requirements for minors seeking abortions were introduced during the same period. Although many states had such laws before the *Casey* decision, not all were being enforced. Many states provide for judicial bypass, which allows a minor to petition the courts for permission for an abortion if she feels she cannot approach her parents or if parents are not able or willing to give their consent. Parental consent and notice requirements are likely to be adopted in more states since such provisions were ruled constitutional under *Casey*.

A third trend involves the use of tax money for abortion. Although public funding for low-income women was not part of the Pennsylvania law, most states had already prohibited use of state funds for abortion with limited exceptions. All states will pay for abortion if the life of the mother would be threatened by continuation of the pregnancy, but only 12 states cover the costs of abortion from assistance funds for most or all circumstances. Twenty states pay for abortion if the pregnancy is the result of rape or incest. Of those, 15 will also pay for an abortion if a fetal defect is likely to result in death. During the 1992 and 1993 sessions more than 60 funding bills were introduced, almost all of them to further limit the use of public money for abortion.

Despite the Supreme Court decision on what types of restrictions are permissible (informed consent, waiting periods and parental notice or consent) and which aren't (spousal notification), further litigation is almost certain.

Pro-life advocates will push for broader restrictions than those approved in *Casey*, but they will have to pass the "undue burden" test. For example, Pennsylvania's statute requires a 24-hour waiting period and was ruled constitutional. But would a 48-hour period be unduly burdensome and therefore unconstitutional? Is it possible a 48-hour wait would be acceptable in cities where clinics are readily available, and unacceptable in rural areas where extensive travel would be involved, requiring time and expense for staying over or a second trip?

The same questions of degree apply to informed consent. How much and what type of information—whether it is provided in verbal or written form and whether it is written by the state, interest groups or health professionals—may make a difference in whether an informed consent requirement could be considered unduly burdensome. Many of the bills introduced during the 1993 session detailed the nature of the information provided and who would publish it, opening the door for further litigation of informed consent requirements.

Pro-choice advocates have been active, too. A number of bills have been introduced protecting the right of choice.

Advocates have also taken on the issue of increased violence aimed at clinics and abortion providers, based on incidents that have troubled many pro-life, as well as pro-choice, supporters. Six states already had statutes on the books that protect health facilities, including those that perform abortions. California and Colorado passed laws during the 1993 session aimed at curbing violence at abortion clinics.

For the most part, the battle is likely to continue over the next few years with the same game plan: Abortion foes will seek to impose limits, rather than bans, and abortion supporters will argue that those limits are unduly burdensome.

But there are two new factors to consider: the impact of Ruth Bader Ginsburg's elevation to the Supreme Court

State Abortion Laws

	Informed Consent	Waiting Periods (in hours)	Public Funding Limited to Rape or Incest*	Parental Consent (C) or Notice (N)	RU 486 Support	Clinic Violence Protection Statute	Pro-Choice Statute	Public Funding Available in Most Cases*
Alabama	X			C				
Alaska	X			C				X
Arizona				C				
Arkansas				N				
California	X			C	X	X		X
Colorado				C		X		
Connecticut	X					X	X	X
Delaware	X	24		C				
Florida	X							
Georgia				N				
Hawaii					X			X
Idaho	X	24	X	N				
Illinois	X			N/C				
Indiana	X	24		C				
Iowa			X					
Kansas	X	8		N		X		
Kentucky	X	2		C				
Louisiana	X			C				
Maine	X	48			X			
Maryland			X	N		X	X	
Massachusetts	X	24		C				X
Michigan	X			C				
Minnesota	X		X	N				
Mississippi	X	24		C				
Missouri	X			C				
Montana	X			N				
Nebraska	X			N				
Nevada	X			N		X	X	
New Hampshire					X			
New Jersey								X
New Mexico				C				
New York								X
North Carolina								X
North Dakota	X	24		C/N				
Ohio	X	24		N				
Oklahoma								
Oregon						X		X
Pennsylvania	X	24	X	C				
Rhode Island	X			C				
South Carolina				C				
South Dakota	X	24		C				
Tennessee	X	48		N				
Texas	X							
Utah	X			N				
Vermont								X
Virginia	X		X					
Washington							X	X
West Virginia				N				X
Wisconsin	X		X	C		X		
Wyoming			X	C				

*All states provide public funding for abortion when the life of the mother is in danger.

Sources: NARAL Foundation, 1993; Information for Public Affairs, Sacramento, Calif.; West Publishing Company, St. Paul, Minn.

and the likelihood that the "French abortion pill" RU-486 will become available in the United States in the next few years.

The Supreme Court has been sharply divided in its views on abortion over the last decade. The *Casey* decision was a 5-4 split. Then Justice Byron White, who dissented on *Roe vs. Wade* and supported a narrower interpretation of the liberties granted by the 14th Amendment, retired. His replacement by Justice Ginsburg, who indicated that both the right to privacy and the right to equal protection support choice in personal reproductive decisions, will affect the Court's treatment of future abortion cases, including those that will weigh the burden of further restrictions imposed by the states.

With a pro-choice president and a pro-life Congress lessening the likelihood of national action on abortion, the states will continue to be the major forum in the abortion debate.

The introduction of RU-486, delayed because its French manufacturer Roussel Uclaf did not want to enter the emotional battle over abortion in the United States or become the target of boycotts and demonstrations by abortion foes, will also have an effect.

RU-486 makes the abortion decision much more private. It can be prescribed by any physician, requires no invasive procedures and eliminates the need to go to an abortion clinic. That lessens the impact of one of the major anti-abortion weapons: clinic blockades and protests, which have been very successful in reducing the number of abortion providers over the last 10 years.

Though four states have passed bills supporting the use of RU-486 when it becomes available, pro-life forces have vowed to find ways to prevent it. Will states pass restrictions on its use and will such restrictions be "unduly burdensome" under the standards set by the *Casey* decision, especially given the changes in the composition of the Court?

Though the focus may have changed for the time being, the abortion debate is far from over. Approximately 300 abortion-related bills are introduced each year; litigation follows the passage of each significant law. Both sides promise not to rest until they win. But in this battle, it's hard to define "win."

A DESIRE NAMED STREETCAR

Eliza Newlin Carney

Eliza Newlin Carney is an associate editor for National Journal *in Washington, D.C.*

Milt Rosenbaum calls it the "white snail": a parade of sleek but frequently empty trolley cars that meander past his store near downtown Baltimore, part of a 22-mile light rail system that cost $364 million to build.

Five years ago, when Rosenbaum first looked over the city's light rail plans, he and other nearby merchants were enticed by the promise of 33,000 riders a day bustling through the downtown shopping district. But there are only 13,000 riders, and the new rail system has forced cars off a three-block section of Howard Street, around the corner from his Hosiery World retail outlet.

"It has left the street as a virtual death valley," says Rosenbaum, who is president of the city's Market Center Merchants Association. "The price that the merchant community has paid to give up one of our major thoroughfares as a personal right-of-way for the Mass Transit Administration is a bigger price than any of us would have been willing to pay initially."

There is a Milt Rosenbaum in just about every American city that has invested in a glitzy new light rail system in the past decade. But in each of those cities, there is also a John Agro. As Maryland's mass transit administrator, Agro explains patiently that light rail in Baltimore is on schedule, that it is gaining popularity, that it will eventually bring enormous intangible benefits to the community. As for the 33,000 riders a day,

Light rail transit hasn't exactly been an economic panacea in many places, but that isn't preventing city after city from craving it.

Agro says, that was never supposed to happen until the year 2010. Rosenbaum and other disappointed merchants misread the timetable.

"Our base-line system is an absolute success," Agro says. "It is the crown jewel of our existing transit system."

That is pretty much the story of light rail transportation in America in the 1990s: tangible disappointment on the ground and unquenchable optimism in the air. Nearly 20 years after the light rail renaissance had its tentative beginnings in the aftermath of the 1973 energy crisis, the evidence in its favor is still modest, but light rail fever continues to gather strength. More than 30 cities are now considering new systems, including Detroit, Orlando, Denver and Minneapolis. There are constant pilgrimages by city officials to Portland, Oregon, San Diego and the others of the relatively few places where light rail has been a demonstrated success. These pilgrims see the crowded trains, the revived downtowns, the improved air quality projections, and they all seem to return home singing the same refrain: If it works there, it can work for us.

But can it? Once you get past Portland, Sacramento and San Diego, you descend very quickly into the ranks of cities where the benefits are yet to be realized. Buffalo is perhaps the most dramatic example.

In Buffalo, plans for an 11-mile, mostly above-ground system were scaled back as a result of community pressure, and most of the system was built underground. As a result, the system covers only 6.4 miles and is too short to reach the fastest-growing suburban population clusters. With a capital investment of $535.8 million, the Buffalo system cost more than $83 million per mile. Yet the $42 million transit mall downtown and the $1 million for artwork at underground stations have done little to placate struggling merchants.

"I think the building of our transit mall was a big mistake," says Richard T. Reinhard, executive director of the Buffalo Place business association. The mall works well on weekdays from spring through fall, says Reinhard, but "the rest of the time is problematic. And the sidewalks seem kind of wide and empty, and very lonely, in large part because there is no vehicular traffic on the street."

Buffalo transit officials say the system has helped stabilize neighborhoods that were going downhill and has stimulated development. Critics counter that the tangible downtown improvements of the past few years, the new baseball stadium and waterfront revitalization, would have happened anyway. In any case, there are no plans for light rail expansion.

"We have made it clear that we are not going to proceed with any extensions unless there is a solid financial commitment from the local communities—primarily for operating assistance," says Robert W. Gower, superintendent of route planning for the Niagara Frontier Transit Metro System Inc.

Finding a way to cover operating costs is *the* challenge for cities hooked on light rail, which tends to rack up big deficits even in the places where it is popular and widely used. Officials in St. Louis, which opened an 18-mile light rail line with great fanfare last July, are pointing with pride to daily ridership figures that have already reached 23,500, considerably more than the 17,000 originally estimated. "I think the level of acceptance in the community has been far greater than any of us expected," says Les E. Sterman, executive director of the East-West Gateway Coordinating Council, the region's metropolitan planning organization.

But what St. Louis officials don't boast about is the $10 million-a-year operating deficit that may force the light rail system to shut down if the state doesn't cover the shortfall on a long-term basis. The city is lobbying the Missouri legislature to approve a funding mechanism for transit systems statewide, most likely in the form of a transportation sales tax.

The sobering financial situation in St. Louis has done little, however, to dampen local enthusiasm for light rail. Plans are in the works for two 18-mile extensions, one across the Mississippi to Scott Air Force Base in Illinois and another traveling west from the airport into St. Charles County. Residents of one Illinois county have already approved a half-cent sales tax to help fund the eastward extension. That tax will not come close to covering the costs of the project, however, and with the federal government unlikely to provide much help, it is far from clear how the extension will be paid for.

Los Angeles is facing the same issues on a much larger scale. The city opened a 26-mile line in July of 1990 (at a cost of $877 million), and has two extensions in the works, one scheduled to open in late 1994 and the other in 1998. As in St. Louis, Los Angeles transit officials say the system is a success: Ridership, which now totals some 40,000 a day, has outstripped projections.

But the L.A. system carries only 39.7 riders per million dollars of spending, less than most of its counterparts in other cities. It covers only 15 percent of its costs from the farebox, a smaller proportion than virtually any other system built in recent years. Meanwhile, a half-cent transportation sales tax passed by L.A. County voters in 1980 has raised less money than originally projected, due in part to the recession, and the Metropolitan Transportation Authority has had to postpone or scale back a number of improvements to the overall transit system.

MTA officials insist that light rail will bring the entire L.A. area significant economic benefits once the system is completed, and some business leaders agree. The Blue Line, they say, has opened the door for affordable housing, retail growth and light industrial development in the communities it serves. The question, however, is whether the price tag for these benefits will ultimately be impossible to meet. "Eventually the MTA will go broke," says James Moore, an urban planning professor at the University of Southern California. "And eventually isn't too far away."

The high costs and modest benefits of so many of the new light rail systems have spawned a nationwide cadre of academic critics like Moore, anti-light rail crusaders who blast the new trolleys as a costly fad that attracts too few riders and is ill-suited to today's metropolitan commuting patterns. Most of the light rail systems built in the 1980s, these critics say, guaranteed their ultimate uselessness by being designed to bring commuters downtown, when an ever-larger percentage of them needs to travel circumferentially from one outer suburb to another. Upgraded bus service, they say, would move more people at far lower cost.

"The rail technology just is the wrong technology," says John F. Kain, an economics professor at Harvard and perhaps the nation's most visible anti-light rail crusader. "A few miles of light rail is just not going to serve the highly dispersed workplaces and residences that you get in these cities."

The scriptural text for Kain and his allies is a controversial 1990 study by Don H. Pickerell, an economist with the U.S. Transportation Department's National Transportation Systems Center in Cambridge, Massachusetts. The conclusion of the study was that early ridership and capital cost estimates have been overly optimistic in nearly all the communities that have built light rail systems in the past decade.

Pickerell found that ridership was a full 66 to 85 percent lower than the initial forecast, not only for troubled systems such as the one in Buffalo, but even for those that, as with Sacramento's system, are cited often as light rail success stories. The study also found capital costs to be 13 to 50 percent higher than originally estimated.

The focus of opposition to the Pickerell study, and of continued enthusiasm for light rail expansion, is the American Public Transit Association, which issued an eight-page rebuttal almost as soon as the study was out. APTA argued that Pickerell chose very preliminary estimates of ridership rather than later, more realistic ones, and ignored outside factors such as falling gas prices and economic recession.

The pro-light rail faction has its academic allies too, such as Vukan R. Vuchic, professor of transportation engineering at the University of Pennsylvania. Light rail, Vuchic says, "is for many cities an excellent combination of high-quality transit service—considerably higher than the buses can offer—and considerably lower cost than rapid [conventional subways] can require."

But the most effective arguments against the Pickerell doctrine come from the handful of cities whose experiences seem to belie it. Portland's 15.1-mile Metropolitan Area Express light rail system, known as MAX, carries 24,500 passengers a day in a medium-sized metropolitan area; fares cover nearly half its costs, more than almost all the others.

Managers of the system claim at least partial credit for a significant improvement in air quality—zero violations of federal health standards in the area last year, compared with as many as 170 in a single year during the 1970s, before MAX existed. Light rail has kept Portland's city center vital, says G.B. Arrington, of the Metropolitan Transportation District, while reducing automobile congestion. "Pickerell's analysis," he says, "is an excellent example of selectively picking data to prove a point."

The news is even better in San Diego, which opened a 16-mile base line in 1981 and has added four extensions since then for a total of 36 miles. The system carries 45,000 riders daily and covers 69 percent of its operating expenses with fares. San Diego had two advantages over many cities: an existing right-of-way that was purchased at low cost, and eager customers among those who commute the 15-mile corridor between downtown San Diego and the U.S./Mexico border. "We attracted a market that had already existed to a higher-speed, more reliable, higher-capacity transit system," says Thomas F. Larwin, general manager of the San Diego Metropolitan Transit Development Board.

Given the popular appeal that light rail continues to generate, it seems a fair bet that many of the 30 or so cities still considering it will find ways to generate the money to get their new systems built. But it is hard to see how most of them are going to resolve the long-term question of operating costs. It's one thing to get the capital funds to build, particularly when federal help is close at hand, as it was during much of the past decade. It's quite another, as St. Louis is now discovering, to find the $13 million to $15 million a year it may take to keep it going.

Typically, mass transit operating funds come from a variety of sources, from regional bond issues to motor vehicle registration fees and state and local sales taxes. In California, a quarter-cent statewide sales tax funds public transportation, including bus as well as rail. In addition, all but three of the state's major urban areas have a full-cent sales tax to help fund both capital and operating expenses for mass transit.

But light rail systems tend to get more costly as time goes on, as maintenance bills mount for aging rail cars. And in the recession years of the 1990s, sales taxes have become a problematic funding source. Transit officials in most big cities with heavy costs for light rail systems eventually find themselves in a tug of war with state legislators who see other pressing needs for the local dollar.

That is a problem that the federal government is now increasingly disinclined to help local governments solve. Local transit officials were pleased with the passage of the 1991 Intermodal Surface Transportation Efficiency Act, which set aside $31 billion for public transportation through 1997 and actually increased funding for "new starts" and extensions to existing transit systems. Much of that "new start" money is bound to go to light rail projects.

But that is only on the capital side. Even as it spends that money, the Clinton administration is considering cutting as much as $800 million from the federal subsidies that the new systems and extensions would need to stay open. "The administration's apparent emphasis on capital funding is very encouraging for light rail," says APTA spokesman Chip Bishop, "but you have to be able to operate what you build."

Even if transit advocates lobby successfully to save the operating subsidies, Congress is losing patience with the never-ending demand for more federal light rail dollars. Under the chairmanship of Michigan Democrat Bob Carr, the House Appropriations Subcommittee on Transportation adopted new economic criteria in 1993 for judging transit projects. Planners seeking federal support must now prove that a system's projected benefits, from improved air quality to eased traffic congestion, stack up against its proposed costs. Some of the systems built and federally subsidized in the 1980s would not pass muster if they came before Carr's subcommittee today.

"These systems seem to get somewhat hooked on the federal light rail dollar," says Carr. "It's very difficult for these systems to say we're completed, we're done.... They've always got one more segment that they want to build. And it's very hard to stop these things. They become monsters because they feed on federal dollars." Carr is more interested in using federal money for upgraded bus systems that travel on high-speed transitways and cost less to

THE LIGHT RAIL REVIVAL
Light rail systems opened in the 1980s and '90s

	Length in miles	Year opened	Average weekday trips	Cost (millions)	Federal funding (millions)	Operating costs covered by fares
Baltimore	22.5	1992	13,000	$364.0	0	25.0% *
Buffalo	6.2	1985	29,900	$535.8	$421.4	32.5%
Los Angeles	21.6	1990	40,000	$877.0	0	15.6%
Pittsburgh	22.6	1987 **	32,500	$539.0	$429.1	27.8%
Portland, Ore.	15.1	1986	24,500	$214.0	$176.3	47.1%
Sacramento	18.3	1987	23,400	$176.0	$98.0	30.9%
San Diego	36.0	1981	45,000	$308.4	$53.4	69.0%
San Jose	21.0	1987	21,000	$500.0	$250.0	11.0%
St. Louis	18.0	1993	22,000	$351.0	$345.6	27.7%

* Projected Baltimore farebox recovery for fiscal year 1994   ** Pittsburgh in 1987 opened a 10.5-mile reconstruction of its existing 22.5-mile system

Sources: Data obtained from local transit officials and from the American Public Transit Association

build and operate. He and other critics complain that urban transit officials are seduced by light rail as a status symbol.

Some cities seem to be responding to that message. In Houston a couple of years ago, local officials rejected plans for a light rail system in favor of a 105-mile system of high-occupancy-vehicle automobile lanes and high-speed transitways. The city has now opened about half of this system, which when complete will feature seven HOV corridors leading out of the city in all directions like spokes of a wheel. "They cost us less per mile than the rail by a good bit," says Mayor Bob Lanier, "and they move more people . . .

not only the transit passengers but also those people that double up or triple up in cars to form car pools."

Even the most zealous light rail advocates concede a part of the critics' point. They recognize that simply plunking down a train track while ignoring buses and broader transit and zoning issues can be a recipe for disaster. The more successful light rail systems—such as the one in Portland—all are part of regional transit plans that include feeder buses, park-and-ride lots, and zoning changes that allow high-density development around stations. The more that light rail proponents couch their

requests for money in this integrated transportation language of the 1990s, the more likely they are to see the requests granted.

But even so, it seems certain than the cities now experiencing light rail fever are going to find the search for dollars tougher than they expect. "In some ways, building a light rail system is a luxury that may have to be postponed to meet more urgent needs," says C. Kenneth Orski, a longtime federal transit administrator. "The costs can be estimated probably more accurately than the benefits, because many of the benefits are highly subjective."

THE FAILURE OF THE
ADOPTION MACHINE

ELLEN PERLMAN

Two men meet unexpectedly on a downtown street in Washington, D.C. They become animated as they catch up on each other's lives. One mentions that he recently bought a rowhouse on Capitol Hill. He suggests that they grab some lunch.

"I wish I could, but I promised my son I'd pick him up early."

"Son? Are you married?"

"No, I adopted."

"Adopted? I know that set you back."

"Not at all. I even got financial assistance. You know, adoption was a lot easier than I thought. No hassles."

That upbeat conversation takes place in a 30-second television commercial, one of several radio and TV ads in a campaign being waged by the city's Child and Family Services Division to get people interested in adoption.

Posters on subway platforms implore single, married or divorced people to "open your heart, open your home" and "help a boy become a man." Segments on the local television news focus on individual children up for adoption. Pamphlets go out to churches, businesses and community groups. Every few months, foster children are brought to a local Wendy's for an "adoption party," where they eat hamburgers and cake and mingle with prospective parents.

The thought of adoption parties and advertising strategies may jar some sensibilities, but programs to peddle adoptable children to adoptive families, as if they were laundry detergents or new cars, seem to be effective. "When you advertise the children, it works," says Wilfred Hamm, chief of the city's Adop-

America's child welfare system keeps thousands of abandoned children floating in foster care hell while stable families wait to adopt them. It's a matter of tragically misplaced priorities.

tion and Placement Resources Branch, who even admits to tucking adoption pamphlets under car windshield wipers. For the 22 children featured in the TV news segments last year, 18 adoptive families have been identified and 10 adoptions have been finalized.

But the District of Columbia's child welfare system cannot be called a success. Far from it. Although Hamm's agency has improved its rate of getting children into adoptive homes—placing 163 children in 1993, compared with 24 in 1992, and approving 200 adoptive homes in 1993, double the number in

the previous year—it still has dozens of children cleared for adoption waiting more than nine months to be placed. And placement is but one piece at the end of a lengthy process.

First, children must survive a roiling, inefficient, understaffed foster care system mired in paperwork that keeps already troubled children suspended for years in what is known as "foster care drift." And what the colorful adoption posters don't reveal is that it took a lawsuit by the American Civil Liberties Union in 1989 to kick the badly lumbering D.C. bureaucracy this far.

"The District's dereliction of its responsibilities to the children in its custody is a travesty," a federal judge told the city in 1991. By the time a child turns 5, he or she is considered a "special needs" child, harder to adopt. Yet the 2,000 children in the city's system had an average stay in foster care of 4.8 years, more than twice the national average. Children were in emergency custody far past the 90-day limit specified in the law. The automated information system could not keep track of them, so the city's Human Services Department couldn't do the record-keeping necessary to get federal funds it badly needed. Social workers were overburdened with cases; some of them even testified against their own agency in court hearings.

The story of the failure of the District of Columbia's adoption machine is far from unique: It is the story of government adoption bureaucracies across the country. The ACLU Children's Rights Project has sued 10 state or local governments to improve services for children stuck in what it calls "tragically mismanaged" child welfare systems. As many as 20 jurisdictions are believed to be operating under some kind of court order.

Government agencies have shown that it is possible to begin to rehabilitate dysfunctional child welfare systems. But for that to happen, it seems to take either litigation or such a heap of children piled up in the system that the public reacts in horror.

And the pileup is awesome. In 1992, 442,000 children were living in foster care, up from 280,000 in 1986, according to the American Public Welfare Association. By 1989, the number entering foster care was 40 percent higher than the number leaving, compared with 6 percent in each of the four previous years. Most child welfare experts think those numbers have only gotten worse. Carol Statuto Bevan, director of public policy for the National Council for Adoption, estimates that the typical stay in foster care is two to seven years—and double that for minority children. "Nobody's getting out," she says.

People working in the adoption field attribute the swell in the number of children entering the system since the late 1980s to the crack cocaine scourge and a dramatic rise in such social ills as poverty and unemployment, along with high teen pregnancy rates and an increase in reporting of child abuse. Illinois fields more than 1,300 calls to its child-abuse hotline each day.

But as more children came in, child welfare agencies, many of them also suffering under budget and staff cuts, got no better at moving children out. Unwieldy bureaucracy isn't the only obstacle. Well-meaning policies aimed at preserving families or matching children with adoptive parents of the same race often keep kids from getting what they need most: a stable, permanent family situation.

Finding enough adoptive families requires vigilance and enthusiasm by an agency. But it can be done if agencies work constantly to recruit for the new crop of children that arrive each year. "We have demonstrated that all kinds of children, with handicaps or with siblings, can be adopted and families can be found," says Betsy Rosenbaum, director of family and child welfare services for the APWA. "First you've got to free the child."

Child welfare work is by nature a messy, emotional, complicated business. This trading in human lives and psyches is most often left to low-paid, overloaded caseworkers and harried judges who must make Solomon-like decisions about which children should be removed from their homes and where they should be assigned.

The process is necessarily time-consuming because the decision to rip apart the bond between a parent and a child to refashion another family, or to return a child to a troubled home, cannot be made lightly. There is no standard procedure. "If ever there were a system where you need to make individual decisions, this is it," says Mac Ryder, who until recently was director of the Illinois Department of Children and Family Services.

But many government agencies compound the inherent difficulties with underfunding, understaffed departments, poor casework and worker training, lack of diligence and unnecessary delays. Lawyers clash with social workers who squabble with judges.

The shame is that, for the most part, public agencies know what ails them. But many governments choose to do precious little until forced to do so by the courts. The children languishing in the care of child welfare bureaucracies have no voice, so governments listen to other budget demands. "If you waited for three hours at the Department of Motor Vehicles, you'd complain," says Marcia Robinson Lowry, director of the ACLU's Children's Rights Project. "If kids are sitting in foster care for five years, who's going to complain?"

Fiscal pressures aren't the only reasons children spend years in foster care hell. In many cases, the goals of finding stable families for children and preserving families seem in conflict. Caseworkers usually try all avenues for keeping a child with his or her natural parents. And if a child has been abandoned, natural parents still must be found so their parental rights can be terminated. That means searching public assistance records, prisons and morgues. Even when children have been removed from abusive parents, the bias is toward reuniting families. Supporters of family preservation say children can be kept out of foster care if agencies help dysfunctional families stay together.

Last year's federal spending bill provided a billion dollars for such efforts. The move horrified many adoption experts, who think the system is weighted far too heavily toward preserving families, even in cases where children have been harmed—where children have been burned with cigarettes or have had their bones broken from beatings. "Judges are extremely reluctant to terminate parental rights until the last drop of blood has been shed," says Ron Haskins, a child welfare expert who is counsel to a congressional committee.

It's hard to see how family preservation efforts can do much for some of the families they are aimed at. Ninety days of counseling, housekeeping assistance and emergency money—the type of support services that preservation programs such as Family First in Illinois provide—can hardly be expected to make complex problems such as drug addiction go away. When bad social work decisions are made about which children should go back to their parents, it can result in the ultimate consequence. Some children who are returned home die at the hands of their families: In Chicago, 3-year-old Joseph Wallace was hanged after being returned to his mother; she has been charged with the murder.

"The research on preservation and its ability to keep a child safe or be successful is underwhelming," says Bevan, of the adoption council. "When chronic, serious, debilitating problems separate kids from their families, they are not helped by family preservation."

While there are bottlenecks for all children in the system, the situation is worse for minority children, who make up about 40 percent of the children in foster care. One reason is policies, sometimes official but in many cases unwritten, that favor adoptions by families of the same race even when non-minority families are waiting to adopt.

There is a growing body of evidence that permanency, even when it means a so-called transracial adoption, is vastly preferable to foster care and that these children thrive in their mixed-race or multi-ethnic families, says Elizabeth Bartholet, a Harvard Law School professor who studies transracial adoption and is critical of policies limiting it.

Texas passed a law last year saying a child's placement should not be denied or delayed based on the race or ethnicity of the prospective family. A similar bill passed the U.S. Senate in March. But the National Association of Black Social Workers calls transracial adoption "cultural genocide." And even when laws or policies require that children be moved to waiting homes with parents of any race, that doesn't mean caseworkers don't have personal beliefs they act on; many social workers will delay adoptions to search for racially matching families.

But while transracial adoptions may slow down the adoption process, adoption experts are quick to point out that some of the biggest hitches come before the child is ever ready to be matched to a family.

The cases of children cleared for adoption can get shelved in deference to emergency cases. Overloaded caseworkers in Montana, for example, routinely delay adoption casework on a child perceived to be in a "safe" foster home to focus on one in imminent danger, concedes Hank Hudson, director of the state's Department of Family Services. In San Francisco, caseworkers investigating child abuse have only about 10 to 15 cases. Those working on reunifying a child with his or her family have about 20 to 30 cases. Those working on what's known as "permanency planning," or getting children adopted, are burdened under 60 cases.

That the adoption system is slow, cumbersome and inefficient most everyone agrees. One more signature always seems to be needed in the back-and-forth paperwork shuffle between the social service agency and the court system. And more resources are perpetually needed. But it doesn't have to be so bad. All the steps could be started sooner and done more quickly, from determining the goal for the child's future to cutting off the rights of abusive parents to investigating homes of prospective parents. Workers need proper training and oversight, agencies need to be funded and properly staffed, and laws need to be enforced.

Granted, the same could be said of all government agencies. But when it comes to child welfare, the courts are forcing governments to speed up the process for the sake of their wards. "The system runs on an adult sense of time, not a kid sense of time. But every month is precious to a two-month old," says Ben Wolf, a staff attorney with the ACLU in Chicago.

Obviously, if there were money to hire enough caseworkers, many of the delays that prove so harmful to children would be eased. In some states, under court order, lawmakers have allocated more funds to child services even while other agencies have been cut.

In the District of Columbia, the child welfare agency's budget got shortchanged during some very tough financial years. With constituents worried about crime and the environment, local leaders seeking reelection have been inclined to spend on the hot issues. "They're not going to talk about adoption at the local meeting when someone's been shot or the garbage hasn't been picked up," says Hamm, the District's adoption agency chief.

After the 1991 court agreement, however, the District was forced to find more money for its child-welfare system. Since then, attempts have been made to jump-start the foster care and adoption bureaucracy. With funds and staff help from the Freddie Mac Foundation, an independent foundation funded by the Federal Home Loan Mortgage Corp., the District is improving its computer system for tracking foster children and parents. With its improved record-keeping, the agency is doing a better job of claiming federal funds for foster care reimbursement: It claimed $12.3 million in fiscal 1993, nearly double the $6.6 million from fiscal 1991.

But the Center for the Study of Social Policy, which was appointed by the court to monitor the city's compliance, says the District should be claiming at least $19 million a year for child welfare services. Burdened as it continues to be with staff shortages and administrative, management and data system problems, however, the District has not managed to complete the complicated eligibility requirements for each child. Because the District is slipping behind on many other requirements, the federal judge who has overseen the case since 1991 in May considered putting aspects of the foster care system into the hands of temporary receivers.

At that contempt hearing, the ACLU said that the agency is failing to refer children who are candidates for adoption to the adoption branch within five days, as required by the court; that dozens of children are waiting more than nine months for adoptive placements when there should be adoptive homes waiting for them as soon as they are freed from foster care; and that the agency is backlogged on investigating neglect cases. The city is missing deadlines "on everything, basically," says the ACLU's Lowry.

It's not hard to see why: Caseloads average 50 per worker when the mandated limit is 12 for foster children with special needs and 20 for children without. Although the District did a good job of hiring social workers in the first year of the consent decree, it couldn't retain them. Since January 1992, 196 were hired but 98 left. The District blames inadequate space and equipment to handle such a quick, huge influx of employees; social workers were doubling and tripling up on phones. Lowry says about 315 social workers are needed; the District has fewer than 200.

While Lowry commends the District's "real progress" in the adoption area, she says the unit was such a disaster that it could only have improved. There had been no adoption chief at all for five years before Hamm arrived in 1992. Still, the ACLU charges, there are simply too many children for whom the District is not finding homes.

Wilfred Hamm doesn't disagree with that assessment, but he reacts in frustration to the adversarial stance of the ACLU and other critics of his agency. They know, Hamm says, how far the District has come in 2½ years. "You don't just walk in and transform a system," says Hamm. "What we've done is phenomenal, but it doesn't mean we don't have a distance to travel. We're a quantum leap from where we were."

Indeed, the District is pioneering some adoption programs that are being closely watched around the country. One Saturday in May, on an Army base nearby in Virginia, the District graduated its first class of prospective adoptive parents recruited from military installations under a federally funded demonstration program. Military bases offer a pool of young people living in a close-knit community with support services. "I want the child today," said an excited graduate, Dianna Toliver, 29, after posing for a group picture with her

HELP A BOY BECOME A MAN

ADOPT

OPEN YOUR HEART

OPEN YOUR HOME

CALL 202-727-0894

To find adoptive parents, D.C. uses posters, ads, pamphlets—even fliers tucked on car windshields.

graduating class. Nationwide, six jurisdictions have grants for military adoption programs.

The District also has a special program to publicize and find adoptive parents for black male children aged 8 to 15, who are considered particularly hard to place. Of 20 the District is seeking homes for by September, 10 have been placed. And the adoption unit has started to focus on child-specific recruitment, developing profiles and videos of children that it takes to churches and other community gathering places.

What the District has shown is that once children can get wrenched free of the foster care system to be adopted, aggressive recruitment can turn up homes and parents for them, even for older or minority children or those with emotional and physical problems. But few adoptions are easy. Any child rejected by his or her parents or removed from them because of abuse is going to come with emotional baggage. Two district girls, Jeanette, 12, and Faye, 9, are on their third adoptive home. They were born to a teenage mother, herself a foster child. By the time they were featured on a local TV news *Wednesday's Child* segment, they had been through two "disrupted placements." In one case, a biological child gave an ultimatum to his parents that it was either him or the girls they wanted to adopt.

Now, however, the girls seem to be doing well with a single woman with whom they were placed last July. However, the prospective parent has yet to file a petition to adopt them, and it generally takes another six to nine months before it is finalized.

But even a finalized adoption doesn't solve child and family problems; it just ends the legal road. Hamm would like to start another unit to provide services to adoptive families. Such programs are being touted in New Jersey and elsewhere as a good approach to keeping children in new homes and recruiting parents apprehensive about adoption.

Solutions for some of the other problems that bedevil the child welfare system are hard to come by. Everyone agrees on the need for incentives to speed up the progress of children through the system. In Illinois, Ben Wolf, the ACLU attorney, thinks the state should consider reducing payments to private agencies with whom it contracts for adoption services the longer a child stays with them. And, he says, governments must do a much better job of training and supervising caseworkers—and firing those who don't perform. Few now are held accountable. "The only way a worker gets fired is if she sends a kid back home and he gets killed. If the kid

drifts forever, the worker doesn't get fired."

Ryder doesn't disagree. The former Illinois child welfare director worries that even when caseloads are reduced, as Illinois must do under court order, some workers won't be any more motivated to close cases because they just get new ones dropped on their desks and have to start over again. He says Illinois has to do a better monitoring job and be aggressive about accountability. Adoption specialists not surprisingly, have become cynical about such promises.

In New York, the sheer number of children in limbo forced the Department of Social Services to try to lift itself up from its knees. The agency needs to find adoptive homes for more than a third of the 60,000 children in foster care. And though 6,000 of those children are free to be adopted, because the rights of their parents have been terminated, they remain in a pre-adoptive state because the paper-gathering exercise is not completed. The agency has set a goal of 15 to 18 months to complete the nagging details, such as getting birth certificates and collating the 12 to 14 other items holding up finalization of the adoptions.

Some states are looking to Alabama's successful efforts at improving its system under court order. Outside consultants have been brought in to train staff members, both in the classroom and in the field—for some veteran employees the first training they've ever received. Alabama's reform plan was "wisely crafted" to proceed incrementally by groups of counties, rather than all at once statewide, says Paul Vincent, director of the state Division of Family and Children's Services. That decision was based on "the observation of states that failed from the sheer weight of reform," he says. The total caseload has actually been reduced over the past 3½ years, to 3,800 from 4,600.

And that, after all, is the ultimate goal. The child welfare system was created to take care of the most vulnerable children in society, the ones who have already suffered rejection or abuse by their own kin. For the crisis to ease, governments will have to act boldly to make the issue a priority. "We don't lack for good ideas," says the APWA's Rosenbaum. "But it requires doing. It requires diligence. It's like a diet. You may know how, but if you don't attend to it every day, it doesn't happen."

Pay now - - - - - - - - - - learn later

Kathy Tyson and Miriam Fordham

Kathy Tyson is a research associate and Miriam Fordham is a research assistant with the National Association of State Treasurers of The Council of State Governments.

The dream is alive for 17-year-old Durone Glymph and his 14-year-old brother Tarik. When Durone enrolls in Florida Agricultural and Mechanical University this fall, he'll be free to pursue an engineering degree without working or seeking loans.

His tuition and his brother's will be paid because of the foresight of their mother Barbara, who enrolled them in Florida's Prepaid College Program four years ago.

A second-grade teacher, Barbara Glymph came from a family of college graduates and wanted her sons to continue the family tradition. A single parent, she found it hard to save enough for two children to go to college back-to-back. "I tried savings bonds and a savings account, but there was always the temptation to use them when I needed money."

Parents in five other states also can prepay their children's college tuition. Wyoming established the first program in 1987 in response to university tuition increases. In addition to state tuition prepayment plans,

about 20 states issue college savings bonds and a handful offer some combination of the two methods to allow parents to save for their children's education.

The tuition prepayment plans are a "pay now, learn later" approach to saving for college expenses. Parents purchase contracts that give their children the right to use the tuition benefit when they enroll. The prices are reviewed and adjusted annually.

"Since the modest beginning five years ago, tuition prepayment plans have enjoyed tremendous popularity in the few states to implement the program," said William W. Montjoy, executive director of Florida's program. "More than 250,000 contracts have been sold, with more than $650 million collected by the six operational states."

Florida has the nation's largest. More than 122,000 prepaid tuition and 34,000 dormitory contracts are active, representing a cancellation rate of less than 10 percent of the 175,000 contracts sold.

Besides Florida and Wyoming, Alabama, Alaska, Michigan and Ohio have prepaid programs. Each is a member of the College Savings Plans Network, formed in 1991 as an affiliate of the National Association of State Treasurers. The network's

members work toward making higher education attainable through state college savings plans.

"Our goal is simple. We want our children to go to college. We believe that our children truly are our most valuable resource," said Brenda Emfinger, vice chair of the network and executive director of Alabama's Wallace-Folsom Prepaid College Tuition Fund, or PACT for Prepaid Affordable College Tuition.

To the surprise of naysayers, Alabama's program has enjoyed tremendous success. "We were told PACT would never work," said Emfinger. "People were real skeptical because the median income in our state is so low and because people were not familiar with the concept."

Alabama's program guarantees the payment of up to four years of undergraduate tuition and mandatory fees at any of the state's 50 public two- and four-year colleges and universities. During the first three enrollment periods, more than 27,000 contracts were purchased.

Not all programs have had smooth sailing. Michigan halted its program following an adverse Internal Revenue Service ruling that was upheld in federal district court. Before the ruling, the Michigan Education Trust had sold 55,000 contracts, representing an investment of $420 million. The state has appealed the ruling that allowed the IRS to tax the earnings on Michigan's Educational Trust Fund. With its prepayment program in court, Michigan imitated programs in some 20 other states and began issuing college savings bonds that are exempt from state and federal taxes.

States typically issue zero-coupon bonds and market them to low- and middle-income families to encourage financial planning and college savings. As with all zero-coupon bonds, college savings bonds are sold at a deep discount, usually with a face value of $5,000. They earn 6 to 8 percent interest annually and mature in five to 20 years.

"The most popular approach to assisting early college savings has been the issuance of bonds," said Barbara M. Jennings, executive director of the Ohio Tuition Trust Authority. "Across the nation there appears to be widespread agreement that it is good public policy to encourage and assist families with planning and saving to cover future college costs."

Ohio was first to offer both a prepayment and a college savings bond program. "Last year, $40 million in bonds were offered as College Savers and were sold in two days," said

State College Savings Programs

Savings Bonds or Earmarked General Obligation Bonds

Arkansas College Savings General Obligation Bonds	Delaware	New Hampshire College Savings Bonds	Oregon Baccalaureate Bond Program	Texas College Savings Bond Program
California Savings Bond Program	Hawaii	North Carolina Capital Appreciation Bond Program	Rhode Island College & University Savings Bond Program	Virginia Tuition Savings Program
Connecticut College Savings Bond Program	Illinois College Savings Bonds	North Dakota Educational Bonds for Savings Program	South Dakota Education Savings Program	Washington College Savings Bond Program
	Indiana College Savings Bonds		Tennessee Baccalaureate Education Savings Program	Wisconsin Higher Education Bond Program
	Iowa College Super Savings Plan			

Prepaid Tuition Program

Alabama-Wallace Folsom Prepaid College Tuition Trust Fund	Alaska Education Trust Fund	Florida Prepaid Post-secondary Education Expense Program	Oklahoma Tuition Trust*	Wyoming Advance Payment of Higher Education Costs
			West Virginia Higher Education Tuition Trust*	

Combined Prepaid Tuition Program and Savings Bonds

Louisiana Education Tuition Trust and Savings Plan Fund*	Missouri College Savings Bond & Missouri Access to Higher Education	Pennsylvania Tuition Account Program and College Savings Bond	Ohio College Savings Program & Ohio Tuition Trust Authority

Combined Trust Fund and Prepaid Endowment Fund Tuition Plan

Kentucky Educational Savings Plan

Inactive or Suspended Operation

Maine Student Educational Enhancement Deposit Act	Michigan Education Trust	Minnesota College Tuition Bond Program	Tennessee Baccalaureate Education System Trust

* — Not yet operational

Source: Dr. Michael Olivas, University of Houston Law Center, Fall 1992

Ohio Treasurer Mary Ellen Withrow. "When families invest in their children's future, they invest in the future of their communities as well."

Withrow marketed state infrastructure bonds as college savings bonds, with proceeds used to finance roads, bridges, sewer systems and water quality systems. The college bonds, backed by the state, are exempt from state, federal and municipal income taxes.

Ohio's prepayment program offers tuition credits through the Ohio Tuition Trust Authority. The price of a tuition credit is adjusted annually, with each credit worth 1 percent of the weighted average of the annual tuition for Ohio's public universities and colleges. Since tuition credits first were offered in 1989, more than 28,000 Ohio children have enrolled in the program, purchasing a total of 1.5 million tuition credits.

States have experimented with variations of prepaid and college bond savings plans. A unique feature of the Alaska Advance College Tuition allows participants to use up to 50 percent of their annual dividends from Alaska's permanent fund to purchase tuition credits. The permanent fund dividends are distributed to qualified Alaskans from the state's oil and gas royalties. The price of tuition credits in Alaska rises annually, differing from guaranteed prepayment plans that offer fixed prices. Approximately 1.3 percent of Alaska residents paid into the program in 1991.

The Kentucky Educational Savings Plan Trust offers competitive savings rates and exempts investment earnings from state taxes. Monies may be applied toward tuition, fees, room, board, books, supplies and other education expenses at any two- or four-year public, regionally-accredited private or non-profit college or university, or vocational-technical school nationwide. In addition, beneficiaries attending Kentucky institutions are entitled to a financial bonus from the endowment trust.

What all state plans have in common is the goal of helping families like the Glymphs save for a college education. Said Withrow, "Families across the country who envision the college dream for their children or grandchildren must plan now for the college costs of the future."

Of LULUs, NIMBYs, and NIMTOOs

Herbert Inhaber

Herbert Inhaber is principal scientist for the Westinghouse Savannah River Company in Aiken, South Carolina.

In high school, we were told by our mathematics teachers that a proof in geometry had to be both necessary *and* sufficient. The present way we choose sites for hazardous and radioactive wastes in this country, replete with elaborate environmental impact statements and risk analyses, is in some ways necessary. But it isn't sufficient. If it were, we wouldn't have so much trouble finding sites for these locally unwanted land uses—LULUs, in the jargon.

Siting protests have become frequent, and some have even turned violent. In April 1990 an anti-LULU riot broke out in Caneadea, New York (in Allegany County). Protesters charged police lines set up to protect officials who were trying to inspect a proposed low-level radioactive waste (LLRW) site. Hundreds took part in the melee, many wearing masks reading, "Allegany, No Dump." Six men riding horses charged the police. A group of elderly citizens chained themselves across a bridge to prevent the state inspectors from getting through. Thirty-nine people were arrested.

A poll taken around that time showed that about 91 percent of local residents were opposed to the site. Feelings ran so high against the proposed facility that the local prosecutor had no luck getting a grand jury to indict the rioters, despite the fact that the violence was captured on videotape and witnessed by many bystanders.

THE PRESENT APPROACH

How can a LULU site be built without setting off riots or endless litigation? The "scientific" approach to finding sites for these LULUs has clearly failed. Everyone is in favor of finding a place for a LULU, as long as it is at least a hundred miles away from them. Is there another way, perhaps market-based, of finding a site? Will those responsible for finding a site for these LULUs always be confronted with counter-acronyms: NIMBY (not in my backyard) or NIMTOO (not in my term of office)?

There *is* a way out of this predicament. It involves simple and proven market principles. Environmental standards, cumbersome as they sometimes are, do not have to be diluted or reduced.

Before I discuss how the market can again solve a seemingly intractable problem, consider the approach leading to the New York riots and many other less violent confrontations. On its face, who could quarrel with it? It is strictly scientific and objective, complete with risk assessments and elaborate ecological studies. As a risk analyst, I cannot quarrel with these studies. Yet, as I noted above, while necessary, these detailed examinations are not sufficient.

The solution envisioned by most siting agencies is education. Who could be against that? To carry this out, public meetings are held in which the potential host communities are lectured by scientists and administrators. The experts usually explain that the risks are very small (which they are) and that the chances of environmental damages from a well-engineered facility are almost negligible (also true). Then they sit back and wait for nods of agreement from the locals.

The nods never come. As University of Southern California professor Elihu Katz has noted, "In spite of the blind belief of advertisers, politicians, some academics and the public that media campaigns are capable of inducing massive changes in opinions, attitudes and actions—always somebody else's, not one's own—the research evidence continues to say otherwise."

In Allegany County, according to one newspaper report, one public information meeting attracted about 5,000 people, "many of them chanting 'no dump,' [who] hooted and hollered their opposition." While this was undoubtedly one of the major examples of public participation in that sparsely populated county's history, it could hardly be described as a meeting in which the people were educated by the scientists.

I was formerly coordinator of the Office of Risk Analysis at Oak Ridge National Laboratory in Tennessee. As part of my job, I attended public meetings dealing with the proposed (and semi-abandoned) Monitored Retrievable Storage system, whereby nuclear fuel rods would be "temporarily" stored until a final repository was built. In

Reprinted with permission from *The Public Interest*, No. 107, Spring 1992, pp. 52-64. © 1992 by National Affairs, Inc.

these meetings, I was nervous about standing up and saying something that could be construed as possibly supporting the viewpoint of the scientists who were being shouted down. So much for public interaction and dialogue, the ostensible purpose of these gatherings.

The system is not supposed to work like this. It is supposed to begin with a neutral evaluation of the need for a facility. Then a map of the state or region under consideration is examined to eliminate unsuitable places, such as swamps and big cities. The narrowing-down process, performed only by experts, continues until a specific, presumably the "best," site is chosen. The inhabitants of that community are told that their increase in risk, as calculated by yet other experts, will be small. After some consideration, they agree, and construction begins.

That is the way it looks on the blueprint. But the preceding examples suggest that the elaborate plan, with its series of milestones and deadlines, rarely is implemented.

EDUCATION AND RISK

While educating the public on any technical subject is a good idea, in the case of LULUs it has worked fitfully at best. Locals often perceive contempt in the attitude of technicians who lecture them along these lines: "Here are the facts. There's no appeal, because we know what the truth is. If you had any sense, you'd accept what we say."

Much of the debate ultimately centers on risk. Risk analysts contend that the hazards are small, but the people in affected areas meet this with disbelief. Part of the disparity in viewpoints is normal, deriving from who is performing the risk analyses, and who is expected to understand them. Chauncey Starr, the former head of the Electric Power Research Institute in Palo Alto, would illustrate this disparity with a story about bread-cutting:

Go to the grocery store and buy a loaf of unsliced bread. When you get it home, start slicing. Note how far your thumb is from the knife. Now call in a neighbor, your spouse, or even a stranger walking down the street. You again hold the loaf, but this time let the other person hold the knife. Now see how far your thumb is from the knife. Chances are it's much farther away.

In other words, when you are in charge of your own risk, you may be nonchalant. If somebody else is controlling the hazards, you are much more cautious.

This proposition was self-evident at the Tennessee meetings I attended. I made a brief observation of the other vehicles pulling into the parking lot. Very few of the drivers and passengers were wearing seatbelts. And the air in the meeting halls was filled with cigarette smoke. Most risk analysts would say that smoking or driving without seatbelts would produce much greater risk than any conceivable LULU.

Such instances may give the impression that the public is somehow irrational about LULUs. It is not. Consider the following imaginary analogy: Suppose it had been shown by batteries of scientists that green cars cause less eye strain, and in addition reduce global warming due to their absorption of certain solar rays. But suppose that consumers preferred red cars. Any manufacturer who decided that customers were unreasonable in ignoring the scientific evidence, and produced only green autos, would soon find himself with shuttered factories. No LULU site will ever be built by debating just who is or is not being logical. If the facilities are to be constructed, fruitless arguments of this type must be put aside.

In truth, those who live around a potential LULU site are exhibiting intelligence, although it may not be readily apparent to the beleaguered scientists and engineers dodging verbal bullets on the platform. As Gail Bingham of the Conservation Foundation writes,

Although it may sound heretical or obvious, local *residents are acting rationally in opposing hazardous waste facilities* [emphasis in original]. Those wishing to site new hazardous waste facilities must begin by acknowledging (at least to themselves) that even good proposals are likely to impose more costs than benefits on local residents. The reason local residents oppose new facilities is that they have every incentive to do so—the new facility makes them worse off. Thus, the most direct way to respond to such opposition is to change the incentives that motivate people's behavior.

THE ROLE OF INCENTIVES

Incentives are key here. Incentives of varying types propel much, though not all, of human behavior. Is it inconceivable that they can be used to find sites for LULUs?

The rush to the barricades begins. "You can't mix the environment with money," the cry arises. "People's health and environmental quality are too important to be rung up on a cash register."

Perhaps the best response to this was offered by a fellow risk analyst at the University of Tennessee. He had long been active in studying the nuclear waste management process, and observed:

In a perfect world, environment and dollars might be in separate compartments, kept apart by an impermeable barrier. But in the real world, they're already intermingled, whether or not the neighbors of a waste site get a penny themselves. The funds to 'educate' the people that the risks are smaller than they imagine have to come from somewhere. They're taken from the pockets of the rest of us, of course. And the various siting commissions spend freely. I should know—some of my research is paid for by them. The states have spent tens of millions of dollars, if not hundreds of millions, without an ounce of radioactive waste being put into the ground. The federal program for high-level radioactive wastes has spent hundreds of millions, with about the same results.

So let's not pretend that there are no incentives in the hazardous-waste siting process. There are plenty of them—but they go to government bureaucrats, university professors like myself, and consulting firms. The people whose lives would be most affected by the waste site see precious few of these incentives.

But does the use of incentives for accepting LULUs constitute a bribe to the local population? In a word, no. Bribery has three elements that a properly designed incentive system does not. First, bribery is only used in pursuit of an illegal act. Finding a LULU site is not only legal, almost every citizen is in favor of it, as long as it's not in his backyard, Second, bribery is almost always done under the table. A viable incentive system would avoid closed doors. It would make the level of payments publicly and widely known. Third, bribes are always targeted. An appropriate incentive system will not zero in on any specific county, town, or other political jurisdiction, as is often done under the "objective" procedure now in place. Rather, it will let the potential site neighbors decide for themselves if the level of incentives matches any level of harm they perceive coming from the site.

Incentives to take socially approved action would not be a new phenomenon if applied to hazardous-waste sites. For example, walk into a post office and chances are you will see photos of real or alleged felons. Above their fuzzy snapshots will be the word "Reward." In a perfect world, we would all be so civic-minded that we would be on continuous outlook for these fugitives, without any thought of recompense. In the real world, the state has found that it can achieve its goals—bringing these individuals to justice—by offering an incentive to do so.

WHY NEGOTIATION FAILS

If incentives should be supplied to the people who would be affected by a LULU near them, what system should be used to set the level? The obvious and intuitive first choice would be negotiation between the siting authority and the affected community.

But that process holds a defect that, as I noted above, will engender charges of bribery, if not worse: the element of secrecy. Most negotiations are carried out behind closed doors. I cannot envision the entire population of a town or county bargaining simultaneously. While negotiation over compensation works in most other contexts, it faces severe difficulty in the LULU context.

The implicit model used for negotiation in trying to site a LULU is that of labor-management bargaining. Admittedly, most labor-management talks end in success, in that a contract of some sort is signed. But these discussions have one element that arguments over LULU siting do not: a deadline. That is, both labor and management know that at some point a strike or lockout can occur. Even when that date is postponed, it still looms in all negotiators' minds.

Nothing of the sort happens in LULU-siting talks. All participants know that any deadlines specified are easily ignored. When Congress passed the Low-Level Radioactive Waste Policy Act of 1980, for example, it required states to form "compacts" that were to build waste-storage facilities. By 1985, all the elaborate deadlines set down in the legislation had passed, so Congress passed amendments to the original law. Seven years after the new legislation got the President's signature, most of the new deadlines have been forgotten. States and localities are still arguing over where the radioactive wastes should go.

About the same thing happened with respect to high-level nuclear waste (mostly spent fuel rods from nuclear reactors). After years of the Department of Energy setting its own deadlines, Congress got involved in 1982, establishing a whole new set. Few if any were met. Five years later, a new law was passed, producing still more deadlines. Even those have been missed by years, due in part to legal wrangling. So when a siting system for a LULU is proposed, with an elaborate schedule of milestones, the targeted community generally knows it can avoid them.

AUCTIONS: DIRECT AND INDIRECT

One way out of the negotiation-deadline trap is a public auction. The reasons for holding auctions of any type were summarized by Ralph Cassady in his authoritative book on the subject, *Auctions and Auctioneering:*

> One answer is, perhaps, that some products have no standard value. For example, the price of any catch of fish (or at least of fish destined for the fresh fish market) depends on demand and supply conditions at a specific moment of time, influenced possibly by prospective market developments. For manuscripts and antiques, too, prices must be remade for each transaction. For example, how can one discover the worth of an original copy of Lincoln's Gettysburg Address except by auction method?

To follow Cassady's reasoning, there would be no point in using an auction system in conjunction with the millions of catalytic converters attached annually to our cars to reduce air pollution. The converters are generally similar. But each hazardous- or radioactive-waste site, or other LULU, is a unique combination of calculated risks, geology, nearby population, engineering design, and, most importantly, the attitudes of potential surrounding neighbors. For this reason, an auction is the best way to decide the appropriate level of compensation.

Although almost everyone has participated in an auction at one time or another, we may be unfamiliar with their use in public policy. One recent example was the siting process for the superconducting supercollider (SSC), the physically largest and most expensive scientific project in history, which took place via an indirect auction among the competing states.

AN AUCTION IN DISGUISE

The gigantic particle accelerator, estimated recently to cost about $8 billion, will dwarf all past scientific endeavors. When finished, it will employ about 3,000 scientists, engineers, and technicians, with an annual payroll of about $270 million.

The SSC was, and is, clearly a desirable installation. It is thus vastly different from a LULU. Yet both share one characteristic: they both can be built in a variety of locations. Because there are then many potential "bidders," an auction could, in principle, have taken place for the SSC.

Almost every state expressed at least some interest in having the lucrative installation within its borders. About two dozen submitted formal applications. Congress wanted the selection to be done in an "objective" way, and so forbade direct financial bids by the states. That is, Pennsylvania could not say, "We hereby offer $500 million for the SSC."

In that sense, there was never any auction held for the accelerator. But as Congress often does, it left a loophole in the law big enough to drive the entire SSC installation through. States were not precluded from bidding *indirectly* on the project. As far as the theory of auctions is concerned, an indirect bid, with goods and services offered instead of currency, is equivalent to a direct bid.

Since all states were aware of the size of competing indirect bids, for all practical purposes an auction was held for the SSC. The auction took place at the same time as the "objective" search by a committee of the National Research Council (NRC), an arm of the National Academy of Sciences.

Of the indirect bids, Texas's was the largest, at approximately $1 billion. Some of it was in the form of an electricity subsidy over the lifetime of the installation, providing electricity at the rate of one cent per kilowatthour. About one-eighth of the current average national rate, this is an enormous indirect subsidy, since the SSC will be a prodigious user of electricity. Illinois offered $570 million in roads, housing, and fellowships. Colorado offered a package of $300 million in road and railroad improvements; many other states offered comparable packages.

The NRC awarded the SSC to Texas, which, as it happens, made the highest indirect bid. So if the "objective" method had been dropped in favor of an auction, Texas would have also won. The results were the same as if an auction *had* been held.

THE REVERSE DUTCH AUCTION

The economic literature is filled with descriptions of many types of auctions. Which one is best to site LULUs?

Consider the English auction, the one with which we are most familiar: this variety is held in Sotheby's, churches, synagogues, and farm yards. In an English auction, the auctioneer's cry might be as follows: "I have ten dollars, ten dollars. . . . Do I hear fifteen? Fifteen—I have fifteen. Now, is there someone at twenty? The gentleman in the back row offers twenty. Anyone for twenty-five?"

The English auction almost always has multiple bids. But this is probably too much to expect when finding a site for a LULU. One adequate volunteer would be sufficient. That would be one more than the number that usually volunteer.

What then is left? The Dutch auction (sometimes called Chinese) starts with a high price that falls. This form is used to speed up the auction process, since the English auction can be time-consuming. The Dutch auction begins with a silent appraisal by the auctioneer of a reasonable price for the goods on the block. For example, he might decide that a consignment of cut flowers is worth about $50. He does not announce this. On that basis, he might start the bidding at $100, hoping that a bid of more than $50 will be made. The cry in a Dutch auction might then be:

> I will start the bidding at $100. Any takers? I will reduce the price to $95. No hands at that price, so I will lower it to $90. Going once, going twice to $85. The lady in the front row raises her hand, so she gets the lot for $85.

The Dutch auction differs considerably from the English version. From the viewpoint of finding LULU sites, the prime dissimilarity is that there is only one bid. In the above example, when the hand was raised at $85, the auction ended immediately. There was no chance for reconsideration or second chances.

This feature then corresponds to what society needs in finding a LULU site: a community that is certain of what it wants and the price it deserves.

HOW IT WORKS

The Dutch auction deals in desirable objects, like flowers or cheese. But a LULU is clearly a different matter. In a Dutch auction, the bidders pay *for* the object on the block. In dealing with LULUs, we have to pay money *to* the community making a bid. This then suggests a *reverse* Dutch auction, in which a community bids to be paid.

In the reverse Dutch auction, another feature of the ordinary Dutch auction is retained. The price level is set by the auctioneer, not the participants. In the example noted above, the auctioneer, if he had been so inclined, could have changed the price in increments of $100 or $1. The participants in a reverse Dutch auction therefore cannot arbitrarily raise the price they will be paid for accepting the LULU. The auctioneer—in this case a siting authority—is in control.

Thus, in a reverse Dutch auction, the price would rise until a town or county came forward with an environmentally acceptable location. After that sole bid the auction would end.

The reverse Dutch auction would of course be proposed via the usual official documents. But if an oral announcement to a meeting of officials from potential siting communities were made, it might sound approximately as follows:

> We have this radioactive waste (or prisoners, or municipal trash, or incinerator) we wish to site. We have abandoned

the previous technique of pretending to listen to you and then forcing the facility on a community regardless of its wishes.

What have we substituted in place of this discredited method? We propose to let the market determine the site, subject to existing environmental regulations. Any community that does not want the facility under any circumstances does not have to participate in the auction. This will ensure that the facility will never be within its boundaries.

The increase in the size of the bonus should draw the attention of those communities that are not absolutely and irrevocably opposed to the facility. Of course, if a community waits too long to decide, it runs the risk of seeing the bonus go to another community.

We are not going to choose the site. You are. Admittedly, most communities don't have the scientists and engineers needed to do any required studies. Feel free to hire as many as necessary, and send the bill to us. But don't employ them to prove you shouldn't have the site in your area. If you don't want the site at any price, just don't bid.

For the first month of the auction, we're offering a $10 million bonus [or any arbitrary amount] to a community that volunteers. After that, the bonus will rise $10 million monthly, until a community comes forward. And we know that one will volunteer, when the price is right. That should end, once and for all, the waste controversy in our state. All unproductive activity—lawsuits, threats, and riots—can now come to an end. We have found the key to making the volunteer community happy that it has stepped forward.

SOURCE OF THE BONUS

Where would the money for the reverse Dutch auction come from? For LULUs built to accommodate wastes the initial source would be the waste generators. Ultimately, of course, the costs will be passed on, in one form or another, to the rest of us. As a nation, we have been crying "NIMBY" without having to pay any price. But the privilege of living ten, one hundred, or one thousand miles from a LULU surely has an economic value. Whatever the level of the bonus in the reverse Dutch auction, it is the true social cost of the facility. Put another way, it's the price the rest of us have to pay so the wastes aren't in *our* backyard.

Waste generators won't like new taxes. But at least they would be getting something for their money. No bonus would be paid until a real site was found and approved. Contrast this to the search for a low-level radioactive waste site in New York State. Roberta Lovenheim, a consultant to the New York State Low-Level Waste Group (an organization of radioactive-waste producers), says that $37 million has been spent to date in the so-far fruitless quest. The federal government has spent hundreds of millions of dollars on a site for high-level waste, battling Nevada and the governors of other states. The nuclear fuel rods still wait patiently in their pools at the reactors. The moral? It's better to pay for a Mercedes, if you're definitely going to get it, than for a Yugo that never appears.

Is this just a technique for foisting LULUs on the poorest communities? Not really. Under the reverse Dutch auction, if a poor community volunteered, it could anticipate a substantial bonus heading its way. The bonus might be on the order of hundreds of millions, depending on the particular facility, the size of the state, the competition in the auction, and other factors. Modern Landfill Incorporated has offered every citizen of Lewiston, New York, $960 annually for the next twenty years for the right to expand a landfill, from which hazardous wastes would be excluded. The price per citizen could very well be higher for hazardous and radioactive wastes, although the bonus would only be decided as the reverse Dutch auction proceeded.

Contrast this with the battle over the low-level radioactive waste site in Allegany County. The state offered to pay the county $1 million annually in lieu of taxes. This works out to about $20 per person each year. Although Allegany County residents have been derided as irrational, in reality they were behaving in accord with economic logic, if a little violently. They were each asked to accept $20 a year for wastes that most people, rightly or wrongly, regard as more dangerous than regular garbage. Yet people three counties away are offered $960 annually to enlarge an ordinary landfill.

A WAY OUT OF THE MAZE

Of course, LULUs do get built, sometimes without significant opposition. Penitentiaries arise and homeless shelters are located, occasionally without the slightest protest. An economist would say that in these instances the perceived social benefits to the nearby community outweigh the costs. For example, in some areas, a prison might be regarded as a valuable source of employment. In those cases, no reverse Dutch auction would be necessary. In others, the odium of the facility may outweigh the promise of hundreds of jobs.

In general, though, LULUs—especially waste sites—will tend to be regarded negatively by most communities. And those who cry "NIMBY" are in an important sense rational. They are telling us that the cost, real or perceived, of a LULU in their vicinity is high *to* them.

One critic has labeled the present system of finding waste sites "DAD," perhaps in honor of its paternalistic nature: "Decide, Announce, and Defend." Under the present system, a siting commission decides on a specific site behind closed doors, announces its decision, and spends the rest of its time defending the decision from the slings and arrows of outraged citizens.

The objections of these citizens have been a useful signal, like a toothache telling us of decay. Now is the time to respond to that sometimes noisy message in a fair and equitable way, using the reverse Dutch auction to settle LULU disputes.

Taking Old McDonald To Court

As the suburban dream encounters the manure spreader, counties are passing a second wave of 'right-to-farm' laws.

ROB GURWITT

Talk to Jackie Stewart, a cattle rancher in eastern Contra Costa County, California, and you'll discover that for a nation whose roots on the farm often go back only a generation or two, we're appallingly forgetful.

Her end of the county, once entirely rustic, has been suburbanizing over the past decade or so, and the encounters between its new residents and its farmers can lack a certain neighborliness. "It's been a real battle to try and live in harmony," says Stewart, who heads the county Farm Bureau.

People let their dogs run loose among cattle. They climb fences to pick fruit in orchards. They roar across fields on dirt bikes. They cut fences and let cattle loose. And, worst of all, they sue farmers for doing what they've always done.

Admittedly, it can be something of a shock for a homeowner in some spanking new subdivision to discover that the brilliant green fields next door get that way because of the manure the farmer spreads on them. But it's no less shocking to the farmer to be hauled into court for creating a "nuisance" as a result.

"The attitude of suburban America toward agricultural land is confused," says Tom Gardner, assistant administrator of Yolo County, just west of Sacramento. "They see it as nice open space, but they don't identify that it has a functional use. Tractors run, water pumps pump, airplanes spray, nut shelling occurs, and it's all loud and noisy and often happens at 5 in the morning."

As a result, Contra Costa appears ready to join Yolo and other California counties that in the past few years have passed local "right-to-farm" ordinances to try to protect farmers from nuisance-based lawsuits. They constitute what

Neil Hamilton, director of the Agricultural Law Center at Drake University in Des Moines, calls a "second generation" of such measures.

The first generation was a set of state right-to-farm laws, most of them dating back to a wave of the legislation in the late 1970s and early 1980s. All 50 states now have them.

Counties began moving in on the action, though, because the state statutes have encountered a fair amount of judicial hostility—which in practice has translated into more decisions favoring homeowners than farmers.

Hamilton sees any number of reasons why the courts look askance at the measures, but chief among them, he wrote in a recent law review article, is that legislatures are in essence "asking the court to sanction conduct" that would fall under the legal definition of a nuisance if the right-to-farm law did not exist. As a result, he argues, courts see such laws as limiting the property rights of the community for the benefit of a few farmers.

The California counties' measures—as well as a handful of similar ordinances that have popped up in Iowa, New York and elsewhere—move the matter two steps beyond the state statutes. First, they attempt to bypass the courts entirely by setting up a grievance commission to which conflicts between farmers and homeowners must be submitted before they can go to court. And second, they require written disclosure to home buyers that the property they want to buy is in an agricultural area and that they will suffer inconveniences as a result.

"It doesn't stop people from being able to voice concerns about odor, dust, noise and so on," says Jack DeFemery,

agriculture commissioner in Contra Costa County, "but it does put a homeowner on notice that he can't just move in and then complain, just like you can't move in next to an airport and then complain about the noise."

The written disclosure also may help farmers deal with another problem, says Edward Thompson, director of public policy at the American Farmland Trust, a Washington, D.C.-based organization that promotes farmland preservation. Thompson is the man who, in an article 10 years ago, first gave a broad public airing to the proposals that counties are now codifying.

"What happens is, the farmer's got to change the time of day he plows, or the irrigation pumps now run all night, so homeowners come in and say that it's an entirely new operation and not covered by the right-to-farm law," says Thompson. "But if you put it in black and white that things could change, a homeowner can't come in and say, 'I didn't know that.'"

Even so, there aren't too many people who believe that this latest wave of county ordinances goes far enough in addressing conflict between suburban and rural values related to the land. As counties come under increasing development pressure, they argue, right-to-farm ordinances can only work if a county is determined enough to protect its farmland that it uses zoning, land use statutes, its comprehensive plan and other measures as well.

"If you're trying to reinforce a long-standing commitment to preserve agricultural land, then a good right-to-farm ordinance will help you do that," says Yolo County's Tom Gardner. "On the other hand, if right-to-farm is the only tool you've got, you're dead meat."

Communities, Fearful of Importing Crime, Bar Routine Businesses

Movies, Arcades, Car Washes Draw Too Many Youths, Say Worried Residents

North Dallas Spurns Cinema

Scott McCartney

Staff Reporter of The Wall Street Journal

DALLAS—When Kathy Coffman heard of plans to redevelop the site of a long-abandoned Kmart in her neighborhood, the housewife and mother of four teenagers hit the warpath.

Joining several hundred other residents of the neat, well-to-do section of north Dallas, Mrs. Coffman helped organize pickets, distribute leaflets and post signs to protest the project. The group collected $26,000 to hire attorneys for the cause and launched an intense lobbying campaign at city Hall. "They want to sacrifice the neighborhood," Mrs. Coffman says.

Sacrifice it for what? Movie theaters.

"Movies," Mrs. Coffman argues, "are not family entertainment. Movies depend on teenagers for revenue." Adds comrade Susan Pardo, mother of two: "We're afraid of gangs."

The reaction surprised city officials and Cinemark U.S.A. Inc., the Dallas-based national theater chain that wants to build a $30 million, 18-screen "Tinseltown" complex on the site. But zoning experts say this is part of a pattern. Across the nation, they say, a new isolationism is emerging as seemingly innocuous developments like parks and footpaths—and theaters—prompt angry not-in-my-back-yard, or "nimby," responses.

Not Just Noxious Things

Of course, neighborhood activism isn't new, and as has long been the case, plans for a prison or a trash incinerator still can rouse communities to arms. But now, driven by perceptions of a rising tide of crime and gang violence, some neighborhoods are resisting any change that they think might expose them to feared outsiders. And that often puts them in direct conflict with city planners, sparking zoning debates that resemble pitched battles.

"It used to be people just protested against noxious-type things," says Jon Perica, a city planner in Los Angeles for 25 years. "But we're seeing socially positive things now targeted by neighborhood opposition."

In Durham, N.C., neighborhood opposition last year forced the rerouting of a greenbelt with a jogging path and nature trail. "I've got nothing against nature," says one homeowner, Guy Gentry. "I just don't want these two-legged nature folks wanting to come through."

In Overland Park, Kan., protests led to the removal of basketball and volleyball courts from a park under development in 1992. Residents of the Kansas City suburb argued that such facilities would attract unwanted youths.

'Trigger-Happy Kids'

In the Queens borough of New York City, residents of one neighborhood defeated a plan in January to convert an abandoned cinema into a laser-gun games center. "That's what we're afraid of—trigger-happy kids," says Wendy Marsh, owner of an optical shop and president of the Union Turnpike Merchants Association, which was instrumental in killing the plan. "We didn't know if they would take it outside after the game."

Police generally discount such effects. They and urban planners even argue that parks, greenbelts and mixed-use developments—the combined office-retail-residential properties now popular in many cities—may help deter crime by getting people out and about in a neighborhood.

"If you're trying to create more livable, cohesive cities, you want to connect complementary uses," says Paul Norvy, Durham's planning director. "We're trying to get back to what made cities more livable. Creating communities where people interact will also be safer."

Try telling that to North Miami Beach, Fla. The Miami suburb last month asked the Chicago-based American Planning Association, a subscription research service for community planners, to send it examples of especially restrictive zoning ordinances from other cities. The reason, it said, was to help it find ways to ban laundromats, telegram offices, car washes, pawn shops and other businesses that might draw outsiders to the area.

The Luxury of Saying 'No'

Planning association staffers, however, soon found that most of the examples they came up with were from North Miami Beach. "We called back and said, 'You already have some of the most restrictive zoning in the country,' " says Marya Morris, senior research associate. She says the association doesn't encourage such zoning, adding that "most cities don't have the luxury of turning everything down."

That is because new businesses mean more tax revenue. Ironically, city officials say, nimby-movement leaders often also complain about higher taxes and lack of police protection—both of which can be linked to insufficient growth in the local tax base. "People right now are opposed to any change, and that creates absolute instability as we go out and try to promote economic development in the city," says Dallas City Councilor Chris Luna.

In many cities, the new isolationists have recourse to laws and regulations born of past nimby successes. In Los Angeles, an ordinance permits the city to act on zoning complaints by shutting down targeted businesses even if they are in compliance with existing codes.

Zoning experts say opposition to a community project often is fueled by a recent, highly publicized crime. In Queens, the plan for a laser-gun games center came just after a gunman killed

six people and wounded 19 on the Long Island Railroad commuter train.

"People are afraid, and they are getting paranoid," says Alvin Lubov, landlord of the property that was to house the Q-Zar laser center. "It was not the right time for this" development.

The Dallas Project

In Dallas, proponents of Tinseltown thought their timing was perfect. The derelict site, positioned amid the area's commercial district, is indeed ripe for redevelopment. Just a quarter of a mile away sits the giant Galleria mall and office tower. Also close by is a strip mall, a major tollway, gasoline stations, more shops and an indoor amusement park. In 1985, the surrounding neighborhood agreed to plans to build three 18-story office towers on the site, but the crash of the Texas economy sank that project.

Eight years later, Cinemark came along. The nation's sixth-largest theater chain, with 157 theaters in 27 states, still had only suburban outlets in its hometown. While traveling to Mexico with a group of businesspeople last July, Mayor Steve Bartlett heard of Cinemark's search for a city site and offered his help.

Cinemark told the mayor a few weeks later that it wanted to use the Kmart site, just blocks from the mayor's house and roundly scorned as an eyesore. The mayor, says Randy Hester, Cinemark's head of corporate development, was "thrilled" with the company's interest.

But as word spread, Mrs. Coffman and her neighbors began to worry that Tinseltown would become a regional draw, particularly for teenagers up to no good. "Gangs come to movies together and run into another gang. Then do they shoot up the neighborhood?" asks D. M. Bland, a retired aircraft engineer who lives 12 blocks from the Kmart site.

The community is one of the safest in a city where statistics show that violent crime has declined for five consecutive years. City officials have

insisted that the predominantly white neighborhood's fear of teen gangs is illogical, and local talk-radio hosts have suggested that their resistance is rooted in racism.

Violence Cited

Residents scoff at such criticism. When explaining their stance, they readily tick off examples of violence in other parts of the city that they think the Cinemark complex would expose them to: a man shot in the neck at an automatic teller machine; a young girl abducted from a soccer field in suburban Plano and then murdered; patrons of a grocery store robbed in the parking lot; a bystander killed in a gang shooting at a suburban mall.

"I could see a young girl or boy disappearing just as easily there as at that Plano soccer field," says Mrs. Coffman, who now watches from her door when her teenage children play outside. "If I can't see my daughter, I get nervous."

In November, residents of the conservative neighborhood, which is dominated by rambling $200,000 and $250,000 homes built in the 1960s and 1970s, formed a group called "Citizens Against Tinseltown" and began marshaling their resources to fight the project. They said the complex would create lots of noise and traffic at night. They offered data from marketing studies showing that the average moviegoer spends 90 minutes near a theater in addition to the time spent in the theater, time enough for youths to make trouble in adjacent residential areas. They enlisted real-estate experts to predict a decline in property values. Mrs. Coffman claimed that based on her own survey of movie listings, Cinemark theaters were more likely than others to run R-rated films. Cinemark, which says it had never before been the focus of fears over plans for a theater, denies that.

The Fight Begins

Cinemark says the city attorney's office assured it that the theater complex and four restaurants met the criteria of a planned-development ordinance approved for the 1985 project and that the City Council's approval was a formality.

Soon, the battle was engaged. Residents shouted down Cinemark officials during a company news conference at the Kmart site. Playing tit for tat, Cinemark then filled City Council chambers with its supporters before the start of a Jan. 12 meeting called to hear both sides of the conflict. Foes of the theater were able to take their seats only after a truce was negotiated by the mayor, who by this time had switched to support his neighbors.

"The [neighborhood's] fears are probably somewhat overblown," Mayor Bartlett says, "but there are legitimate questions."

Cinemark presented a letter in which police officials testified that its existing theaters weren't crime centers. The company also got a former mayor of nearby Garland to stump for its cause, praising a Cinemark megatheater in his town.

Beyond City Hall, the neighborhood group continued picketing and posting signs, including a "STOP CINE-MARK" Christmas-light display on the roof of one home. Cinemark mailed slick promotional fliers to the neighborhood to announce: "We're Coming!" It said it had conducted a mail-in poll in which area residents approved of its plan, 406–71.

The company, saying it had all the needed administrative approvals, issued a veiled threat that if the City Council didn't sign off on the project, members could be held personally liable. And in an 11th-hour attempt to woo councilors before a vote, Cinemark said it would build a theater in economically depressed south Dallas if its north Dallas plan was approved.

The neighborhood group, counting only seven votes on its side among the 15 council members, went to the meeting prepared for defeat. It brought along an attorney who carried a lawsuit to be filed immediately after the vote. But at the last minute, a councilor switched sides giving Mrs. Coffman and her cohorts an 8–7 victory.

"I don't think the neighborhood should only be allowed to speak out if it's a prison or a lead smelter coming in," an exuberant Mrs. Coffman said soon after the vote.

Since the late-January vote, Cinemark has taken its case to court. It is asking a Texas court to order the city to approve the Tinseltown plan. And it has filed suit in federal court in Dallas against the city, the mayor and the seven city councilors who voted against it, asking millions in damages. City attorney Sam Lindsay says the city will be "vigorously defending both lawsuits."

Cinemark's supporters, including a few local merchants and even some of Mrs. Coffman's neighbors, worry that the council's decision bodes ill for Dallas's future. "If we are at the point where we are afraid of a family entertainment center, then we all better live in a steel box," says Richard Jaffe, owner and manager of the strip mall near the site.

Complains Councilor Luna, chairman of the council's economic-development committee and a Cinemark supporter: "The public is saying, 'Do something about the city,' and when you do, they say, 'Don't do it here.' This is classic nimby taken to an extreme."

Credits/ Acknowledgments

Cover design by Charles Vitelli

1. Early Commentaries

Facing overview—Carnegie Library of Pittsburgh photo.

2. Intergovernmental Relations

Facing overview—WHO photo by Kalisher.

3. Linkages between Citizens and Governments

Facing overview—Sygma photo by A. Tannenbaum.

4. Government Institutions

Facing overview—Connecticut Department of Economic Development photo by Dominick J. Ruggiero.

5. Cities and Suburbs

Facing overview—United Nations photo by Milton Grant.

6. Finances and Economic Development

Facing overview—Las Vegas News Bureau photo.

7. Service Delivery and Policy Issues

Facing overview—Dushkin Publishing Group/Brown & Benchmark Publishers photo.

ANNUAL EDITIONS ARTICLE REVIEW FORM

■ NAME: _____ DATE: _____

■ TITLE AND NUMBER OF ARTICLE: _____

■ BRIEFLY STATE THE MAIN IDEA OF THIS ARTICLE: _____

_____

_____

_____

_____

■ LIST THREE IMPORTANT FACTS THAT THE AUTHOR USES TO SUPPORT THE MAIN IDEA:

_____

_____

_____

_____

_____

_____

■ WHAT INFORMATION OR IDEAS DISCUSSED IN THIS ARTICLE ARE ALSO DISCUSSED IN YOUR TEXTBOOK OR OTHER READING YOU HAVE DONE? LIST THE TEXTBOOK CHAPTERS AND PAGE NUMBERS:

_____

_____

_____

_____

_____

_____

■ LIST ANY EXAMPLES OF BIAS OR FAULTY REASONING THAT YOU FOUND IN THE ARTICLE:

_____

_____

_____

_____

■ LIST ANY NEW TERMS/CONCEPTS THAT WERE DISCUSSED IN THE ARTICLE AND WRITE A SHORT DEFINITION:

_____

_____

_____

_____

_____

*Your instructor may require you to use this Annual Editions Article Review Form in any number of ways: for articles that are assigned, for extra credit, as a tool to assist in developing assigned papers, or simply for your own reference. Even if it is not required, we encourage you to photocopy and use this page; you'll find that reflecting on the articles will greatly enhance the information from your text.

ANNUAL EDITIONS:
STATE AND LOCAL GOVERNMENT, Seventh Edition
Article Rating Form

Here is an opportunity for you to have direct input into the next revision of this volume. We would like you to rate each of the 67 articles listed below, using the following scale:

1. **Excellent: should definitely be retained**
2. **Above average: should probably be retained**
3. **Below average: should probably be deleted**
4. **Poor: should definitely be deleted**

Your ratings will play a vital part in the next revision. So please mail this prepaid form to us just as soon as you complete it.
Thanks for your help!

Rating	Article	Rating	Article
	1. The Federalist No. 17		34. In Search of the Toughest State Ethics Law
	2. The Federalist No. 45		35. The Buddy System
	3. Nature of the American State		36. Business Flees to the Urban Fringe
	4. The *New* Federalism		37. The Impossible Commute
	5. Federal Government Mandates: Why the States Are Complaining		38. Bend or Die
	6. Tightening the Screws on 'Takings'		39. A Tale of Two Suburbias
	7. The Gorilla that Swallows State Laws		40. Indianapolis and the Republican Future
	8. A Declaration of War		41. Block Watch: Not in Your Backyard, Say Community Panels in Suburban Enclaves
	9. Local Options		42. The Sweet Smell of Secession
	10. Should States or Regions Set Clean Air Rules?		43. Revenue-Raising Partners
	11. The Mirage of Campaign Reform		44. Our Outmoded Tax Systems
	12. Seismic Shift in the South		45. It's Not a Miracle, It's a Mirage
	13. It Isn't the Gender		46. The Tax the Public Loves to Hate
	14. Dickering Over the Districts		47. The Quagmire of Education Finance
	15. If Term Limits Are the Answer, What's the Question?		48. Balancing the Budget with Billboards & Souvenirs
	16. Should Judges Be Elected?		49. A Bankruptcy Peculiar to California
	17. My Life As a School Board Candidate: Lessons Learned in Local Politics		50. Budget Chicken: The Newest High School Sport
	18. All Politics Is Local		51. Taxing Travelers to the Hilt
	19. Store Wars		52. The Third Wave of Economic Development
	20. Boycott Madness		53. Romancing the Smokestack
	21. Swiss Cheese *Journalism*		54. The Strange Career of Enterprise Zones
	22. Civic Strategies for Community Empowerment		55. Wild about Convention Centers
	23. Is the Initiative Process a Good Idea?		56. Government at Bat
	24. The Legislature 2010: Which Direction?		57. The Tricky Path to Going Private
	25. Our Beleaguered Institution		58. Private Firm to Run Schools in Hartford
	26. The Political Virtue of Partisan Deadlock		59. School Choice *and* Reality
	27. Term Limits Change Ohio's Landscape: Groans about 'Dead-End' Jobs, Cheers for Looser System		60. Do We Need More Prisons?
			61. Abortion: The Never Ending Controversy
	28. Reviewing Political Science on a Local School Board		62. A Desire Named Streetcar
			63. The Failure of the Adoption Machine
	29. Wisconsin's 'Quirky' Veto Power		64. Pay Now . . . Learn Later
	30. The Lure of the Strong Mayor		65. Of LULUs, NIMBYs, and NIMTOOs
	31. The States' Lead in Rights Protection		66. Taking Old McDonald to Court
	32. View from the Bench: A Judge's Day		67. Communities, Fearful of Importing Crime, Bar Routine Businesses
	33. Justice by Numbers		

(Continued on next page)

ABOUT YOU

Name_____ Date_____

Are you a teacher? ☐ Or student? ☐

Your School Name _____

Department _____

Address _____

City _____ State _____ Zip _____

School Telephone # _____

YOUR COMMENTS ARE IMPORTANT TO US!

Please fill in the following information:

For which course did you use this book? _____

Did you use a text with this Annual Edition? ☐ yes ☐ no

The title of the text? _____

What are your general reactions to the Annual Editions concept?

Have you read any particular articles recently that you think should be included in the next edition?

Are there any articles you feel should be replaced in the next edition? Why?

Are there other areas that you feel would utilize an Annual Edition?

May we contact you for editorial input?

May we quote you from above?

ANNUAL EDITIONS: STATE AND LOCAL GOVERNMENT, Seventh Edition

BUSINESS REPLY MAIL

First Class   Permit No. 84   Guilford, CT

Postage will be paid by addressee

**Dushkin Publishing Group/
Brown & Benchmark Publishers**
Sluice Dock
Guilford, Connecticut 06437

DPG